HONG KONG'S LINK TO THE US DOLLAR

HONG KONG'S LINK TO THE US DOLLAR

Origins and Evolution

Second Edition

John Greenwood

HKU
PRESS
香港大學出版社

Hong Kong University Press
The University of Hong Kong
Pokfulam Road
Hong Kong
https://hkupress.hku.hk

ISBN 978-988-8754-08-3 (*Hardback*)

British Library Cataloguing-in-Publication Data
A catalogue record for this book is available from the British Library.

10 9 8 7 6 5 4 3 2 1

Printed and bound by Hang Tai Printing Co., Ltd. in Hong Kong, China

CONTENTS

APPENDICES AND BOXES

CHARTS, TABLES, AND FIGURES

Key to Symbols Used in the Charts	
%RP	– Percentage <u>R</u>ate of change over <u>P</u>receding period
%RS	– Percentage <u>R</u>ate of change over <u>S</u>ame period of preceding year
SA	– <u>S</u>easonally <u>A</u>djusted
SAAR	– <u>S</u>easonally <u>A</u>djusted at <u>A</u>nnualised <u>R</u>ate
% YOY	– <u>P</u>ercentage change <u>Y</u>ear-<u>O</u>n-<u>Y</u>ear (i.e. over same month or quarter of previous year).

FOREWORD

The monetary crisis in Hong Kong, starting in September 1982, following Mrs. Thatcher's failed visit to Beijing, and culminating in September/October 1983, threatened both the economic and the political identity of this unique city. It was, of course, primarily a politically induced crisis. Mrs. Thatcher had gone to meet Deng Xiaoping to try to renegotiate and to extend the lease on the New Territories of Hong Kong. She was turned down. Without the New Territories it was generally agreed that Hong Kong would not be a viable entity; so the ending of the lease, in 1997, would effectively mean the transfer of sovereignty from the colonial power, UK, to the Mainland authorities at that same time.

This was a signal for Hong Kong residents to diversify assets abroad, and a large capital outflow ensued. With a floating exchange rate, and no domestic monetary anchor (as John explains in his first few chapters), the Hong Kong dollar began to depreciate rapidly. The Mainland authorities appeared to interpret this depreciation as the result of the British trying to strip the colony of its wealth before departure, and there were — or so it was claimed — threats that they would have to march into Hong Kong immediately, rather than wait until 1997, in order to protect what was (rightfully) their own property. This only aggravated the capital outflow. The pace of external currency depreciation accelerated. Internally domestic prices began to rise dramatically, and signs of panic (e.g. runs on stores to stockpile necessities) developed. It had become a major crisis.

This crisis was stopped dead by the monetary regime reform of October 1983, introducing the link between the US dollar and the Hong Kong dollar (at HK$7.80 to US$1). The regime change was brilliantly successful in that respect. As described by John in the Epilogue, considerable changes have been made in the system since then, and it has endured even through many difficult periods, notably in 1997/98. By all reasonable standards this regime change was a triumph. Outside the government John was the analytical author and progenitor of the regime that was introduced. I was myself a bit-part player in this exercise, as John explains in his book, and I remember reading his *Asian Monetary Monitor* issue of September/October 1983 (Chapter 5 below) on the plane flying out to Hong Kong, alongside David Peretz of HM Treasury, to advise the Hong Kong government on what they should do. It was, in effect, his proposal 2B that was put into operation.

This proposal was for a (version of a) currency board adjusted to take account of several of Hong Kong's peculiar monetary features. What a list of peculiarities these were! There was no central bank, nor was one wanted. The note issue was undertaken by two (later three) note-issuing commercial banks, but the seignorage accrued to the government, because each note had to be backed by a Certificate of Indebtedness (CI), issued by the government. Such CIs were issued against sterling until 1972, against US dollars from 1972 until 1974, but could be paid for in Hong Kong dollars from then on, as John records in Chapter 2. Cheque and payments clearing was run by the leading commercial bank, the Hong Kong and Shanghai Banking Corporation (HSBC), which also carried out a few quasi-central-bank functions. Interest rates on deposits and loans were set by a government-sponsored cartel, the Hong Kong Association of Banks (HKAB), over whose decisions the authorities had some limited leverage.

Against this background, the decision was made to go to a system of partial convertibility, with the banks exchanging bank notes into US dollars, or the reverse, rather than full convertibility (allowing the general public the same right). This is very nicely discussed in a box in Chapter 8 (p. 188). As described there, this meant that arbitrage worked less immediately, and that the new regime had to be "managed", rather than work automatically.

One, very minor, quibble that I have with John's book is that it does not, in my view, emphasize the key, central role of the HSBC enough in this respect. In the early 1980s, HSBC had much greater clout in Hong Kong than the monetary authorities. Much of the credit for the successful early management of the Link should go to them and their, very competent, General Manager Mr. John Gray. Of course, it was in the long-run interest of HSBC to have a stable monetary system in Hong Kong, but people do not always see what is in their own best interest. While on personalities, my impression was that the key figure amongst the officials was Sir Philip Haddon-Cave, the Chief Secretary, who had been the Financial Secretary (FS) in the 1970s, rather than Sir John Bremridge (the FS at the time) or Douglas Blye (Secretary of Monetary Affairs), neither of whom had much background in monetary theory — fortunately Blye had the support of Tony Latter, an economist seconded from the Bank of England, who did, and who also had experience in monetary policy operations.

Even so, such partial convertibility and indirect management led to various frictions and problems in the operation of the Link. As John notes, these could have been resolved in one of two ways, either:

(a) by moving to full convertibility and a more automatic currency board system, or

(b) by moving to a system in which the authorities were put into a position to operate so as to manage the Link more directly and more effectively.

Under the patient, astute and wise leadership of Joseph Yam as Director of the Office of the Exchange Fund from 1991 to 1993 (he had been Deputy Secretary for Monetary Affairs from 1985 to 1991) and as Chief Executive of the Hong Kong Monetary Authority (HKMA) from 1993 onwards, the second course was followed, effectively endowing HKMA from 1998 with all the operational powers of a full-fledged central bank. The twists and turns, and arguments for and against, these changes are set out well in Chapters 11–13.

As John notes in his introduction, he came to Hong Kong in 1974 as a young graduate monetary economist to work for GT Management Asia Ltd. He found in Hong Kong a complex monetary system, with very little data available and no clear anchor nor determinant to the monetary base, the money stock (or to interest rates). In seeking to make sense of all this, he developed an analytical platform that he decided to make public with the publication of the *Asian Monetary Monitor* (AMM) starting in September 1977. From then on until John left Hong Kong in 1993 (and the AMM ceased publication in 1995) the AMM was a pre-eminent source of information and analysis on Hong Kong's monetary affairs; indeed until 1994 when HKMA began to publish its own *Quarterly Bulletin* it was about the only good, regular, source of analysis on Hong Kong monetary affairs.

This book reproduces twelve of his more important and influential AMM papers, Chapters 1 to 12, plus a short introduction and a most useful epilogue, Chapter 13, reflecting with the benefit of mature hindsight how Hong Kong monetary affairs have developed. Given John's central role in all this, the reproduction of these chapters is of importance to preserve the historical record. In addition each chapter is preceded by a most useful short additional introduction giving the context in which the article was originally written, and an (extremely open and honest) assessment of how he now (i.e. in 2006) sees the strengths and weaknesses of his own earlier arguments.

As a judge and analyst of the technicalities of Hong Kong's monetary set-up, John Greenwood was, in the late 1970s and early 80s, quite outstanding, there was no one else like him. Since then, of course, a new generation of experts has grown up. If I may be permitted another tiny quibble, to my mind he does not emphasize quite enough the wider economic (and political) conditions that made a quasi-currency-board system so suitable, enduring and robust in Hong Kong, notably the strong fiscal position, the flexibility of wages and prices, and the desire to have a quasi-automatic stable system, without political direction.

Whether the answer to Hong Kong's 1982/83 monetary crisis would have been found without John's guidance is a counter-factual no one can ever know. The truth is that it was his scheme (Proposal 2B) that formed the template for the regime change. In that sense the Link is his begetting. My own small bit-part in the resolution of this crisis is one of the highlights of my own career. John must, and should, be very proud of his own much larger role.

Charles Goodhart, CBE, FBA
Professor Emeritus of Banking and Finance,
London School of Economics and Political Science

INTRODUCTION TO THE FIRST EDITION

This book contains a selection of articles written in the bimonthly journal *Asian Monetary Monitor* during the years 1981–89. The focus of the journal, as its title implies, was the analysis of contemporary monetary issues in the East Asian economies from Japan down to New Zealand and across to India. The particular selection in this book concentrates on Hong Kong's monetary crisis and its solution during the decade of the 1980s. Chapters 1 to 5 focus on the developing crisis in Hong Kong during the years 1981–83. Chapters 6 to 10 trace the initial resolution of the crisis via the restoration of a currency board mechanism in October 1983, and the immediate aftermath as the economy adjusted to the fixed exchange rate. These chapters also highlight some of the shortcomings of the new mechanism — shortcomings which were later to cause serious difficulties for Hong Kong during the Asian Financial Crisis of 1997–98. Chapters 11 and 12 deal with the package of measures introduced in July 1988, and the subsequent response of the restored currency board system to the Tiananmen Square crisis of June 1989. The book closes with an Epilogue which updates the story of Hong Kong's monetary developments between 1990 and 2005.

The book is aimed at students, economists and financial market analysts. It is intended to provide a detailed analysis of Hong Kong's monetary system in the years leading up to the currency crisis of 1983, the breakdown of that system under the pressure of capital outflows during the Sino-British negotiations over the future of Hong Kong after July 1997, the introduction of the "linked rate system" pegging the Hong Kong dollar to the US dollar, and the subsequent gradual process of reform and refinement of the currency board mechanism. Each chapter is preceded by an introductory narrative that puts the analysis in its historical context and places the economic argument in perspective. The book also provides some of the key documents of record that helped shape Hong Kong's unique monetary institutions in the years before the hand-over of sovereignty in 1997.

The story begins with my arrival in Hong Kong in May 1974 from Tokyo, where, as a graduate student at Tokyo University, I had spent the preceding three years studying the Japanese language and conducting economic research. My topic had been the relation between fluctuations in the money supply and the Japanese business cycle from the foundation of the Bank of Japan in 1882 to modern times. One of the first challenges I faced as I settled down to do macro-economic research in Hong Kong for Hutchison-GT (later to be known as GT Management Asia Ltd.), an investment manager of pension funds and unit trusts, was to build a statistical framework for understanding the Hong Kong economy. Immediately I found a huge contrast between the wealth of data on the Japanese economy and the relative paucity of data on the Hong Kong economy.

In view of the lack of computing power — personal computers did not become available until the early 1980s — I needed a theoretical framework that would enable me to make reliable predictions with a minimum of relevant data. Monetary analysis had proved its value to me as a consultant to banks in Tokyo, and in making predictions for the Japanese economy even during the dramatic events of the early 1970s — the closing of the gold window by President Nixon in August 1971, the consequent end of the Bretton Woods system and the shift to floating exchange rates in February 1973, the first oil crisis in late 1973, and the surge of inflation in 1973–74. It therefore seemed plausible that a similar kind of monetary analysis should be applicable in Hong Kong.

However, few if any of the economies in the East Asian region produced money supply data in the early 1970s. Fortunately, data on the notes and coin in circulation in Hong Kong were available on a monthly basis, and data showing the consolidated balance sheets of the licensed banks were also available in the Monthly Digest of Statistics. Therefore within a week of my arrival I was able to start compiling rudimentary statistics for the Hong Kong money supply consisting of the total notes and coin *less* cash held by the banks, *plus* customers' deposits (divided into current, time and savings) at the banks. The reference library at City Hall enabled me to obtain historical data so that within a fairly short space of time I had several monetary series from the early 1960s to 1974, and I was able to relate these to the key data for the Hong Kong economy. Before long this database had expanded into a system of charts and underlying statistical datasheets covering the relation between the money supply and stock prices, some rather limited indices of manufacturing output (e.g. electricity consumption), real GDP, and inflation. The data were by no means as comprehensive as I had come to know in Japan, but at least the basic relationships appeared to make sense.

So far so good, but one problem kept gnawing at my mind. What or who determined the money supply in Hong Kong at any point in time? In Japan there was a central bank, which, together with the Ministry of Finance and the Economic Planning Agency, was clearly responsible for the formulation of monetary and economic policy, and it was possible, for example, to link decisions to cut interest rates or reserve requirements to accelerations in the money supply. In Hong Kong, by contrast, there was no such obvious linkage. Hong Kong at this time had no central bank; the licensed banks appeared to set deposit interest rates largely independently of the government through the Hong Kong Association of Banks; the interbank clearing and settlement system was run by a consortium of the leading banks; and banknotes were still issued by two of the local banks. There was certainly no user-friendly manual to explain to itinerant monetary economists how the system worked, and as I soon discovered the Monetary Affairs Branch of the government (which was effectively the monetary authority) was obsessively secretive not only about disclosing its balance sheet but also about its general role and functions. For example, at this time the authorities did not even publish the quantity of foreign exchange reserves held by the Exchange Fund of the Hong Kong government.

Faced with an unusual institutional framework for the monetary system, limited data, and an official attitude that distrusted external analysts, it was several years before I was able to come to a proper understanding of how the monetary system of Hong Kong really worked. Initially my analyses were circulated only among the clients of GT Management. Two key milestones were the publication of *Asian Monetary Monitor* (from September 1977) which brought the analysis to the attention of a much wider audience, and a eureka moment in 1981 when I was able to prove convincingly that there was something fundamentally wrong with the monetary system in Hong Kong at the time (Chapter 2, pp. 30–31). The essays that follow show how various pieces of the jigsaw gradually fell into place.

None of my involvement in resolving the currency crisis of 1983 might have happened had it not been for three individuals. Richard Thornton, the "T" in GT, had read some of the economic papers I had been writing from Tokyo, and it was he who persuaded me to come to Hong Kong primarily to discuss things Japanese with his team of investment managers there. Second, Robert (Bertie) Boyd, then Managing Director of GT in Hong Kong, encouraged me to extend my monetary analysis of Japan to other economies in Asia, and gave me the resources to do so.

The third person was Donald Storey, publisher of the *Bank Credit Analyst* (BCA). After I had attended and spoken at a conference organized by the BCA in Bermuda in September 1974, Don visited Hong Kong in 1975, and made a deal with Richard Thornton whereby I would write regular contributions to the international edition of the BCA covering Japan and Australia. For a while this worked well, but gradually I was put under pressure to transfer to Montreal where the BCA's editor, Tony Boeckh, was based. I countered with a proposal to set up an Asian edition of the BCA, saying that it made no sense to attempt to cover Asia from Montreal, but this idea was turned down. The net result was that in 1977 the arrangement with BCA ceased and I set up *Asian Monetary Monitor* (AMM) in Hong Kong, with the blessing of Richard Thornton and with GT participating as a shareholder but carrying most of the overhead expenses. These arrangements continued until 1996, when, following my transfer to San Francisco, publication ceased.

With the exception of Chapter 13, the essays in this collection originally appeared in *Asian Monetary Monitor.* They have all been reproduced from the original, edited only to remove duplication, and, in the case of Chapter 12, to change the title. Some minor editorial corrections and updates have been made (e.g. replacing "Euro-dollar" with "US$" to avoid confusion since the introduction of the euro). Also, since the original chapters were published as stand-alone articles, some repetition occurred which it has not been possible to remove without substantial revisions.

AMM was not only a unique publication covering financial developments in Asia from a consistent, monetarist perspective, but it also became a vehicle for writing more in-depth macro-economic articles — in contrast to the type of strategy pieces that were normally written for investment managers. It was therefore able to attract the attention of academics, businessmen and central bankers, and consequently carried more influence than a regular investment newsletter. For me personally as publisher and editor, AMM provided a platform for exploring Asia's monetary history as well as current monetary developments in Asia either with members of my team at GT, or sometimes relying on external contributors.

I am grateful to numerous colleagues at GT and *Asian Monetary Monitor* for their contribution over the years to the special quality of AMM analysis, particularly to my colleagues and co-writers Christian Wignall, Hugh Sloane and Tim Lee. John Blundell, now Director General of the Institute of Economic Affairs in London, but then at the Institute of Humane Studies in the United States, deserves a special mention for providing a string of brilliant young interns — including George Selgin, Randall Kroszner, Kurt Schuler and Chris Culp — to work as interns in Hong Kong on AMM. Tony Latter, previously Executive Director (Research) at the HKMA, made valuable suggestions on an early draft of the narrative sections at the head of each chapter, and on the Epilogue. I am also grateful to Hans Genberg, Research Director of the HKMA, and Matthew Yiu and his colleagues at the HKIMR for their help and support in preparing the manuscript for publication.

ADDENDUM: INTRODUCTION TO THE SECOND EDITION

The second edition of this book includes an amended Chapter 13 (previously entitled "Epilogue", now retitled "Building Resilience and Automaticity, 1983–2005") and a new Chapter 14 ("Establishing Credibility, 2005–2020"). The discussion of the optimum monetary system for Hong Kong, previously in the final section of Chapter 13, has been transferred to Chapter 14 and updated. In all other respects the new edition is unchanged from the first edition.

I am grateful to Steve Hanke of Johns Hopkins University, Kurt Schuler of the Center for Financial Stability, and Hans Genberg, Executive Director at SEACEN in Kuala Lumpur, for comments on a draft version of Chapter 14. Lillian Cheung, Executive Director, Economic Research Department of the HKMA and her colleagues Li Ka-fai and Kevin Li provided helpful comments on both the text and the data.

June 2021

Notes on the Arrangement of the Book

1. A new commentary, in a sans serif typeface, is placed at the beginning of each chapter.
2. The main body of each chapter, placed under an AMM heading in a serif typeface, is reproduced from original AMM articles (except the new Foreword, Introduction, and Epilogue).
3. Boxes from original AMM articles, with a shaded background, provide in-depth commentary on subjects discussed in the chapter.

CHAPTER 1

CURRENCY ON THE SKIDS

May–June 1981

Starting in January 1977 the trade-weighted index of the Hong Kong dollar began a persistent decline lasting almost four years, interrupted only by a brief upturn in 1979–80. This shows that the currency depreciation began long before the Sino-British negotiations over the future of Hong Kong in 1982–83, and could not be due simply to a flight of capital following Margaret Thatcher's visit to Beijing in September 1982. Considering the contrast with the sustained strength of the Hong Kong currency between 1972 and 1976, the depreciation posed some serious questions: was there something fundamentally wrong with the Hong Kong monetary system that predisposed the currency to persistent weakness? And why did the currency weakness begin in 1977 rather than in 1974 or 1975, soon after the Hong Kong dollar was floated?

The answer given in this article to the first question focuses on the relative money growth rates in Hong Kong compared with the money growth rates in Hong Kong's five major trading partners, and finds a systematic tendency for Hong Kong's money supply to grow more rapidly than was consistent with currency stability on a trade-weighted basis. The article does not discuss the causes of the problem, but refers to previous AMM articles that had pointed out the "structural reasons" for Hong Kong's monetary difficulties. The next article (Chapter 2) gives a consolidated summary of the structural faults in the monetary system.

In answer to the second question the article argues that until 1977 currency market participants regarded the Hong Kong dollar as part of the US dollar area, but that thereafter they began to view the HK$ as trading independently of the US unit. While the argument is plausible, it does not have the decisive strength of the empirical data used in answering the first question. One reason why market participants may have continued to regard the HK$ as part of the US$ area was that they did not realize that a fundamental break with currency board principles had occurred in 1972 (See Chapter 2). The fact that the HK$ had remained stable or even strengthened against the US$ for just over two years after floating in November 1974 led to a feeling that the Hong Kong authorities could somehow manage and maintain the HK$/US$ rate just as they had maintained the HK$-sterling rate in the preceding decades.

As writers and editors of AMM we were never afraid to give our readers a punchy forecast or investment conclusion stemming from the logic of our analysis. This was always provided in the concluding "Summary and Forecast" paragraph. The investment conclusion at the end of this article — two years ahead of the currency collapse in 1983 — was uncompromising: "Until structural reforms in the monetary system are implemented... there is only a remote chance that the Hong Kong currency will retain its purchasing power. Long term investors would be therefore well-advised to hedge their Hong Kong dollar investments on a continuous basis..."

A S I A N   M O N E T A R Y   M O N I T O R
Vol. 5 No. 3 May–June 1981

The value of the Hong Kong dollar against the US dollar has plunged in recent months. From a level of HK$5.37 in March this year, the Hong Kong dollar has skidded almost without interruption to nearly HK$6.00 per US dollar. To some extent the weakness of the Hong Kong dollar against the US dollar simply reflects the general strength of the US currency against all other currencies. Hence in Chart 1.1 the Hong Kong dollar has been rising against the Pound, against the Yen, and against the Deutsche Mark for much of this year. But the currency's trade-weighted index has fallen inexorably since its peak in late 1976/early 1977 to its lowest levels since the base-date of the trade-weighted index in December 1971.

From the time of the Smithsonian Conference in December 1971 until June 1972 the Hong Kong dollar was pegged to sterling. From July 1972 until November 1974 the currency was pegged to the US dollar (with an upward revaluation on February 15th 1973). During the first three years shown in Chart 1.1, therefore, the currency was not free to reflect economic forces and its trade-weighted value was more a by-product of the policy of pegging against other currencies than an economically significant price or value in its own right.

However, after the Hong Kong dollar was floated in November 1974 the situation changed. The appreciation or depreciation of the trade-weighted index became a meaningful independent measure of the relative performance of the Hong Kong currency against other currencies in a world of generally floating exchange rates, rather than a reflection of the performance of the currency (sterling or the US dollar) to which the Hong Kong dollar was pegged.

In the first three years after floating the performance of the Hong Kong dollar on this trade-weighted exchange rate basis was pretty good. The currency generally held its own or appreciated against other major currencies. It was only in late 1977 and then in 1978 that the Hong Kong dollar began to weaken significantly against other currencies. Throughout the period 1974–78 the Hong Kong dollar remained close to the US dollar in

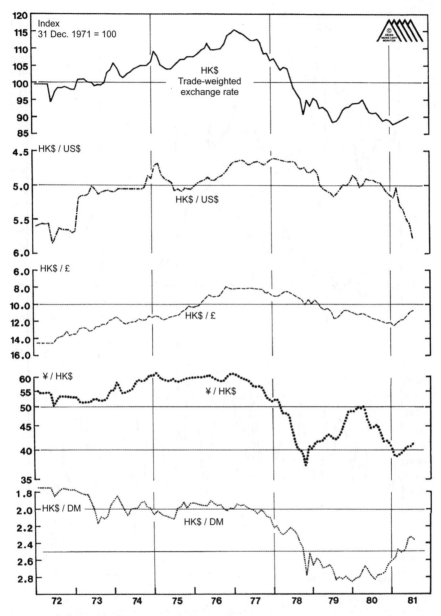

Chart 1.1 Exchange Rate of the Hong Kong Dollar

terms of its foreign exchange value and therefore the fall in the trade-weighted exchange rate index can be viewed largely as a reflection of the enormous strength of the yen, the DM and Swiss Franc against the US dollar between mid-1977 and November 1978.

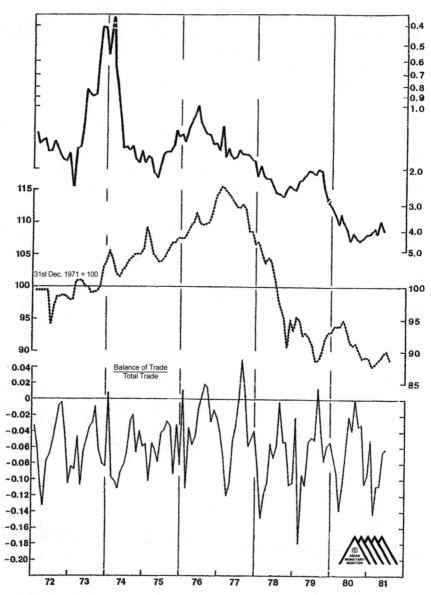

*   Change in Hong Kong data series from M_2 to M_3
** (Money growth in Hong Kong) ÷ (Weighted average of money growth in USA, W. Germany, Japan, UK and France)

Chart 1.2   Determinants of the Trade-Weighted Exchange Rate Index

In other words, during the early years of floating the Hong Kong currency was in the US dollar camp, with changes in its value largely reflecting changes in the international value of the US dollar. Recently, however, the Hong Kong currency has moved sharply downwards against the US dollar, and although it has strengthened somewhat against sterling and the Deutsche Mark, the trade-weighted exchange rate has weakened to near-record lows. Thus the Hong Kong dollar appears at last to have broken away from its position as a US-dollar linked currency in the perception of traders and investors.

In the light of this more variable relationship with the US dollar and the continuing variability of the relationship between the Hong Kong dollar and other currencies it would seem desirable to have some idea of what determines the trade-weighted value of the Hong Kong dollar in a fundamental sense. The theory we have experimented with is a variant of purchasing power parity theory which relates changes in the exchange rates between two currencies over the long term to differences in the inflation rates between those two countries. The problem in applying this theory in the short term is that the various indices of inflation commonly used are themselves affected by exchange rate changes, and in addition it is hard to find truly comparable price indices in different countries. One way round these difficulties is to take one step further back in the inflationary process, and look at relative money growth rates rather than relative price changes which are the outcome of differing monetary growth rates.

Applying this idea to explaining the movement of the trade-weighted exchange rate index of the Hong Kong dollar requires compilation of a similar weighted index of money supply growth rates for Hong Kong's main trading partners. Although this is feasible, we cut short this process in two ways — first by using the money supply growth rates of just five major countries (which are also large trading partners of Hong Kong), and second by weighting them according to the size of their GNPs rather than the amount of trade they actually did with Hong Kong. It is probable that, assuming all the data could be readily obtained, the trade-weighted index of money supply growth rates would not be significantly different from the results we actually obtained. (See Chart 1.2.)

Before describing the quantitative results it should be mentioned that we have not been able to establish any significant relationship between Hong Kong's trade balance and short term movements of the currency. In Chart 1.2 the trade balance is shown as a ratio to the value of total trade. If the invisible and capital accounts (data for which are not collected in Hong Kong) were assumed to remain unchanged, one would expect the strength of the currency to vary directly with the size of the trade account surplus or deficit. However as Chart 1.2 shows, there are at least as many upward spikes in the trade balance/total trade ratio coinciding with strength in the trade-weighted index as there are downward spikes. Without more knowledge of the invisibles, capital movements and official transactions it does not seem feasible to investigate any further the relationship between movements of the currency and the overall or partial balance of payments.

The only alternative is to use proximate indicators which will necessarily be less useful over the shorter term, but which may yet shed some light on the long term relationships involved. For this purpose we have taken the ratio of monetary growth in Hong Kong to monetary growth in five major countries and divided the period from 1971 to the present (1981) into four sub-periods, taking periods starting and finishing six months later in each case for the trade-weighted exchange rate index. Taking the average values for the money growth ratios and for the weighted exchange rate index for each sub-period gives the results tabulated below.

Average Ratio of Money Growth in Hong Kong to Money Growth in 5 Major Countries		Average Trade-Weighted Exchanged Rate Index of HK$ in periods starting 6 months later		Percentage Appreciation or Depreciation
Jan 72 – Jun 73	1.525	Jul 72 – Dec 73	99.68	–
Jul 73 – Jul 76	1.314	Jan 74 – Jan 77	107.08	+ 7.4%
Aug 76 – Dec 79	2.054	Feb 77 – Jun 80	99.82	– 6.8%
Jan 80 – Dec 80	4.010	Jul 80 – Jun 81	89.33	–10.5%

Chart 1.3 shows these subperiod averages as steplike lines superimposed on the same underlying data as in Chart 1.2. In the period July 1973–July 1976 the money supply in Hong Kong grew relatively more slowly than it did in January 1972–June 1973. In the six-month trailing period January 1974–January 1977 the Hong Kong dollar appreciated by 7.4% compared with the period July 1972–December 1973. Thus the mysterious strength of the Hong Kong dollar over much of the January 1974–January 1977 period could be explained as a consequence of the relatively slow money growth in Hong Kong over the July 1973–July 1976 period.

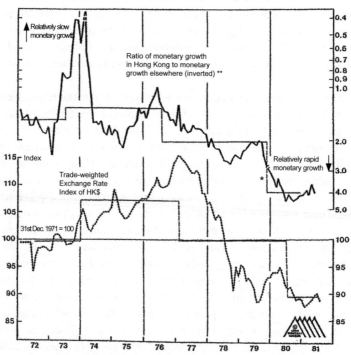

* Change in Hong Kong data series from M_2 to M_3

** (Money growth in Hong Kong) / (Weighted average of money growth in USA, W. Germany, Japan, UK and France)

Chart 1.3 Determinants of the Trade-Weighted Exchange Rate Index

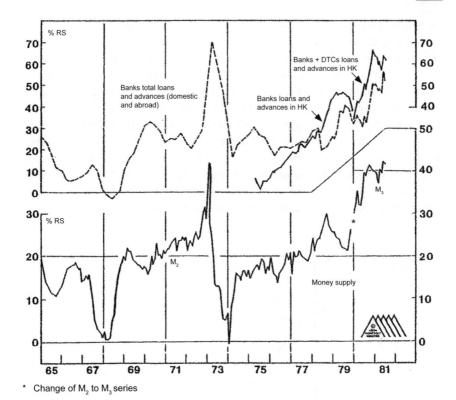

* Change of M₂ to M₃ series

Chart 1.4 Money and Credit Growth

From its peak in January 1977 the trade-weighted index fell steeply without much pause until the turnaround in the fortunes of the US dollar in the autumn of 1978. It is also true that the monetary growth rate in Hong Kong had accelerated somewhat so that from a trough of 1.1 times the money growth rate elsewhere it had accelerated to almost 3 times the money growth in 5 major countries by late 1978.

Again, therefore, the pattern of monetary growth — in this case acceleration — was consistent with the currency movement — depreciation by 6.8% compared with its average level in January 1974–January 1977.

Shifts of deposits from banks to deposit-taking companies (DTCs) make the M_2 statistics for 1979 somewhat misleading, so from January 1980 onwards Charts 1.2, 1.3, and 1.4 shift to a new monetary data series (M_3). The average growth rate of money in Hong Kong over the period January 1980–December 1980 accelerated again to just over 4 times the growth rate of money in the five major countries chosen for comparison. Once again the exchange rate index shows a further depreciation in the subsequent six-month trailing period July 1980–June 1981 — this time by 10.5%.

The question is, what is an appropriate money growth rate in Hong Kong in order for the weighted exchange rate index to remain stable? The data quoted above give us sufficient information to answer that question, at least approximately. By plotting the average ratio of money growth in Hong Kong to the money growth in five major countries against the percentage appreciation or depreciation of the weighted exchange rate index in the corresponding six-month trailing period we have been able to calculate the line which best fits these data points. The result is shown in Chart 1.5. Now, by starting at the point on the vertical axis which shows zero appreciation or depreciation of the currency we can follow the dashed line across to the point on the fitted line and then down from the point of interception to the horizontal axis which indicates the relative money growth rate ratio required for stability of the weighted exchange rate index — about 1.9. In other words, in order for the Hong Kong dollar's weighted exchange rate to be stable on average over an extended period of time — say, two years — the money supply in Hong Kong should not grow faster than 1.9 times or about twice the weighted average money supply growth rate of its major trading partners.[1]

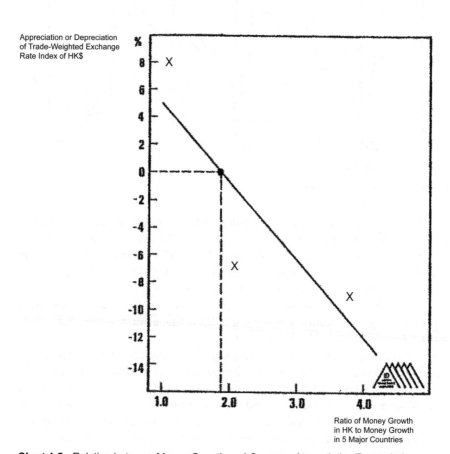

Chart 1.5 Relation between Money Growth and Currency Appreciation/Depreciation

---

1. See Appendix 1.1 for derivation and assumptions.

This number seems reasonable to us in that the real growth rate of Hong Kong's economy is about twice the average real growth rate of Japan, Germany, the USA, Britain and France, so we would expect the permissible monetary growth rate to be that much higher in Hong Kong. Conducting the same exercise for the *difference* between the money growth rate in Hong Kong and the money growth rate in 5 major countries gives similar results. The recent record shows that average money growth in the 5 major countries has been around 11%. A similar computation to that conducted above suggests that money supply growth in Hong Kong could afford to be 9 percentage points higher (i.e. around 20% per annum) without producing any long term depreciation of the trade-weighted exchange rate.

SUMMARY AND FORECAST

For structural reasons explained in previous issues of AMM the supply of money in Hong Kong (or its near-counterpart, the volume of bank credit) continues to grow at a very rapid rate. In the past year (1980–81) the rate of money growth in Hong Kong has averaged four times the rate of money growth in five major trading partners, or about twice the rate of growth which would seem to be compatible with stability in the trade-weighted exchange rate index. (A money growth rate in Hong Kong of 1.9 times the weighted average growth rate of money in the same five major trading partners was found to be compatible with stability in the trade-weighted exchange rate index.) Now that the Hong Kong dollar is no longer so closely identified with the US dollar bloc of currencies its movements can be expected to be more independent of the American currency, but this also suggests that investors and traders will pay more attention to the impact of such local factors as monetary growth, the trade balance and inflation in determining the external value of the Hong Kong dollar. Until structural reforms in the monetary system are implemented which enable the authorities either to regulate directly the quantity of base money (and hence the total money supply) or to maintain a particular exchange rate (as in the pre-1972 system), there is only a remote chance that the Hong Kong currency will retain its purchasing power. Long term investors would be therefore well-advised to hedge their Hong Kong dollar investments on a continuous basis against whichever major currency they estimate to be the strongest, while borrowers would be wise to maintain their liabilities in Hong Kong dollars. High interest rates in Hong Kong provide no assurance that the local currency will stabilise, being as much a symptom of inflation as a sign that funds are in short supply. Whatever the destiny of Hong Kong as an international financial centre, the medium and long term outlook for the local currency is for continuing weakness.

APPENDIX 1.1

Derivation of Relation between Money Growth and Currency Appreciation/ Depreciation

We start with a quantity theory identity for two countries:

Country ① $MV = Py$;   Country ② $M'V' = P'y'$

where M is the stock of money, P is the general price level, y is real income per annum, and V (income velocity) is the ratio of nominal income per annum (Py) to the money stock, M; and similarly for country ②.

Divide ① by ②

$$\frac{MV}{M'V'} = \frac{Py}{P'y'}$$

$$\frac{M}{M'} = \frac{P}{P'} \left(\frac{V'}{y'} \cdot \frac{y}{V} \right)$$

Assume the factors in parentheses remain constant [k]. Expressed in terms of growth rates we have:

$$(\dot{M} - \dot{M}') = (\dot{p} - \dot{p}') + [\dot{k}]$$

i.e. $\left\{ \begin{array}{l} \text{Difference in money} \\ \text{supply growth rates} \end{array} \right\}$ $\begin{array}{l} \text{should} \\ \text{explain} \end{array}$ $\left\{ \begin{array}{l} \text{Differences in} \\ \text{inflation} \end{array} \right\}$ assuming other factors (real growth, income velocity) remain unchanged.

and $\left\{ \begin{array}{l} \text{Differences in} \\ \text{inflation} \end{array} \right\}$ $\begin{array}{l} \text{should} \\ \text{explain} \end{array}$ $\left\{ \begin{array}{l} \text{Exchange Rate} \\ \text{changes} \end{array} \right\}$ assuming other factors remain unchanged.

Hence, $\left\{ \begin{array}{l} \text{Relative money} \\ \text{supply growth rates} \end{array} \right\}$ $\begin{array}{l} \text{should} \\ \text{explain} \end{array}$ $\left\{ \begin{array}{l} \text{Exchange Rate} \\ \text{changes} \end{array} \right\}$ assuming other factors remain unchanged.

CHAPTER **2**

TIME TO BLOW THE WHISTLE
July–August 1981

Between the publication of this article and the preceding one the HK$ had fallen further against the US currency. There could now be no escaping the conclusion that there was something seriously amiss with Hong Kong's monetary arrangements. But, far from addressing the causes of the problem, the authorities appeared to be tackling only the symptoms by intervening in the foreign exchange markets to support the local currency. Normally such intervention ought to succeed if it was supported by other policy measures, but it was quite clear to me that — given Hong Kong's institutional structure — such measures could not possibly succeed in halting the slide in the currency. It was therefore time to "blow the whistle" on Hong Kong's monetary arrangements, pointing out as forcefully as possible the inherent weaknesses of the prevailing structure, and to insist again that reforms were necessary if the currency slide was to be stopped and inflation was to be avoided.

The article that follows is in some respects a comprehensive restatement of previous ideas and proposals published in AMM in 1979 and 1980, but it also contains two critical additions to previous arguments which considerably sharpened the critique — (1) a list of the steps that the authorities had taken in 1972 that had undermined their ability to hold the exchange rate steady at some specified nominal rate against the US$, and (2) the tabular presentation of a series of transactions from the T-form balance sheets of the Exchange Fund, the commercial banks and the non-bank public. These proved conclusively that foreign exchange intervention by the authorities under these arrangements was futile.

It should be noted that at this time I was still thinking in terms of a central bank as the only feasible alternative to Hong Kong's prevailing monetary arrangements — not a reformed currency board system. In this connection there are two boxes in the article: one that critiques the government's case for maintaining the status quo ("Central Bank or No Central Bank?"), and points out the key differences between the accounting arrangements of Hong Kong's monetary system versus other monetary systems, and another that explains how a monetary authority can operate without government debt (since this was often cited as a reason why Hong Kong could not have a central bank). An interesting sub-plot in this article is that the government, by adopting mistaken remedies to deal with symptoms resulting from monetary problems, threatened to damage the wider economy of Hong Kong, for example imposing rent controls to suppress rising rents.

If the authorities were to continue to hold out against the arguments in AMM they would now have to prove that the principles demonstrated in "Time to Blow the Whistle" were incorrect in logic. It was not long before they showed their cards. As author of the article I received a call requesting that I attend a meeting with the Financial Secretary, John Bremridge, at 4.30 p.m. on Monday October 12th 1981. Also present was Douglas Blye, Secretary of Monetary Affairs, who did most of the talking. He said that the article was destabilizing to Hong Kong, and contained serious mistakes. When asked for specifics he pointed out a couple of factual errors (subsequently corrected), but when asked if the principles underlying the relationship between the Exchange Fund and the banking system were wrong, I received no answer. The stand-off was to continue for two more years.

A S I A N M O N E T A R Y M O N I T O R
Vol. 5 No. 4 July–August 1981

During the recent precipitate slide of the Hong Kong dollar from around HK$5.40 per US$ towards HK$6.00, there were several occasions on which it was reliably reported that the Hong Kong government had intervened to support the local currency on the foreign exchange market.

Such intervention, when carried out by a central bank in an orthodox banking system, can be effective in supporting the local currency. But in the case of Hong Kong's peculiar and unorthodox banking structure such intervention is utterly pointless and futile.

To understand why this is so it is necessary to see (a) how a normal central bank and banking system operates and how intervention in the foreign exchange market can be made effective, (b) how Hong Kong's automatic adjustment mechanism under a fixed exchange rate operated in effect like any orthodox central bank would have done, (c) how errors of policy caused Hong Kong's banking system to come off the rails in 1972–74, and how the system now differs from orthodox banking systems around the world and hence (d) why operations in the foreign exchange market by the government or Exchange Fund under present institutional arrangements neither tighten the money market nor reduce monetary growth.

(A) INTERVENTION IN AN ORTHODOX BANKING SYSTEM

When a central bank in a normal banking system faces a balance of payments deficit and wishes to support the local currency, it will sell foreign currency. To do this it simply calls up any foreign exchange dealer and places an order to sell foreign currency. Assuming the dealer can find a willing purchaser, the central bank's foreign exchange holdings will be reduced. At the same time the buyer (or dealer) must pay the central bank an equivalent amount in domestic currency for the foreign exchange, so will write a cheque drawn on his bank, payable to the central bank. When the central bank receives this cheque it does not redeposit it in the banking system, but merely debits the account of the paying bank at the central bank.

If we assume the central bank records no other subsequent transaction, the net effect is to reduce the reserves of the commercial bank in question (i.e. its deposits at the central bank), and thus of the commercial banks as a whole. With less reserves the banks must now reduce their loans if they are to maintain their previous deposit/reserve ratio. But as they reduce their loans, so their deposits will decrease. This adjustment process will continue until a new equilibrium is reached where the new level of bank reserves (set by the central bank via its original sale of foreign exchange) is compatible with the banks' desired or required deposit-to-reserve ratio, and until the public has adjusted its level of cash currency holdings to the new deposit level. The crucial point is that at the end of the whole process, the money supply would have declined by some multiple of the original amount of domestic currency purchased by the central bank.

The original intervention in the foreign exchange markets "supported" the currency in the sense that the central bank came into the market as a buyer of domestic currency, but the more important effect was that intervention produced a multiple contraction in the banking system. This tightening of the money supply would raise interest rates in the first instance, slow down domestic expenditures, and in time produce a correction in the balance of payments both through induced capital inflows and through reducing the demand for imports as the growth of domestic spending declined. All these effects would tend to strengthen the currency, which was what the original intervention was intended to achieve.

However, in the case of Hong Kong today almost none of these effects occur. And this is not because Hong Kong does not have a central bank. In the period of fixed exchange rates before 1974, the mechanism as described here did operate in Hong Kong. To see that, however, one must make one or two small qualifications because the system described above is not immediately recognisable as the system which used to operate in Hong Kong, although in principle the mechanism was identical.

(B) HONG KONG'S AUTOMATIC ADJUSTMENT MECHANISM DURING THE ERA OF FIXED EXCHANGE RATES

With just two small modifications the mechanism described above for an orthodox central bank system also explains the operation of the classical adjustment process system in Hong Kong.

First, instead of Hong Kong's commercial banks holding reserve deposits at the "central bank" or Exchange Fund, they only held Certificates of Indebtedness, or authorisations to print bank notes. In effect bank notes — or their counterparts, the CIs — were the only "reserves" in the system.

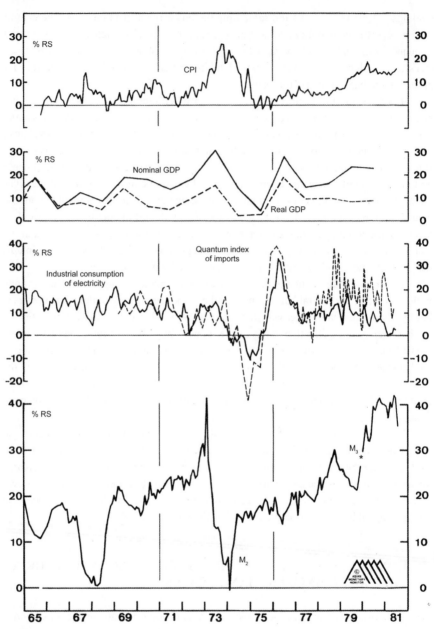

* Change of M_2 to M_3 series

Chart 2.1   Money, Output Indicators, and Prices

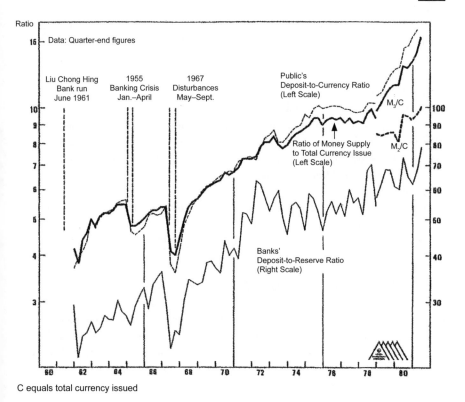

Chart 2.2   Monetary Determinant Ratios

Second, the Exchange Fund's only assets used to be foreign exchange whereas the orthodox central bank we were describing in the preceding section might have held a variety of other assets denominated in domestic currency. As long as the Exchange Fund only held foreign currency assets and the sole counterpart to these was CIs, i.e. the notes held by the banks and public (rather than deposits of banks), it could not deliberately alter the quantity of reserves in the system of its own accord.

As a consequence, the supply of reserves or notes was a passive process resulting partly from the balance of payments, partly from the public's demand for currency, and partly from changes in the amount of notes the banks wanted to hold in their tills as vault cash. Reserves were not actively or deliberately determined by the Exchange Fund; what the Exchange Fund did was to fix the "price" of those reserves, i.e . the value of the HK$ in terms of other currencies. As a corollary, the money supply in Hong Kong was not "deliberately determined". The quantity of money at any point in time reflected (1) the interacting decisions of the banks and public about the relative amounts of deposits or currency they wished to hold, and (2) the state of the balance of payments given the particular exchange rate chosen by the Exchange Fund.

In our example of the operation of an orthodox banking system it was a balance of payments deficit which triggered off the intervention to support the currency and resulted ultimately in a multiple contraction of the assets and liabilities of the banking system. In the classical automatic adjustment mechanism operating in Hong Kong, reserves were also depleted by a balance of payments deficit, but this was more the outcome of the process than the trigger to the adjustment. The balance of payments adjustment or change in the money supply occurred primarily through the impact of private portfolio decisions. If the demand for imports or overseas assets increased, the banks' foreign assets would be depleted leaving them less foreign currency with which to buy CIs (to print notes). This would mean that to meet increased demand for banknotes the banks faced a choice:

Either they must reduce their loans and sell HK$ to acquire the necessary foreign currency to purchase the CIs,

or   they must reduce the amount of cash they held in their tills (vault cash) relative to deposits.

The first course of action would reduce the amount of deposits, and in time reduce spending, ultimately leading to a lower demand for banknotes. The second, which would involve cancelling CIs in exchange for foreign currency, would run the risk of banks being caught short of banknotes with which to meet customers' needs, and would probably only ever be undertaken temporarily. In short, a sustained shift towards balance of payments deficit (due to an increase in demand for imports or net capital outflows) would ultimately force the banks to call in their loans, and this would have a contractionary effect on the money supply.

Over long periods of time variations in the banks' deposit-to-reserve ratio were not important. In other words most of the growth in the money supply occurred through conversions of foreign currency remittances (i.e. via the balance of payments), but from time to time changes in this ratio have been significant, for example the period 1971–72 (see Chart 2.3).

Similarly there have been long periods when the public's demand for currency relative to deposits has not altered much, but from time to time large scale conversions of deposits into currency have been crucial determinants of the overall quantity of money, as for example during the banking crises of 1961 and 1965, and during the 1967 disturbances (see Charts 2.2, 2.3 and 2.4).

To summarise, the level of reserves under the old Hong Kong system was the simultaneous outcome of the balance of payments and the money supply, with the money supply also being affected by the portfolio decisions of the banks and the public concerning their respective deposit-to-currency ratios. In normal times changes in reserves and the overall balance of payments would have been well correlated together, but variations in the banks' and the public's deposit-to-currency ratios would have served at times to cushion and at other times to amplify the direct impact of the balance of payments on the money supply. In a statistical sense therefore changes in the balance of payments or reserves were the dominant influence on the money supply in the longer term.

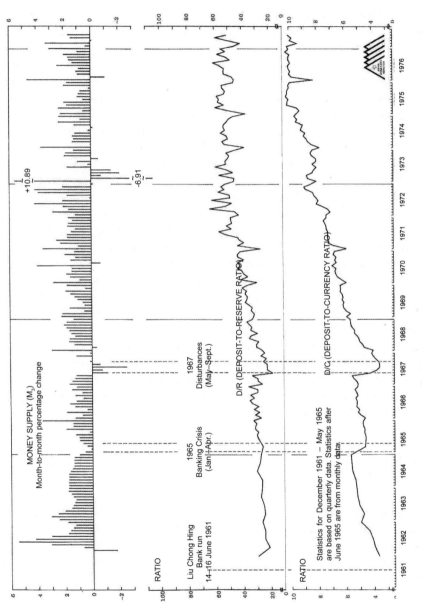

Chart 2.3 Money Supply and Determinant Ratios

The essential difference between the orthodox central bank in our previous example and the Exchange Fund in the latter is that changes in the reserves in the orthodox central bank system were *deliberately engineered*, while changes in the Exchange Fund system occurred *passively*. In the first case deliberate intervention to maintain a particular foreign exchange rate (with no offsetting action) produced a multiple contraction. In the Hong Kong case a balance of payments deficit also used to produce a multiple contraction, but the contraction occurred as a by-product of decisions by the private sector, and the Exchange Fund remained essentially passive. In both cases any variations in the deposit-to-reserve ratio of the banks or the deposit-to-currency ratio of the public would amplify or modify the direct link between the balance of payments and the money supply and, though critical from time to time, shifts in these ratios were relatively rare so their importance was limited to those occasions when public behaviour did alter (as in the 1965 bank runs, or the 1967 disturbances).

However, the essential similarity of the two mechanisms was that the effects of slower monetary growth in Hong Kong on the local currency would have been exactly analogous to the effects of slower monetary growth under the orthodox system: higher interest rates, slower growth of expenditures and ultimately a correction in the balance of payments. So although the initial decisions which produced the change in reserves were different in each case, the end results of the process for the economy were identical. Thus, for example, just as the fixed exchange rate and explicit intervention by the Bank of Japan operated so as to keep traded-goods prices in Japan in line with prices in the USA throughout the period 1949–1971, so a fixed rate in Hong Kong without explicit intervention but with the Exchange Fund passively supplying currency kept prices in Hong Kong in line with prices elsewhere.[1] The fact that Japan had a central bank and Hong Kong did not is, as we have shown, a difference of form, not of substance. The adjustment mechanism in both economies worked so that at the end of the day the two economies "adjusted" to external circumstances (the fixed exchange rate and the inflation rate overseas), inflating when countries to whose currencies they were pegged inflated, and deflating when they deflated.

(C) HOW HONG KONG'S MONETARY SYSTEM WENT OFF THE RAILS, 1972–74

During the late 1960s and early 1970s Hong Kong's authorities had to deal with many external difficulties. Among the most important and worrying of these was the devaluation of sterling in 1967, and the subsequent protracted negotiations in the early 1970s about how to diversify Hong Kong's reserves without putting undue strain on sterling itself.

---

1.   An article in AMM Vol. 3 No. 3 May–June 1979 had provided a demonstration of this proposition for Japan, and AMM Vol. 3 No. 4 July–August 1979 provided a demonstration of the same proposition for Hong Kong. See also Chapter 4, pp. 83–86.

From the standpoint of Hong Kong's domestic monetary system two types of changes were introduced. First there were outward and visible changes, and second there were the technical, internal accounting changes, not very much publicised at the time but nonetheless highly significant in terms of their impact on the operation of the classical adjustment mechanism.

Starting in June 1972 the external value of the HK$ was unpegged from sterling and pegged to the US$. In other words the Exchange Fund no longer issued CIs at a price quoted in sterling, but quoted a price in US$. At the same time and following discussions with officials from the IMF and elsewhere, the authorities introduced a band within which the price of the HK$ per US dollar could move. Aside from introducing more variability into the relationship between the balance of payments and the money supply these moves were unfortunate because the US$ itself was losing credibility as a stable store of value as American inflation accelerated. Also, with the American economy experiencing a strong monetary expansion at home, all those Asian economies with currencies pegged to the US dollar began to experience massive balance of payments surpluses which explicit central bank intervention naturally translated into huge monetary expansions. Hong Kong was no exception (the only difference being that the Exchange Fund was a passive participant in the process), and in 1971–72 monetary growth exploded, with M_2 going from 22% year-to-year growth at the start of 1972 to 41% in January 1973.

As the effects of this monetary explosion became evident in a soaring stock market, a booming real estate market and accelerating consumer price inflation, the balance of payments switched from surplus to deficit putting the whole process into reverse. The money supply turned down (recording absolute declines in each of the months from February to May 1973, for a total decline of 10.8% in four months), the stock market crashed, and property values plunged.

As if the gyrations on the domestic money markets and stock markets were not enough for the Hong Kong government to cope with, the gradual move towards floating exchange rates in the international economy from August 1971 onwards combined with the impact of the 1973–74 oil crisis, plus the switch from generally expansionary monetary policies to tight monetary policies around the world meant that the US dollar was fluctuating quite widely on foreign exchange markets against many other currencies. If the Hong Kong dollar was pegged to the US dollar but floating against all other currencies, then why not allow it to float against the US$ also?

The logic of this view seemed to be confirmed by the futility and frustration which the Hong Kong authorities were newly experiencing as they tried actively for the first time to peg the currency within a band. The new tools for intervention came from some technical and internal measures not publicised very much at the time, but which changed the structure of the Hong Kong banking system in a basic and fundamental way. For, having given an undertaking to maintain the Hong Kong dollar within a band vis-a-vis the US dollar, it was soon realised that the Exchange Fund had no Hong Kong dollars which it might be able to sell if the market rate threatened to move up against the upper limit of the band. To give them the necessary ammunition the authorities did three things:

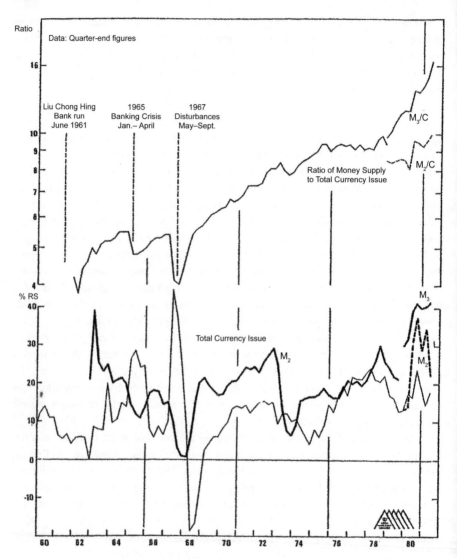

C equals total currency issued

Chart 2.4   Money Supply and Cash Currency

(1) they set up deposit accounts[2] in Hong Kong dollars for the Exchange Fund with the two main note-issuing banks;

(2) they borrowed Hong Kong dollars from the commercial banks to provide a temporary cushion which they could use in emergency; and

(3) to repay their borrowings and to ensure they would have a source of HK$ in the future the authorities asked the note-issuing banks to pay for Certificates of Indebtedness not in foreign currency but in HK$ by crediting the new HK$ deposit accounts of the Exchange Fund at the banks. (Presumably the authorities felt they could do this because having earned a handsome yield for many years on their foreign exchange reserves, the assets of the Exchange Fund were now well in excess of the minimum 105% cover required to guarantee the note issue.)

On the surface these measures appeared to enable the Exchange Fund to intervene in the foreign exchange market to shore up (or hold down) the HK$ because now the authorities had the necessary resources in both foreign and domestic currency to intervene on either side of the exchange rate. However, and to the acute discomfort of the officials concerned, they soon discovered that any intervention which they undertook was embarrassingly ineffective and did not seem to achieve any results. On occasion huge quantities of reserves were fruitlessly used up in the vain attempt to hold the Hong Kong dollar to some elusive and arbitrary parity band. Accordingly the authorities finally abandoned the struggle and in November 1974 the HK$ was allowed to float.

To summarise, the machinery for the "passive" expansion and contraction of money had been left intact, but the central pivot on which the old adjustment mechanism had depended — namely the fixed external value of the currency — was abolished since the currency was allowed to float. Worse still, tacked on to the old structure were the Exchange Fund's new accounts in HK$ at the licensed banks, together with the new practice of issuing CIs (permits to issue banknotes) in exchange for HK$ credit. The net result to put it crudely, was a free float *and* a free currency issue.

Since 1974 some minor changes have been made to patch up the system as it stands, but the key elements of the new edifice, namely the Exchange Fund's accounts in HK$ with the licensed banks, the practice of accepting HK$ assets as payments for CIs, and the freely floating exchange rate, have all remained intact. Moreover, the money supply has continued to grow rapidly, giving the lie to any supposed control the authorities claim to have over it through interest rates, moral suasion, or any other weapon. Many people are increasingly concerned that there is something seriously wrong with Hong Kong's monetary system, but few can specify exactly what it is, or what needs to be done.

---

2. These may not have been entirely new: the Exchange Fund may have kept small HK$ deposits before to meet petty expenses, but the practice of accepting and depositing HK$ funds against CIs must have raised the size of transactions on such accounts to an entirely different level of magnitude, at the same time as transforming the monetary implications of issuing CIs.

CENTRAL BANK OR NO CENTRAL BANK?
A CRITIQUE OF THE OFFICIAL CASE

The official case against establishing a central bank in Hong Kong was formally set out by P.W. Allsopp, Deputy Secretary for Monetary Affairs in a speech on November 27th 1980. His procedure was to define a central bank in terms of its functions, listing 12 typical functions ("in no particular order of priority"):

(a)   acting as financial adviser to the Government;

(b)   supervising the private deposit-taking sector (including the banks);

(c)   regulating the exchange rate;

(d)   managing the economy's foreign currency reserves;

(e)   acting as banker to the Government;

(f)   issuing notes and coins;

(g)   managing the Government's debt;

(h)   carrying out open market operations;

(i)   acting as lender of last resort to the money market;

(j)   acting as banker to the banking system;

(k)   organising emergency support for banks and other deposit-taking institutions; and

(l)   operating or supervising exchange control.

He then asked the question, which of these functions is already carried out by the monetary authorities in Hong Kong? In answer to this he proceeded to demonstrate that almost every function was currently being performed by the Exchange Fund itself (or by the Monetary Affairs Branch of the Government Secretariat, or by the Commissioner of Banking and Deposit-Taking Companies).

In respect of items (a) to (f) the implicit conclusion was that since the Hong Kong authorities already perform all of these tasks, a new central bank as such was not necessary. The Hong Kong and Shanghai Banking Corporation acted as lender of last resort to any particular bank in the money market (i), but the foreign exchange market was the "residual source of liquidity" for the banking system as a whole (j). The Commissioner of Banking has powers to intervene in the running of a bank that gets into solvency difficulties (k), and the Monetary Affairs Branch would be likely to take a lead in making the ad hoc arrangements for an emergency support operation.

In regard to (l), there is no foreign exchange control in Hong Kong so this can be left on one side. That leaves two functions not so far covered: items (g) and (h).

In respect of managing the government's debt (g), which is really the counterpart of managing the foreign currency reserves, there is no such debt to be managed so the issue doesn't arise.

With respect to carrying out open market operations, Allsopp correctly points out that while other governments can use open market operations to immobilise "the banking system's unlent resources", the Hong Kong government cannot because there isn't any such debt. Even if the Exchange Fund instructed the licensed banks to place Special Deposits (required reserves in American terminology) with it, he argued, in Hong Kong's circumstances the funds thus acquired by the Exchange Fund would not be immobilised but would have to be channelled back into the banking system.

"It is not the absence of a central bank which would make these circular movements of funds", he concluded, "but the absence of government debt".

Wrong.

Even if HK Government debt instruments existed, the movement of funds would still be circular. The reason is precisely analogous to the explanation of why intervention in the foreign exchange market does not work in Hong Kong.

In effect Allsopp's methodology was to ask what were the similarities between the functions of an orthodox central bank and the functions currently performed by the Hong Kong authorities. Instead it would have been more fruitful to have started with the question, what is it that is different about the operations of the Exchange Fund as compared with orthodox central banks?

As explained in the accompanying text the crucial differences between the Hong Kong system and other monetary systems do not so much concern the functions of a monetary authority as the accounting relationships between the authority and the banks, and the consequences which these imply for the banking system as a whole. Specifically:

(1) Instead of the commercial banks or licensed banks holding HK$ deposits with the monetary authorities, the Hong Kong monetary authorities hold domestic currency deposits with the commercial banks — the exact opposite to orthodox systems.

(2) This undermines the multiple expansion or multiple contraction mechanism which is fundamental to the operation of an orthodox central bank system or, for that matter, the traditional colonial currency board system of which Hong Kong's Exchange Fund is a variant.[*]

---

[*] Multiple expansion or contraction does still occur in Hong Kong through variations in the monetary determinant ratios (shown in Charts 2.2 and 2.3), and through the impact of the balance of payments. However the Exchange Fund no longer has the key role in this process whereas it used to have the (passive) role of setting the foreign currency price for the HK$, which in turn determined the balance of payments.

(3) It also effectively relegates the Exchange Fund from the status of an institution which can directly or indirectly control monetary growth to an institution which is on a par with any other large corporation holding deposits in the banking system.

This is what Allsopp refers to as the circular movement of funds consequent upon any operations by the Exchange Fund, and it is this which constitutes the basis for the official policy that it is not feasible to manage the foreign exchange rate or control the money supply.

Correct — insofar as it goes.

But the official conclusion that there is no operational case for the creation of a central bank in Hong Kong is, in our submission, not the end of the story. It is true that so long as Hong Kong has, in Allsopp's phrase, these "rather idiosyncratic institutional arrangements" (whereby the Exchange Fund holds HK$ deposits with the banking system), the Monetary Affairs Branch or the Exchange Fund is prevented from acting effectively like any orthodox monetary authority to expand or contract the money supply.

However, that begs the whole question of whether these "idiosyncratic institutional arrangements" can, in the light of the events of the recent past, be considered any longer desirable for the long term health of the economy.

In our view these arrangements have not served Hong Kong well, and it is time to review them.

(D) WHY INTERVENTION IN HONG KONG'S FOREIGN EXCHANGE MARKET DOESN'T WORK

Under the orthodox central banking system described in section (A) intervention in the foreign exchange market was successful because the central bank's transactions produced a reduction in the quantity of bank reserves, and hence tightened the money supply. In the classical pre-1972 system in Hong Kong a similar result was achieved even though the Exchange Fund was a passive participant in the process. In both systems the formal pegging of the exchange rate worked because balance of payments surpluses or deficits at any given exchange rate produced a corresponding multiple expansion or multiple contraction of bank credit or deposits which in turn induced adjustments in the economy that tended to correct the original source of the problem. This self-correcting mechanism in Hong Kong was "automatic" in the sense that the Exchange Fund was a passive participant in the process in contrast to the orthodox central bank case where the intervention was explicit and discretionary.

However, the new Hong Kong dollar accounts of the Exchange Fund with the licensed banks (actually with the two largest note-issuing banks), activated and enlarged in 1972–74 to meet the need to intervene actively in the foreign exchange market, do not have comparable multiple expansion or multiple contractionary effects (see tables on pp. 30–31).

If the authorities wish to stop the Hong Kong currency depreciating, the Exchange Fund will buy Hong Kong dollars in the foreign exchange market from private sector owners of those deposits who will receive foreign currency deposits in exchange. The problem is that the Exchange Fund nowadays deposits the Hong Kong dollars it receives from such support operations back in the banking system, where the funds are again lent out, so there is no material change in the size of banks' balance sheets — only a transfer in the ownership of HK$ deposits from the private sector to the Exchange Fund.

Similarly, if the authorities were in the enviable position of wishing to limit an upward appreciation of the HK$ exchange rate, they would be equally powerless to do anything about it. The Exchange Fund would buy foreign currency from private individuals or corporations in the market and sell Hong Kong dollars to them. Insofar as the Exchange Fund is a seller of Hong Kong currency this would keep the currency down momentarily, but as soon as the authorities had no more Hong Kong dollars to sell the effectiveness of their intervention would be at an end. The net effect would be a transfer of deposits between the Exchange Fund and the private sector, but with no multiple expansion of the banking system as a whole. So the old adjustment mechanism, whereby the money supply expanded until the balance of payments was corrected by increased spending on imports or capital outflows (both induced by the monetary expansion), no longer operates.

In other words deposits "withdrawn" from the banking system by Exchange Fund are not withdrawn at all, they are merely redeposited with the banking system. Conversely deposits "injected" into the system by Exchange Fund intervention to keep the HK$ rate down are not really new additions to the system at all, they are merely transfers of deposits from the government sector to the private sector with no effect on the overall size of licensed bank balance sheets.

A useful way of looking at the situation today (1981) is to regard the Exchange Fund as if it were just any large corporation. (The Exchange Fund happens to have the special privilege of enjoying the seignorage from the issues of CIs, but that is not material to the argument here.) If the Exchange Fund buys or sells foreign exchange through the banking system its transactions are just like those of any other large corporation. If the Exchange Fund Corporation buys Hong Kong dollars and the ABCD Corporation sells Hong Kong dollars the end result is a transfer of the ownership of deposits, not a change in the total quantity of deposits. This is quite a different result from the intervention operations of the orthodox central bank described in section (A) where sales and purchases of foreign currency for domestic currency led respectively to a multiple contraction or expansion in the total money supply.

The only other peculiarity of the Exchange Fund in comparison with other public corporations is that under legislation introduced in 1979 the Exchange Fund can arrange

Table 2.1 The Multiple Contraction Process in an Orthodox Banking System — How Intervention Works

STAGE 1: STARTING POINT

Central Bank

Foreign Exchange 600	Banknotes	550
	Deposits of banks	50

Commercial Bank

Banknotes	50	Deposits	5000
Deposits at Central Bank	50		
Loans and investment	4900		

Non-Bank Public

Banknotes	500
Deposits	5000
Money Supply:	5500

Banks' Deposits/Reserve ratio*: 50
Non-bank public's D/C ratio*: 10

(EQUILIBRIUM)

* These are assumed to be the desired ratios in each case.

STAGE 2: INTERVENTION

Central Bank

Foreign Exchange 590	Banknotes	550
	Deposits of banks	40

Commercial Bank

Banknotes	50	Deposits	4990
Deposits at Central Bank	40		
Loans and investment	4900		

Non-Bank Public

Banknotes	500
Deposits	4990

Banks' Deposits/Reserve ratio: 55
Non-bank public's D/C ratio : 9.98

(DISEQUILIBRIUM)

STAGE 3: EQUILIBRIUM RESTORED
(figures have been rounded)

Central Bank

Foreign Exchange 590	Banknotes	541
	Deposits of banks	49

Commercial Bank

Banknotes	49	Deposits	4916
Deposits at Central Bank	49		
Loans and investment	4818		

Non-Bank Public

Banknotes	492
Deposits	4916
Money Supply:	5408

Banks' Deposits/Reserve ratio: 50
Non-bank public's D/C ratio: 10

(EQUILIBRIUM)

Original intervention: −10
Monetary contraction: 5408-5500 = -92

Table 2.2 The System in Hong Kong — Why Intervention Doesn't Work

STAGE 1: STARTING POINT

Exchange Fund

Foreign Exchange	600	Certificates of Indebtedness (CIs)	600

Commercial Banks

CIs	600	Banknote issue	600
Till Cash	100	Deposits	5000
Loans and investments	4900		

Non-Bank Public

Banknotes	500
Deposits	5000
Money Supply:	5500

Banks' Deposits/Reserve ratio*:	50
Non-bank public's D/C ratio*:	10
(EQUILIBRIUM)	

* These are assumed to be the desired ratios in each case.

STAGE 2: INTERVENTION

Exchange Fund

Foreign Exchange	590	CIs	600
HK$ Deposits	10		

Commercial Banks

CIs	600	Banknote issue	600
Till Cash	100	Deposits of non-bank public	4990
Loans and investments	4900	Deposits of Exchange Fund	10
Foreign assets	10	Foreign currency deposits of non-bank public	10

Non-Bank Public

Banknotes	500
Deposits	4990
Money Supply:	5490
Foreign currency deposits	10

Banks' Deposits/Reserve ratio:	50
Non-bank public's D/C ratio:	9.98
(DISEQUILIBRIUM)	

STAGE 3: EQUILIBRIUM RESTORED
(figures have been rounded)

Exchange Fund

Foreign Exchange	590	CIs	599
HK$ Deposits	9		

Commercial Banks

CIs	599	Banknote issue	599
Till Cash	100	Deposits of non-bank public	4991
Loans and investments	4900	Deposits of Exchange Fund	9
Foreign assets	10	Foreign currency deposits of non-bank public	10

Non-Bank Public

Banknotes	499
Deposits	4991
Money Supply:	5490
Foreign currency deposits	10

Banks' Deposits/Reserve ratio:	50
Non-bank public's D/C ratio:	10
(EQUILIBRIUM)	

Original intervention:	-10
Change in money supply:	-10

to have its Hong Kong dollar deposits treated either as deposits of a bank (in which case they must be 100% covered by so-called liquid assets), or it can have them treated as deposits of a normal corporation or individual (in which case they are subject to the standard 25% liquid asset ratio). Official assertions to the contrary notwithstanding, this facility has no monetary significance whatsoever. Switching deposits from one category to the other may affect the distribution of bank credit (i.e. the form of bank assets), but it has no effect on private sector holdings of deposits or the money supply properly conceived. (There may be a small statistical effect, but that is because the "money supply" in Hong Kong is mistakenly defined to include the ordinary deposits of the authorities and to exclude those designated as "bank"-type deposits, not because the public's holdings of money have changed.)

It is not surprising in view of these fundamental deficiencies in the Hong Kong banking system that the money supply has continued to balloon and periodic government intervention in the foreign exchange market has had no effect. Since intervention is not effective under present institutional arrangements it is not surprising that the government is reluctant to manage the exchange rate in the way that Australia, Malaysia, Singapore and other economies have done in recent years. But this should not be allowed to remain an excuse for inaction. Active intervention may have proved futile given the present system, but that does not necessarily mean that another set of institutional arrangements could not be effective. In particular there is nothing sacrosanct about the new HK$ accounts that the Exchange Fund set up around 1972. If they were to be properly rearranged in such as way as to correct the mistakes of 1972–74, then there would be some prospect that Hong Kong could return to the exemplary path of high real growth with low inflation and a strong currency.

However, under present institutional arrangements neither pegging the exchange rate nor controlling the reserves of the banks as a means of controlling the money supply is feasible. The plain fact is that given the present set-up with the Exchange Fund holding local currency deposits in the banking system (rather than the other way round) there is no way of successfully controlling the supply of money either directly via the reserves of the banks or indirectly through managing the foreign exchange rate — despite all rhetoric about the "interest rate weapon".

The solution to Hong Kong's monetary problems requires rectifying the mistakes of 1972–74, and instituting a simple and effective banking structure which ensures that in the long term Hong Kong can again enjoy overall price stability. At the same time it is desirable that the characteristics which have made Hong Kong's economic performance so successful are preserved. The options available together with the basic legislative changes required to implement them were set out in *Asian Monetary Monitor* two years ago (AMM Vol. 3 No. 2, March–April 1979), and still hold good today.

Briefly the two options are *either* to control the quantity of money directly by first redefining and second regulating the quantity of HK$-denominated reserves held by the banks, *or* to control the external value of the currency in such a way that the adjustment mechanism operates to regulate monetary growth in Hong Kong so as to keep overall prices in Hong Kong internationally competitive at the chosen exchange rate.

However, the first thing to be done before either of these proposals can be effective is for the Exchange Fund to close down its HK$ accounts with the two note-issuing banks, and having done that, *either* to revert to its passive role of supplying CIs (or authorisations to print bank notes) at some announced rate — which need not be constant — in terms of foreign currency (or currencies) with the basic idea of setting the external value of the currency and leaving the domestic money supply to look after itself, *or* to decide once and for all to become an honest-to-goodness central bank with the full panoply of instruments necessary to vary the reserves of the banks (or the monetary base) in such a way as to regulate the overall rate of monetary growth.

A MONETARY AUTHORITY WITH NO GOVERNMENT DEBT[†]

It is sometimes stated by private bankers and by public officials that the lack of any government debt in Hong Kong hinders the establishment of a central Bank. This argument is mistaken. There is no reason why a monetary authority or central bank needs to conduct its operations in government debt, nor any reason why the Monetary Authority should hold any government debt as a part of its assets.

Consider the situation in Japan from 1949 to 1973. Throughout most of that period the Japanese government maintained a budget surplus so there was virtually no government debt, and yet the Bank of Japan supplied reserves to the banks either by purchasing foreign exchange and selling yen to the City Banks, or by discounting private sector export bills or by making direct loans to the banks. The Bank of Japan held almost no government debt. Yet despite this, the Bank of Japan was able to influence monetary growth upwards or downwards, and Japan accordingly experienced distinct phases of monetary acceleration alternating with periods of monetary deceleration.

Consider the situation in Singapore today. The Government of Singapore issues substantial quantities of debt, but almost all of it is purchased by the Post Office Savings Bank and the Central Provident Fund; almost none is purchased is by the Monetary Authority of Singapore (MAS). The assets of the MAS consist mainly of foreign exchange (92% as at the end of March 1978) and the MAS conducts its operations for the most part in the foreign exchange market. Government debt exists, but, except for small-scale operations in Treasury Bills, it is not central to the conduct of monetary policy.

[†]   The text in this box was originally published in AMM in March–April 1979.

It is true that Central Banks such as the US Federal Reserve System or the Bank of England conduct their open market operations largely in government debt, but there is absolutely no reason why this should necessarily be so. The US Federal Reserve could purchase Commercial Paper or Bankers Acceptances instead of Treasury Bills and Government Securities, and the Bank of England could equally well buy or sell private sector paper instead of Treasury Bills whenever it wishes to adjust liquidity in the system. Indeed the Fed and the Bank of England do buy and sell private sector debt instruments in the course of their open market operations.[‡] The crucial point is that irrespective of the particular instrument employed in these central bank operations, there will be a multiple expansion effect or a multiple contraction effect on the banking system as a whole resulting from the original purchase or sale by the central bank.

In short, the proposition that Hong Kong's lack of government debt makes it difficult to establish a Monetary Authority or central bank is a red herring. The only logical consequence is that the assets of the monetary authority would have to be comprised of instruments other than government debt, i.e. foreign exchange or private sector debt instruments such as export bills or commercial paper.

[‡]   Between October 1981 and October 1982 the Issue Department of the Bank of England bought GBP6.7 bn. (net) of private commercial bills, and sold government securities worth GBP6.5 bn. (net).

The details of the transition from the present system to a central bank system controlling money supply are straight-forward in principle but would be complicated to implement and would require a wide measure of cooperation from government departments and the licensed banks. Moreover, once implemented such a system would encounter tricky problems involved in defining the operating procedures, in maintaining the impartiality appropriate to a central bank, and in deciding on a rate of monetary growth appropriate to Hong Kong's circumstances. (See AMM March–April 1979 Vol. 3 No. 2 p. 15 for further disadvantages of this scheme.)

But the key question which the authorities will have to face sooner or later is how long can Hong Kong afford to continue with the present makeshift monetary system? How far does the exchange rate have to decline and how high does inflation have to rise before it is time to call a halt?

Already in December 1979 rent controls were imposed on private residential accommodation in a misguided attempt to suppress the symptoms of inflation instead of tackling the root causes of the problem. Like governments in other countries which have embarked on such a programme the Hong Kong government has claimed that rent control is purely a temporary measure. Yet the clamour for extension of the legislation when it expires in December 1981 is likely to be overwhelming. As the inflation intensifies more and more lobby groups are clamouring for special interest legislation to protect them from the effects of higher prices — public bus users who want fares to be subsidised, small shopkeepers who want rents on commercial premises to be controlled, and so on. The danger is that Hong Kong will progressively abandon the free market which has served it so well because the authorities are failing to deal with the problem of inflation at its source by correcting the deficiencies of the monetary system.

Meanwhile by imposing rent controls and thus preventing the property market from acting as the hedge against inflation that it normally would be, the rent control legislation is encouraging more and more people to look elsewhere and particularly abroad for a safe haven from the depreciating domestic purchasing power of the currency. That trend has been accentuated by the loss of confidence in the stock market. As a consequence it is likely that the Hong Kong dollar will continue to depreciate on the foreign exchange market, and then the danger is that the depreciation of the Hong Kong dollar will be blamed for inflation. Next, the wrong diagnosis could elicit further mistaken treatment, such as credit controls or another attempt to reinforce the Interest Rate Agreement, which would further damage the vital fabric of Hong Kong's free market economy and yet the disease would still persist . . .

It is time to blow the whistle on Hong Kong's monetary system.

CHAPTER 3

MONETARY DOWNTURN COMPOUNDS TRADE WOES

May–June 1982

Between 1980 and 1982 the developed world experienced two back-to-back recessions, with the US having recessions from January 1980 to July 1980, followed by another from July 1981 to November 1982 according to the National Bureau of Economic Research. Not surprisingly this led to a sharp downturn in Hong Kong's external trade, as reflected in the original title of this next article. Of more significance, perhaps, from the standpoint of elucidating the monetary mechanism at work in Hong Kong was that the trade downturn was accompanied by an abrupt slowdown in monetary growth. If previous articles had given the impression that Hong Kong's monetary system had a tendency to generate excess money growth, here was an opportunity to test that idea, or alternatively to devise a more robust hypothesis that was consistent with the empirical data.

The hypothesis I proposed ("A Hypothesis for the Hong Kong Trade Cycle") in the face of this new situation was essentially an application of the real bills doctrine. This is the proposition advanced in the eighteenth century by Adam Smith (among others) that money and credit should expand and contract to meet the needs of trade. It featured prominently in the bullionist controversy of the early nineteenth century, when it was repudiated by Henry Thornton and David Ricardo, who argued that controlling the volume of bills discounted (i.e. the quantity of high-powered money) was more important to overall economic stability than allowing flexibility of supply since there was no other limit to the depreciation of the currency "than the will of the issuers" (David Ricardo, see *The New Palgrave: A Dictionary of Economics,* 1987). The real bills doctrine appeared again in the Federal Reserve Act of 1913 and in the deliberations of the Fed in its first two decades. It was one of intellectual factors contributing to the Great Depression of 1931–33 (see Allan Meltzer, *A History of the Federal Reserve System,* 2003).

It should be recalled that I was continuously grappling with the problem of how, in the absence of a central bank in Hong Kong, one could explain the accelerations and decelerations of the money supply. In view of the global economic slowdowns of 1980–82 it was natural for Hong Kong's external trade to slow down, and this could be extended to explain the behaviour of money and credit. The additional twist to the hypothesis was the idea that, since the banks in Hong Kong set their deposit rates through the Hong

Kong Association of Banks (HKAB) and lending rates were derived from these regulated rates, money growth and bank credit growth could in turn be viewed as a result of whether interest rates were set too high or too low by the HKAB cartel. If rates were set too low, or lower than equilibrium levels, this would generate excess money growth, whereas if rates were set too high this would generate inadequate money growth.

A global recession and the downturn in Hong Kong's trade, together with the delayed adjustments in HKAB interest rates, produced exactly the set of conditions that could explain the sharp downswing in Hong Kong's money growth in 1982. Moreover, the temporary stabilization of the exchange rate during the global recession would also be consistent with the idea that Hong Kong's monetary system was subject to a real bills mechanism. Although nothing can ever be conclusively proved in the real world from economic theory, it would be hard to replicate a situation that more closely conformed to a textbook case of the real bills doctrine than that in Hong Kong between 1974 and 1983.

The analysis places strong emphasis on the desirability of monetary base control, or at least a quantitative approach to monetary control. In part this approach was designed to highlight the defects of the Hong Kong monetary framework in an era when the authorities had no direct means of managing expansions or contractions in the system; in part it reflected the academic spirit of the times which featured Paul Volcker at the Federal Reserve System attempting to implement monetary base control, and Margaret Thatcher's first government in the UK attempting to control the broader monetary aggregates. An updated analysis would be more sympathetic to the use of interest rates as a means of indirectly achieving monetary stability, but it would still home in on the lack of suitable monetary instruments available at the time, and the inappropriate structural or accounting relationship prevailing between the Hong Kong authorities and the banking system.

A S I A N   M O N E T A R Y   M O N I T O R
Vol. 6 No. 3 May–June 1982

The downturn in world trade is slowly but surely affecting the economic performance of Hong Kong. Not only is the slowdown apparent in the external sector, but it is also having a pronounced effect on domestic activity.

The performance of Hong Kong's export sector is illustrated in Chart 3.1 and shows that total export growth (i.e. domestic exports plus re-exports) peaked at a growth rate of between 40% and 50% in 1979 and has been slowing down ever since. In US$ terms domestic export growth had came to a virtual standstill by mid-1981, and it was only the 20% depreciation of the Hong Kong dollar against the US$ which kept up the appearance of a continuing export boom. But even in Hong Kong dollar terms the slowdown is now undeniable: domestic exports for May 1982 were virtually unchanged from May 1981, and imports were actually down by 3% (both figures in nominal terms). In real terms, too, the downturn has arrived: after zero growth in the first four months of the year the quantum index for domestic exports then plunged 7% in May.

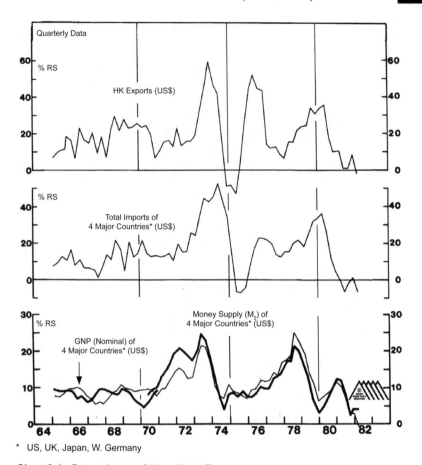

Chart 3.1 Determinants of Hong Kong Exports

In the domestic economy there is ample evidence that growth has come to a near-standstill. Retail sales have fallen, the output of cement for the local building industry fell by 7.4% in the final quarter of 1981 and by 6.7% in the first quarter of 1982. The supply of new residential premises had slowed up by the third quarter of 1981, and unfilled commercial office space rose sharply in the subsequent six months to March 1982.

A key factor in the international backdrop to the Hong Kong recession is the marked slowdown in global monetary growth over the past two years. Measured in US$ the range for the aggregate money supply growth for four major countries has declined to between 2% and 12%, a range comparable with the pre-1971 era. In Chart 3.1 some of the fluctuation in the global money supply total arises from exchange rate fluctuations (so a strong US$ lowers US$-denominated monetary growth) but in all major economies monetary expansion has decelerated to a slow pace, and this has brought down the total.

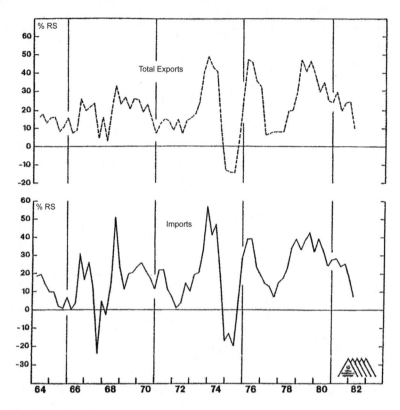

Chart 3.2   Hong Kong's Total Exports and Imports

However, an equally important factor has been the shift in monetary policy in Hong Kong itself. For the first time in several years monetary growth has finally slowed down, and this has been reflected in numerous domestic economic indicators.

Since the formation of the Hong Kong Association of Banks (a statutory body under the HKAB Ordinance replacing the Exchange Banks Association) in 1981 the authorities in Hong Kong have placed increased emphasis on the setting of interest rates (or, in their words, "the interest rate weapon") as the key instrument of monetary policy (see box on pp. 46–48). In effect the authorities have admitted that the peculiarities of Hong Kong's financial system make direct or indirect control of the money supply impossible. Direct control via regulating the monetary base or bank reserves is impossible because Hong Kong's banks and DTCs do not hold reserves in the conventional sense of holding deposits with the monetary authorities; indirect control via setting the exchange rate is impossible because intervention in the foreign exchange markets by the authorities in Hong Kong does not have multiple expansionary or multiple contractionary effects. In other words, because the system is not a conventional fractional reserve banking structure the authorities lack the standard instruments to enforce policy in either of these two ways.

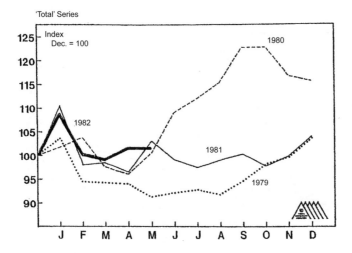

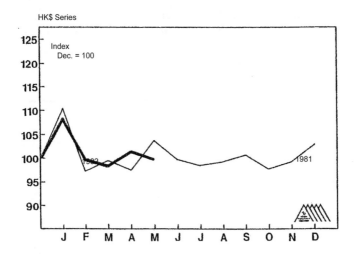

Chart 3.3 Index of Money Supply (M₁)

Controlling reserves and hence directly affecting the money supply is, in the case of most major economies, the best option. Managing the exchange rate and hence allowing the balance of payments to influence the money supply is usually the second best option, except in the case of small countries where it is sometimes the best option. But undoubtedly the worst option is the method of managing interest rates and hence allowing fluctuations in the demand for credit to influence the money supply. Yet this is the option chosen by Hong Kong. As indicated in the box on pp. 46–48, this can result in a money growth rate which is determined in the first instance by the demand for credit, and ultimately by the fickle trend of expectations.

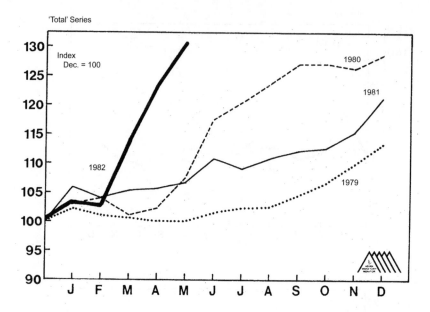

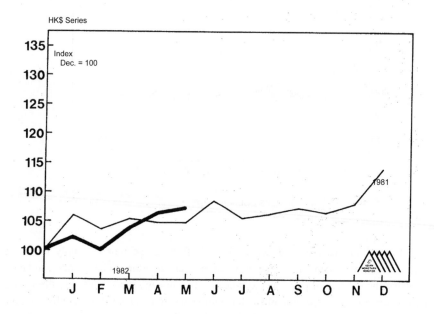

Chart 3.4   Index of Money Supply (M$_2$)

'Total' Series

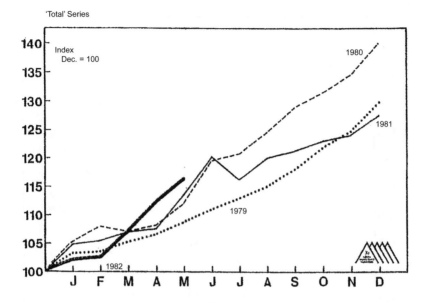

HK$ Series

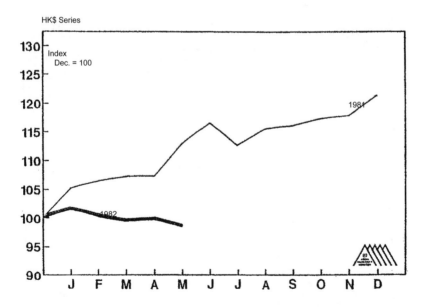

Chart 3.5 Index of Money Supply (M₃)

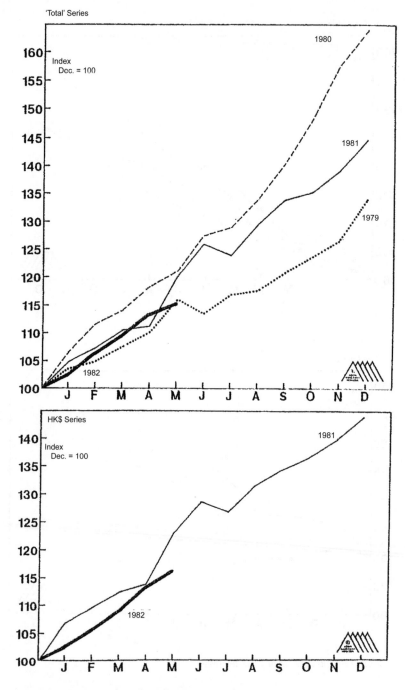

'Total' Series

Index
Dec. = 100

1980

1981

1979

1982

J F M A M J J A S O N D

HK$ Series

Index
Dec. = 100

1981

1982

J F M A M J J A S O N D

Chart 3.6   Index of Total Domestic Loans and Advances

Not surprisingly, monetary growth in Hong Kong has consequently been highly erratic, varying from excessive expansion last year to virtually zero growth this year. A hypothesis to explain the mechanism underlying the violent cycle of monetary expansion and contraction in Hong Kong is set out on pp. 46–48.

Apart from the general policy of maintaining high interest rates to restrain money and credit growth, two factors have affected the money aggregates in Hong Kong. First, there has been a shift of funds since the Hong Kong budget of February 24th this year which abolished the 15% withholding tax on foreign currency deposits, and simultaneously reduced the withholding tax on HK$ deposits from 15% to 10%. The main effect has been to encourage banks and deposit-taking companies (DTCs) to book in Hong Kong foreign currency loans and deposits which previously were placed offshore to avoid the withholding tax. This shows up very clearly in the Total M_2 series which consists of cash held by the non-bank public, plus demand, time and savings deposits at the licensed banks in local and foreign currencies. Since HK$$M_2$ has grown very little since the start of the year, and the bulge in Total M_2 growth starts in March it is clear that the growth is due to the growth of foreign currency deposits since the Budget. (See Chart 3.4.)

A second factor affecting the monetary aggregates has been the erosion of the market share of the registered DTCs. Under Hong Kong's new legislation regulating bank and DTC behaviour, registered DTCs can only solicit deposits in excess of HK$50,000 and with minimum maturity of three months. Since much of their deposit base previously derived from deposits of less than three months' maturity registered DTCs are being forced to relinquish this type of business and depositors are being forced to place these funds with the licensed banks. An intermediate category of institutions, the so-called licensed DTCs, are not benefiting since they can only take deposits exempt from the Interest Rate Agreement in amounts in excess of HK$500,000. Thus there is a steady flow of funds from the DTCs back to the licensed banks which is helping to boost HK$$M_2$ at the expense of HK$$M_3$. (HK$$M_3$ includes DTCs; HK$$M_2$ excludes DTCs. Compare Charts 3.4 and 3.5.)

Loan growth continues at quite a strong pace both in HK$ and in foreign currencies (see Chart 3.6), which must mean that a significant volume of loans is being funded from foreign currency sources. Insofar as this indicates an inflow of funds to Hong Kong — effectively non-residents lending to residents — this borrowing by Hong Kong entities from abroad has helped to offset the trade deficit and to keep the Hong Kong currency reasonably firm against other currencies. However, if there should for any reason be a decline in confidence in foreigners' perceptions of the investment environment in Hong Kong those inflows could easily evaporate and the currency would rapidly weaken unless the authorities stepped in to support it. This would not mean that the banks could not continue to extend credit — there are plenty of ways for Hong Kong banks to do that — but it does suggest that in the absence of a satisfactory system of monetary control Hong Kong's currency is peculiarly dependent upon foreign currency inflows and particularly vulnerable to adverse shifts in sentiment.

IN THEORY,

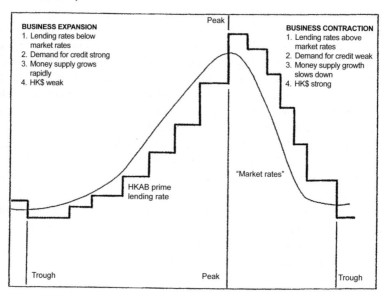

BUSINESS EXPANSION
1. Lending rates below market rates
2. Demand for credit strong
3. Money supply grows rapidly
4. HK$ weak

BUSINESS CONTRACTION
1. Lending rates above market rates
2. Demand for credit weak
3. Money supply growth slows down
4. HK$ strong

Peak

"Market rates"

HKAB prime lending rate

Trough   Peak   Trough

AND IN REALITY . . . .

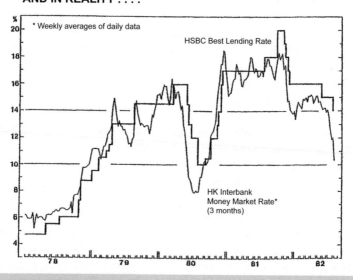

* Weekly averages of daily data

HSBC Best Lending Rate

HK Interbank Money Market Rate* (3 months)

Chart 3.7 Hong Kong Credit Cycle in Theory and in Reality

A HYPOTHESIS FOR THE HONG KONG CREDIT CYCLE

In any system where prices are regulated, markets will not clear. Accordingly demand for the commodity in question will tend to be either above or below the amount that could be offered at that price.

In the market for bank credit the same principles apply. When interest rates are fixed too low, the demand for credit will be very strong, and consequently credit expansion and money supply growth will tend to be very rapid. Conversely when interest rates are fixed too high, the demand for credit will be very weak, so that credit creation and money supply growth will tend to slow down.

In Hong Kong interest rates are set by a committee of the Hong Kong Association of Banks (HKAB) which is a legalised banking cartel. Its deliberations are directly influenced by the Financial Secretary and the Secretary for Monetary Affairs. The licensed banks are obliged to abide by the so-called Interest Rate Agreement on customer deposits of less than 18 months maturity and under HK$500,000. Banks individually set their lending rates depending on the cost and source of their deposit bases, but in practice the rates are fairly uniform. These "prime" or "best" lending rates are the key rates. Because the committee meets just once a week (it used to be fortnightly) and because the agreed rates tend to reflect the authorities' view of where rates should be (or where the exchange rate should be) rather than actual market forces these lending rates are somewhat rigid, and they tend to lag behind developments in the market.

During the expansion phase of the business cycle the demand for credit will be growing as trade and business activity pick up, as investment in property, capital equipment and inventories accelerate, and as inflationary expectations rise. Typically free market interest rates will run ahead of bank lending rates, and because lending rates will appear cheap relative to market rates or relative to inflation the demand for credit will be extremely strong. Bank credit and money growth will grow very rapidly so that despite the rising trend of interest rates the Hong Kong dollar will tend to be weak.

Gradually, as fears about overheating, speculation, inflation and a weakening HK$ intensify, the authorities and the HKAB will agree on the need to take action. Right at the peak of the business cycle they will finally jack up lending rates above "market" rates, just as they did in October 1981.

Conversely during the contraction phase of the business cycle the demand for credit will be weakening as business activity and trade slow down, as plans for investment in property development, capital equipment and inventories are shelved, and as the inflation psychology gives way to a deflationary mentality. Because bank lending rates are now above free market rates, and because lending rates will appear high in relation to the falling inflation rate, the demand for credit will be weak. Bank credit and money growth will grow more slowly so that despite falling interest rates the Hong Kong dollar will tend to be strong.

Finally, as fears about recession and unemployment increase, and as a strengthening HK$ discourages an export-led recovery the authorities and the HKAB will at last agree to get the economy moving again. Right at the trough of the business cycle they will allow lending rates to drop below "market" rates, and the whole process will start all over again...

HONG KONG'S MONETARY MUDDLE-THROUGH

Leaving aside direct quantitative credit controls, there are three main avenues of approach to the problem of controlling monetary growth.

Lever	Fulcrum	Impact
1. Direct control of bank reserves	Money multiplier	Money supply will grow at a known rate, but interest rates and the exchange rate will fluctuate in response to domestic and foreign economic conditions. Inflation cannot be "imported" because monetary growth is domestically determined.
2. Managing the exchange rate	Balance of payments	Money supply will grow at varying rates depending on the state of the balance of payments. Interest rates respond to fluctuations in the demand for credit at home and abroad. Inflation will approximate to the inflation rate in the country (or countries) to whose currency(ies) the local currency is pegged.

| 3. Controlling interest rates | Demand for credit | Money supply will grow at varying rates depending on the demand for credit at the particular interest rate set. The exchange rate will fluctuate in response to the relative demands for credit at home and abroad. Inflation will depend on the money growth rate which will depend on the demand for credit, which in turn will depend on whether interest rates are set too high or too low. |

To control monetary growth and hence inflation one can either control the *quantity* of money via regulating the availability of reserves (1), or the price of money in terms of foreign currency (2), or the cost of credit (3).

- The Hong Kong authorities cannot control bank reserves (1) because the Exchange Fund does not exercise any influence on bank reserves, and Liquid Assets are not amenable to control.

- The exchange rate (2) represents the price of money in an absolute and definable sense; it is the quantity of foreign currency which a unit of the domestic currency can purchase at any given time.

- Interest rates (3), however, are not such a reliable tool because interest rates are the price of credit (rather than the price of money), and as such they only relate the present and future values of usable funds, which is a highly elastic and variable measure.

In practice the Hong Kong authorities have muddled through by employing interest rates as an indirect method of affecting the exchange rate. Since the collapse of the Hong Kong dollar in August/September 1981 they appear to have tried to keep the HK$ in a band somewhere between HK$5.80 and HK$6.00 to the US currency, but since the US$ has been exceptionally strong over this period the result has been that HK$-denominated monetary growth has virtually come to a halt. In other words, in accordance with the theory set out on pp. 46–48, Hong Kong has swung from excessive money growth in 1979–80 to the opposite extreme today.

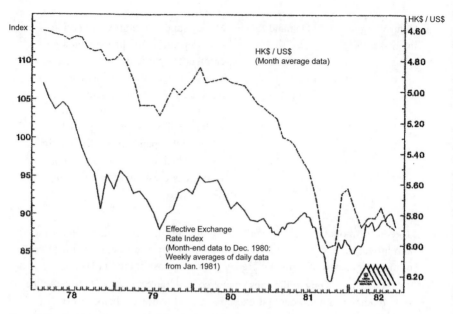

Chart 3.8　HK$/US$ Rate and Effective Exchange Rate Index

FORECAST

The Hong Kong dollar is normally weak during booms and strong during recessions. This tendency stems from the peculiarities of the interest rate mechanism adopted during the past few years in Hong Kong, and occurs because of the inherent likelihood that rates will be kept too low during the business cycle upswing, and will be kept too high during the business cycle downswing. During a trade recession the downturn in economic activity will be compounded by the tendency for HK$-denominated money supply to slow down very rapidly, thus squeezing domestic purchasing power. Although this has a beneficial effect in forcing Hong Kong to adjust its cost/price structure rapidly, it has some equally important side effects which tend to make economic activity, property prices and equity prices highly volatile. The current downturn is only just beginning to affect Hong Kong seriously, and any sudden weakening of confidence in the trade outlook or in the stock and property markets could temporarily undermine the currency as well.

CHAPTER **4**

HONG KONG'S FINANCIAL CRISIS
History, Analysis, Prescription
(November–December 1982)

In September 1982 Margaret Thatcher made her infamous visit to Beijing to discuss with Deng Xiao-ping and other Chinese leaders the future of Hong Kong after June 30th 1997, when the British government's lease over Hong Kong's New Territories was due to expire. From the viewpoint of the people of Hong Kong the visit went badly. Not only had Margaret Thatcher tripped and fallen on the steps of the Great Hall of the People in Tiananmen Square — an ill omen in Chinese eyes — but following these discussions Sir Geoffrey Howe, the British Foreign Secretary, had confirmed in Hong Kong that it would not be possible for Britain to maintain sovereignty in Hong Kong beyond June 1997. At this stage there was no official indication of the terms on which Hong Kong might be handed back, and therefore Hong Kong people were left to fear the worst — that there might be a complete transfer to communist rule. In this atmosphere a capital flight from Hong Kong started, causing the currency to tumble again. Between June and November 1982 it fell from an average of HK$5.86 per US$ to HK$6.67, a depreciation of 13.8%.

Having made it clear by means of the T-form balance sheets (in Chapter 2) why the Hong Kong authorities could not stop the currency slide through intervention in the foreign exchange markets, and having been brushed aside by government officials in August 1981, the only course of action that seemed open to me was to offer a comprehensive restatement of the entire range of monetary problems facing Hong Kong. This was the role of this extended article (69 pages in the original AMM) in December 1982.

The broad-brush argument — set out in sections 1 and 2 — was that the Hong Kong authorities had been treating the symptoms of the territory's monetary and financial problems instead of dealing with the underlying causes. For example, the authorities treated bank and DTC insolvencies only by introducing increased regulation and supervision. Similarly, they dealt with stock market booms and slumps by tightening securities regulation, whereas in AMM's view it was monetary instability that was causing both banking and DTC problems, as well as stock market and property market booms and busts. Furthermore the wide cyclical fluctuations in the economy, and a growing problem of inflation since 1974 were also evidence of underlying monetary problems. Because the Hong Kong government and banking circles at the time focused almost exclusively on "prudential" solutions to Hong Kong's problems, the text necessarily spends much time critiquing these approaches, attempting to offer corrective analysis of the true nature of the problems facing Hong Kong. Indeed the original section 3, which has been edited down here to eliminate repetition, exhaustively presented the four major instruments of monetary policy (liquid assets, interest rates, a government borrowing scheme, and intervention in the foreign exchange market), and why each of them did not work. In this chapter only the first three are reproduced in full; the fourth is summarized.

Section 4 (pp. 73–92) deals with the widespread misunderstanding in Hong Kong at the time of how the business cycle worked. One particular feature of business cycle analysis as presented in the government's budgetary statements of this period was the complete separation of developments in the real economy from monetary developments. Whereas monetary economists view fluctuations in financial markets and in economic activity and inflation as part and parcel of the transmission process of monetary policy, Hong Kong government officials had developed a view of the business cycle that entirely omitted money and its impact on the economy.

Some of the analysis may seem redundant today (e.g. the integration of the monetary and real sectors with inflation), but some of it remains very relevant (e.g. how a small open economy with a fixed exchange rate or with a currency board arrangement adjusts to external changes, and how its business cycle relates to the global or external business cycle). Sub-sections F and H (p. 83 and p. 86), dealing with Japan between 1949 and 1971, when Japan's real GDP averaged 9.4% p.a. and the yen-dollar rate was pegged at 360 yen per US$, are especially relevant to China today.

Section 5 (pp. 92–98) concludes by reviewing the two key proposals for reforming the monetary system that had appeared previously in earlier issues of AMM — either to control the quantity of money by converting the Exchange Fund, Hong Kong's monetary authority, into a central bank (e.g. by requiring the banks to hold reserve accounts at the Exchange Fund), or to manage the exchange rate with a central bank or modified Exchange Fund. Both proposals would have required a fundamental change in the relationship between the existing Exchange Fund and the banking system, a change that the authorities were not ready to consider at this stage. Moreover, it is clear from the article that a return to orthodox currency board arrangements was not considered one of the leading contenders for reforming Hong Kong's monetary system. In effect, of the three possible solutions that were to be offered by AMM in September 1983, none was regarded as remotely relevant in December 1982.

ASIAN MONETARY MONITOR
Vol. 6 No. 6 November–December 1982

1. OUTLINE OF THE ARGUMENT

1. *The Problem:* In 1979–81 Hong Kong experienced excess credit creation which was the major source of the boom in the property market and the boom on the stock exchanges, but since 1981 this has been followed by a sharp contraction in the rate of growth of money and credit, leading to a fall in property values, a crash on the stock market, and serious liquidity problems for many of the quasi-banks which helped to finance the boom. To date no less than eight deposit-taking companies (DTCs) have been suspended or are in various stages of liquidation. It is this boom and bust cycle in money and credit which is at the root of the current financial crisis in Hong Kong — a crisis which would probably have occurred for economic reasons alone, even without the added uncertainty injected by the political negotiations in Peking over Hong Kong's future.

2. *Current Stop-Gap Measures:* The present approach by the banks and the authorities to the crisis is a form of fire-fighting rather than fire prevention. It is of course essential to put out the fires and ensure the surviving banks and deposit taking companies (DTCs) are both liquid and solvent, but is that enough? Without sensible, fundamental reforms can there be any assurance that the whole boom-bust cycle will not be repeated all over again in the future?

3. *The Future:* Given the present banking structure and assuming that no fundamental changes are implemented before the next economic expansion gets under way, it is almost certain that Hong Kong's whole boom-and-bust cycle will be repeated once again sometime in the late 1980s or early 1990s.

4. *The New Banking Legislation of 1978–80:* The series of revisions to the Banking and DTC Ordinances of 1978–80 did nothing to regulate the growth of money and credit on any sound basis. Far from making changes at a fundamental level, the new legislation simply imposed an artificial 3-tier compartmentalisation of financial institutions by size and maturity of deposit. This was itself discriminatory, and, by its timetable of implementation, has accentuated the financial crisis among the DTCs. The new Ordinances also brought into being a statutory cartel — the Hong Kong Association of Banks (HKAB) — which enshrined interest rates as the key regulatory mechanism for controlling credit and money creation. But the experience of the past year or two and the wide fluctuations in money and credit growth have amply demonstrated the futility of that approach. In addition, at a time when the rest of the world was abandoning interest rates as an unreliable device for the control of money growth it is at the very least appropriate to question the wisdom of adopting interest rates as the primary instrument of monetary policy. It is hardly surprising that they should have turned out to be such a weak reed.

5. *The Official Case* underlying the need for a 3-tier banking system is tenuous. Moreover, the official case against the kind of thorough-going reform previously set out in AMM is either unpublished or unconvincing. (See box in Chapter 2, pp. 26–28, "Central Bank or No Central Bank? A Critique of the Official Case".)

6. *The limited measures* devised and implemented in 1979 and 1981 — namely the 100% liquid asset requirement placed on short term government deposits and the official scheme to borrow funds in the money market in order to affect interest rates — have been entirely unsuccessful in moderating the wide fluctuations of money and credit growth. While they may have occasionally been used to some effect in raising the interbank rate by a fraction or temporarily defending some particular exchange rate, there is no evidence to suggest they have been anything other than useless in countering the broader problem of the huge amplitude of fluctuations in money and credit growth to which the Hong Kong economy has been subjected.

7. *The Business Cycle* can probably never be eliminated entirely — least of all in a highly open economy such as Hong Kong — but there is much to be said in favour of moderating the fluctuations of the business cycle by instituting monetary policies which do not actually promote instability (in the way that Hong Kong's peculiar system has done). Hong Kong would be better off with a mechanism which tended to restrain the economic upswing and moderate the downswing. In the belief that now is the time to be making plans for the longer term stability of Hong Kong's economy, some proposals are again put forward here which would accomplish these ends.

2. BACKGROUND TO HONG KONG'S PRESENT BANKING LEGISLATION

Thanks to the laudable reluctance of the Hong Kong government to intervene in the private sector, major pieces of banking legislation and other financial arrangements have usually been introduced to Hong Kong only in the aftermath of some crisis.

— The 1964 Banking Ordinance was brought in as a direct response to the 1961 banking crisis.

— The interest rate agreement was introduced in 1966 in the aftermath of the 1965 Banking Crisis.

— The Office of Commissioner for Securities, the Securities Ordinance, and the Protection of Investors Ordinance were all introduced in 1974 in response to the stock market boom and crash of 1972–74.

— The DTC Ordinances from 1976 onwards were brought in to regulate a part of the financial sector which was growing at such a pace that it posed a direct threat to the Licensed Banks and their interest rate agreement.

— More recently a 3-tier banking system has been brought into being with the specific aim of protecting the Licensed Banks' "interest rate agreement" which was rapidly being eroded by the competitive, free market interest rates offered by the deposit-taking companies (DTCs) for deposits in excess of HK$50,000 (about US$7,500).

From an analytical standpoint, however, this type of "reactionary" legislation has inevitably produced a somewhat curious and makeshift banking structure. The peculiarities of the Hong Kong system have resulted in a system which, in our view, positively promotes monetary instability because the authorities are virtually powerless to affect the rate of monetary growth, while the banks are not restricted by any external constraint on the rate of credit and money creation and consequently they are free to alternate between phases of exuberant credit expansion and extreme cautiousness and timidity. This results in wide swings in money and credit growth. (The non-bank public is for the most part not responsible for these wide swings in money and credit growth, but from time to time there have been episodes involving large scale conversions of deposits into currency by the public — such as in 1965 and 1967 — precipitating a sudden monetary contraction.)

In more orthodox banking systems the role of the authorities is to limit money and credit growth in the expansion phase of the business cycle by restricting the availability of bank reserves, a process which is usually reflected in rising interest rates as a symptom of tight money, while in the contraction phase the role of the authorities is to ensure that banks still have loanable funds by continuing to provide ample reserves, a process which is normally reflected in falling or low interest rates as a symptom of easy money.

The most recent monetary contraction (see Chart 4.1) has been followed by a collapse of property prices, a slump on the stock market, and a rash of bankruptcies in the property sector. Predictably, the cry is going up for more supervision, tighter control over bank lending to the property sector or to individual borrowers, tougher disclosure requirements, more vigorous scrutiny of the ownership of public companies, and more exacting standards for the registration of DTCs.

But if our analysis is broadly correct the real problem which requires attention is the fundamental instability of the monetary system as a whole. For as long as money and credit growth alternates between phases of dangerously rapid expansion and phases of abrupt curtailment or contraction, bankers and businessmen will inevitably make greater mistakes and get caught in a more severe financial squeeze than they would otherwise have done under a system which promised more stable money and credit conditions throughout the cycle. Responding to the present crisis by instituting tougher, more extensive supervision only treats the symptoms of the credit crisis, it does not treat the underlying causes.

Prudential arrangements and supervision are one problem; monetary stability is another problem. More detailed supervision will not control fluctuations in money and credit, but controlling money will limit potential disturbances in the system, and in so doing avoid the need for the extensive, interventionist type of supervision which Hong Kong is gradually drifting towards in the wake of each financial crisis.

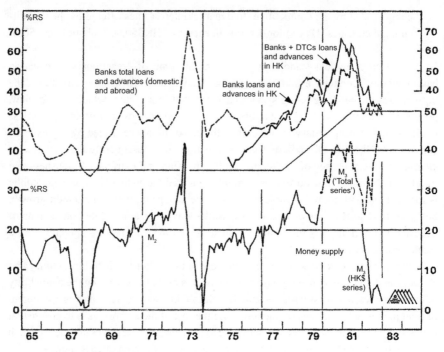

Chart 4.1   Money and Credit Growth

*   Change of M_2 to M_3 series

It is true that there have been abuses associated with the recent boom-and-bust cycle, but reforms aimed only at increasing supervision without improving the underlying processes which determine the growth of money and credit do not tackle the root cause of monetary instability, namely the ability of banks and DTCs in Hong Kong to create (or not to create) credit more or less at their own discretion. Before 1972 banks in Hong Kong did not have such discretion, and consequently the ups and downs of the normal business cycle were not so severe.

The origins of Hong Kong's monetary instability since 1972 are to be found in (1) the technical innovations affecting the operation of the Exchange Fund in 1972–74 and (2) the failure of the subsequent misdirected banking legislation to counteract those measures.

(1)   The 1972–74 changes in Hong Kong's financial system removed the external constraints on excess money and credit growth but failed to substitute any internal discipline in the form of any domestic means of restraint or control. It is most important to understand this proposition because all too often the mere suggestion that Hong Kong should introduce any method of controlling money and credit is dismissed as outright interventionism or a failure to appreciate the benefits of Hong Kong's free market, laissez-faire philosophy. Yet the fact is that in all the years up to 1972 there was a very real control on the rate of monetary growth in Hong Kong. (The pre-1972 mechanism is explained on pp. 80–86). The fact that this mechanism of control was not an overt, explicit one does not mean that it was not effective. Indeed, the beauty of it was that it was automatic and unseen (even if not widely understood). Basically the authorities did three things in 1972–74 to undermine the operation of the old automatic monetary control system:

(i)   they changed the note issue mechanism in 1972 by allowing the note issuing banks to issue HK$ notes in exchange for local currency rather than foreign currency;

(ii)   they set up or greatly expanded the use of Exchange Fund deposit accounts in HK$ with the commercial banks, thus making the Exchange Fund a client of the banking system rather than the sole source of bank reserves; and

(iii)   the Hong Kong dollar was allowed to float free in November 1974, thus ending any formal link between the price level or inflation rate in Hong Kong and the price level or inflation rate overseas.

(2)   The new banking and DTC legislation has been based largely on the premise that the money supply and bank credit expansion can be satisfactorily influenced (if not successfully controlled) by means of regulating interest rates through the licensed banks' interest rate agreement. The legislation has not been aimed at rectifying the measures taken in 1972–74 and has instead attempted to impose some degree of order on the banking system by (a) compartmentalising it into three sectors and (b) formalising the mechanism through which deposit interest rates are set by the licensed banks. However both of these measures are much too nebulous to have any precise effect on money and credit growth. They also assume a much tighter link between any given level of deposit interest rates and money growth than actually exists, and they leave completely untouched the mechanism by which money (banknotes or deposit money) is created in the Hong Kong banking system.

Other sections of this analysis will explain first why Hong Kong's present monetary instruments don't work, second how the pre-1972 adjustment mechanism operated and how it was undermined, and finally we reiterate some proposals for reform first made in AMM three years ago and which we believe still hold valid today.

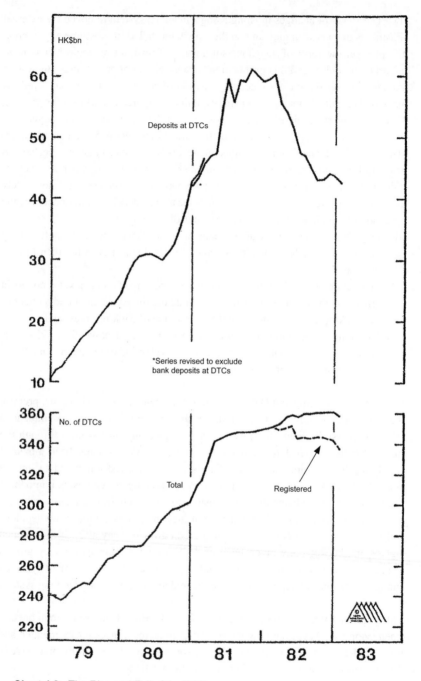

Chart 4.2   The Rise and Fall of the DTCs

3. HONG KONG'S MONETARY INSTRUMENTS AND WHY THEY DON'T WORK

(A) Liquid Assets — Their Shortcomings as an Instrument of Monetary Control

Liquid assets were intended as a prudential device but in Hong Kong they have come to be used as a monetary instrument. As a prudential device liquid assets are inferior to other methods of protecting depositors; as a tool for regulating monetary growth they do not work.

Liquidity ratios were first introduced to the British banking scene in 1955 when the clearing banks were required to observe a 30 per cent minimum ratio of liquid assets to deposits. In 1964 the ratio was reduced to 28 per cent. From 1946 to 1971 there was also a narrower cash ratio of 8 per cent applicable to London clearing banks. In 1971 both ratios were replaced with a so-called reserve asset ratio of 12.5% of eligible liabilities, though this excluded assets which were also liabilities of the Bank of England such as vault cash.

The importance of these British practices for Hong Kong was that in the period following the run on the Liu Chong Hing Bank in 1961, recommendations were made for Hong Kong by Mr. H.T. Tomkins of the Bank of England which relied heavily on British practice, and in particular on the intellectual framework adopted by the Report of the Radcliffe Committee on the Working of the (British) Monetary System (1959). These recommendations were enshrined in the Banking Ordinance of 1964 which under Section 18 imposed on Hong Kong's licensed banks the obligation to hold certain specified liquid assets equal to at least 25% of their Hong Kong dollar deposits. The 25% ratio was divided into two categories, 15% was required to be held in certain "super-liquid" assets and the remaining 10% could be held in assets deemed to be slightly less marketable. Over the years there have been some changes in the definition of liquid assets, but they have remained unaltered in principle.

As a prudential device to protect depositors the ratios were dramatically put to the test by the banking crisis of 1965, the year following their introduction. Evidently they did not stop bank runs, and their definition was therefore tightened up so as to permit only net balances with other banks in Hong Kong to qualify as a part of the extensive amendments to the Banking Ordinance in 1967.

The problem with liquid asset ratios as a prudential device is that while they may ensure that at least a proportion of bank deposits is matched by readily marketable assets, they cannot protect depositors to any greater extent than the liquid assets themselves if other bank assets or bank capital are not available due to illiquidity or insolvency. In this respect they are inherently inferior to deposit insurance as a means of protecting depositors.

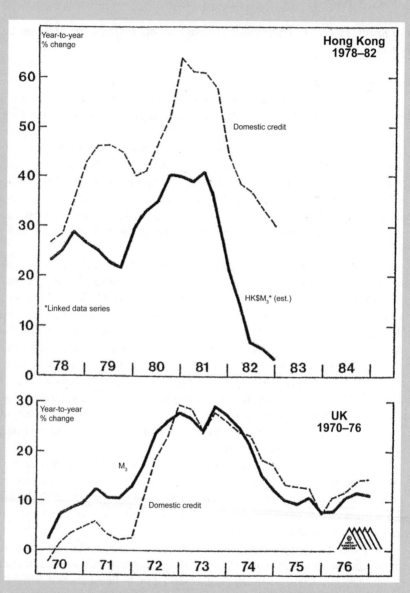

Chart 4.3 The UK Secondary Banking Crisis and Hong Kong's DTC Crisis: A Striking Parallel

THE BRITISH SECONDARY BANKING CRISIS OF 1973–74
AND THE HONG KONG DTC CRISIS OF 1982–83:
SOME STRIKING PARALLELS

1. With the accession of Edward Heath's conservative government in June 1970 and following the publication of "Competition and Credit Control" in 1971 by the Bank of England loan ceilings on the larger banks and finance houses were scrapped, money and credit growth exploded, a variety of quasi-banks authorised under section 123 of the 1967 Companies Act flourished, and the property market took off. In Hong Kong finance companies which had grown up outside the licensed banks' interest rate agreement started to be regulated by the Deposit-Taking Companies Ordinance of April 1976, though no effective restrictions were placed on their growth, so that by April 1981 (when registrations were suspended) there were no less than 350 registered DTCs. Meanwhile money and credit growth had soared, and the property market was booming. By the end of 1981 DTCs had captured one third of the deposit market.

2. As a part of the financial U-turn away from the "Dash for Growth" the Heath government imposed a general prices and incomes standstill in Britain in November 1972, to include all commercial rents. With the economy showing signs of overheating in many sectors, the pound under pressure and the balance of payments deteriorating, MLR (Minimum Lending Rate) was finally raised from 7.5% to 9% on July 20th 1973 and then to 11.5% on July 27th. Banks' base lending rates rose to 11%. By September 1973 the Bank of England was requesting the banks to exercise "restraint on lending for property development and financial transactions". These belated attempts to curb the boom sowed the seeds of the 1973–74 secondary banking crisis.

    In exactly the same kind of build-up to the DTC crisis of 1982 the Hong Kong authorities first extended rent controls to all residential accommodation in December 1980. In May 1981 the Financial Secretary introduced legislation to restrain the growth of DTCs, and explained the necessity for a 3-tier banking system. As the economy became more overheated and inflation took hold the Hong Kong dollar plunged in September 1981, until finally in September and October 1981 interest rates were sharply raised taking prime to 20%, well above prevailing interbank rates. These belated initiatives during 1981 caused the property market to turn, and set the scene for the DTC crisis of 1982–83.

3. Perhaps the most striking parallels in the British and Hong Kong cases are the extraordinary similarities in the growth profiles of money and credit over the whole period in both countries, and the authorities' attitude

towards the use of interest rates in both places. The similarity in the growth profiles of money and credit is abundantly clear from the charts on p. 60. Also, in both places the authorities failed to raise interest rates sufficiently in the early stages of the credit expansion to choke off the demand for loans, and consequently the money supply ballooned. Subsequently both governments had to see to it that rates were raised sharply and far enough to choke off credit demand. The result in both cases was a painful and far-reaching downturn.

These experiences suggest it would have been better in each case to have restrained money and credit growth earlier during the upswing by some reliable mechanism (not necessarily interest rates), and then such a drastic downswing would probably not have been precipitated, and the associated financial crisis in each case would have been greatly alleviated.

The problem with liquid assets as a device for monetary control is that usually those assets defined as liquid assets do not correspond to the liabilities of the monetary authority, and therefore the monetary consequences of changes in the supply of liquid assets are not predictable. Moreover, since both the government and the private sector can issue liquid assets, the monetary authorities cannot control the amount that may be available to the banks to acquire.

In Hong Kong the authorities generally used to acknowledge that the liquidity ratios were a prudential device rather than a device for monetary control, yet in 1979 the regulations were altered for specifically monetary control purposes. The banks were required to maintain 100% liquid asset cover against any deposits of the Exchange Fund designated as short-term deposits. The authorities' belief was that by requiring banks to hold liquid assets corresponding to such short-term deposits they would sterilise the inflationary note issue mechanism that had been introduced in 1972. However, money is a uniquely fungible commodity, and there can be absolutely no assurance that any particular asset on a bank's balance sheet corresponds to any particular deposit liability, so provided that banks can obtain or create liquid assets without any difficulty (as any Hong Kong banker will cheerfully attest) it is evident that there is a still major loophole in the system.

To put it another way, so long as the banks can manufacture liquid assets to match any local requirement, there is likely to be very little effective restraint from this source on their willingness to create credit. The fact that Hong Kong's licensed banks have persistently been able to maintain average liquidity ratios of well over 45% as against a required ratio of 25% suggests that meeting the minimum requirement is not exactly arduous. To argue, as one official has, that a 50% liquidity ratio makes Hong Kong one of the most liquid financial centres in the world is plain silly; it could equally well be said that Hong Kong's liquidity ratios are among the easiest in the world to satisfy!

THE LIQUIDITY RATIO — A MISLEADING INDICATOR

Two Distinct Meanings of Liquidity

Much confusion in economic or financial affairs arises from a failure to define one's terms. A good example is the use of the word "liquidity". There are two quite distinct senses in which the word is popularly used, and it is vital to separate them. First there is liquidity as applied to an individual bank or other financial institution. Liquid in this sense means either that the bank or finance company has prudently matched the maturities of its assets and liabilities, or that a significant proportion of its assets are of very short maturity and hence easily realisable (i.e. marketable). Second, liquidity is sometimes used in reference to the financial system as a whole. Typically when interest rates are low people say that the financial system is highly "liquid". Conversely when interest rates are high fears are expressed that the system is "illiquid".

"Liquidity" under the Banking Ordinance

Under Section 18 of Hong Kong's Banking Ordinance the licensed banks are required to observe and maintain certain Specified Liquid Asset Ratios. These requirements were introduced in 1964 following a minor banking crisis, to ensure that individual banks were "liquid" in the first sense by requiring every bank to hold minimum ratios of certain kinds of assets to deposit liabilities. In effect the ratios provided a minimum prudential standard. In addition, Section 23 of the Banking Ordinance restricts loans to any single customer of a bank to 25% of the bank's paid-up capital and reserves, while Section 24 restricts unsecured loans to directors, their relatives or related companies. Finally the Ordinance places restrictions on shareholdings and loans for real estate not used for banking purposes. "Liquidity" in this prudential or balance sheet sense, however, has nothing to do with liquidity in the aggregate or macro-economic sense.

"Liquidity" and Inflation

Liquidity in a broader sense can refer to the quantity of money in relation to the volume of goods and services produced by the economy. In this sense "excess liquidity" occurs when the supply of money persistently grows more rapidly than the demand for it at any given overall price level. In the early stages the greater quantity of money available leads to lower interest rates. At the next stage business activity is stimulated as spending increases. The ultimate result is a general rise in prices (as well as wages, rents, interest rates etc.). If the growth of the money supply now slows down this is typically accompanied by a further rise in interest rates and a "credit crunch" or "liquidity squeeze".

One way to avoid inflation, therefore, is for the monetary authorities to design a system which regulates or controls liquidity in the second sense i.e. the quantity of money relative to the quantity of goods and services produced in the economy. In order to avoid runs on banks, or to ensure prudent banking behaviour, or to protect depositors from loss, or to protect bankers from overextending themselves to individual borrowers it may or may not be regarded as desirable to specify a whole variety of ratios and restrictions along the lines of the Banking Ordinance. But even the most complex and far-reaching controls on liquidity in this balance sheet sense provide absolutely no guarantee that there will not be excess liquidity in an aggregate, macro-economic sense. Hong Kong's Liquidity Ratio is therefore potentially misleading because even if every single bank conforms minutely to the liquidity requirements, the stability of the financial system as a whole may nevertheless be threatened more by the general disturbances that accompany inflation resulting from excess liquidity in the second sense than by any individual instance of illiquidity in the first sense.

(B) Interest Rates — What's Wrong with Them as an Instrument of Monetary Policy?

• **Theory**

If one wants to control the market for any commodity it is necessary either to control the *price* of that commodity or to regulate the output or *quantity* produced. The same holds true for money.

The price of a unit of money is not interest rates, but what has to be given up to obtain that unit. For example, one Hong Kong dollar may purchase one orange, or fifteen US cents. So the price of money in Hong Kong (or elsewhere) may be expressed either in terms of the goods and services that must be foregone (or sold) to obtain that money, or in terms of units of foreign currency. Rather than attempting to regulate the amounts of goods and services that must be foregone to obtain a unit of Hong Kong currency the authorities generally take the sensible view that it is futile to try to control the price of every commodity or service, and they leave this process to the free market. In the good old days, however, they used to define the value of a Hong Kong dollar in terms of sterling (1935–72) or US dollars (1972–74). This meant in effect that the authorities stood willing to supply (sell) or take back (buy) an indefinite number of units of foreign currency for Hong Kong dollars at the pre-defined price.[1] In those days one could say the authorities controlled the *price* of Hong Kong dollars, but allowed the *quantity* of Hong Kong dollars to be whatever was necessary to keep Hong Kong's overall price level in line with price levels of overseas economies.

When they abandoned this system in 1972–74, it would have been logical and sensible for the Hong Kong authorities to go from a system of setting the *price* of Hong Kong dollars to a system of controlling the *quantity* of Hong Kong dollars, i.e. the money supply. In Japan, West Germany, Switzerland and more recently in Britain and the USA the authorities have moved to controlling the quantity of money by means of monetary base control, or direct control of the amount of central bank money as a means of regulating the aggregate money supply. The Hong Kong authorities unfortunately chose not to do this, and ever since they have been tinkering with a makeshift structure in which neither control of the *price* nor *quantity* of money is possible.

Worse yet, instead of sticking with the two basic options of controlling the *price* or the *quantity*, they have sought to affect the quantity of money by exerting their influence over interest rates. To do this they have brought in extensive new banking legislation, created an officially sanctioned bank cartel to enforce regulated deposit interest rates, and imposed an artificial 3-tier banking structure.

But the problem is that interest rates are not the price of money, so there is no assurance — even assuming the authorities could have any precise influence on the whole spectrum of interest rates — that their influence would be effective in regulating the quantity of money.

Interest rates are the cost of credit i.e. the cost of renting money for a specified period of time. When an individual (or company) places money on deposit at a bank he (or it) can obtain some rent in the form of an interest payment, and the bank in turn is able to lend out that money as a means of payment to a needy borrower for a similar payment of rent which will normally include some "spread" that varies with a host of factors such as the creditworthiness of the borrower, the competitiveness of the credit market, and the efficiency of the bank's administrative operations. Because interest rates are often loosely referred to as the "cost of funds" or the "cost of money" it is nevertheless highly probable that many people including Hong Kong's monetary authorities do indeed think of interest rates as the cost or price of money, and hence they are led to believe that if only they can control this "price", then they can somehow control the quantity of money. Alas, this is not so.

In a system where deposit interest rates are controlled the main effect on holders of money will be to affect not the amount of money they hold in absolute

---

1. As in other colonies the Hong Kong authorities only dealt in banknotes (or certificates of indebtedness) and coin. As a rule they did not intervene on the open foreign exchange market.

terms, but only in relation to their total assets. If interest rates are held too low, there will be little incentive to hold assets in the form of money, and people will try to spend this money in an effort to reduce their money holdings as a proportion of their assets. The result of the whole community trying to spend this money simultaneously will be to drive up prices to the point where people feel that the amount of money they hold is once again at the right level as a proportion of their total assets. Conversely if interest rates are fixed too high there will be a clear incentive for the public to build up its money balances relative to other assets by holding back on expenditures, leading to a general slowdown in economic activity and falling prices until an equilibrium has been restored. So to be successful in controlling deposit interest rates as a means of regulating the money supply and keeping inflation under control the authorities must know precisely how much money the community collectively wishes to hold in relation to its other assets at any given level of interest rates.

On the other side of banks' balance sheets, in a system where bank lending rates are controlled, the main effect will be on the rate of credit creation by the banks. If bank lending rates are set too high borrowers will be dissuaded from drawing down credit lines, and banks will find themselves with excess funds which they will either lend to other banks at lower rates, so the interbank rate will fall, or they will buy already existing credit instruments (CDs, bonds etc.) bidding up their price and forcing down their yield. The rate of new credit creation will tumble, and the yields on existing marketable credit instruments will fall, encouraging borrowers to resort to these other credit instruments rather than borrowing from the banks at the high fixed rates. Bank lending will decline, but bank holdings of bonds and other investments will rise i.e. the *form* of credit will change, but the aggregate amount may not. Conversely if bank lending rates are set too low, borrowers will be encouraged to draw down and even increase their credit lines, and banks will find themselves short of funds, and they will bid up interbank rates as they try to borrow from other banks or they will sell credit instruments such as bonds and CDs which they hold as investments. New credit creation by the banks will soar, and yields on existing instruments will rise. Bank lending will expand at the expense of other forms of credit instruments, but once again aggregate credit creation may not alter.

•   **Application**

In Hong Kong's financial system alternative forms of credit instrument other than bank credit are relatively few and underdeveloped. Accordingly the main effect of bank lending rates being set too high or too low is probably on the rate of overall credit creation since there will be relatively little switching between types of credit instrument as occurs in financial markets with a more diversified range of financial instruments.

The direct implication of this analysis is that in Hong Kong credit creation will tend to alternate between being too fast and too slow, depending on whether bank lending rates are set too low or too high. Examination of the recent pattern of bank credit creation certainly seems to bear this out. Moreover, the controls on deposit interest rates will tend to amplify the effects of unstable credit growth because when deposit interest rates are too low people will tend to spend more in an attempt to reduce the amount of money they hold in relation to other assets, thus adding to the effects of excess credit creation when bank lending rates are too low. Conversely, when deposit interest rates are too high people will tend to spend less in an attempt increase their money balances in relation to other assets, thus intensifying the effects of the drying up of credit when bank lending rates are too high.

Thus the basic explanation for Hong Kong's boom-bust cycle is that interest rates are first an inefficient and very indirect way of controlling the money supply, and second, they tend to alternate between being too low for much of the business cycle (thus encouraging excess credit creation, a rapid acceleration of spending, booming property and stock prices, ultimately resulting in generalised inflation and a depreciating currency), and too high for the other part of the cycle (as when the Financial Secretary, Mr. Bremridge, finally forced the banks to raise their prime rates to 20% in October 1981, thus precipitating a sharp credit contraction, a downturn in spending, and the subsequent property and stock market crash).

In conclusion, the elaborate and openly discriminatory 3-tier banking system which was designed to protect the interest rate agreement turns out to have feet of clay. The intricately designed 3-tier system was intended to ensure, in the then Financial Secretary Haddon-Cave's words, "that an effective interest rate agreement is available as an instrument of monetary policy". Instead, it turns out not to be a dependable instrument at all (and this is basically why central banks elsewhere have abandoned interest rate controls). Rather, it has bequeathed to Hong Kong a system which virtually guarantees monetary instability in the shape of periods of excess credit creation and rapid money growth resulting in massive spending binges by Hong Kong's entrepreneurs and consumers alternating with periods of money and credit contraction bringing on sharp corrections to the property and stock markets and to the overall growth rate of the economy.

In retrospect Haddon-Cave's second reason for introducing the 3-tier structure has a bitterly ironic flavour to it. "The second reason," he said, "for creating this three-tier structure is to protect the smaller deposit-taking companies from cut-throat competition which would, in turn, undermine the general stability of our monetary system at least for a period." What he meant was that if the banks were finally to tear up the interest rate agreement and compete openly for deposits, the deposit-taking companies would find it very hard to compete and some might go under in the ensuing struggle. In practice what has happened is that the general instability of Hong Kong's monetary system (together with the reforms which were supposed to cure it) has undermined the property market, leading to a collapse in the collateral or security against which many DTCs had lent, and a drying up of the income of numerous borrowers who are now unable to pay interest or repay the principal. At the same time the DTCs have been deprived of their access to short-term deposits by explicit legislation, and their credit lines for interbank funds have also been restricted. So the combination of the general credit contraction associated with the interest rate agreement and the simultaneous introduction of a three-tier banking structure has hit deposit-taking companies on both sides of their balance sheets, and in doing so has precipitated a financial crisis broadly comparable to the secondary banking crisis in Britain in 1973–74.

• Conclusion

The interest rate agreement is obsolete and should be scrapped. First, its original raison d'être is no longer valid. Second, its current justification is manifestly unsound. Third, it is more likely to have a destabilising influence on Hong Kong's financial system than to provide a stabilising effect.

The original raison d'être for the Hong Kong Association of Banks' interest rate agreement dates back to the period 1958–64. During this period there was free competition among the licensed banks for deposits. During the most intensely competitive phase, in 1963, local banks were prepared to pay rates as high as 0.9 per cent per month on 12-month time deposits, and 0.5 per cent per month on 7-day call deposits. The competition for deposits combined with the lack of any required liquidity ratios for the banks (which were not introduced until the 1964 Banking Ordinance) led to dangerously low levels of liquidity among some of the smaller banks. According to Dr. Y.C. Jao the average liquidity ratio for the banking system declined from 53.3% in 1955 to 34.3% in 1961, but since this latter figure was simply an average for the industry, the more venturesome banks were probably operating with liquidity ratios well below 20%. Among such banks a deterioration in business standards followed, and resources were severely stretched. In addition, the 1961 boom on the property and stock markets encouraged a crop of irregularities in management and business methods. Finally, a wild scramble for a two new issues on the stock market (Kowloon Motor Bus and Jardine Matheson) drained funds from the small banks, which, together with the circulation of malicious rumours precipitated a run on the Liu Chong Hing Bank (June 14–16, 1961).

Although the Liu Chong Hing affair ultimately led to the Banking Ordinance of 1964 and the imposition of liquid asset ratios, it did not spell an immediate end to the interest rate war. In September 1961 the Hongkong and Shanghai Banking Corporations' subsidiary Wayfoong Finance Ltd. sparked off the next phase by raising its deposit rates for 1-year to 3-year deposits from 6% to 7%, while the parent bank also raised its rates for 6 to 12 month deposits to 6.5%. "These moves by the largest bank and its subsidiary came like a bombshell, and were widely interpreted, especially by the Chinese banks, as an attempt to monopolise the banking business" (Y.C. Jao: "Banking and Currency in Hong Kong", Macmillan 1974, p. 240). In this atmosphere of mutual distrust attempts by the Exchange Banks Association to work out an agreed rate structure failed to produce any agreement until July 1st 1964, and then only under the threat that non-signatories would be prohibited from use of clearing facilities, causing their cheques to be subject to a penalty tax.

It is not easy today to disentangle the rights and wrongs of this ancient dispute, but some conclusions may be drawn. First, free competition among the banks was generally good for depositors who benefited from competitive deposit interest rates. The only serious threats to the stability of the banking system as a whole came from illiquidity, capital inadequacy, and instances of malpractice among the more aggressive banks which then became prone to bank runs. Illiquidity was a problem which the Banking Ordinance of 1964 was supposed to address. (In fact it was not until the Ordinance was revised in 1967 that the liquidity requirements became sufficiently stringent to ensure that banks did indeed have positive net liquid assets.) The problem of capital adequacy has been dealt with in recent years by increasing the capital requirements of licensed banks (and DTCs), which means that banks have ample capital to finance any temporary adverse trend in spreads. Tighter supervision and more careful safeguards against the abuse of depositors' funds by directors or bank management have helped to reduce the more obvious malpractices, but it would be naive to pretend that there will not again be cases of abuse in the future.

Nevertheless, the current regime of liquid asset ratios (despite all their shortcomings in other respects), larger capital requirements and tougher conditions for entry to the Hong Kong banking market mean that Hong Kong's banks are liquid enough, strong enough, and sufficiently well-managed to be able to offer their depositors competitive interest rates on deposits. To argue that the interest rate agreement is still necessary in today's environment is to ignore all the improvements in supervision and control which have occurred over the past twenty years. For these reasons we believe the interest rate agreement is obsolete.

Although there are occasional (and in our view misguided) attempts to defend the interest rate agreement on the grounds that free competition for deposits would be worse than having the present day banking cartel, the primary justification for the HKAB is that the interest rate agreement is the government's only effective tool of monetary policy. Without it, the official argument goes, the authorities could exercise no significant influence on the growth of money and credit. However, it can easily be shown that money and credit growth have been ill-behaved rather than well-behaved even under the interest rate agreement, with money and credit fluctuating widely and pro-cyclically, amplifying the instability of Hong Kong's business cycle. One is forced to conclude that the much-vaunted effectiveness of the interest rate weapon as a tool of monetary policy is highly dubious. More important, the discrimination which the interest rate agreement imposes on the small depositor might be excusable if the interest rate cartel were properly effective as an instrument of monetary policy, but even that is very much open to question (see above, pp. 64–66). In our view these current justifications for continuing with the interest rate agreement simply do not stand up to rigorous examination.

Finally, the third and perhaps the best reason for scrapping the interest rate agreement is that it can be clearly shown to contribute to *instability* in Hong Kong's financial system rather than to be a force for stability. First, pegged interest rates contribute to unstable money growth on the domestic side (see box, pp. 46–48), but second, pegged interest rates will tend also to contribute to short-term instability in the foreign exchange market. For the more rigid domestic rates are, and the larger the proportion of domestic deposits that are covered by the fixed rate agreements, the more significant this instability will become. Interest rates, spot exchange rates and forward exchange rates are more or less locked together through the interest parity theorem. Consequently if interest rates are rigidly pegged and there is no central bank undertaking to stabilise the foreign exchange market, much of the variability in the demand for and supply of credit will show up in the foreign exchange market.

If the interest rate agreement could be shown to serve depositors and at the same time it could be shown to contribute materially to stability in Hong Kong's financial system, there would be a good case for continuing with it. However, the obvious discrimination against small depositors (under HK$500,000), and the manifest instability of the behaviour of Hong Kong's monetary aggregates only reinforce the grave doubts which theoretical examination suggests as to the value of the interest rate agreement.

While it may seem neat and tidy from a bureaucrat's standpoint to have all banks offering virtually identical deposit interest rates, such tidiness is more apparent than real because where price competition is prohibited, non-price competition will flourish. However, for all its virtues non-price competition will not solve the fundamental shortcoming of the interest rate agreement, namely ensuring that the quantity of money in Hong Kong grows at a pace consistent with either equilibrium in the balance of payments at a particular exchange rate or (assuming a floating exchange rate) overall price stability in the domestic economy.

To summarise and conclude, the original raison d'etre for the interest rate agreement has long since vanished, it currently fails to do the task it is purported to do (promote monetary stability in Hong Kong), and it is probably actually contributing to instability by encouraging alternately excessively fast and slow money growth. Moreover, the agreement is irrelevant to a more soundly based reform of Hong Kong's monetary system, and it should therefore be allowed to wither and die as and when more thorough-going legislation along the lines suggested elsewhere in AMM is introduced.

(C) The Exchange Fund's Borrowing Scheme: A Twist on Operation Twist

Concerned at the persistently excessive growth of money and credit, and acknowledging the fact that the authorities had only a consultative role in setting interest rates, the Hong Kong government worked out a scheme in November 1981 whereby the Exchange Fund was going to influence money market rates directly.

The plan was outlined in Legislative Council on December 9th 1981 by Financial Secretary John Bremridge:

"A scheme has now been implemented to enable the Government through the Exchange Fund to influence the level of money market rates. Briefly, the Exchange Fund can bid through one or another of its major bankers in Hong Kong for deposits in the money market in the short end (say one week to one month). This will increase the demand for funds in the market. The Exchange Fund then holds the funds it has taken off the market for one or two weeks, or even longer, so that the supply in the market is not increased to match the increase in demand. That will tend to push up, or to hold up, interest rates at the short end. When market participants come to accept that the tightness in the market is not a temporary aberration, the Exchange Fund will lend out the deposits it has taken at the longer end of the market (maybe three to six months) and, if possible, at a higher rate of interest.

"If the tightness in the domestic money market pushes interest rates to a higher level than banks or deposit-taking companies needing local funds are willing to pay, they will have to borrow foreign currency, usually US dollars, with which to buy Hong Kong dollars. That will directly support the exchange rate of the Hong Kong dollar. At the same time the higher level of these interest rates will be passed on to the cost-of-funds (HIBOR) customers as their drawings are rolled over.

"This mechanism will be most effective when local interest rates are rising, or when they are stable and no downward movement is expected in the next few weeks or months. If an imminent downward movement is expected there is little incentive for a bank or deposit-taking company to borrow funds in the three to six months range, and so to lock in what may prove to be an expensive interest rate. Conversely when rates are rising they may be glad to lock in an interest rate which may prove to be cheap.

"I must emphasize that Government is using, and will use, this new weapon in their monetary armoury selectively and cautiously. It is certainly not a panacea. Nor do we intend to be operating constantly in the money market."

This apparently ingenious innovation has two noteworthy features. First, if the funds borrowed by the Exchange Fund are not utilised i.e. if the funds are not spent by drawing a cheque against the loan, it is questionable whether there is any sense in which the money is "taken off the market". It is rather like bidding for shares on the stock market and so pushing the price up, and then not taking delivery. Ultimately the price of the shares must come back down again. Similarly the Exchange Fund's scheme will not really affect interest rates because it does not affect the aggregate amount of funds available in the way that central bank open market operations do; it does not remove the funds from banks' balance sheets or initiate a multiple contraction process in the way that central bank sales of securities would do.

Second, insofar as the Exchange Fund borrows short and lends long it is simply imitating the long discredited Federal Reserve tactic known as "operation twist". This trick was practised in the following manner. In November 1960 and in 1961 the Fed wanted to lower long term rates to encourage domestic corporate investment while holding short term rates up to safeguard the balance of payments against short term capital outflows.[2] Accordingly it sold (or did not buy) short term Treasury bills and bought roughly corresponding amounts of long term paper. The initial effect was to push up short rates and to lower long rates, i.e. to "twist" the yield curve. But subsequently the private sector responded by shifting funds from longer term instruments which were now less attractive to shorter term instruments which were now more attractive. Also, long term capital, though less internationally mobile than short term capital at the time, was discouraged from flowing into the USA, further undermining the Fed's intentions.[3] In other words the redistribution of funds which the Fed sought to produce by its operations was soon negated by the response of private sector investors at home and abroad to the now distorted rate structure. The experiment was therefore abandoned. Yet exactly twenty years later the Hong Kong authorities have introduced a variant of the same scheme.

To conclude, in our view it is highly dubious whether the scheme actually works as it is purported to do, and in any case the response of the private sector to such artificial rate distortions is likely to undo their effects within a short period of time.

(D) Intervention in the Foreign Exchange Market — Why It Doesn't Work in Hong Kong

Under orthodox central banking systems of the Bretton Woods era, intervention in the foreign exchange markets was successful when it produced accompanying multiple expansions or contractions of the local monetary system. Purchases of foreign exchange intended to prevent an appreciation of the local currency would generate an increase in the volume of local money supply, thus helping to offset the initial shortage in the foreign exchange market. Conversely, sales of foreign exchange intended to prevent a depreciation of the local currency would result in a decrease in the volume of local money supply, thus helping to offset the initial excess in the foreign exchange market. The problem for Hong Kong in the years after 1972 until the early 1980s was that as Hong Kong no longer had an orthodox monetary system, this mechanism could not be expected to work. The reason for the failure of attempted intervention in the foreign exchange market in Hong Kong was explained in Chapter 2, section D, pp. 28–33 and was reproduced at this point in the original AMM, but will not be replicated here.

The solution to Hong Kong's monetary problems requires rectifying the mistakes of 1972–74, and instituting an orthodox banking structure which would ensure that in the long term Hong Kong can again enjoy overall price stability. The alternative options available are presented in section 5.

---

2.   See Milton Friedman and Anna Schwartz, *A Monetary History of the United States* (NBER and Princeton University Press) pp. 633 and 636.

3.   See Leland B. Yeager, *International Monetary Relations* (Harper & Row, 2nd edition) p. 569.

4. THE OLD AUTOMATIC ADJUSTMENT MECHANISM — HOW IT OPERATED AND HOW IT WAS UNDERMINED

Summary

1. The adjustment mechanism is the process by which economic activity and the price level in one economy *adjust* to economic activity and the price level in other economies.

2. The adjustment mechanism is not simply the change in the growth and composition of the GDP but a much broader process, which may be characterised in three stages. The first stage involves the balance of payments and its impact on the banking system. The second stage concerns the impact of changes in the money supply on total spending in the economy, and the third stage concerns the feedback effect of greater aggregate spending (i.e. higher output and prices) on the balance of payments again.

3. This three stage process occurs in all economies; it is not unique to Hong Kong. What was different about Hong Kong (and other colonial economies) was the way in which the balance of payments impacted the banking system. The other two stages of the process were the same in Hong Kong as elsewhere.

4. The crucial difference between Hong Kong and other economies was therefore not so much in the sequence of events making up the adjustment process as in the way that the authorities (i.e. the Exchange Fund) participated in the adjustment process. In a typical orthodox central banking system the authorities participated (a) actively and (b) in direct response to the balance of payments, whereas under the Colonial Currency Board systems the authorities participated (a) passively and (b) only in response to the demand for banknotes, not in response to the balance of payments.

5. Hong Kong's adjustment mechanism was drastically undermined by the changes that were made to the financial system in 1972–74. Today the authorities are no longer passive, but they are powerless in the sense that they neither have the means effectively to control the quantity of money nor the ability to regulate systematically the exchange value of the Hong Kong dollar. It is the banks who now take the lead in the adjustment process through their discretionary power to create credit, and the exchange rate then alters to adjust the price level in Hong Kong to prices overseas. Hong Kong would benefit by implementing institutional changes which would restore control of the adjustment mechanism *either* to the authorities (by moving to a central bank) *or* to the old automatic mechanism (by reverting to a modified form of the pre-1972 system).

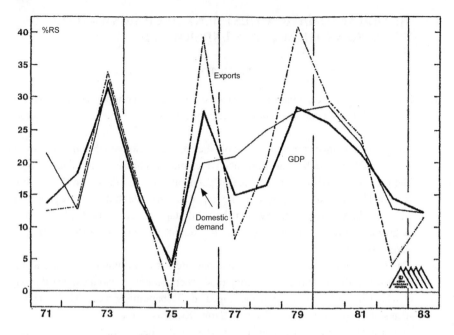

Chart 4.4   Hong Kong GDP and Components (at current prices)

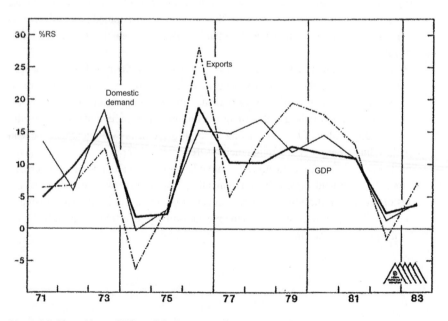

Chart 4.5 Hong Kong GDP and Components (at constant prices)

(A) A Superficial View of the Automatic Adjustment Mechanism

In his lengthy analyses of the Hong Kong economy, the previous Financial Secretary frequently referred to the operation of the automatic adjustment mechanism. A careful reading of his speeches reveals three distinguishable phases which the Hong Kong economy could be considered to experience: 1) An equilibrium state when all components of the GDP were growing at the same rate, 2) a stage during which exports (or overseas demand) was growing more rapidly than domestic demand, and 3) a stage during which domestic demand was growing more rapidly than foreign demand.

The actual experience of the Hong Kong economy in nominal and real terms is shown in Charts 4.4 and 4.5 (p. 74). As can be seen, the actual behaviour of the components of the GDP conforms roughly to the theoretical pattern depicted in Chart 4.6. (p. 76) In other words, periods in which domestic demand grows more rapidly than foreign demand tend to alternate naturally with the periods when foreign demand grows more rapidly than domestic demand. Occasionally both these components grow at similar rates, but this is rare.

However, the reason that these phases of faster and slower growth in the components occur is purely a result of arithmetic — it has nothing to do with the automatic adjustment process.

$$
GDP = \begin{pmatrix} \text{Private} \\ \text{Consumption} \\ \text{Expenditure} \end{pmatrix} + \begin{pmatrix} \text{Government} \\ \text{Expenditure} \end{pmatrix} + \begin{pmatrix} \text{Private} \\ \text{Investment} \\ \text{Expenditure} \end{pmatrix} - \left(\text{Imports} \right) + \left(\text{Exports} \right)
$$

(Domestic)	(Domestic)	(Domestic)	(Domestic)

$$
= \quad \begin{matrix} \text{Domestic} \\ \text{Demand} \\ \text{Components} \end{matrix} \quad + \quad \begin{matrix} \text{Foreign} \\ \text{Demand} \\ \text{(Exports)} \end{matrix}
$$

Since the GDP can be defined as the sum of domestic and foreign demand, if one component is growing faster than the total, then the other component must be growing more slowly than the total. But there is nothing unique to Hong Kong about this process: it happens in all other economies too. Nor is there anything automatic about it except in an arithmetic sense which also applies to all other economies. Clearly, this is not an adequate description of the automatic adjustment mechanism.

Indeed, this description of the interaction of the different components of the GDP is only a very superficial account of the business cycle in that it omits any reference to developments in the balance of payments and their impact on the banking system, or the link between changes in money and credit in the banking system and changes in domestic expenditures.

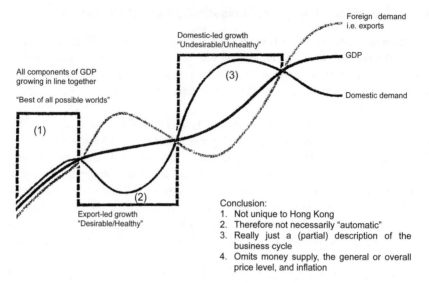

All components of GDP
growing in line together

"Best of all possible worlds"

(1)

Domestic-led growth
"Undesirable/Unhealthy"

(3)

Export-led growth
"Desirable/Healthy"

(2)

Foreign demand
i.e. exports

GDP

Domestic demand

Conclusion:
1. Not unique to Hong Kong
2. Therefore not necessarily "automatic"
3. Really just a (partial) description of the
   business cycle
4. Omits money supply, the general or overall
   price level, and inflation

Chart 4.6   Haddon-Cave's Concept of "Automatic Adjustment" — A Post-mortem

(B) A More Comprehensive View of the Business Cycle

A more complete description of the business cycle requires integration of the balance of payments, the banking system, money and credit, their impact on output and prices, and finally the feedback effect of changes in output and prices on the balance of payments.
Under a system of fixed exchange rates a surplus on the balance of payments will be reflected in an excess of foreign currency on the foreign exchange market, which will either lead to an increase in the reserves of commercial banks, or at least an increase in their lending ability. The combination of increased receipts from abroad in the hands of domestic residents or increased lending by the banks will show up as an increase in the money supply (Chart 4.7, phase 2). As these money balances increase relative to total incomes, individuals and businesses will tend to increase their spending, thus setting off a general increase in total spending (or GNP). The upward pressure of demand will trigger increases in output until supply shortages occur, whereupon there will be increases in prices as well.

Increased spending on all goods and services will be reflected in a greater demand for imports, and consequently a deterioration of the balance of payments. Similarly, higher domestic prices will result in less competitive exports and hence a worse performance on international markets. The end result will be a switch from a balance of payments surplus to a balance of payments deficit, whereupon the whole adjustment process will go into reverse (Chart 4.8).

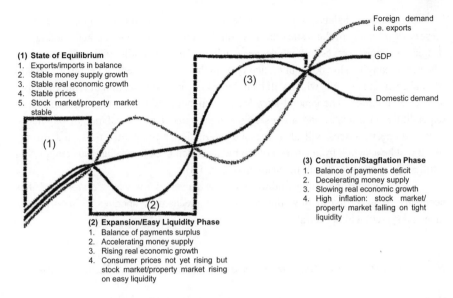

(1) State of Equilibrium
1. Exports/imports in balance
2. Stable money supply growth
3. Stable real economic growth
4. Stable prices
5. Stock market/property market stable

(3) Contraction/Stagflation Phase
1. Balance of payments deficit
2. Decelerating money supply
3. Slowing real economic growth
4. High inflation: stock market/ property market falling on tight liquidity

(2) Expansion/Easy Liquidity Phase
1. Balance of payments surplus
2. Accelerating money supply
3. Rising real economic growth
4. Consumer prices not yet rising but stock market/property market rising on easy liquidity

Chart 4.7 Characteristics of the Business Cycle

Outline of the adjustment process,

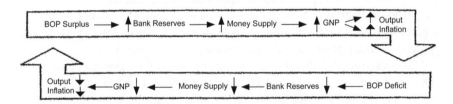

And Its application to two economies:

Chart 4.8 Outline of the Adjustment Process and Its Application to Two Economies

Conversely, a balance of payments deficit will be reflected in a shortage of foreign currency (or excess of domestic currency) on the foreign exchange market, leading to a decrease in bank reserves and/or a decrease in banks' lending ability (Chart 4.7, phase 3). The accompanying slowdown in monetary growth will tend to reduce the rate of growth of total spending or GNP, which will be reflected in some combination of reduced output and lower inflation. The general slowdown in spending will also show up in reduced expenditure on imports, and a consequent improvement in the balance of payments. Lower domestic prices will also improve international competitiveness, and the net result will be a switch from balance of payments deficit back to surplus, thus completing a full cycle of the adjustment mechanism (Chart 4.8).

To see why Hong Kong's adjustment mechanism is (or was) *"automatic"* it is necessary to look first at how this adjustment mechanism operates in an orthodox financial system with a central bank.

(C) The Adjustment Mechanism in an Orthodox Central Bank System

Under a fixed exchange rate system (such as Bretton Woods) the central bank in a country experiencing a sustained balance of payments surplus was obliged to take corrective action. The mechanism was that the central bank stood ready to purchase the excess foreign currency offered on the foreign exchange market. When it intervened in the foreign exchange market the central bank purchased foreign currency, thus adding to its foreign currency reserves. This addition to the central bank's assets was matched by a simultaneous crediting of the commercial banks' accounts at the central bank, their accounts being credited with an equivalent amount of domestic currency at the fixed exchange rate. As a result of this process both sides of the central bank's balance sheet expanded. In contemporary parlance, the monetary base was expanded.

The provision of additional domestic currency reserves (or deposits at the central bank) to the commercial banks enabled them in turn either to expand their lending in domestic currency or to credit the deposit accounts of their exporter customers (who were earning the foreign currency remittances) in domestic currency. Such new lending or conversion of net foreign remittances into domestic deposits fuelled an increase in the domestic money supply which was gradually reflected in greater domestic expenditures via the same process as that described in connection with Chart 4.8.

A precisely analogous set of consequences was set in motion by a balance of payments deficit, starting with sales of foreign exchange by the central bank and ending with a reduced rate of growth of total spending.

During the expansion phase following on from a balance of payments surplus the central bank participates in the adjustment process in two quite different respects. In the first instance it participates actively and deliberately (though of course it is in a sense under an obligation to do so) in the foreign exchange market to supply new reserves to the banking system (see Chart 4.9). Second, as domestic expenditures increase so the demand for banknotes will grow — typically in line with consumer spending —

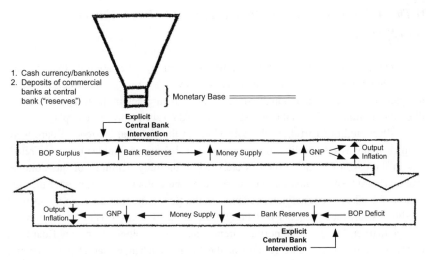

Chart 4.9 Adjustment Mechanism under Orthodox Central Bank System

and banks will draw down on their reserve accounts at the central bank to pay for the banknotes which will be passed on to bank customers. These two activities — supplying reserves to the banks and supplying new banknotes (and coin) to meet the demand for currency — are the hallmarks of any central bank.[4] Conversely, during the contraction phase following from a balance of payments deficit the central bank will tend to be draining reserves from the system and reducing or slowing down the supply of banknotes. On the liabilities side of their balance sheet central banks may or may not perform other functions (such as accepting deposits from the government or the general public), and on the assets side of their balance sheet they may buy or sell a greater or lesser range of financial instruments in the foreign exchange market or the domestic money market, but the really crucial point so far as the analysis of the adjustment process is concerned is that there are two distinct liability-side activities involved: supplying bank reserves and supplying banknotes. The supply of reserves is an active and conscious process in which the central bank has discretion to offset or not to offset balance of payments surpluses or deficits; the issue of banknotes is one in which the central bank is essentially passive, with the central bank responding to the natural fluctuations in the public's demand for banknotes which are conveyed from the general public to the commercial banks and thence to the central bank via the commercial banks' decisions to convert reserves to currency and vice-versa.

It is the deliberate, active supply of bank reserves by the central bank which prevents one from applying the phrase *"automatic"* adjustment mechanism to economies with central banks.

---

4.   As we shall see, a colonial currency board differs from a central bank in that it only performs the second of these functions.

(D) The Adjustment Mechanism in a Typical Colonial Currency Board System

The typical Colonial Currency Board system was simply a variation of the standard fixed exchange rate system described above. However, whereas in the orthodox central bank system the central bank bought and sold foreign currency in the foreign exchange market, the traditional Colonial Currency Board had no such active role to play.

As illustrated in Chart 4.10, the sole assets of the Colonial Currency Board were foreign currency assets (sterling in the case of British Colonies and Dominions, French francs in the case of French Colonies etc.), while the only liabilities of the Colonial Currency Board were the notes and coin issued by the Colonial Government. Since the commercial banks did not maintain accounts at the Board, the Board was in no position to credit or debit their reserves if it bought and sold foreign currency in the foreign exchange market. Moreover, in normal circumstances the Colonial Currency Board did not play an active role of intervention in the foreign exchange market like a central bank. The only role which the Colonial Currency Board played was to supply banknotes or coin passively in response to fluctuations in the public's demand for currency. In terms of the diagram opposite, this function occurred towards the end of the adjustment process, not at the beginning as in the case of central bank intervention.

Instead of relying upon central bank-type intervention Colonial Currency Board systems relied upon the operation of market forces in the private sector to bring about the adjustment of business activity or prices in the colonial economy to the level of activity or price level of the metropolitan economy. In an orthodox central bank system commercial banks could sell excess foreign currency balances for their customers to the central bank, but in a Colonial Currency Board system it was assumed that the exchange rate was immutable and commercial banks were therefore taking no material risk in crediting their customers with the domestic currency equivalent of whatever foreign currency amount they were due. Since the commercial banks had to pay foreign currency to the Board only to obtain new banknotes, the process of monetary expansion was ultimately held in check only by the amount of net foreign currency balances held by the private sector. Thus during periods of balance of payments surplus when the private sector was in net receipt of foreign currency remittances, the banks could either lend more in local currency (which would be reflected in the growth of local currency deposit accounts) or obtain more banknotes and coin from the Colonial Currency Board. Conversely during periods of balance of payments deficits when the private sector was a net spender of foreign currency, the banks would find they could not both increase their loans and obtain more banknotes because their foreign currency position would be run down. The first process gave rise to a monetary expansion, the second to monetary contraction.

But at no time did the Colonial Currency Board *actively* participate in this process. The adjustment process was "automatic" in the sense that the switch from monetary expansion to contraction (and vice-versa) occurred as a direct result of the switch from balance of payments surplus to deficit (or deficit to surplus) in the private sector without the government or Currency Board taking an active role.

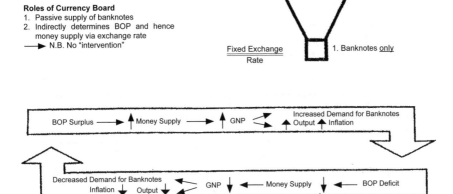

Roles of Currency Board
1. Passive supply of banknotes
2. Indirectly determines BOP and hence money supply via exchange rate
→ N.B. No "intervention"

Chart 4.10 "Automatic" Adjustment Mechanism under Colonial Currency Board System

The only modification which is necessary to make this description applicable to the case of the Hong Kong is to note that banknotes in Hong Kong were not issued by the Exchange Fund itself but by certain commercial banks against Certificates of Indebtedness (CIs) issued by the Exchange Fund. However, to obtain the CIs the note-issuing banks had to pay foreign currency to the Exchange Fund, so in effect the banknotes were issued on government authority but at one remove. The Exchange Fund held the foreign currency assets which were the ultimate 'backing' for the note issue, but commercial banks actually printed and distributed the notes. In every other respect the operation of the automatic adjustment mechanism in Hong Kong was identical to its operation in other colonies.

The distinguishing feature of the "automatic" adjustment process so far as Hong Kong (and other colonies) were concerned was that the authorities through the Exchange Fund did not and could not actively participate in adjusting the rate of monetary expansion in the colony to the exigencies of overseas economic activity or price levels overseas, and were obliged to allow the process of adjustment to occur "automatically" through the private sector.

(E) How the Adjustment Mechanism Worked to Align Price Levels

During the post-war years two types of banking system co-existed side by side under the Bretton Woods agreement. For the most part independent nation states had orthodox central banks at the core of their financial systems, with commercial banks operating as customers of the central bank and maintaining reserve accounts at the central bank. Given the adherence to pegged exchange rates by all these central banks, fluctuations

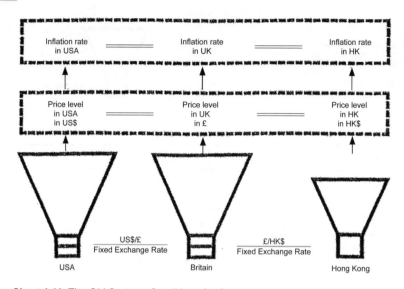

Chart 4.11 The Old System: Conditions for Success

in the balance of payments had to be met by the central banks buying or selling foreign currency and supplying or withdrawing a corresponding amount of domestic currency in the form of reserves via the accounts of the commercial banks at the central bank. These fluctuations in commercial bank reserves translated into periods of acceleration or deceleration in the monetary aggregates, which were almost invariably followed by periods of business expansion or contraction respectively. The expansions were typically accompanied by some overheating in the economy and prices would rise more rapidly leading to a deterioration in the balance of payments; the contractions were typically followed by some slowdown in inflation leading to an improvement in the balance of payments. In practice the balance of payments acted as a constraint on excessive expansion or contraction keeping the price levels in different economies from diverging too far.

In the colonial economies which did not have central banks but had some form of Colonial Currency Board system the adjustment process operated to produce the same result (i.e. preventing price levels or inflation from diverging too far), but instead of the process of adjustment being initiated by explicit central bank intervention in the foreign exchange market, the adjustment process occurred without explicit intervention by the authorities — the adjustment occurred "automatically" through the private sector. In most other respects the process of converting external surpluses of the private sector into monetary accelerations and hence into business cycle expansions or booms and the converse process of converting external deficits into business cycle contractions or recessions were identical in colonial economies and in orthodox central bank-type economies.

Obviously there were variations in duration, diffusion, and amplitude of business cycles, but the general process by which stimulatory policies at the core of this whole system (i.e. in the USA) were transmitted to other central bank system and colonial economies differed only in the way in which the authorities in any particular economy reacted. In the colonial economies with Colonial Currency Board monetary systems we have shown that the authorities did not enjoy any discretion in the adjustment process and as such the transmission mechanism was "automatic". Indeed, insofar as the authorities were only involved to the extent of passively issuing or retiring banknotes in response to private sector demand the whole adjustment process was "automatic" in the sense of not requiring or depending on government action or intervention to initiate it.

Properly defined the term *"automatic adjustment mechanism"* refers to the maintenance of compatible and consistent price levels in different economies via the Colonial Currency Board system whose central characteristic is the essentially passive nature of its operations, implying in particular an inability to supply or withdraw reserves in the manner of a central bank. Chart 4.11 offers a schematic diagram of the outcome of this process.

(F) How the Orthodox Adjustment Mechanism Worked: Japan and the USA, 1949–71

The operation of the adjustment mechanism is best illustrated by reference to some actual examples drawn from the history of post-war Asian economies. To illustrate the operation of the orthodox adjustment mechanism under a central bank system we may examine Japan and the USA; to illustrate the operation of the automatic adjustment mechanism under a Colonial Currency Board type of system we may study the example of Hong Kong.

The basic lesson to be drawn from Chart 4.12 is that once Japan had fixed its exchange rate at ¥360 to the US dollar in April 1949 under the Bretton Woods arrangements, the level of wholesale or traded goods prices in Japan was closely tied to the level of similar prices in the USA throughout the period of fixed rates. This was not only true for prices, but also for economic activity; the two economies virtually moved in step together, with the Japanese economy being obliged to dance to the tune of the dollar. As the Japanese economy was growing more rapidly than the US economy the amplitude of its business cycle fluctuations tended to be larger than those of the USA, hence the popular saying, "If the US economy catches cold, Japan catches pneumonia."

The mechanism involved in the process of keeping Japanese and American prices in line was a monetary one. If Japanese prices were "too high", Japanese exports would begin to slow down, Japanese imports would begin to accelerate and the balance of payments would switch from surplus to deficit. To make good the deficit and balance Japan's international payments at ¥360 per US$ the Bank of Japan had to supply dollars by purchasing yen, and in so doing it reduced the reserves of the Japanese banking

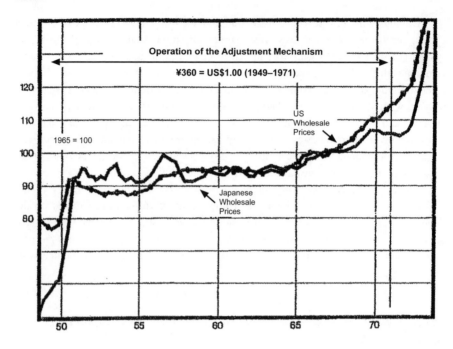

Chart 4.12 The Bretton Woods System: USA and Japan

system, causing the money supply to decelerate. The deceleration of the Japanese money supply led to a slowdown in the Japanese economy, a shrinking of the demand for imports and a decline in the price level. Ultimately as exports became more competitive again, the balance of payments reverted to surplus. Then the converse process would operate, with a balance of payments surplus producing an expansionary monetary policy, and finally a general rise in prices. Thus the obligation of the Bank of Japan to intervene in the exchange market provided Japan with the classic form of adjustment mechanism — a process by which monetary expansions and contractions brought Japan's price level into line with the price level in the United States.

(G) How the Automatic Adjustment Mechanism Worked: Hong Kong, 1952–74

The automatic adjustment mechanism which operated in Hong Kong up until the floating of the exchange rate in November 1974 operated in such a way as to produce effects which were precisely the same as the effects resulting from the orthodox central bank system described for Japan in the previous section. The only difference lay in the mechanism by which the process of monetary expansion and contraction was achieved: in the case of the orthodox central bank system it required explicit intervention in the

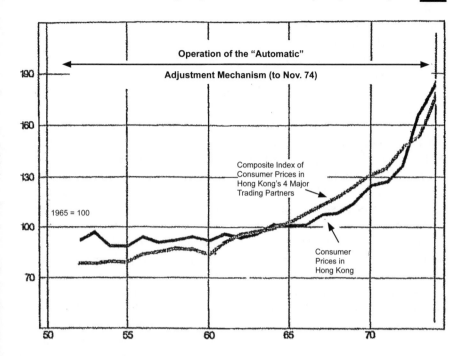

Operation of the "Automatic"
Adjustment Mechanism (to Nov. 74)

Composite Index of
Consumer Prices in
Hong Kong's 4 Major
Trading Partners

1965 = 100

Consumer
Prices in
Hong Kong

Chart 4.13 The Bretton Woods System: Hong Kong

foreign exchange market while in Hong Kong's modified Colonial Currency Board system no such explicit intervention normally occurred.

To see the effects of the operation of the automatic adjustment mechanism it is only necessary to compare the behaviour of the price level in Hong Kong with the price level in overseas economies. As Chart 4.13 shows, Hong Kong's price levels were indeed determined by the level of prices in its major trading partners which were all linked through pegged exchange rates. Given the fixed rate between the Hong Kong dollar and sterling up until June 1972 (or the US dollar until November 1974), it was not possible for Hong Kong's price level to deviate far from the price levels in its leading trade partners' economies. Relatively "low" price levels in Hong Kong would have soon led to a highly competitive trading position for Hong Kong which would soon be reflected in a balance of payments surplus and an accelerating money supply which in time would have led to higher prices in Hong Kong and a correction of the original competitive advantage. Conversely, relatively "high" prices in Hong Kong would have led to a disadvantageous trading position for Hong Kong which would soon be reflected in a deteriorating balance of payments and a decelerating money supply which in time would have led to recession and lower prices in Hong Kong, thus correcting the original competitive disadvantage.

Two conditions necessary for the successful operation of the automatic adjustment mechanism wherever it operated were:

(1) the guaranteed convertibility of the colonial currency into the currency of the metropolitan country at a fixed rate, and
(2) the inability of the monetary authority in the colony to undermine or offset the operation of this mechanism so long as they lacked the means to intervene either in the foreign exchange markets or the domestic money markets.

In Hong Kong's case the first condition was ultimately violated by the decision to float the Hong Kong currency in November 1974, but essentially that followed from the initial undermining of the second condition in 1972. For in that year the authorities made some crucial changes in the way the monetary system operated (see Chapter 2, section C, pp. 22–25). When the decision was taken to abandon the fixed rate against sterling in June 1972 and to adopt a fixed rate against the US dollar, instead of requiring the note-issuing banks to pay for Certificates of Indebtedness (i.e. the authorisations to print banknotes) in US dollars or sterling, the authorities permitted the banks to make payment in domestic currency. Superficially this appeared to give them the means to intervene on either side of the foreign exchange market.[5] Moreover, the authorities then redeposited that domestic currency back in the banking system, contributing greatly to Hong Kong's monetary explosion in late 1972 and early 1973. Most of Hong Kong's subsequent monetary problems result from the mistakes of policy made at this time. Before returning to the specific case of Hong Kong it is useful to see how the traditional adjustment mechanism broke down elsewhere and how it was replaced with a more satisfactory system because, notwithstanding the chorus of voices to the effect that somehow Hong Kong is different and therefore what applies elsewhere does not apply in Hong Kong, these lessons are particularly relevant to Hong Kong.

(H) How the Orthodox Adjustment Mechanism Broke Down: Japan, 1971–74

Just as there were two main ingredients of the success of the automatic adjustment mechanism, so there were two similar conditions necessary for the success of the orthodox adjustment mechanism under central bank-type systems:
(1) the guaranteed convertibility of the domestic currency into US dollars at a fixed rate, and
(2) the willingness of the central bank not to undermine or offset the operation of the adjustment mechanism by intervening in the domestic money markets.

---

5. "Superficially" because in reality Exchange Fund intervention operations did not result in the normal multiple expansion or multiple contraction effects (see Chapter 2, section D, pp. 28–33).

As with the previous example, violations of the second condition frequently led to either a change in the pegged rate or an erosion of confidence that domestic currency would be exchangeable into foreign currency at a known rate, hence fuelling speculation and making the job of maintaining the fixed rate more costly in terms of official foreign exchange reserves.

So long as the USA, the core economy in the Bretton Woods system of fixed exchange rates, pursued sober and stable monetary policies there was no serious disruption of other economies. However when in the late 1960s management of the American money supply began to be less stable, larger disturbances in the US economy were transmitted via the fixed exchange rate system to all other economies which maintained pegged rates against the US dollar. The authorities in these other economies faced the choice of *either* going along with US policies and maintaining fixed rates which would have meant exposing their economies to wide fluctuations in the balance of payments and hence a highly unstable monetary growth pattern, *or* offsetting to some degree the impact of the balance of payments on the domestic economy by domestic money market operations, *or* actually altering the parity of the pegged exchange rate.

The West German authorities opted for the third of these courses when they revalued the DM against the US dollar in 1961 and again in 1969.

In Japan, however, the authorities adopted the second course of action. The Bank of Japan's offsetting actions began in November 1962 with limited purchases and sales of bonds between the Bank of Japan and other financial institutions. These operations were extended in January 1966 with the issue of long term government bonds, and the techniques further refined until by July 1969 the procedures were not markedly different in their effects from standard open market operations.[6]

In terms of the above two conditions necessary for successful operation of the old system, the Bank of Japan adhered to the first condition but in respect to the second it said in effect, unless we intervene in the domestic money markets to absorb the excess liquidity resulting from the balance of payments, there will be excessive growth of money and credit which will destabilise our economy. As a consequence, instead of inflating along with the USA from 1968 onwards, the Bank of Japan resisted by trying to offset external surpluses with sales of bonds in the domestic money markets. As a result monetary growth in Japan was not as rapid as it would otherwise have been, and consequently Japan's wholesale price level steadily diverged from that in the USA so that by mid-1971, despite the fact that the exchange rate remained unaltered at ¥360 per US dollar, there was a gap of more than 10% between the two price levels (circled in Chart 4.14). With Japanese prices on average 10% lower than those in the USA it was hardly surprising that Japan was experiencing enormous current account surpluses.

---

6. See Yoshio Suzuki, "Money and Banking in Contemporary Japan", Yale University Press 1980, Chapter 11 pp.188–195 for a complete description of the development of BOJ offsetting operations. It is clear from Dr. Suzuki's account that the burgeoning external surpluses of the late 1960s and early 1970s acted as a major stimulus on the Bank of Japan in the development of open market operations.

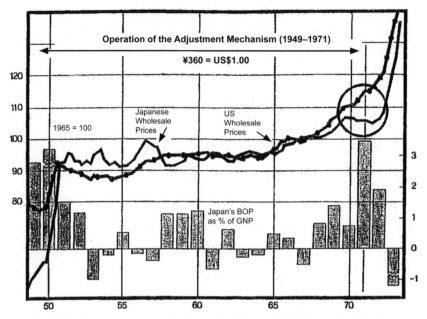

Chart 4.14 Breakdown of the Bretton Woods System (1971): USA and Japan

In a historical sense the breakdown of the Bretton Woods fixed parity system was triggered by the decision of the Nixon administration in August 1971 to close the gold window (i.e. to refuse to pay one ounce of gold for every US$35 submitted by foreign central banks to the US Treasury), thus signalling to foreign central banks that they should revalue their currencies upward against the US dollar if they wished to continue to exchange their reserves for gold at the US Treasury. (In fact the Treasury never permitted this, and the world moved from a gold-dollar exchange standard with fixed rates to a paper standard with floating or managed exchange rates.)

In terms of our analysis the underlying cause of the breakdown of the Bretton Woods fixed parity system was the general unwillingness of other central banks to go along with the disturbances generated at the centre of the system by the Federal Reserve in the USA and transmitted abroad by the operation of the adjustment mechanism under fixed rates. As these disturbances became greater under the more expansionist monetary and fiscal policies of Presidents Johnson and Nixon, and as the price levels between major economies began to diverge more, an intolerable strain was placed on the system, finally causing it to disintegrate.

To express the analysis differently, the general level of prices in each satellite economy had been subject to the law of one price — namely the fixed exchange rate — via the impact of the balance of payments on the money supply and hence on the general domestic price level. After this system was overturned the leading central banks gradually moved from a regime of fixed rates with an uncontrolled money supply and an uncontrolled domestic price level to controlling the money supply and hence controlling the overall price level while allowing the exchange rate to vary. The problem in Hong Kong was that when the decision to float was made no corresponding decision was taken to control the money supply, and, as it subsequently transpired when the problem began to be seriously addressed in 1978, the tampering with the monetary mechanism that had occurred in Hong Kong in 1972 meant that no scheme for monetary control could be introduced without radical reforms.

As a postscript it should be noted that, having abandoned the external "discipline" of the fixed Yen-US dollar exchange rate between 1971 and 1973, the Japanese authorities substituted an internal discipline by deciding to control domestic monetary growth from July 1974 onwards. From that time until the Plaza and Louvre agreements of 1985 and 1987 the Japanese authorities concentrated almost exclusively on regulating the quantity of money rather than the external price of the yen.

(I) The Hong Kong Monetary System in 1982

The Hong Kong monetary system today (1982) is neither an orthodox central bank system nor is it any longer a variant of the old Colonial Currency Board system. There are three crucial differences:

(1) the value of the currency is not defined in terms of a fixed number of units of sterling or US dollars, and the exchange rate is generally freely floating,

(2) the note-issuing banks are not required to pay foreign currency in exchange for the authorisations necessary to print banknotes, but they pay in domestic currency, so the issue of currency is not subject to any external constraint, and

(3) the monetary authorities maintain their accounts with the commercial banks (rather than the commercial banks maintaining their accounts with the monetary authority). This means that instead of being "outside the system" and able to influence the growth of (say) reserves and hence the money supply, the authorities are reduced to being clients of the banking system with little more influence on it (in terms of their transactions) than other major corporations who are also clients of the banking system.

This combination of idiosyncratic features makes it impossible for the Hong Kong authorities to manage the money supply or the exchange rate in a manner which is likely to produce predictable and dependable results, and provides a fundamental explanation for the instability of Hong Kong's financial system. Until reforms are introduced which restore a means of either controlling the money supply directly or managing the exchange rate (and hence regulating the money supply indirectly) it is likely that Hong Kong's financial system will continue to be highly unstable with wide fluctuations in monetary growth over the business cycle.

It is thanks to these idiosyncrasies (presented schematically in Chart 4.15) that the Hong Kong authorities have persisted in the belief that, contrary to the experience of the rest of the world, there must be another way out of their difficulties. That other way is via

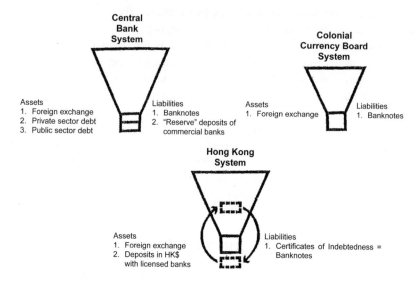

Chart 4.15 Where Are We Now?

the partial control of interest rates through the Interest Rate Agreement, an arrangement whereby the Licensed Banks set deposit interest rates on deposits under HK$500,000 and with maturities up to 12 months. To enable foreign banks to participate in this cartel arrangement without becoming liable to Anti-Trust actions in their home countries the authorities introduced the notion of a statutory body, the Hong Kong Association of Banks, to which all Licensed Banks are required to belong. This official legal sanction makes behaviour which some banks would not contemplate at home acceptable abroad.

(J) The Options Facing Hong Kong's Monetary Authorities

If it is accepted that the present monetary system in Hong Kong is prone to periodic instability, inappropriate to a major international financial centre, the authorities are confronted with three possible courses of action:

Either (1) To tinker with the present system in a bid to patch up the flaws and to hope that next time round something will turn up to avoid the embarrassment of repeating the violent monetary fluctuations of 1972–74 and 1979–82,

or (2) To move towards the introduction of an orthodox central bank in order to enable the authorities directly to control the money supply via the injection and withdrawal of bank reserves,

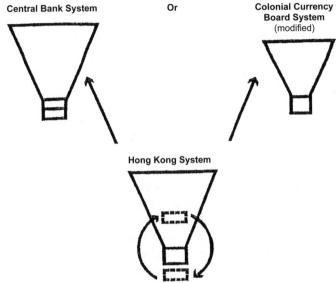

Chart 4.16 Where Next?

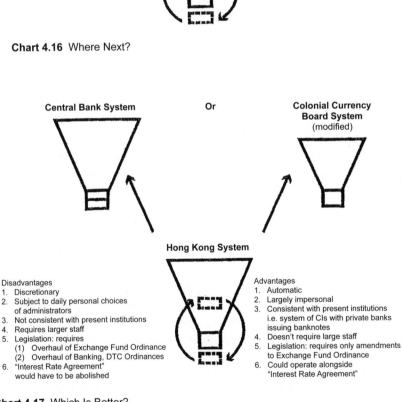

Disadvantages
1. Discretionary
2. Subject to daily personal choices of administrators
3. Not consistent with present institutions
4. Requires larger staff
5. Legislation: requires
   (1) Overhaul of Exchange Fund Ordinance
   (2) Overhaul of Banking, DTC Ordinances
6. "Interest Rate Agreement" would have to be abolished

Advantages
1. Automatic
2. Largely impersonal
3. Consistent with present institutions i.e. system of CIs with private banks issuing banknotes
4. Doesn't require large staff
5. Legislation: requires only amendments to Exchange Fund Ordinance
6. Could operate alongside "Interest Rate Agreement"

Chart 4.17 Which Is Better?

or   (3)   To move back towards the pre-1972 system i.e. a modified Colonial Currency Board, which implies setting the HK$ exchange rate and allowing the old "automatic" adjustment mechanism to operate i.e. to set the price of the HK$ and to allow the quantity of Hong Kong dollars (the money supply) to adjust "automatically" so as to keep the balance of payments in approximate equilibrium.

In our view the first option offers no solution at all. The problem is that the business cycle is long enough for one Financial Secretary to claim credit for the boom on the upswing and to attribute the downswing to factors beyond his control, and then to retire from the post before the whole cycle repeats itself, thus avoiding the reprimand which he would otherwise incur for repeating the mistakes of the past.

The second and third options (summarized in Chart 4.16) have been examined in past issues of AMM, and to date no satisfactory refutation nor any better solution has been offered either by the authorities or — to our knowledge — by anyone in the private sector. The advantages and disadvantages of each option are briefly summarised in Chart 4.17 but in our view either solution would be preferable to the present structure.

5.   PROPOSALS FOR A REFORM OF HONG KONG'S MONETARY SYSTEM

In seeking to stabilise the value of the Hong Kong dollar and to reduce inflation in Hong Kong, the Government faces only two alternative basic courses of action.

Either   the authorities must move to control the *quantity* of money

or   they must peg the *price,* that is, the exchange rate of the currency.

Numerous variations on these two alternatives are of course possible, but irrespective of the final course of action chosen, the best solution will be either one or the other, but *not* a mixture of the two.

Since 1979 several attempts have been made to rectify the flaws in the Hong Kong banking structure, but they have all avoided tackling the quantity-of-money or price-of-money options head-on. On the quantity side the critically important reserve base of the banking system on which Hong Kong's deposit and credit pyramid is erected has been left untouched. On the price side the Hong Kong dollar has essentially been allowed to float quite freely so that the money supply has not been subject to any balance of payments constraint.

Unless further steps are taken to bring the quantity of money more directly under control, these various measures will turn out to have been incomplete. While the government's moves in the direction of controlling interest rates have been welcomed in many quarters, it is by no means clear that controlling the quantity of money (or money supply) via interest rates or via any other means is the best answer for Hong Kong. The question of what is the right solution is the issue we examine here.

The second course of action — pegging the external value of the currency — sounds at first like a return to the pre-November 1974 system when the Hong Kong dollar was pegged to a fixed nominal value of sterling or to a fixed nominal value of the US dollar. However, the drawback of those fixed parity systems was that the value of the foreign currency to which the Hong Kong dollar was pegged proved to be unstable and ultimately resulted in inflation in Hong Kong. The challenge in designing a revised system is to insulate Hong Kong from the consequences of mistaken monetary policies abroad while preserving all the virtues of Hong Kong's open, adaptable, free market economy.

*   *   *   *   *   *

Before setting out our two alternative schemes for reforming the Hong Kong banking system it is necessary to recognise that the acceptability of any set of proposals will depend largely on the criteria by which those proposals are judged. Without specifying some criteria in advance we run the risk of arousing criticisms which are based not on the explicit mechanisms or instruments we recommend, but on the implicit ends which we seek to achieve. Before embarking on the details of our proposals we therefore enumerate below some of the aims and characteristics which any proposals for reform should have in our opinion.

Premises

1. That the agreed aim of the reformed system should be to stabilise the internal purchasing power of the Hong Kong dollar, i.e. to achieve overall domestic price stability in Hong Kong dollar terms — and thereby to moderate even if not eliminate the extremes of the boom-and-bust cycle to which Hong Kong has been subjected.
2. That the reformed mechanism should take account of Hong Kong's special position in the world economy by interfering as little as possible with free market forces, and should not require or encourage extensive governmental intervention in individual financial markets. This would retain the famed flexibility and adaptability of the Hong Kong economy.
3. That any proposals be compatible as far as possible with the existing institutional framework in Hong Kong, and be impartial as between locally incorporated and foreign incorporated banks.

*   *   *   *   *

Scheme 1: Controlling the Quantity of Money

The best way to control the money supply is through regulating the monetary base. Alternative attempts to control the money supply by direct methods such as placing ceilings on bank lending (or "corsets") have been made in several countries but the drawback with these approaches is that they require extensive governmental interference in the process of determining who shall and who shall not be allowed to borrow. Ceilings discriminate amongst the banks to the disadvantage of the borrowers, depositors and shareholders, and they impose an additional reporting burden on private banks, or additional monitoring costs on the government. But more important, loan ceilings are a bad way of controlling the money supply because they only impact a certain part of banks' assets, and they may not affect total bank credit, especially if banks and businesses are adept at devising new credit instruments.

Control of the monetary base — that is, the reserve base of credit expansion — is a better method of controlling the money supply because it leaves market forces intact; the allocation of credit among sectors is not distorted and individual banks are free to compete for whatever share of the market they can obtain. By controlling the quantity of bank reserves, control over the money supply can be quite accurate. It is most accurate when banks' eligible reserve assets are directly controllable, and this is best achieved by defining them narrowly as HK$ liabilities of the monetary authority. This is because the monetary authority can always control the size of its assets or liabilities. For example, if Government debt or short term loans to certain financial institutions (such as the Discount Houses in the UK) are included in the definition of eligible reserve assets, the banks may be able to sidestep a move by the monetary authority to reduce the monetary base by obtaining other reserve assets in place of those being absorbed by the monetary authority.

A narrow definition of reserve assets would obviate three flaws in the present Hong Kong Banking Ordinance. First, it would prevent the banks from being able to create reserves at will as they are currently able to do by borrowing foreign currency. Second, it would end the anomaly which results from translating foreign reserve assets into Hong Kong dollars at the current exchange rate; at present when the exchange rate depreciates the value of bank reserves expressed in Hong Kong dollars increases. Third, it would eliminate the same anomaly which occurs through including gold as a reserve asset; under the current system whenever the exchange rate falls and the value of gold in HK$ terms rises, to the extent that banks hold gold their reserve assets increase.

The simplest alternative to the current multiple reserve (or specified liquid asset) structure would be to require all licensed banks to hold deposits at the Exchange Fund equal to a fixed proportion (say 5 pct) of their Hong Kong dollar deposit liabilities. The authorities could then control the available quantity of such reserve assets by open market operations in foreign exchange, in government securities, or in commercial bills issued by the private sector. At present the markets in government securities and commercial paper in Hong Kong are still at an early stage of development, and with the tendency of government to run a fiscal surplus there is little likelihood of much growth in this sector, so operations would be concentrated in the foreign exchange market for the time being. As and when markets in private and government sector paper develop the monetary authority could of course extend its operations to these areas. (See box in Chapter 2, pp. 33–34, "A Monetary Authority with No Government Debt".)

The attraction of these proposals is that they require minimum alteration of Hong Kong's current institutional arrangements:

1. Private commercial banks could continue to issue bank notes as in the present system. Certificates of Indebtedness (CIs) would continue to be issued in exchange for domestic deposits or foreign assets placed with the monetary authority, and the three note-issuing commercial banks would continue to issue bank notes against CIs.

2. The government could retain its accounts with the commercial banks as at present. In monetary systems where the government's deposits are maintained at the central monetary authority and not at the commercial banks the irregular pattern of tax collection and expenditure causes fluctuations in the volume of credit creation by the commercial banks unless deliberate offsetting action is taken. The advantage of the government keeping its accounts with the commercial banks as at present is that these disturbances would be avoided.

3. Supposing there was a change in policy resulting in the Hong Kong Government shifting to a persistent budget deficit, it would be highly desirable if the automatic monetisation of this debt could be prevented, thus avoiding the inflationary effects of such a policy. Provided the government maintains its fiscal accounts at the commercial banks it is in an analogous position to ordinary corporate entities: if it experienced a cash deficit it would have to borrow temporarily from the banks, or the public. In neither case is new money created. But if the government maintained its accounts only with a monetary authority the temptation to finance the deficit by creating the necessary new funds whenever the need arose would be substantially greater. In other words the privileged position of the government would make it more difficult for the monetary authority to resist financing short term government requirements by simply printing the money. Our proposals do not place the government in any such privileged position.

The main disadvantage of these proposals is that although the structure of the revised banking system and the Exchange Fund is easy enough to set out, the operating procedures for the monetary authorities are much more difficult to define and much more difficult to reconcile with our criteria of non-intervention and impartiality. In the first place it has to be decided at what rate the reserve base of the system should be allowed to grow, and it is by no means easy to select the rate which would be right for Hong Kong's changing circumstances.[7] Meanwhile there would be the clear danger of overshooting or undershooting the appropriate rate with accompanying disruptions to the domestic

---

7. Technically the right rate requires calculating the demand for money function etc.

economy. Second, once it was clear that the authorities had discretion to influence interest rates and exchange rates in the short run, no doubt political pressures would build up in favour of offsetting each disturbance that happened to occur, and before long the officials operating the monetary authority would face substantial temptations to interfere. Even if they acted with the best of motives, their powers to interfere would be enormous, and it is doubtful if they would long be able to resist the political pressure to "do something" for various pressure groups (e.g. exporters, home-buyers, or wage-earners).

Scheme 2: Controlling the Exchange Rate

The major disadvantage of Scheme 1 is that the guidelines for monetary policy are uncertain and left to the discretion of the administrators. There are few checks to ensure that the monetary policy is compatible with long-run price stability. Through error or design the rate of growth of the money supply may deviate from the rate required for long-run price stability — but the consequences of such deviations will not become apparent in the economy until several months or even years later. In other words the feed-back to the monetary authorities of the consequences of their policies is delayed.

This is of course a problem faced by all countries whose monetary authorities aim to control the quantity of money. Like the pilot of an oil tanker, the authorities may not realise the ship is running onto the rocks until it is too late to change course. There is a danger that monetary policy will oscillate between over-expansion and over-correction with the consequent familiar stop-go effects on economic activity.

If instead of using economic indicators within the Hong Kong economy as guidelines for monetary policy an "external" rule could be devised to regulate monetary expansion then the tendency for monetary policy to waver in response to the consequences of earlier mistakes would be avoided. To extend the analogy, if the only guide for steering the oil tanker is a light on the bow, then the man at the helm will be aiming at a target which moves in response to his own actions and the ship will wander erratically on the ocean. If instead the helmsman could aim for a lighthouse on the horizon, then his course would be steady, and his target would be independent of the movements of the ship.

In the 1960s the lighthouse was a fixed rate of the Hong Kong dollar against Sterling. The Exchange Fund bought and sold foreign exchange in whatever amounts were necessary to keep the exchange rate fixed. The money supply adjusted, and the price level in Hong Kong also varied, but the *automatic consequence* of the pegged exchange rate was that the price level in Hong Kong *in the long-run* followed the price level in the UK.

The target of the Exchange Fund was neither the domestic price level, nor the money supply nor interest rates (which were all like lights on the bows of the ship), and these variables were all left to market forces, but nevertheless the long-run trend in the price level was effectively linked to the trend in prices in the UK.

The problem with the pegged exchange rate was that the currency to which the HK dollar was pegged was not inflation-proof: as first the pound sterling, then the US dollar succumbed to inflation the HK dollar was dragged into the same mire. If the HK dollar could be pegged to a currency which was guaranteed inflation-proof then HK would also be free from inflation. Although from time to time a few countries achieve virtual price stability for short periods there can be no assurance that they will continue to follow non-inflationary policies in the future, so an alternative might be to adjust the peg for inflation in the other currency.

As an example, and only as an example, suppose the Exchange Fund were to follow a rule that it must aim to keep the purchasing power of the Hong Kong dollar constant in terms of the commodities comprising the wholesale price index in the USA. Then the Fund would buy and sell US dollars at an exchange rate which moved at the rate of increase of wholesale prices in the USA. Suppose at the beginning of the year the exchange rate of the HK$ was HK$5.00 = US$1.00 and the rate of inflation in wholesale prices in the USA is estimated at 10% per annum, then the Exchange Fund should guide the Exchange Rate to HK$5.00 = US$1.10 by the end of the year or HK$4.55 = US$1.00. If this guideline is followed then in the long run prices in Hong Kong, adjusted for exchange rate changes, cannot move far out of line with prices in the USA. Since the exchange rate of the Hong Kong dollar rises at the same rate as US prices this ensures that long-run price stability is maintained regardless of the inflation rate in the USA.

There are a number of problems associated with this policy:

Firstly, wage/price controls, exchange rate manipulations; political instability and many other factors can distort the US wholesale price index and/or the exchange rate of the currency with third countries against which the Hong Kong dollar is to be compared. To minimize these dangers, the single currency could be replaced by a basket of currencies each appropriately adjusted for inflation, so abnormalities associated with any one currency would have less effect.

Secondly, the appropriate measure of inflation in each currency is open to debate: should it be a wholesale price index, consumer price index, export price index or GNP deflator or some combination of these? This is really not a serious problem. The world is not perfect and inflation is an imprecise concept; as long as some index is agreed upon and the guideline followed, inflation in Hong Kong will be negligible.

Thirdly, a more sophisticated approach would be to use "expected inflation rates". Since inflation responds only with a lag to excessive monetary expansion, adjusting merely for present inflation rates would not prevent excessive monetary growth overseas generating a monetary explosion in Hong Kong and a subsequent inflation. Though the price rises would be eliminated eventually by the exchange rate policy the inflation and subsequent deflation would cause unnecessary instability. By adjusting the exchange rate relative to expected inflation rates i.e. with regard to monetary policy in other countries and not merely their current inflation rates such disturbances could be reduced. The estimation of expected inflation rates would however involve personal judgments and subjectivity which would reduce the "automatic" nature of the system. This problem would also be reduced by including a large number of currencies in the basket, so the leads and lags of monetary policy and inflation in any one country would have less effect on the Hong Kong economy.

Fourth, the appropriate disclosure policy must be carefully considered. Would announcement of the exchange rate policy rule lead to speculation and exchange market instability as operators try to out-guess the authorities? Most countries which "peg" their currencies to a basket do not disclose the weighting of the currencies in the basket or their precise policy of intervention on the foreign exchanges. There is considerable and mounting evidence that both Singapore and Switzerland have adopted policies similar to the proposals outlined here and they have also maintained a deliberate policy of vagueness and secrecy with regard to their exchange rate intervention.

It is not intended to give a detailed description of the "real exchange rate" proposal here, but merely to discuss the issues involved. As far as we can judge it requires very few changes to the existing monetary system.

1.   The Exchange Fund must revert to the situation of the 1960s when only foreign currency assets could be held by the fund. In order to issue new banknotes the commercial banks would have to submit foreign currency at the exchange rate announced by the Exchange Fund, in return for Certificates of Indebtedness. The commercial banks would no longer be able to submit Hong Kong dollar deposits.

2.   The "real exchange rate" system requires no change to the existing specified liquid assets system described in the Banking Ordinance. Though far from ideal the existing arrangements are irrelevant to the operation of the "real exchange rate" system.

3.   There would be no need to set up a new monetary authority or increase the powers of the Exchange Fund; there would be no need for controls on interest rates or credit expansion since these would be regulated by the balance of payments. In effect Hong Kong would return to the automatic adjustment mechanism which operated until 1974, only this time the Hong Kong dollar would be pegged to an artificial inflation-free currency.

SUMMARY AND CONCLUSION

In order to stabilise the domestic purchasing power of the Hong Kong currency and stop inflation, while at the same time preserving the free market strength and adaptability of Hong Kong's economy and maintaining the present institutional structure, the monetary authorities can *either* control the money supply *or* peg the currency.

If they choose the former, this brings with it the danger of more extensive government intervention, and it will certainly require some institutional changes if it is to work successfully. If they choose the latter — pegging the exchange rate — it will be important to peg to an artificial unit of stable value rather than to a nominal foreign currency of unreliable value. At the same time it will be essential for the authorities to abandon any attempt at controlling the money supply because of the logical impossibility of both pegging the currency *and* controlling the money supply.

At present, however, the authorities are *neither* effectively controlling the money supply *nor* pegging the currency to a stable unit of value. Unless further action is taken along the lines suggested here it is more than likely that Hong Kong will again experience the same pattern of excess money and credit creation followed by an abrupt curtailment of money and credit growth whereupon an overheated economy, and booming stock and property markets will give way to a sudden downturn in economic activity, and a collapse of equity and property prices. A decision in favour of the status quo implies a vote for a rerun of recent history — not an attractive path down which to steer the Hong Kong economy, but unless there is some fundamental rethinking which yields some soundly based proposals for reform, Hong Kong is destined to repeat the excesses of the last few years over the course of the next business cycle.

CHAPTER **5**

HOW TO RESCUE THE HONG KONG DOLLAR
Three Practical Proposals
September–October 1983

This is the article written at the height of the HK$ currency crisis in September 1983 that ultimately formed the basis for the government's plan for a return to a currency board mechanism in October 1983. As a development of the arguments previously put forward in AMM for a reform of Hong Kong's monetary system (e.g. in Chapter 4), the main innovation is the fuller treatment of the case for a currency board arrangement — the third proposal (called 2B in the article).

One part of the story concerns the origins of the third proposal (for a return to a fixed rate under an orthodox currency board), and the circumstances that caused this proposal to become a key part of the overall argument. A second strand of the story of the HK$ crisis is how, from my perspective, the key players in the decision to restore the currency board were brought into the process.

*　*　*　*　*

I have explained in the Introduction how I transferred from the University of Tokyo to GT Management in Hong Kong in 1974. Among the topics in monetary history that I had studied while in Japan was the early history of the Japanese monetary system before and after the foundation of the Bank of Japan in 1882. Initially Japan had been on the silver standard, but after the war with China in 1894–95, Japan obtained a large indemnity in gold, and used this as the basis for switching from the silver standard to the gold standard in 1897. Japan and Hong Kong therefore shared a historical adherence to the silver standard, but whereas Japan had first introduced a central bank and then abandoned silver in favour of the gold standard, Hong Kong had persisted with no central bank and maintained the silver standard until 1935. Thereafter Hong Kong had shifted from the silver standard to the sterling standard, but still did not introduce a central bank. China, by contrast, had abandoned the silver standard in 1935 and had in effect moved to a fiat or paper standard under a central bank, with ultimately disastrous consequences. By the late 1940s China's monetary system had degenerated into hyperinflation as the external value of the currency disintegrated. I was therefore aware of the possibility of operating a monetary system without a central bank, provided the underlying monetary standard was sound and credible.

During 1982 and early 1983 I had met with various Hong Kong government officials on an informal basis, and these encounters had conveyed the message that any proposals to introduce a central bank along with a far-reaching restructuring of the institutional framework of the banking system would not be seriously considered. This was how things stood when I left Hong Kong for a scuba-diving holiday in Palau (Micronesia) in August 1983.

From Palau I telephoned Hong Kong from time to time to get updates on the financial markets. What I heard was most alarming: the downward slide of the Hong Kong currency was accelerating. From an average of HK$7.18 per US$ in July the exchange rate slid to $7.44 in August. It became clear to me that I needed to write another article in AMM that would provide a practical solution to the government's problem, while at the same time avoiding any large-scale institutional changes. One day at a rest stop between dives on one of Palau's many small islands I was lying under a coconut tree turning over this problem in my mind when it dawned on me that Hong Kong's monetary problems could be solved almost in one fell swoop and without any institutional upheaval if the 1972 changes (see Chapter 2) could be reversed and a price for issuing and redeeming Certificates of Indebtedness (the HK$-denominated permits that gave banks the right to issue bank notes) could be fixed in US$. I promptly decided to return to Hong Kong and recast my proposal that Hong Kong should introduce a central bank either to manage the money supply or to manage the exchange rate as a three-part proposal: (1) a central bank to manage the money supply, (2A) a central bank to manage the exchange rate, or (2B) a return to the traditional currency board arrangement with no central bank.

The first part of the following article re-works the arguments for monetary control (pp. 106–111). For example, the T-form balance sheets highlighting why intervention in Hong Kong's foreign exchange market didn't work (pp.112–113) are presented in a way that is quite different to AMM of July–August 1981(Chapter 2), yet complementary to the earlier version.

The argument sought to show that, if the adoption of a central bank (under schemes 1 and 2A) was not acceptable for institutional or other reasons, then the exchange rate could in effect be controlled by the re-introduction of a currency board system (scheme 2B) without far-reaching institutional changes. The discussion of schemes 1 and 2A repeats some key arguments, but touches on some theoretical and practical questions (pp.114–120) that would have arisen had either of these schemes been adopted.

The presentation of scheme 2B focuses on some issues that perhaps would generate little interest today, such as the stability of the monetary determinant ratios, and how cash arbitrage would work under the restored currency board (pp.120–128). In retrospect both these points derived from my understanding of the gold and silver standard mechanisms, and my view at the time that, just as arbitrage between gold and currency notes under the gold standard was critical to the automatic corrective features of the gold standard, a similar kind of arbitrage would be critical to the currency board mechanism. In fact this turned out to be a mistake and a blind alley. It was not until the Asian Financial Crisis of 1997–98 that Hong Kong learned the need for the currency board to offer not only a fixed rate for currency note issues, but also a more or less fixed US$

rate to banks for the conversion of their reserves or HK$ settlement balances. In practice, the wholesale transactions of banks in the foreign exchange market and through the inter-bank settlement system were the fulcrum of the system, not the transactions of the public in banknotes.

The operation of scheme 2B is linked to a discussion of the balance of payments and the operation of the adjustment mechanism (pp.120–128), and followed by some topical questions of a predictive nature (How would the money supply and inflation behave under the proposed arrangements? How would interest rates behave?). The conclusion (pp. 128–129) clearly echoes earlier AMM arguments.

The three appendices (pp. 130–135) apply familiar academic theories of the time to the particular circumstances of Hong Kong. Appendix 5.1 explains why interest rates are a bad tool for monetary control. It should again be remembered that in the early 1980s monetary base control (MBC) was a monetary remedy proposed by a number of leading academic economists and by a number of market practitioners both in the US and in the UK, and hence the emphasis on the quantitative aspects of monetary control. In practice few if any central banks ever adopted monetary base control. In the US the Federal Reserve adopted a modified version of MBC from October 1979 until September 1982. According to Charles Goodhart, the volatility of short-term interest rates in the US increased fourfold during this period, while the experiment also resulted in greater volatility of the targeted aggregate, M_1.(For details see "Monetary Base" in *The New Palgrave Dictionary of Economics,* Macmillan, 1987.) In the UK, despite toying with the idea, the authorities formally rejected MBC and only ever targeted M_3, and that only for a while.

Although there are some interesting theoretical points made in the original article, especially in the context of Hong Kong, these arguments could not be used today. In practical terms the distinction between money and credit is even more difficult to pinpoint nowadays, and the current consensus (in 2006) is that, aside from exceptional cases such as Japan's episode of deflation between the late 1990s and 2006, managing short-term interest rates is regarded as the only practical way for central banks to conduct monetary policy. By raising or lowering short-term rates, not only does a central bank influence the incentives to borrow and lend (which in turn affects the quantity of money at the same time), but it also influences the prices of a whole range of securities (e.g. bonds, equities and derivatives), currencies and other assets (e.g. commodities, real estate etc.) in a way that reinforces the effect of the initial interest rate change. In this way the central bank's changes in interest rates percolate outwards to influence financial asset prices, economic activity, and the overall price level. Changes in the quantity of money are nowadays regarded as simply one step in the transmission process rather than an immediate or intermediate objective of monetary policy.

Appendix 5.2 shows how tampering with the liquid asset ratios would have failed to bring any long-term solution to Hong Kong's monetary problems. While this issue has less urgency today because the distinction between matters of prudential supervision and matters of monetary control are better understood, the fact that it merited a separate appendix shows how central the topic was in the debates over Hong Kong's money and banking systems at the time.

*   *   *   *   *

The second strand of the story concerns my efforts to ensure that, following two years of apparent inaction since my meeting with the Hong Kong authorities in August 1981, my proposals would be seriously considered this time. Since the government had given no indication that they had any reforms in mind, and there was certainly no consensus in favour of my earlier proposals for a central bank to manage the money supply or the exchange rate, I felt that my ideas had fallen on deaf ears. On this occasion I therefore resolved to obtain strong endorsement for my proposals from the best academic brains I could muster. Such backing would bolster my confidence in dealing with a sceptical Monetary Affairs Branch and an even more hostile academic community in Hong Kong. My tactics were therefore twofold: first to ensure a proper hearing in Hong Kong, and second to obtain external endorsement of the highest quality.

Within Hong Kong the growing atmosphere of crisis ensured that any proposals for ending the currency crisis would obtain a wide audience. Within days of the Thatcher visit to Beijing the previous September, capital outflows from Hong Kong had commenced. The Hong Kong dollar had depreciated — at first slowly, and subsequently with increasing rapidity, until in mid-September 1983 there was a true run on the currency. Inflation surged to 18% and there were runs on grocery stores and supermarkets. As the currency tumbled, hyperinflation seemed imminent. This was the atmosphere in which this article was prepared. My final tactical move to ensure that the article was not cold-shouldered on this occasion was to send copies to various government departments, notifying them that I planned to publish the article and release it to the press in about 10 days' time.

I subsequently learned that there were two officials within the government — the Deputy Secretary for Monetary Affairs, Tony Latter, and the Government Economist, Dr Alan McLean — who, recognizing that a central bank was a non-starter, began to lend their support to the AMM idea of a return to a pre-1972 style currency board. At one stage Tony Latter had showed me an internal memorandum that had been circulated within the Monetary Affairs Branch diagnosing the problems of Hong Kong's monetary system, although it was nowhere near as radical or outspoken as the AMM article. Had it not been for pressure from these two individuals within the administration, action might have been delayed significantly longer. Another point to note is that in a formal sense the British government left Hong Kong to run its own economic policy and would not have wished to be seen to interfere (especially while the British were arguing in Beijing for a high degree of autonomy for Hong Kong), still less to dictate to the local administration, notwithstanding the acute circumstances. It was greatly preferable that any initiative for change should be seen to come from the Hong Kong authorities — as it ultimately did — and not from London.

On the external front I was fortunate in having some exceptional contacts in the field of monetary research. I have already explained that AMM was read by a number of academics and central bankers. Its circulation among such readers was of the order of 50 to 100 at this time. Among those readers was Milton Friedman, who I had met several years earlier and who was already an avid fan of AMM. Naturally I mailed him a copy of my draft paper on the "Three Practical Proposals". He responded enthusiastically, permitting me to telephone him several times to discuss some of the detailed points of the argument during the 2 to 3 weeks of the crisis. (See Milton and Rose Friedman, "Two Lucky People: Memoirs", p. 326). Having been provided with a ringside seat during the crisis, Milton was particularly helpful in drafting some of the key passages.

The next academic whose help I enlisted was Professor Maxwell Fry. I had met Max some weeks previously, when he gave a paper entitled "Monetary and Exchange Rate Policies in Asia" to the Hong Kong Economic Association on July 26th. He was at the time working on a project with the Asian Development Bank in Manila, but had a keen interest in the Hong Kong problem. He reviewed the draft of my paper and made several helpful suggestions, tightening up the argument significantly.

The third academic I consulted was Alan Walters (later Sir Alan Walters), who at this time although living in Washington DC was still an adviser to Margaret Thatcher. Richard Thornton of GT volunteered to take my analysis to Washington by Concord, and Alan soon called me back with a series of questions. Overall he agreed with my diagnosis and my proposals. Moreover, he immediately understood the need for urgent action in view of the on-going negotiations between Britain and China over the future of Hong Kong. Fortuitously the crisis in Hong Kong occurred immediately ahead of the IMF/World Bank meetings in Washington, and not only were the most senior Bank of England and Treasury officials due to attend, but also the Prime Minister was on a State visit to Canada, and due to call on her friend President Reagan in Washington. Thanks to Alan's appreciation of the problem in Hong Kong and his influence with the PM, a meeting was promptly arranged between the Chancellor of the Exchequer (Nigel Lawson), the Governor of the Bank of England (Robin Leigh Pemberton), visiting Bank and Treasury officials, Alan Walters and the PM at the British Embassy in Washington on Tuesday, September 27th. At the meeting the PM asked Walters to go out to Hong Kong and review the plan in detail. For personal reasons he was unable to go, but on October 6th and 7th a delegation of two (Charles Goodhart from the Bank and David Peretz from HM Treasury) did visit Hong Kong to vet the scheme and give Hong Kong officials the necessary seal of approval.

From our phone conversations at the time I recall Alan saying to me that the main question which would concern the British authorities was whether the Bank of England's reserves might be put at risk by the obligation to maintain the HK$ fixed rate (see Margaret Thatcher, "The Downing Street Years", pp. 489–490). We agreed that if the HK dollar was put under pressure, interest rates in Hong Kong would rise sharply, but the Bank of England would not be called on to lend its reserves because high interest rates in Hong Kong at a broadly unchanged fixed exchange rate would attract inflows back into the territory. As Alan had envisaged, the question did come up at the embassy conference, but more importantly the analysis that Hong Kong would never need to call on the Bank of England's reserves also turned out to be correct.

A S I A N   M O N E T A R Y   M O N I T O R
Vol. 7 No. 5 September–October, 1983

INTRODUCTION[1]

A previous issue of AMM showed that each of Hong Kong's monetary instruments suffered from serious defects from a monetary control point of view and that, given present arrangements, none of the four monetary instruments could be expected effectively to permit the authorities either to control the money supply or to defend the exchange rate. We also argued that these defects in the monetary system were to a large extent responsible for the wide amplitude in Hong Kong's business cycle fluctuations, and the persistent weakness of the Hong Kong dollar over the past four years. We went on to say that the key to moderating the boom-and-bust cycle in the future and the key to rescuing the currency was in correcting the flaws in the monetary system rather than in tightening up prudential controls on banks and DTCs. In this article we explain the practical steps necessary to implement our proposals to control the money supply or manage the exchange rate.

THE NEED FOR MONETARY CONTROL

Why is it so important that the authorities should have some workable system of monetary control?

First, there is the empirical fact that the ups and downs in Hong Kong's business cycle have been closely linked to accelerations and decelerations in money and credit. In our view, by mitigating the tendency of bankers to oscillate between exuberant lending sprees which produce faster money growth and hence inflation, and bouts of extreme caution which restrict bank credit and money, and hence intensify recession, the authorities would go a long way to stabilizing the Hong Kong economy.

Second, there is the irrefutable fact that under present monetary arrangements the authorities have been powerless to prevent the persistent depreciation of the Hong Kong dollar. The precise mechanics of this impotence were explained in Chapter 2. However, if anybody was not completely convinced by that theoretical demonstration then the pathetic collapse of the Hong Kong currency in recent months despite repeated attempts by the authorities to shore it up ought at least to prompt questions about the workings of current monetary system. We see no reason why the Hong Kong dollar should not be able to remain firm, even in the face of widespread uncertainty over Hong Kong's future after 1997, *provided a sensible and workable system of monetary control is adopted.* Under

---

1. The author is indebted to Professor Max Fry for penetrating comments on the first draft of this paper.

present arrangements, however, we see no prospect of the authorities or the HKAB[2] cartel being able to stop the slide for long. Unless some serious steps are taken towards monetary reform it is entirely conceivable that the Hong Kong dollar will continue to slide inexorably downwards. This would be a disaster for Hong Kong, leading first to widespread social unrest as prices for imported food and fuel increase again and again, and could ultimately climax in a massive flight from the local currency.

Third, there is a more basic point of principle. Most people would agree that two of the fundamental springs of success of the Hong Kong economy are the existence of the rule of law and the minimal degree of government intervention in commercial activity. One important element of the rule of law is the equality of all individuals before the law or, to put it the other way, the lack of any class or classes which are peculiarly favoured by the law. Another basic element of the rule of law is the sanctity of contract, which implies a legal sanction to enforce contracts. The role of government in enforcing the rule of law is to provide a *framework* within which individuals can live their lives in whatever manner they choose provided their activity does not cause harm or damage to others.

Since money is the medium of exchange in which all contracts are expressed, it behoves a government which adheres to the principles of the rule of law to provide a *framework* which preserves the value of the medium of exchange. As we have argued consistently in many previous issues of AMM, the value of Hong Kong's money can only be preserved through the provision of a sensible monetary framework which ensures that, over time, the real value of the Hong Kong dollar is preserved.

Events over the past two or three years on the exchange rate front and events in the local money markets this summer have cast serious doubt on the ability of Hong Kong's present monetary system to preserve the value of the Hong Kong dollar, and it is high time in our view the authorities took a proper grip of the situation. It is no use protesting that regulating the value of the Hong Kong dollar or controlling the quantity of Hong Kong dollar money supply would be inimical to "positive non-interventionism". That argument is plainly nonsense since throughout the period 1935–1974 the value of the Hong Kong dollar was fixed, and yet there was, except in the war years, a greater degree of laissez-faire then than there is today.

The fact is that a method of monetary control does exist which is entirely compatible with a stable value of the currency (in real terms) and the continuation of laissez-faire or positive non-interventionism in every other respect. In addition, this scheme of monetary control is largely consistent with existing institutional arrangements (the issue of banknotes by private banks, the absence of foreign exchange controls, the 3-tier banking structure etc.) *and requires zero government intervention in the foreign exchange market.*

Clearly government has to act or make changes to the present monetary system to the extent necessary to bring about monetary control, but we believe this could be

---

2. The Hong Kong Association of Banks.

achieved at minimal cost (in terms of manpower or financial resources) while bringing significant long term benefits to the economy. Therefore, under one of the alternative schemes which we propose, no "intervention" (i.e. active purchases and sales of foreign exchange in the commercial markets to fix the HK$ exchange rate) would be required. In other words, *monetary control is quite feasible without "intervention"*.

Accepting the view that some form of monetary control is desirable (and in our opinion almost any form of control would be better than the present arrangements), the question is how to achieve control of the money supply or control of the exchange rate with minimum disruption to the famous flexibility and adaptability of Hong Kong's free market economy.

It goes without saying that any proposals for reform of the Hong Kong monetary system must be based on a complete and accurate diagnosis of what is wrong with the present system, and such proposals must correct those errors without an unacceptable degree of disruption to existing institutions. In this spirit we present our two basic alternative solutions, one of which has two possible variants, giving three possible schemes. There are some further subvariants of each scheme, but we do not pursue these. We also show again why the interest rate mechanism, which is the focal point of current monetary control arrangements, is a fundamentally unsound fulcrum on which to base any long term solution to Hong Kong's financial problems (Appendix 5.1). Finally we show why certain proposals to tighten up liquid asset requirements put forward by some banks and individuals in Hong Kong would not achieve their purported aims (Appendix 5.2).

DIAGNOSIS OF THE LACK OF CONTROL IN CURRENT ARRANGEMENTS

The essence of the lack of monetary control in Hong Kong's financial system lies in the fact that the Exchange Fund neither controls the quantity of base money nor guarantees its convertibility in terms of foreign currency at any specified price. Yet in all other countries of the world, so far as we know, the monetary authority performs one of these functions, either regulating the size of the monetary base (with a view to controlling the aggregate money supply), or setting the price of its currency in terms of foreign exchange. It is true that authorities elsewhere have vacillated between different policy instruments and objectives — switching between quantitative targets, exchange rates and interest rates according to shifts in the political or economic climate — so that performance has generally not matched intentions. But that does not deny the ability of the authority to determine the *price* of each unit of the monetary base or the *quantity* of base money, *should they choose to do so*. In Hong Kong, however, the authorities have chosen — perhaps unwittingly — not to determine either since the early 1970s. How did this come about?

Between 1935 and 1972 Hong Kong's monetary system was a classic automatic adjustment mechanism that operated under a modified colonial currency board called the Exchange Fund. Instead of designing, engraving and printing the banknotes itself

Table 5.1 Consolidated Balance Sheets for the Current Hong Kong Monetary System
(September 1983)

CONSOLIDATED BALANCE SHEETS FOR THE CURRENT HONG KONG MONETARY SYSTEM (SEPT. 1983)

Assets   EXCHANGE FUND   Liabilities

Foreign Exchange Assets	Certificates of Indebtedness
	Coins Issued
HK$ Deposits at Banks	E.F. Borrowings from Banks
- - - - - - - - - - -	- - - - - - - - - - - - -
HK Government Balances	Debt Certificates
Others	Net Worth

LICENSED BANKS

Certificates of Indebtedness	Notes Issued
- - - - - - - - - - -	- - - - - - - - - - - - -
HK$ Notes and Coin	HK$ Deposits of Public
HK$ Loans and Investments	HK$ Deposits of Exchange Fund/Govt.
HK$ Interbank Balances	HK$ Interbank Borrowings
- - - - - - - - - - -	- - - - - - - - - - - - -
Fx Notes and Coin	Fx Deposits of Public
Fx Loans and Investments	
Fx Interbank Balances	Fx Interbank Borrowings
- - - - - - - - - - -	- - - - - - - - - - - - -
Others	Net Worth

Note: The notional accounts of the Exchange Fund shown in the balance sheet above (and
hereafter) reflect the two roles of the Exchange Fund as monetary authority and as
fiscal agent of the government. For clear thinking and for analysis of the monetary
consequences of Exchange Fund transactions it is important to separate these two
functions. We have therefore divided the Exchange Fund balance sheet with a dashed
line, the upper section containing items relevant to its monetary role, the lower
section containing items relevant to its role as fiscal agent. The fiscal role of the
Exchange Fund dates from a decision in 1977 to transfer to the Fund the Treasury's
Hong Kong dollar balances (apart from working balances) against the issue of interest-
bearing Debt Certificates, the bulk of the Treasury's foreign currency balances having
been transferred in 1976. Between 1972 and December 1981 the Exchange Fund's HK$
assets (and some of its foreign currency assets) therefore comprised (a) the counterpart
of accumulated budgetary surpluses - i.e. the Government's fiscal reserves - and (b) HK$
balances against the issue of CIs. When the Exchange Fund's borrowing scheme was
introduced in December 1981 the HK$ assets would have begun to reflect these
transactions.
Since the authorities do not publish the Exchange Fund's accounts for public scrutiny
it is not possible to put exact figures on these balance sheet items. However, that
does not in the least affect the principles governing the interaction of the Exchange
Fund and the banking system - i.e. the mechanisms of monetary control.
The balance sheets for the licensed banks are divided into four sections: (i) the
note-issuing function of the two note-issuing banks (In a full consolidation of the
authorities and the banks Certificates of Indebtedness cancel out leaving the Notes
Issued as an effective liability of the monetary authorities who hold the backing
for those Notes); (ii) the HK$ domestic banking segment; (iii) a foreign currency
banking segment; and (iv) residual items and net worth. The notional balance sheets for
DTCs are basically the same as (ii), (iii) and (iv) except that they do not include HK$
deposits of the Exchange Fund or Government. For simplicity we have omitted DTCs from
this analysis, but statements applying to the non-note issuing banks can be taken as
applying to DTCs also.

and issuing these colonial notes to the banks, the Exchange Fund permitted three private banks to continue to issue notes as they had done before 1935.[3] In order to issue new HK$ banknotes the note-issuing banks had to submit sterling to the Exchange Fund in return for Certificates of Indebtedness (CIs) at a fixed rate of exchange. These are non-interest bearing certificates denominated in HK$ permitting the bank in question to issue specified amounts of HK$ banknotes. (See illustration below.) Until the early 1970s the Exchange Fund's assets would therefore have been almost entirely in sterling.[4]

However, in June/July 1972 the Hong Kong dollar was unhitched from sterling and pegged to the US$. At the same time the note-issuing banks were permitted to "pay" for CIs in HK$. To the extent that the Exchange Fund now began to hold HK$ balances at those commercial banks against CIs it was altering the basic nature of the monetary standard from something which was equivalent to a fixed amount of foreign currency (HK$5.65 = US$1.00 at the time) to a monetary standard which was only defined in terms of itself, even though the stated policy objective was to keep the HK$/US$ rate pegged at a fixed rate. Not surprisingly the authorities soon had difficulty keeping the exchange rate within the target bands.

This process culminated in the decision in November 1974 to allow the Hong Kong dollar to float freely on the foreign exchange market.

In effect the decision meant that the monetary standard was now a pure Hong Kong dollar standard. But having removed the guarantee of external convertibility at a fixed *price* no provisions were made at the time to control or regulate the *quantity* of Hong

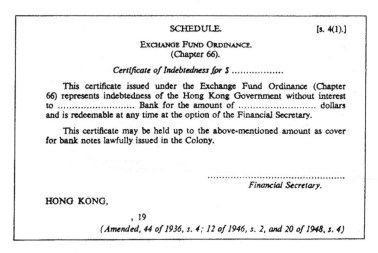

Figure 5.1 A Certificate of Indebtedness (Source: Exchange Fund Ordinance, Chapter 66 of the Revised Edition, Laws of Hong Kong 1971)

---

3.   The Mercantile Bank no longer issues notes, leaving two note-issuing banks in 1983. Since 1994, the Bank of China has become a note-issuing bank, restoring the number of note-issuing banks to three.

4.   See Y.C. Jao, "Banking and Currency in Hong Kong". Macmillan, 1974.

Kong dollars. Hong Kong was therefore left with a system in which neither the *price* nor *quantity* of money was controlled.

One problem in sorting out the current Hong Kong monetary system is the curious arrangement whereby the Exchange Fund issues base money (Certificates of Indebtedness) in exchange for commercial bank *liabilities* (Exchange Fund deposits at the note-issuing banks) — which are another form of money. In other words, in Hong Kong base money is issued by the authorities in exchange for deposit money issued by the banks. In one sense this problem is perhaps more illusory than real. For, although in other orthodox monetary systems, by contrast, the authorities issue "base money" (notes, coin, or reserve deposits) against the purchase of *assets* of the commercial banks, such new issues of base money enable the banks to create more loans and deposits. Thus the difference between the "new" Exchange Fund deposit and a deposit generated by a loan is no more than equivalent to the difference between a primary deposit and a derivative deposit.

In another sense, however, the fact that the Exchange Fund holds domestic currency deposits with commercial banks — in its monetary capacity as opposed to its role as fiscal agent for the government — is disastrous because it undermines the potential for multiple expansion or multiple contraction effects from transactions between the authorities and the banks. If increases or decreases in Exchange Fund balances at the banks encouraged or discouraged bank credit creation in any permanent way (i.e. had some permanent effect on the monetary multiplier) this might provide some offset to the decision not to control the base. But both statistical evidence (on the stability of the monetary multiplier) and casual market observation (on the short-lived effectiveness of Exchange Fund intervention in the domestic money markets or the foreign exchange market) suggest there is no such effect.

The contrast between the Hong Kong system and other systems is illustrated by the notional balance sheets on pp. 112–113.

Type of Monetary Standard	Operating Rule of the Monetary Authority	Choice of Mechanism	AMM Proposal
A pure Hong Kong dollar standard	To determine the quantity of base money	Discretionary	1
		Automatic	–
A foreign currency standard	To determine the price of base money	Discretionary	2A
		Automatic	2B

The three schemes tabulated above and presented on the following pages derive from the view that the monetary authority can only determine either the quantity of base money or the price of base money. In both cases there is the option to adopt either a discretionary mechanism or an automatic mechanism. This gives four possible approaches to reforming the monetary system. For various reasons we omit consideration of what would be 1B (equivalent to a pure commodity standard), leaving three possible options for Hong Kong's monetary standard.

Table 5.2a Annotated Balance Sheet of the Hong Kong Banking System

In an orthodox monetary system...

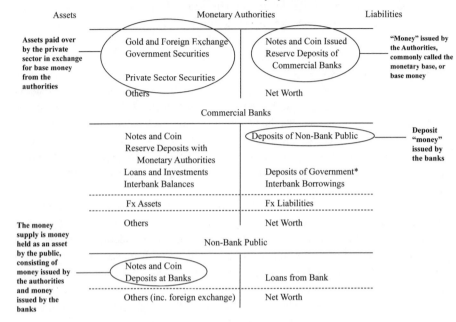

.... there are 3 crucial elements of monetary control

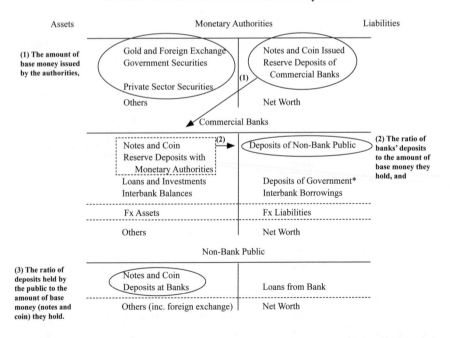

* In some countries government deposits are held at the commercial banks, in some countries at the central bank, and in others at both. To clarify the analysis they are shown here at the commercial banks, which is also the case for Hong Kong.

Table 5.2b Annotated Balance Sheet of the Hong Kong Banking System

In the Hong Kong Monetary System…

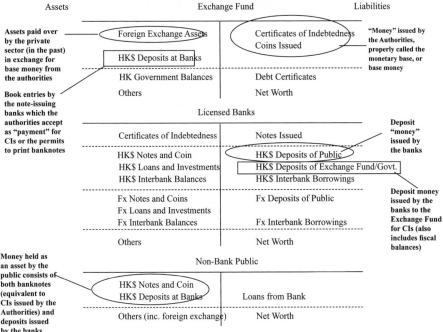

Assets	Exchange Fund	Liabilities
Assets paid over by the private sector (in the past) in exchange for base money from the authorities	Foreign Exchange Assets	Certificates of Indebtedness / Coins Issued	**"Money" issued by the Authorities, properly called the monetary base, or base money**
	HK$ Deposits at Banks		
	HK Government Balances	Debt Certificates	
Book entries by the note-issuing banks which the authorities accept as "payment" for CIs or the permits to print banknotes	Others	Net Worth	

Licensed Banks

	Certificates of Indebtedness	Notes Issued	**Deposit "money" issued by the banks**
	HK$ Notes and Coin	HK$ Deposits of Public	
	HK$ Loans and Investments	HK$ Deposits of Exchange Fund/Govt.	
	HK$ Interbank Balances	HK$ Interbank Borrowings	
	Fx Notes and Coins	Fx Deposits of Public	**Deposit money issued by the banks to the Exchange Fund for CIs (also includes fiscal balances)**
	Fx Loans and Investments		
	Fx Interbank Balances	Fx Interbank Borrowings	
	Others	Net Worth	

Non-Bank Public

Money held as an asset by the public consists of both banknotes (equivalent to CIs issued by the Authorities) and deposits issued by the banks	HK$ Notes and Coin / HK$ Deposits at Banks	Loans from Bank	
	Others (inc. foreign exchange)	Net Worth	

…. two elements of monetary control have major defects

Assets	Exchange Fund	Liabilities
(1) Neither the price nor the quantity of base money is controlled in any way. The price of the Hong Kong Dollar is no longer fixed in foreign currency terms; it is only fixed in terms of itself. Nowadays one dollar of bank money (deposits) buys one dollar of base money (CIs)	Foreign Exchange Assets	(1) Certificates of Indebtedness / Coins Issued	
	HK$ Deposits at Banks		
	HK Government Balances	Debt Certificates	
	Others	Net Worth	

Licensed Banks

	Certificates of Indebtedness	Notes Issued	
	HK$ Notes and Coin (2)	HK$ Deposits of Public	
	HK$ Loans and Investments	HK$ Deposits of Exchange Fund/Govt.	
	HK$ Interbank Balances (net)	HK$ Interbank Borrowings	
	Fx Notes and Coins	Fx Deposits of Public	
	Fx Loans and Investments		
	Fx Interbank Balances	Fx Interbank Borrowings	
	Others	Net Worth	

Non-Bank Public

	HK$ Notes and Coin / HK$ Deposits at Banks	Loans from Banks	
	Others (inc. foreign exchange)	Net Worth	

(2) The Hong Kong authorities do not rely on the ratio of base money held by the banks to their deposits for monetary control. Instead, Hong Kong has a system of specified liquid assets for prudential purposes, under which every item in the dashed line boxes contains eligible assets which can satisfy the liquidity requirements. Consequently it is relatively easy for banks to meet the liquidity requirements, but these specified liquid asset ratios do not provide a mechanism for monetary control

Table 5.3 Proposed Scheme 1

PROPOSED SCHEME 1

Assets | EXCHANGE FUND | Liabilities

Assets	Liabilities
Foreign Exchange Assets	Certificates of Indebtedness
	Coins Issued
HK$-denominated paper	'Special' or Reserve Deposits
	of Banks
- - - - - - - - - - -	- - - - - - - - - - -
HK Government Balances	Debt Certificates
Others	Net Worth

LICENSED BANKS

Certificates of Indebtedness	Notes Issued
- - - - - - - - - - -	- - - - - - - - - - -
HK$ Notes and Coin	HK$ Deposits of Public
HK$ 'Special' or Reserve	HK$ Deposits of Government
Deposits at E.F.	
HK$ Loans and Investments	
HK$ Interbank Balances	HK$ Interbank Borrowings
- - - - - - - - - - -	- - - - - - - - - - -
Fx Notes and Coin	Fx Deposits of Public
Fx Loans and Investments	
Fx Interbank Balances	Fx Interbank Borrowings
- - - - - - - - - - -	- - - - - - - - - - -
Others	Net Worth

SCHEME 1: TO CONTROL THE MONEY SUPPLY

A fundamental flaw in Hong Kong's monetary system today is that the Exchange Fund does not control the quantity of base money because it issues Certificates of Indebtedness (equivalent to banknotes) passively on demand.

To eliminate the passive element in the lack of control the Exchange Fund could purchase either HK$ commercial paper or HK$-denominated bonds or foreign exchange from banks or brokers, crediting the settling banks with the proceeds *in HK$* in newly constituted reserve accounts at the Exchange Fund. The non note-issuing banks would be able to draw on these accounts to obtain notes from the note-issuing banks (in exactly the same way as they draw today on their clearing accounts with the note issuers to obtain notes). This arrangement would mean that notes, CIs and reserve deposits were in effect interchangeable — a homogeneous form of base money.

This would immediately have three effects:

(i) it would mean that each participating bank would hold some combination of (a) reserve deposits at the Exchange Fund and (b) notes (equivalent to CIs issued by the Exchange Fund),

(ii) it would give the Exchange Fund direct control over the joint total of CIs (i.e. notes) and bank reserves, i.e. total base money, and

(iii) it would provide the Exchange Fund with the means to control the money supply (and hence liquidity or money market interest rates in the short term) on a discretionary basis.

If the Exchange Fund were now to sell, say, HK$ commercial paper via a broker, the broker would have to write a cheque in favour of the Exchange Fund which would be settled *not by crediting an Exchange Fund account at a bank but by debiting the account of the settling bank at the Exchange Fund*, thus reducing its reserves and obliging that bank either to lend less or to bid for more reserve deposits. Both sets of actions — the sale of the commercial paper and the reaction of the banks — will tend to push up interest rates and thus tighten the credit markets which in turn would reduce the money supply.

The exact extent of the impact of this monetary tightening operation will depend upon (i) the size of the selling operation by the Exchange Fund, i.e. the change in the base, (ii) the amount by which banks have to reduce their lending and hence their deposits in order to maintain a specified or desired ratio of reserves to deposits, and (iii) the amount by which the non-bank public have to adjust their holdings of deposits and currency to restore their desired ratio of deposits to currency.

While it is possible to conceive of this scheme only being operated with the two note-issuing banks it would clearly be desirable if all banks were to participate. This is because with all banks participating, following any change in the total quantity of reserves or base money by the Exchange Fund, market forces would operate evenly on all banks, transmitting the authorities' desire to tighten or ease money market conditions uniformly throughout the system. If the authorities were to operate only via the note-issuing banks this would give those banks the unparalleled advantage of having exclusive access to or knowledge of the authorities' intentions and this would enable them to position themselves in the market accordingly. This would be highly prejudicial to the development of properly competitive financial markets, and would no doubt soon lead to widespread discontent among the less privileged banks. Often in Hong Kong such banks are reluctant to express their discontent too openly for fear of discriminatory treatment or for fear of jeopardising their current status. This is obviously a thoroughly unhealthy situation and is not conducive to an evenly competitive banking environment. Nevertheless it is currently tolerated or at least accepted as one of the costs of doing business in Hong Kong.

Some related issues:

(1) Clearing Arrangements

If all banks were to participate in the scheme it would soon become apparent that the existing clearing arrangements with the note-issuing banks were somewhat superfluous. At present most banks in Hong Kong maintain clearing accounts with one of the two note-issuing banks. Since under Scheme 1 all banks would maintain accounts at the Exchange Fund it would be quite natural for banks to wish to transfer their clearing accounts to their newly constituted accounts at the Exchange Fund, and these would soon become an integral part of the interbank market as banks who were low on reserves bid for funds from those who were flush with reserves.

(2) Would Reserve Requirements Be Necessary?

In many countries where banks hold reserve deposits with the central bank there are legal provisions or rules requiring banks to maintain ratios of these deposits to their non-bank deposit liabilities in domestic currency. But are these minimum ratios a necessary condition for monetary control? Some quite simple algebra shows that control of the money supply can be achieved without required reserves, provided the base is controlled.

Let C = currency held by the public
D = deposits held by the public
R = vault cash plus licensed bank deposits with the Exchange Fund
M = money supply
B = monetary base

Then M = C + D   (1)
and B = C + R   (2)

Now divide (1) by (2):

$$\frac{M}{B} = \frac{C+D}{C+R} = \frac{C/D+1}{C/D+R/D} \tag{3}$$

Hence $M = B \cdot \left(\dfrac{C/D+1}{C/D+R/D} \right)$ (4)

If R = 0, then $M = B \cdot \left(\dfrac{C/D+1}{C/D} \right)$ (5)

Even if banks held zero reserves (which is inconceivable since they must hold some vault cash to meet customers' needs), the money supply is still some determinate multiple of the base.

(3)   The Exchange Fund as Lender of Last Resort

Today in Hong Kong the two note issuing banks are effectively the lenders of last resort, partly by reason of their dominant size in the market, but also because the authorities have not previously acted in a banking capacity in the sense of issuing deposits to banks and others. However, under Scheme 1 the Exchange Fund could act as lender of last resort insofar as it could always create new reserves by purchasing the assets (HK$ instruments or foreign currency) of any bank in distress and crediting the accounts of that bank at the Exchange Fund in HK$. There should be no need to operate a special discount facility, any more than the Hong Kong and Shanghai Bank does now. But obviously the Exchange Fund would stand by to provide "liquidity" (i.e. reserves) in any emergency, just as private banks do today.

(4)   Transition Arrangements

Whenever this type of scheme is proposed there are some who protest that official purchases of foreign exchange (or HK$-denominated instruments) would somehow weaken the HK$. This objection seems groundless to us because in the initial stages of setting up the scheme the authorities would not be selling HK$ on the open market; they would be merely crediting the newly created reserve accounts of the banks at the Exchange Fund with new HK$. The transactions could be conducted at the market opening at an average of the previous day's rates or at a rate specified by the Exchange Fund which would soon become a guiding rate for the rest of the market. These HK$ credits to banks would not constitute an increase in the HK$ money supply because these accounts are not included in the money supply.

(5)   The Attitude of the Chinese Banks

There are some who maintain that the mainland Chinese banks in Hong Kong would never accede to join such a scheme. This seems unlikely in view of the fact that the Bank of China (HK) Ltd is already subject to inspection by the Commissioner of Banking in respect of its compliance with the Banking Ordinance. Furthermore China has a very real interest in Hong Kong's financial stability and the strength of the Hong Kong dollar since as much as one quarter or one third of its foreign exchange earnings derive from Hong Kong.

SCHEME 2A: TO MANAGE THE EXCHANGE RATE (WITH INTERVENTION)

Another fundamental flaw in the present Hong Kong monetary system is that intervention operations in the foreign exchange market by the Exchange Fund are not effective in determining the price of the HK$. This is because intervention in the foreign exchange market does not affect the quantity of base money in the Hong Kong banking

Table 5.4 Proposed Scheme 2A

PROPOSED SCHEME 2A

Assets	EXCHANGE FUND	Liabilities
Foreign Exchange Assets	Certificates of Indebtedness Coin Issued 'Special' or Reserve Deposits of Banks	
- - - - - - - - - - -	- - - - - - - - - - - -	
HK$ Government Balances	Debt Certificates	
Others	Net Worth	

LICENSED BANKS

Certificates of Indebtedness	Notes Issued	
- - - - - - - - - - -	- - - - - - - - - - - -	
HK$ Notes and Coin HK$ 'Special' or Reserve Deposits at E.F. HK$ Loans and Investments HK$ Interbank Balances	HK$ Deposits of Public HK$ Deposits of Government HK$ Interbank Borrowings	
- - - - - - - - - - -	- - - - - - - - - - - -	
Fx Notes and Coin Fx Loans and Investments Fx Interbank Balances	Fx Deposits of Public Fx Bank Borrowings	
- - - - - - - - - - -	- - - - - - - - - - - -	
Others	Net Worth	

system. Consequently there is no tightening or easing of the domestic money markets in the direction desired by the authorities since the size of banks' balance sheets remain essentially unaltered by official intervention operations. (See Chapter 2, pp. 30–31.)

To overcome this problem the authorities could set up Scheme 2A which is a variant of the arrangements under Scheme 1, with the difference that instead of selling or purchasing both foreign exchange and HK$-denominated instruments the Exchange Fund would restrict its operations to the foreign exchange market. Thus the monetary assets of the Exchange Fund — aside from the strictly fiscal balances of the government — would consist of foreign currency assets only. (This refers only to the part of the Exchange Fund balance sheet above the dashed line on p. 118; see footnote on p. 109.)

Under Scheme 2A the Exchange Fund would always either (1) buy HK$ against the sale of foreign exchange, or (2) sell HK$ against the purchase of foreign exchange, with a view to keeping the exchange rate for the HK$ at some predetermined rate or within some agreed range against one currency or against a basket of currencies.

In the first type of operation banks' reserve accounts at the Exchange Fund would be debited with the HK$ equivalent of the amount of foreign currency sold. The reduction in banks' balances at the Exchange Fund would force them to restrict their HK$ lending, thus slowing or reducing HK$ deposit growth. This type of multiple contraction effect in the aftermath of local currency support (i.e. purchase) operations would automatically and immediately produce a tightening in the local money markets which would reinforce the authorities' original intervention operation.

Conversely, sales of HK$ against purchases of foreign currency by the Exchange Fund would lead to a crediting of banks' balances at the Exchange Fund, thereby increasing total reserves and enabling banks to increase their HK$ lending and accelerating deposit growth. This multiple expansion effect would immediately start to ease local money markets, reinforcing the authorities' original sale of Hong Kong dollars.

The beauty of such intervention operations under Scheme 2A is that foreign exchange rate movements and money market interest rate movements would both be in *complementary* directions, and this mutual reinforcement would virtually guarantee success for official foreign exchange intervention operations. This is in contrast to present arrangements under which the Hong Kong dollars bought in support operations are not debited to any banks' reserve accounts but are credited back to their deposits with the net result that deposits are merely transferred from the private sector to the government and there is no contractionary effect on the banking system as a whole.

It is important in the debate over the exchange rate to separate the problem of political confidence from the problem of monetary mechanics. There is little that the monetary authorities can do about the politics of the 1997 negotiations in Peking; however there is much that they can do about the monetary system in Hong Kong which would help to protect the Hong Kong dollar from persistent erosion.

Related Issues (1)–(5)

Despite the difference in operating rules between Scheme 2A and Scheme 1 (i.e. the exchange rate rather than the monetary base), the comments applying to (1) clearing arrangements, (2) reserve requirements, (3) the Exchange Fund as lender of last resort, (4) transition arrangements and (5) the attitude of the Chinese banks in respect of Scheme 1 would all apply to Scheme 2A because the institutional changes implied by the adoption of either scheme are essentially the same.

Conclusion on Schemes 1 and 2A

There can be little doubt that Scheme 1 would provide the technical tools necessary to control the monetary base and hence the money supply, and that Scheme 2A would provide the tools necessary to manage the HK$ exchange rate. Clearly the introduction of these discretionary mechanisms would mark a further departure from Hong Kong's traditionally non-interventionist monetary policy, but would they be consistent with the preservation of its predominantly free market for labour, for financial and physical assets, and for goods and services?

The schemes described above are exactly the same in principle as many other central bank/fractional reserve banking systems operating in the world today. The primary objection to such systems is that they are discretionary, depending on the personal decisions of administrators, and they offer numerous temptations to the central bank or government to exceed their proper role of providing a stable monetary framework (i.e. a currency of stable internal and external value), and to become involved in the allocation of resources.[5]

A second objection to these discretionary schemes is that the transformation of the Exchange Fund from a passive issuer of CIs to an active central bank regulating the growth of the monetary base would clearly involve extensive institutional changes which many concerned individuals would be most reluctant to contemplate. It is not that institutional changes are wrong in themselves, but if monetary control can be achieved without major structural changes, then so much the better.

A third objection applicable to Scheme 1 in Hong Kong's current circumstances is that even the provision of stable money growth might not be sufficient to prevent erosion of the exchange value of the Hong Kong dollar if confidence in the future were to be undermined. Under these conditions even stable money growth could be quite consistent with a falling exchange rate, rising prices and rising income velocity of circulation.

While Scheme 1 and 2A are practically feasible they imply extensive structural and institutional changes at a difficult moment in Hong Kong's history, and a degree of governmental discretion which could further diminish the operation of the free market in Hong Kong. For these reasons it would seem preferable to examine alternative arrangements.

SCHEME 2B: TO MANAGE THE EXCHANGE RATE (WITHOUT INTERVENTION)

Each of the two previous schemes essentially involves converting the Exchange Fund into a central bank, and using the new apparatus to regulate the amount of base money either as a means of influencing the money supply (Scheme 1), or as a means of managing the exchange rate of the HK$ (Scheme 2A). Both schemes depend on the same two basic propositions: (1) that it is necessary for the authorities deliberately to control the quantity of base money in the economy, and (2) that there is some fairly well-defined relation between the amount of base money and the money supply i.e. the ability of the banking system to multiply up base money into loans and deposits.

---

5.   See Milton Friedman, "A Program for Monetary Stability", Fordham University Press, New York 1960.

However, suppose the authorities are humble enough to admit that they do not know exactly how much new base money they ought to supply in any year (Scheme 1), and suppose that they would prefer to avoid the task of daily intervention in the foreign exchange market to peg the price of the Hong Kong dollar (Scheme 2A). How can the monetary system be controlled now? The only answer to this question that we have been able to advance is that the authorities must devise a system for setting the exchange rate such that the rate of monetary growth is automatically related to the state of the overall balance of payments at the chosen exchange rate. Balance of payments surpluses would permit a degree of monetary expansion, while balance of payments deficits would imply some monetary contraction until the payments position returned to equilibrium.

To avoid the need for the authorities to intervene actively in the foreign exchange markets and hence to allow the amount of base money to be regulated passively it is necessary that whatever serves as base money (CIs or notes in Hong Kong) should be available *in unlimited amounts at a stated price in foreign currency*, and that it should be redeemable on similar terms in indefinite quantities. In technical terms, the supply curve for base money should be horizontal at some stated price in foreign currency. In other words the authorities should stand willing to supply or redeem currency (or CIs) at the stated price, thus allowing the amount of base money to expand or contract in line with the needs of the non-bank public and the banks, given the state of the overall balance of payments at the chosen exchange rate.[6]

The second requirement of such a system is a guarantee of convertibility or interchangeability or perfect substitutability between base money and the deposit money issued by the banks. The reason is that in this type of automatic adjustment mechanism the link between total money supply and the amount of base money is not dependent upon any required or legislated ratios; rather it depends on (a) the desired deposit-to-currency ratios of the banks and the non-bank public, and (b) the efficient operation of market forces.

(A) Determinant Ratios of the Banks and the Non-Bank Public

Both the banks and the non-bank public hold base money. Because the banks issue deposit money which the public can convert into cash on demand, they will tend (collectively) to hold some fraction of their deposit liabilities in the form of notes and coin (base money). That fraction will depend on such things as the maturity structure of their deposit liabilities (i.e. the relative sizes of their demand, time and savings deposits, and their respective convertibility into cash), the efficiency of their vault cash management operations, and the habits of payment of the community (i.e. cash vs. bank transfers, seasonal payment patterns etc.).

---

6.   This is comparable to the classic gold standard mechanism with the nominal money supply adjusting to international specie/payments flows at a fixed price level.

Table 5.5 Proposed Scheme 2B

PROPOSED SCHEME 2B

| Assets | EXCHANGE FUND | Liabilities |

EXCHANGE FUND	
Foreign Exchange Assets	Certificates of Indebtedness Coin Issued
- - - - - - - - - -	- - - - - - - - - - -
HK Government Balances	Debt Certificates
Others	Net Worth

LICENSED BANKS

LICENSED BANKS	
Certificates of Indebtedness	Notes Issued
- - - - - - - - - -	- - - - - - - - - - -
HK$ Notes and Coin HK$ Loans and Investments HK$ Interbank Balances	HK$ Deposits of Public HK$ Deposits of Government HK$ Interbank Borrowings
- - - - - - - - - -	- - - - - - - - - - -
Fx Notes and Coin Fx Loans and Investments Fx Interbank Balances	Fx Deposits of Public Fx Bank Borrowings
- - - - - - - - - -	- - - - - - - - - - -
Others	Net Worth

Provided these determinants of the amount of banks' cash currency assets relative to their deposit liabilities remain stable over time there is no reason why the link between base money held by the banks and the total volume of deposits should not behave in a quite predictable way. There will of course be seasonal fluctuations in the ratio, and there may be gradual changes over time, but we can find no valid objection to reliance on this lever as one of the keys to regulating monetary growth. (Certainly it is more dependable than interest rates!)

Ask any Hong Kong banker for his reaction to this proposition, and he will protest that the amount of currency his bank holds is insignificant in relation to deposits, and probably he will swear that he has never paid any attention to his bank's deposit-to-currency ratio as such. However, he and his deputies have tried to ensure that idle cash lying in bank tellers' drawers is reduced to a minimum, and, yes, he would be interested in any device that improved bank security... The fact is that a combination of technological and economic forces have combined to make the banks' deposit-to-currency ratio for the Hong Kong banking system as a whole quite stable over long periods. (See Charts 5.1 and 5.2, pp. 123–124.)

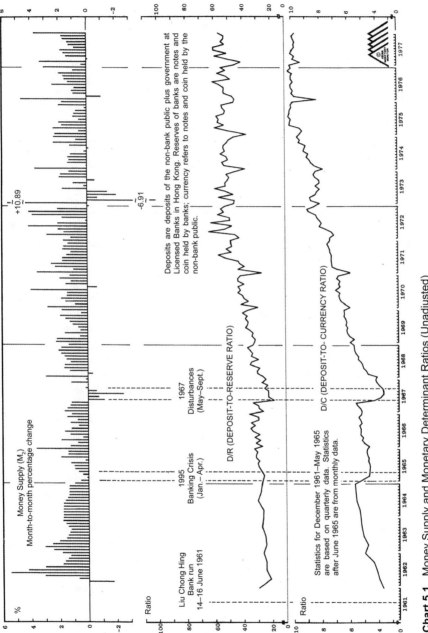

Chart 5.1 Money Supply and Monetary Determinant Ratios (Unadjusted)

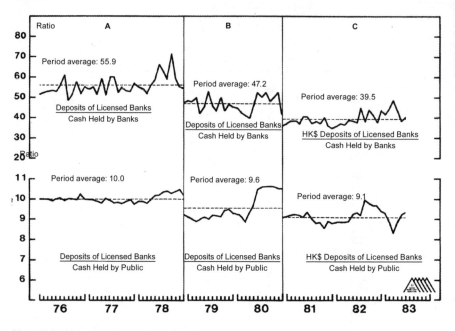

Chart 5.2   Monetary Determinant Ratios (Adjusted)

Notes: (1)   The three panels (A, B, C) in the chart reflect changes in the collection of monetary data in Hong Kong in recent years. Panel A records data collected by the Commissioner of Banking showing gross deposits at licensed banks in Hong Kong including foreign currency deposits and deposits of DTCs. In 1979 a slight improvement in data collection occurred with the separation of DTC deposits from those of the public (Panel B), but foreign currency deposits were still included. In 1981 with the passage of the Monetary Statistics Ordinance a further improvement was made (Panel C) with the separation of HK$ deposits from foreign currency deposits. Unfortunately from an analytical point of view Hong Kong's data still do not separate government and Exchange Fund deposits from deposits of the non-bank public.

(2)   Data are collected for the last banking day of each month, and consequently there appear to be random disturbances due to differing cash withdrawal patterns on different days of the week.

(3)   Another major seasonal problem is Chinese New Year. This is an annual public holiday in the January–March period set according to the lunar calendar, when substantial cash withdrawals are made by the Hong Kong population. Although the actual disturbances the festival produces may be assumed to be regular, as the banks first prepare cash currency inventories, then pay them out, and finally take the cash back in again and redeem the notes, the statistical recording of these events by the official banking data is quite random. In some years data are heavily affected by the incidence of Chinese New Year at month-end, while in other years the data may not be affected at all, while in still other years the official data may capture only the start of the process or only the tail-end of it.

The data in Chart 5.1 are unadjusted. Accordingly most of the downward spikes in the January–March period of any year are due to Chinese New Year.

The data in Chart 5.2 have been "adjusted for Chinese New Year" by a simple statistical smoothing technique, but other seasonal adjustments have not been attempted.

The non-bank public also holds some fraction of its deposits in the form of currency or base money, and again, provided the determinants of the division between deposits and currency can be shown to be reasonably stable, there is little reason to be concerned about leaning on the public's ratio of deposits-to-currency as a policy tool. The determinants of the fraction of money held as currency by the public will include the relative returns on cash versus deposits, the payment habits of the community, and perhaps the level of real income (as a proxy for the level of financial sophistication). Confidence will also play a significant role: whenever the Hong Kong public has lost confidence in the banks or DTCs, the ratio of deposits to currency has fallen sharply as people have converted deposits into currency and awaited the return of confidence in the system. Such bank runs (Charts 5.1) have been the only major source of instability in Hong Kong's monetary determinant ratios in the past two decades for which we have data (1962–1983). However, assuming that the prudential requirements for and careful supervision of the banking system is enforced, there is again little reason to fear that the non-bank public would behave in such a way as to destabilise the banking system.

To summarise: stable behaviour by the banks and the non-bank public in respect of their holdings of base money or currency relative to deposits combined with appropriate prudential supervision should be quite sufficient, without legislated reserve requirements, to ensure stability of the monetary system as a whole.

(B) The Role of Market Forces in the Automatic Adjustment Mechanism

The quantity of base money issued by the authorities in Scheme 2B is not directly controlled — it is the indirect result of the demand for currency or vault cash by the banks and the public combined, at the particular exchange rate set by the authorities. The authorities are essentially passive, except to the extent that they fix the price at which the base money is supplied.

Assuming the authorities will only issue base money to banks and will not deal with members of the non-bank public, banks will have a choice on a day-to-day basis between extending more loans (or making investments) in HK$, or holding more HK$ cash currency. Clearly they will prefer to make more loans so long as they can satisfy any liquidity requirements, since these are earning assets as opposed to currency which is a non-earning asset. As the quantity of loans (and hence deposits) increases, spending in Hong Kong will increase and the balance of payments will deteriorate. This will show up in the commercial T.T. market as a weakening of the HK$ spot rate relative to the Exchange Fund's offered rate for CIs.

Suppose the Exchange Fund rate (stated in US$ for argument's sake) is HK$7.50 and the T.T. rate falls to HK$7.55. The banks now have a choice: either they may sell HK$ to the Exchange Fund at HK$7.50 and obtain US$, or they can sell HK$ in the commercial market at the less favourable HK$7.55 rate.

At some stage there will be a clear incentive for banks to sell cash or CIs back to the Exchange Fund at the Exchange Fund's rate, rather than make new loans. These redemptions of HK$ base money at the Exchange Fund will cause a contraction of the total quantity of base money, and the banks as a whole will feel under pressure to slow down their lending. If they slow their lending under conditions where the demand for credit is strong, clearly this will lead to upward pressure on interest rates in Hong Kong, helping the commercial T.T. rate for HK$ to move back towards the Exchange Fund's offered rate. The rise in interest rates in turn will induce a decline in the demand for money balances consistent with the monetary contraction which stems from reduced credit demand at these higher interest rates. *In short, as long as the overall balance of payments was negative, pressure would be brought to bear on bank lending and the money supply until the original deficit was corrected.*

Let us examine the process in reverse, i.e. in the case where the T.T. rate was stronger than the Exchange Fund's offered rate for CIs. Let the Exchange Fund rate be at HK$7.50 again, and the T.T. be HK$7.45. This time the banks have a choice of buying US$ from the Exchange Fund at HK$7.50, or obtaining US$ at HK$7.45 in the commercial/T.T. market. Clearly they will prefer the latter, which means that currency will not be redeemed at the Exchange Fund and no pressure will be put on bank's holdings of cash, enabling them expand their lending. Lower interest rates from the increased supply of credit will encourage an increased demand for money balances consistent with the monetary expansion. *In other words, as long as the overall balance of payments was positive, there would be no pressure to restrict bank lending and the money supply until the surplus was eliminated.*

The beauty of this mechanism is that it is *automatic*, it requires no intervention by the authorities, and it requires minimal changes in Hong Kong's present institutional structure. To minimise the spread between the Exchange Fund's offered rate and the commercial or T.T. rate, however, it would be desirable to allow market forces to operate throughout the system as freely as possible. This could easily be accomplished by permitting banks other than the note-issuers to have access to the Exchange Fund's conversion facilities. These other banks would obviously submit notes rather than CIs to the authorities, who would pay the banks foreign exchange *at the same rate* as that received by the note issuers. The authorities would simultaneously cancel the equivalent amount of CIs, notifying the note issuers. The authorities' holdings of notes could of course be returned to circulation whenever a note-issuing bank was willing to pay over more foreign exchange for CIs in the normal way.

In essence this mechanism (i) makes notes and CIs interchangeable, thereby making base money homogeneous, and (ii) it greatly enhances the efficiency of the arbitrage between the Exchange Fund's rate for banknotes and the commercial/T.T. rate for foreign currency in the markets. (As all first year students of economics will know, homogeneity of product and free entry to the market place are two basic conditions for perfect competition.) The greater the possibilities were for this arbitrage, the less would be the divergence between the Exchange Fund's offered rate and the commercial/T.T. rate, and the more rapid would be the adjustment of the money supply to the balance of payments and vice-versa.

What are some of the practical implications of Scheme 2B?

- ## How would the foreign exchange markets operate?

Since Scheme 2B is essentially a return to the old automatic adjustment mechanism one would expect exchange rates to behave much as they did in the years before 1972, with the commercial or T.T. rates fluctuating narrowly on either side of the Exchange Fund's offered rate for CIs in line with the balance of payments. The commercial market rate for the HK$ would be at a slight premium to the Exchange Fund's rate for CIs when the balance of payments was in surplus, and at a slight discount to the Exchange Fund's rate for CIs when the balance of payments was in deficit.

As suggested in AMM Vol. 3 No. 6 (Nov.–Dec. 1979, pp. 18–22) there would be no need for the authorities to keep the rate for CIs pegged rigidly against one currency; they could aim simply at stabilising the trade-weighted index for the HK$, announcing their rate for CIs daily (or weekly or monthly) against one particular currency; or define the HK$ in terms of SDRs.

- ## How would the money supply and inflation behave?

Under Scheme 2B the ultimate constraint on bank credit and money supply expansion is the amount of base money held by the banks.

In the long run the money supply could only accelerate continuously if the community as a whole had sufficient foreign currency to pay over to the Exchange Fund for new CIs (or new note issues). This would only occur as long as Hong Kong was paying its way in the world (i.e. running an overall balance of payments surplus), and there would be no harm in monetary acceleration under these conditions. Conversely the money supply would only slow down continuously if the community as a whole was caught short of foreign exchange — e.g. when the domestic economy became overheated; but again there would be no harm in that. (Indeed, this was exactly what was required at the time of the 1980–81 property boom, but unfortunately the automatic adjustment mechanism had been rendered inoperative by the monetary changes of 1972–74.)

In the short run there would of course be some elasticity in the relation between the money supply and the amount of base money, but the underlying stability of the monetary determinant ratios documented in Charts 5.1 and 5.2 (pp. 123–124) would ensure that this short term elasticity did not undermine longer term monetary stability.

Under Scheme 2B inflation — that is, the general or overall price level — would be indirectly controlled by the authorities' choice of exchange rate for CIs. If they wished to have a low rate of inflation they would gradually move the rate for CIs upwards against other currencies. If they wanted to have an inflation rate approximating to that of Hong Kong's main trading partners the obvious thing to do would be to base the rate for CIs on a trade-weighted index of the Hong Kong currency. This is because in each case the inflation rate would be the outcome of whatever the money supply growth rate was at the chosen exchange rate. And the money supply in turn would reflect the balance of payments at that exchange rate, accelerating if the balance of payments was strong, decelerating if the balance of payments was weak.

- **How would interest rates behave?**

As in all other economies the level of nominal interest rates in Hong Kong would be the result of two interacting channels of transmission. First, there is the domestic supply and demand for credit. In Scheme 2B the supply of bank credit is ultimately regulated by the banks' access to base money, and the Exchange Fund would indirectly control the amount of base money by setting the price for CIs. On the demand side the more stable behaviour of the money supply (at least under normal conditions) should mean greater stability for domestic demand generally and hence for credit demand in particular.

Second, there is the influence of foreign interest rates as transmitted via the foreign exchange markets (i.e. from international trade transactions, from foreign capital markets, from interest arbitrage transactions etc., etc.). The current and expected level of the HK$ exchange rate is obviously crucial to this set of influences, and here again the Exchange Fund would play a key role via its pricing of CIs, because, as explained above, market exchange rates could be expected to vary within quite a narrow range on either side of the Exchange Fund's rate for CIs.

In short the Exchange Fund would play a crucial part in determining the environment for interest rates through its impact on both the domestic and foreign channels of influence. Its role would be indirect (for it would not be involved directly in any of the commercial credit markets) and impartial (for it would not favour any particular interest groups), yet pervasive.

The HKAB's Interest Rate Agreement is clearly irrelevant to the operation of these mechanisms. The Agreement could continue to exist, but it would be superfluous if not counterproductive to the automatic adjustment of the money supply to the balance of payments and vice-versa at the chosen exchange rate. In time the Interest Rate Agreement would be eroded as the credit and foreign exchange markets became more efficient, and then gradually it could be dismantled *without any harm to the machinery of monetary control* — indeed its abolition would positively enhance the automatic adjustment mechanism.

CONCLUSION

The three schemes described in the preceding pages provide a logical and coherent package of solutions drawn from a common and consistent framework of analysis. These proposals are substantially the same as those put forward by AMM in 1979 — the only significant difference being that we have adapted the money supply control proposal there to enable the exchange rate to be managed (Scheme 2A). Our own preference among these three is for Scheme 2B not only since it requires least alteration to the present institutional structure in Hong Kong (and therefore is possibly the least politically unacceptable of the three schemes), but, more importantly, in the longer term Scheme 2B implies less intervention by the authorities in the operation of the financial system.

At the core of our analysis is the view that the internal and external anchors of monetary control were unknowingly thrown overboard in 1972–74 by decisions to change the note issue mechanism and to float the exchange rate, and those anchors have never been satisfactorily replaced. Since that time there have been several attempts at patching up the system, but none of this official tinkering was based on a sound, fundamental analysis of how the monetary system as a whole operated. As a result the 100% Liquid Asset Requirement against short-term deposits of the Exchange Fund (1979), the much vaunted 3-tier banking structure and HKAB's Interest Rate Agreement (Jan. 1981), and the official money market borrowing scheme (Dec. 1981), have *all* failed to correct the fundamental problems of Hong Kong's monetary system.

Until some effective action is taken based on a sound analytical framework such as that presented here, readers are advised to be highly sceptical of the ability of the authorities to do anything whatever to rescue the crumbling Hong Kong dollar. In 1981 we blew the whistle on the Hong Kong monetary system, and although the authorities heard the whistle, they failed to take effective action. How far must the Hong Kong dollar fall before a soundly based rescue plan is put into effect?

APPENDIX 5.1

Why Interest Rates Are a Bad Tool for Monetary Control

First, in Hong Kong the authorities cannot control any particular interest rate under present monetary arrangements. More importantly, neither the banks nor the authorities can determine interest rates conceived in the broad, fundamental sense of the marginal productivity of investment, the returns (pecuniary and non-pecuniary) on assets such as businesses, real estate, and durable goods, or the returns on credit instruments. Only the market can do that. Policies designed to set bank deposit or bank loan rates stem from a basic confusion between the returns from holding money and the price of credit in the "money" (i.e. credit) markets.

Second, if three month deposit interest rates are set at, say, 8%, how do we know that this is the "right" level? And which are the "right" interest rates to follow? With an inflation rate of 10%, 8% interest rates could be too low; but with a 5% p.a. money supply growth rate, 8% interest rates could be too high. There is no way of knowing.... If the authorities were to focus on the exchange rate and set that directly (as in Scheme 2A or 2B), rather than allow the exchange rate to be whatever happens to be the outcome of the HKAB Interest Rate Agreement, we would at least be able to predict the consequences in terms of inflation. For example, by pegging the HK$ to the US$, Hong Kong could expect to average the same inflation rate as in the United States over a period of a few years. By pegging to a basket of currencies Hong Kong could expect to average an inflation rate approximating to a composite of the inflation rates in those countries whose currencies comprised the basket. But pegging interest rates gives no such assurance.

Third, even in an orthodox monetary system controlling interest rates leads to instability, with monetary growth alternating between excessive rapidity (which produces inflation) and insufficiency (which brings recession). This is because, in part, controlling interest rates is a highly inefficient way of achieving the objective at hand. In the words of Milton Friedman commenting on the UK Green Paper of March 1980[7] on Monetary Control: "Trying to control the money supply through 'fiscal policy and interest rates' [to quote the Green Paper] is trying to control the output of one item (money) through altering the demand for it by manipulating the incomes of its users (that is the role of fiscal policy) or the prices of substitutes for it (that is the role of interest rates). A precise analogy is like trying to control the output of motor

---

7. "Monetary Control: A Consultation Paper by H.M. Treasury and the Bank of England". Cmnd. 7858, March 1980.

cars by altering the incomes of potential purchasers and manipulating rail and air fares. In principle, possible in both cases, but in practice highly inefficient. Far easier to control the output of motor cars by controlling the availability of a basic raw material, say steel, to manufacturers — a precise analogy to controlling the availability of base money to banks and others."[8]

These shortcomings apply in orthodox systems where, if the monetary base is allowed to accommodate passively, the pegging of one interest rate is at least feasible — though only in the short term. They apply a fortiori in Hong Kong where there is no control of the base either in terms of its price (i.e. foreign exchange value), or in terms of its quantity.

---

8.   Quoted in M.J. Artis and M.K. Lewis, "Monetary Control in the United Kingdom", Philip Allan Publishers Ltd., 1981, p. 124.

APPENDIX 5.2

Why Amending the Liquid Asset Ratios Will Not Work

Numerous proposals have been made in recent years to improve monetary control in Hong Kong by amending the system of liquid asset ratios (S. 18 of the Banking Ordinance) in such a way as to restrict credit creation. Here we deal with the two most frequently voiced proposals, and then generalise the analysis.

(1) A Compulsory Minimum Cash Ratio

One proposal put forward by the Hong Kong and Shanghai Banking Corporation's monthly Economic Report (August 1982, p. 2) is to introduce a compulsory cash ratio for the licensed banks which would require banks to hold notes and coin equivalent to some fixed percentage (3–5%) of their deposit liabilities in HK\$. At first sight this appears similar to AMM's Scheme 2B insofar as both rely on the link between the quantity of HK\$ deposits and the quantity of base money — i.e. the multiple expansion/contraction process which is at the heart of fractional reserve banking systems — to control money growth. However, the HSBC cash ratio proposal nowhere mentions any device for limiting the cash or base money which forms the numerator of their ratio.

If the Exchange Fund were to continue to issue CIs *passively* and on demand against Exchange Fund deposits at the note-issuers (i.e. at virtually nil cost) as it does at present, how would the total quantity of base money behave? The note issue would swell rapidly as the demand for cash by banks rose, and bank spreads might be widened slightly to compensate for banks' need to hold more non-earning assets, but the world would go on very much as before.

Unless the authorities were simultaneously to introduce a mechanism to limit the quantity of notes or base money issued, the proposal would make no contribution to monetary control. But if the authorities were to introduce a mechanism to limit the quantity of notes or base money, a compulsory cash ratio would, in our view, almost certainly be superfluous, if not positively harmful in that it would impose an unwarranted degree of uniformity on the banks, discouraging some healthy specialisation in the banking sector.

(2) Closing the Foreign Asset Loophole for Manufacturing Liquidity

A second proposal which is often put forward is that banks should not be able to "manufacture liquidity" by counting as specified liquid assets their *gross* assets at call in foreign currency with banks outside Hong Kong. This technique is felt by many to be *the* major loophole in Hong Kong's monetary system and the source of an unfair advantage to foreign banks. The idea behind the proposal is that by restricting the range of assets which count as liquid assets, the credit-creating capacity of banks will be reduced, and then only those banks with bona fide HK$ liquid assets or with genuine *net* foreign assets will be able to expand credit in Hong Kong.

What would happen if this proposal was implemented?

Assuming banks had some leeway to set off capital against liquid assets, implementing this proposal would immediately lead to new injections of foreign capital and other fund-raising exercises necessary to show "net" foreign assets for Hong Kong branches, and/or it would lead to a scramble for those HK$ assets which qualified as "liquid assets". Suppose for a moment the Exchange Fund did not undermine the proposal by continuing passively to issue liquid assets (i.e. CIs or notes), all that would happen is that other qualifying HK$ assets (such as, foreign exchange bills, sight drafts, MTR bonds etc.) would go to a slight premium (i.e. a lower yield), encouraging private sector borrowers to issue more of these eligible credit instruments, until supply had adjusted to demand. *Unless the authorities can actually control the total supply of liquid assets it is pointless to tamper with the liquidity ratios because market forces will rapidly be set in motion to create those instruments which will most easily satisfy banks' requirements.*

Perhaps more important, there is no assurance that any of this would occur at all if, as one might suspect, the only effect was to reduce the aggregate liquidity ratio for the Hong Kong banking system from around 49% to nearer the minimum 25% required ratio.

Address the Fundamentals

To generalise, the basic objection to these and other similar proposals is that they do nothing to address what we have called the two *fundamental* flaws in Hong Kong's monetary system, namely (1) the inability of the Hong Kong authorities under present arrangements to control the supply of base money, and (2) the failure to define or treat as reserves of the banks only those assets which correspond to liabilities of the Exchange Fund. Since 1979 AMM has consistently advocated correcting these fundamental flaws in the system rather than tampering with the liquidity ratios. How far does the Hong Kong dollar have to fall before the authorities get to grips with what is *fundamentally* wrong?

APPENDIX 5.3

SUMMARY OF PROPOSED SCHEMES

OBJECTIVES   **REQUIREMENTS**

Scheme 1

To control
the money supply

1. All Licensed Banks to establish HK$ deposit accounts at Exchange Fund.

2. Exchange Fund to regulate the volume of these reserve deposits either

   (a) by purchases and sales of foreign exchange, or

   (b) by purchases and sales of HK$ denominated instruments

   - each against credits or debits to the Licensed Banks' reserve deposit accounts at the Exchange Fund

Scheme 2A

1. All Licensed Banks to establish HK$ deposit accounts at the Exchange Fund.

2. Exchange Fund to regulate the volume of these reserve deposits only by purchases and sales of foreign exchange against credits or debits to Licensed Banks' accounts at the Exchange Fund.

Scheme 2

To manage
the exchange rate

Scheme 2B

1. The Exchange Fund would transfer its HK$ deposit accounts with the Licensed Banks to the Government's fiscal account. It would no longer operate such HK$ deposit accounts in its monetary capacity.

2. The Exchange Fund would only set a price in foreign exchange for CIs and it would be willing to buy or sell an indefinite amount at that price. The Exchange Fund would only operate in the market for CIs (= banknotes); it would not intervene in the regular foreign exchange market.

IMPLICATIONS

1

1. Effectively this amounts to establishing a central bank

2. Difficult decisions need to be made on the appropriate rate of monetary growth.

3. While there need be no change in the note issuing arrangements, it would be preferable for the clearing facilities to be operated at the Exchange Fund or central bank rather than at HSBC as at present.

4. For best operation of the scheme adequate disclosure will be required on goals (monetary targets), and on operations (publication of Exchange Fund balance sheet etc.) on a regular basis.

2A

1. Effectively this amounts to establishing a central bank, the sole difference being that money market operations will be conducted only in foreign exchange.

2. A simple decision is required on whether to peg the currency to one single currency or to some basket (e.g. a trade-weighted index).

3. While there need be no change in the note issuing arrangements, it would be logical to transfer bank clearing facilities from HSBC to the Exchange Fund.

4. For best operation of this scheme the appropriate disclosure policy on targets will need to be decided. It will make for better public understanding if the overall balance of payments data (including changes in official reserves) are published on a regular basis.

2B

1. Effectively this amounts to returning to the pre-1972 system in Hong Kong i.e. a colonial currency board type of system with the authorities issuing notes (or CIs) and coin, but not regulating bank reserves.

2. Under this system the authorities' only decision is whether to set the foreign exchange price for bank notes (or CIs) in terms of one currency (e.g. a fixed rate for US$) or to vary the price (in terms of one currency or in terms of a basket or index).

3. While there need be no change in the note issuing arrangements there is some advantage in all banks being able to buy or sell CIs or notes at the Exchange Fund because this improves the arbitrage between the market for banknotes and the market for commercial deposits and foreign exchange.

4. The only disclosure required by the Exchange Fund will be a daily (or weekly or monthly or even irregular) announcement of the foreign currency rate at which the Exchange Fund is willing to buy and sell CIs.

CHAPTER 6

THE STABILISATION OF THE
HONG KONG DOLLAR

November–December 1983

This chapter looks back on how the HK$ was stabilised in October 1983. The six appendices (pp. 157–167) reproduce some of the key documents of record in the stabilization process, and a memorandum from the author addressed to the Financial Secretary dealing with arrangements that might have been necessary if the new scheme had been implemented immediately with "full convertibility" for the public of their HK$ deposits into US$ (or other currency), instead of waiting three weeks and not providing convertibility to the man-in-the-street.

The main body of the article presents a combination of theoretical discussion and historical narrative of the events between late September and mid October when the new scheme was adopted. On the theoretical side, there is an extended discussion of why the "interest rate weapon" failed (pp. 141–143). On the historical side, in Sections 1 and 2 (pp. 138–143 and 143–146) there is an account of some of the international political events (the Sino-British negotiations over the future of Hong Kong) and local dramas (the run on the supermarkets) that formed the background to the currency crisis. Within Section 2 there is another document of record, namely the government's holding statement issued on September 25th, hinting at the re-introduction of a currency board mechanism (p. 144).

Section 3 discusses various important issues in a currency stabilisation such as the choice of monetary standard, whether to adopt partial or full convertibility (for the public) of HKD banknotes to USD at the fixed rate, the choice of currency, and the choice of exchange rate (pp. 146–153). Section 4 of the main article outlines the institutional arrangements of the new scheme, anticipating some of the later discussion of the cash arbitrage process. One can debate which of these topics are most interesting to present-day readers, but all have featured in discussions about the Hong Kong monetary system at different times.

While the tone of this AMM article appears to applaud the fact that the Hong Kong government had closely followed the core proposals set out in Chapter 5, there were in fact defects in the original design that did not become apparent immediately. The gradual rectification of these flaws forms a continuous thread through the next two decades (see Epilogue, Ch. 13).

A S I A N   M O N E T A R Y   M O N I T O R
Vol. 7 No. 6 November–December 1983

INTRODUCTION

At noon on Saturday October 15th, 1983 Hong Kong's Financial Secretary Sir John Bremridge announced a unique scheme to stabilise the value of the Hong Kong dollar. His announcement came exactly three weeks from Black Saturday, September 24th when the value of the Hong Kong dollar had plunged in a free fall, sending the US$ to a price of HK$9.55 on the local foreign exchange market, and nearly ten years from the ill-fated decision of November 1974 to float the Hong Kong dollar from its parity of HK$5.65 to the US dollar. The new scheme, which was to be implemented from the opening of the foreign exchange markets on Monday October 17th, would operate by restoring a fixed rate against the US$ for the issue and redemption of Certificates of Indebtedness, equivalent to Hong Kong dollar banknotes, this time at HK$7.80 per US dollar.

After a decade of drift the Hong Kong dollar had at last been rescued.

In large measure the scheme adopted by the Hong Kong Government puts into practice the proposals set out in Scheme 2B of the September–October issue of *Asian Monetary Monitor* ("How to Rescue the Hong Kong Dollar: Three Practical Proposals"). There are a few minor points of difference, but the fundamental principles set out in the paper (Chapter 5) have been substantially incorporated in the new scheme. In this article section 1 analyses the collapse of the Hong Kong dollar in the period up to September 24th, section 2 describes some of the events of the next three weeks during which the stabilisation plan was evolved, and section 3 outlines the basic theoretical elements of the new scheme. Finally, section 4 provides an account of the detailed institutional arrangements of the stabilisation plan, and notes the differences between the actual plan adopted and the original AMM proposals.

1.   A MONETARY ANALYSIS OF THE COLLAPSE OF THE HONG KONG DOLLAR

Under the barrage of incessant daily propaganda from the communist Chinese press — which circulates freely in Hong Kong — there was mounting anxiety in the colony during September about the future of the territory after 1997. These anxieties could have been largely contained were it not for the fact that Hong Kong's monetary system suffered from certain basic defects as a result of technical changes made in July 1972 concerning the issue of banknotes in Hong Kong, which ultimately led to the floating of the Hong Kong dollar in November 1974.

(A) An Inherently Unstable System

The net result of these defects was that in Hong Kong's unorthodox monetary system neither the price of money nor the quantity of money was controlled. Technically, Hong Kong's monetary arrangements constituted an indeterminate, meta-stable equilibrium system. This meant that for any given level of money supply and prices in Hong Kong, the exchange rate would adjust to that price level; alternatively, given any level of the exchange rate, money supply and domestic prices would adjust to that exchange rate.

Since the world abandoned fixed exchange rates (i.e. fixing the price of money) around 1973 most major industrial countries (USA, Japan, UK and West Germany) have moved, to a greater or lesser extent, to control the quantity of money (i.e. the money supply). These countries have been able to do this because they have central banks which can supply or withdraw base money (or high powered money) on a discretionary basis. (Base money or high-powered money consists of the monetary liabilities of the central bank i.e. notes and coins plus commercial banks' deposits at the central bank. In practice it is only banks' deposits at the central bank which can be adjusted in a discretionary manner by the central bank.)

In the case of Hong Kong, the decision was taken in November 1974 to float the currency (i.e. to vary the price of money) but no corresponding provisions were made to control the quantity of money. Although official government statements were not couched in these terms, the reason that the Hong Kong government could not control the money supply was that the banks did not hold deposits with the monetary authorities, and therefore the authorities were not in a position to supply or withdraw base money in a discretionary fashion.

Instead, Hong Kong had a form of Colonial Currency Board called the Exchange Fund, whose main function was — and is — the issue of so-called Certificates of Indebtedness which authorise the two note-issuing banks to issue banknotes, but the issue and redemption of banknotes could not be done on a discretionary basis. In sum, neither the money supply nor the exchange rate had been controlled. Consequently there was no fixed point within the system around which money, prices or the foreign exchange rate could find equilibrium. The only "prices" over which the monetary authorities exercised any influence were the interest rates on retail deposits at licensed banks and the associated Best Lending Rate (BLR) of the licensed banks. Until August 1983 Hong Kong had been lucky: as long as expectations about the future were buoyant and therefore perceived real rates of return on capital were at "normal" levels, the banks' interest rate cartel had been sufficient to keep the Hong Kong dollar exchange rate reasonably stable. (N.B. It had not, however, been capable of keeping the money supply stable — see Chapter 3, pp. 46–48, "A Hypothesis for the Hong Kong Credit Cycle").

(B) Failure of the "Interest Rate Weapon"

However, under the barrage of Peking propaganda on the one hand, and given the British confidentiality over the talks in Peking and the inevitably slow progress of those talks on the other, Hong Kong people's hopes about the future were beginning to crumble. In the money markets, this translated itself into lower perceived real returns on businesses and property in Hong Kong, stimulating a consequent capital outflow. But in practical terms businesses and property could not be exported; they first had to be sold, and then the Hong Kong dollar proceeds in turn had to be sold on the foreign exchange market. Since the only way people in Hong Kong could export capital under the existing floating exchange rate system was to sell Hong Kong dollars to somebody else, the Hong Kong dollar was driven down on the foreign exchange markets, and domestic prices began to rise as the velocity of circulation increased and the exchange rate declined.

This was the process which resulted in the collapse of the foreign exchange value of the Hong Kong dollar in September, and a situation of near panic in Hong Kong as people started to hoard rice, cooking oil, toilet paper and other basic essentials ahead of the inevitable price inflation.

With capital fleeing Hong Kong in search of higher returns elsewhere, surely this was the moment to bring the "interest rate weapon" to bear. The rate structure had not been altered since late July (when rates were lowered by 1 percent), and the currency had ended the month at HK$7.31 per US dollar. By September 7th the exchange rate had fallen to HK$7.74 and the Hong Kong Association of Banks agreed to raise deposit interest rates by 1.5%. Simultaneously the Prime Lending Rate was raised to 13%.

Initially there was some impact, and the currency closed at $7.67 on September 10th, but by September 13th it had started to fall again, closing at $7.78. On September 17th the HK$ crashed through the psychological $8.00 level, hitting $8.40 two days later. By the time the bankers met again on September 19th they were increasingly reluctant to take all the strain on interest rates, and decided not to raise them. Perhaps, in part, they sensed the futility of another rate hike; perhaps, in part, they felt that if they were to lose loan business by raising interest rates, the government should at least provide more intervention to support the exchange rate as a quid pro quo.

On September 22nd and 23rd the Fourth Round of Sino-British talks was held in Peking. On September 23rd the HK$ suffered its sharpest fall to date, plunging to $8.83 against the US$ following the release of a bare one sentence joint statement in Peking which merely said the two sides "held further talks on the question of Hong Kong ... and the fifth round will be held in Beijing on October 19 and 20".

On Saturday, September 24th the Hong Kong dollar went into an uncontrolled tailspin. In the words of the *South China Morning Post* (on Sunday, September 25th), "The Hong Kong dollar's free-fall continued on the foreign exchange markets yesterday, dropping to yet another all-time low against the American dollar at $9.45/55, and triggering a huge surge in the local gold price.

"Following hard on the heels of yet another non-statement at the conclusion of the latest round of Sino-British talks on Hong Kong's future it can leave absolutely no doubts as to the political nature of the Colony's fast dwindling exchange rate.

"Trade was thin and one-way with much of the demand for US dollar emanating from gold merchants using US dollars as the intermediate currency on almost panic buying of taels at gold shops throughout the territory.

"The local gold price consequently closed sharply higher at $4,705 a tael — significantly trading at premium on the international bullion price of US$418/419 an ounce despite the modest discount that has ruled since the beginning of the year — after touching yet another 3 1/2-year high earlier in the day at $4,750.

"This $409 spurt is the sharpest single day's gain in the tael price since January 1980.

"The Hong Kong dollar's slump, meanwhile, was aggravated by a marked reluctance on the part of US dollar holders to sell at any price, in addition to some minor commercial demand for greenbacks.

"The local unit opened at $8.70/80 vis-a-vis the American dollar, compared with the late $8.80/90 ruling on Friday, and sank as effortlessly through the psychological $9 barrier as it did through the $8 mark last Saturday.

"The decline and fall of the local currency continued unabated until the local forex markets closed at 12.30 pm, by which time the Hong Kong dollar was $9.45/55 against its American counterpart.

"Spreads remained at banana republic levels all morning, blowing out at one stage to an incredible 3,000 points with a Hongkong and Shanghai Bank quote at $9.20/50.

"The dollar's vertiginous plunge was manifest in a massive 4.5 point slump in the trade-weighted index to another nadir of 57.2.

"Against a backdrop of a plummeting exchange rate now clearly out of control, the Hong Kong Association of Banks announced after its usual Saturday morning meeting that it had decided 'to maintain the present interest rate structure unchanged'."

The interest rate weapon had failed.

(C) Why the Interest Rate Weapon Failed

Why was it, fundamentally, that raising interest rates had proved futile in the face of this crisis?

After all, just two years earlier the government had placed its faith in the "interest rate weapon", enshrining the Interest Rate Agreement of the Exchange Banks Association in an elaborate legal and quasi-legal structure comprising a new three-tier banking system (from January 1981), and a supporting system of licensing or registration requirements, reporting procedures, and channels for consultation with the government. The Interest Rate Agreement of the licensed banks was given pride of place in the new banking framework, and it was reinforced by the prohibition on registered deposit-taking companies (DTCs) soliciting deposits of under HK$50,000 and of less than three-months maturity, and the prohibition on licensed DTCs soliciting deposits of less than HK$500,000 for any maturity. This compartmentalisation of the deposit market was supposed to ensure that while free market rates might hold sway in some sectors of the deposit market, there would be one area in which the government, in consultation with the licensed banks through the newly created Hong Kong Association of Banks (HKAB), would have a reasonably firm grip on interest rates, and hence on bank credit creation and thus supposedly on the money supply.

Sadly for Hong Kong this elaborate edifice was critically flawed in three respects. In the first place it made the classic error of confusing the price of money with the price of credit by explicitly suggesting that interest rates were the price of money and hence an effective lever through which the quantity of money could be controlled. In fact the price or purchasing power of a nominal unit of money is what has to be given up to obtain it (e.g. a certain amount of goods and services, or a certain amount of foreign exchange). Interest rates, which are the price of credit, are what has to be paid to rent money for a specific period.

In common with the experience of other countries, the use of interest rates as the basic tool of policy in Hong Kong from the early 1970s onwards had contributed significantly to widening the amplitude of Hong Kong's business cycle fluctuations by encouraging periods of excess bank credit creation and excess money growth alternating with periods of credit restriction and monetary contraction. The first episode of excess money growth was in 1972–73, just after the change in currency-issuing procedure in July 1972, followed by a collapse of money and credit growth in 1973–74; a second episode of excess money and credit growth occurred in 1978–81, and a second episode of contraction in 1982–83. (See Chapter 3, pp. 46–48, "A Hypothesis for the Hong Kong Credit Cycle" for the details of the theory underlying this proposition).

A second basic problem with using interest rates as *the* tool of monetary policy began to be evident in September 1983. Growing scepticism at the possibility of a favourable outcome from the Peking talks was leading to lower perceived rates of return on capital in Hong Kong *over the long term* and hence to a capital outflow. Consequently it would have required an extraordinarily high level of interest rates *in the short term* to make the perceived yields on capital in Hong Kong equal to the perceived yields on capital elsewhere. As neither the banks nor the authorities were willing to raise interest rates to such a level, the exchange rate inevitably gave way under the pressure of Hong Kong dollar selling.

Thus the interest rate weapon not only failed as a tool of monetary policy in normal times due to the fundamental misconception that interest rates were the "price" of money, but the interest rate weapon also failed in the moment of crisis in September 1983 because there was no level to which *short term* interest rates could reasonably be raised which would compensate for the lower rates of return on capital in Hong Kong *in the long term* which the supposed outcome of the Sino-British talks in Peking were believed to imply.

In addition the Hong Kong dollar crisis of September 1983 highlighted a third fundamental problem — the problem of the distinction between nominal interest rates and real interest rates. For while central banks and governments may be able temporarily to fix a limited number of nominal interest rates, they have no such ability to control *real* interest rates i.e. the real rates of return on the whole range of capital goods including land and buildings, industrial plant and machinery, durable goods such as vehicles, electrical appliances and so on. Yet it was the change in Hong Kong people's perception about the expected long term *real* rates of return on capital — especially businesses and properties in Hong Kong — which, in our hypothesis, precipitated the currency crisis.

As people began to lose confidence in the outcome of the Peking talks over Hong Kong's future, real rates of return on capital or other assets outside Hong Kong began to be perceived as more attractive than returns inside the territory, and consequently capital in the form of buildings, businesses, and monetary assets were being sold to enable their owners to switch to the higher perceived real rates of return available abroad.

In effect the prices of capital assets in Hong Kong were being driven down to levels necessary to equate yields in Hong Kong with yields overseas. Given the fact that Hong Kong had a floating exchange rate, and, under the existing monetary framework, no workable mechanism for supporting the exchange rate, the currency could theoretically have been driven to the point where Hong Kong dollars were virtually valueless as residents attempted to export capital through the foreign exchange market. In such circumstances it is hard to conceive what the government could have done with the available tools to raise *nominal* interest rates in Hong Kong sufficiently to offset the abrupt change in the public's perception of *real* rates in Hong Kong versus *real* rates abroad.

With the failure of the interest rate weapon the monetary standard, the value of the local unit of account, collapsed. The Hong Kong dollar, in short, was only worth what people were prepared to pay for it, and in September 1983 that amount was plummeting. By September 24th the value of a Hong Kong dollar had fallen to only just above a dime or 10 cents in US currency (HK$9.55 per US$1.00). The desperate problem facing the monetary authorities was how to stop the slide in the short term — with stopgap measures if necessary — and, in the longer term, how to restore Hong Kong's monetary standard to a sound and secure basis which would survive in the critical years up to 1997 and possibly beyond.

2. A STOPGAP ANNOUNCEMENT

Faced with a flight from the currency and a crisis of public confidence in the ability of the monetary authorities to protect people's money, the government urgently needed a concrete, workable plan. To be successful any such plan would require three characteristics: it would need to be theoretically sound, operationally feasible in Hong Kong's particular circumstances, and politically acceptable in Hong Kong, London and Peking.

With the Financial Secretary (Hong Kong's equivalent of Secretary of the Treasury or Minister of Finance and Governor of the Central Bank) away from the colony attending the Commonwealth Finance Minister's Conference in Trinidad and scheduled to go to Washington the following week for the annual meetings of the IMF and World Bank, there was no possibility of implementing a comprehensive currency stabilisation package involving fundamental monetary and political issues over the weekend of September 24–25th. But in an atmosphere of mounting tension and anxiety government officials were determined that something meaningful needed to be said or done to arrest the currency slide, restore public confidence and provide some breathing space for a plan to be developed.

The recognition that such a plan was needed represented a major turning point — the official view up until this time having been that nothing was fundamentally wrong with the floating exchange rate system and therefore no serious reform was required.

Accordingly an emergency meeting was called for 11.00 a.m. on Sunday, September 25th with a view to discussing the available options. Those present included senior government officials from the Monetary Affairs Branch, the Commissioner for Banking, representatives from the two note-issuing banks — the Hongkong and Shanghai Bank and the Standard Chartered Bank — government economists, and the editor of AMM.

Following that meeting, which lasted until late afternoon, the Acting Financial Secretary who was also the Secretary for Monetary Affairs, released the following announcement to the press:

Hong Kong Government Statement Issued September 25th 1983

As a result of the recent unwarranted depreciation of the local currency the Acting Financial Secretary Mr. Douglas Blye has been in consultation throughout the weekend with the note-issuing banks and other advisers.

Various proposals have been considered. A basic pre-requisite of all of these proposals was full convertibility of the currency.

One proposal which is being actively developed involves a substantial revision of the mechanics for issuing and redeeming Certificates of Indebtedness to the note-issuing banks in such a way as to produce an exchange rate which would more accurately reflect the fundamental strength of the economy. The proposal will mean the assumption by the Exchange Fund of a more significant role in the exchange rate determination mechanism.

In the meantime the Exchange Fund retains its existing capability to intervene in the foreign exchange and money markets.

The following day was Monday September 26th, and most foreign exchange dealers were at their desks especially early. For the most part they were baffled by the Acting Financial Secretary's statement. In effect he had promised convertibility, but failed to deliver. No price was mentioned, and many people in any case did not understand how there could be a connection between the domestic note issue process referred to in the press statement and the daily commercial foreign exchange rate which, as the previous few days had so dramatically shown, was entirely determined by the free market. Accordingly there was immense uncertainty about the immediate outlook and this was duly reflected in the huge spreads quoted by dealers. Prior to market opening some dealers were quoting HK$8.00–9.00 for the US dollar — a spread of 10,000 basis points.

When the market opened at 9.00 a.m. spreads narrowed to between 7,000 and 5,000 basis points, but volume was minimal and some traders simply were not prepared to deal at all.

At 10.00 a.m. the Hong Kong Association of Banks announced a hike in deposit interest rates of 3 percentage points, and the two leading banks raised their best or prime lending rate to 16%. At this time the HK$ was being quoted at 7.90–8.40. However, the foreign exchange market was disappointed by the rise in rates, since dealers had, perhaps optimistically, expected some more far-reaching package of monetary measures, not simply the same ineffective instruments. The effect of the 3-percentage point hike in rates lasted about ten minutes, and the exchange rate then dropped back to the 8.20–8.60 range. Combined intervention by the Government and two note-issuing banks seemed to have little impact. Towards the end of the day spreads narrowed a little, and the HK$ closed at 8.32–8.42, in the words of the *South China Morning Post* "with Government support for the flagging currency manifest".

The next day, Tuesday September 27th spreads were generally narrower, though still at abnormally high levels, with the prevailing uncertainty being reflected in wider swap costs for US dollars. However the main event of the day occurred after market closing when the Legislative Council met in an emergency 15-minute session during which a bill to empower the government to take over the Hang Lung Bank, the Hang Lung Bank (Acquisition) Bill 1983 was taken through the necessary three readings. The Hang Lung Bank, a local bank with 28 branches, had been the subject of a bank run in September 1982, and had been known to be having liquidity difficulties for some time. The Financial Secretary — who had arrived back in Hong Kong on Monday evening — said the bank had reported to the Commissioner of Banking that it was unable to meet in full its liabilities to the Clearing House in respect of cheques drawn by its customers. The Chartered Bank was not prepared to cover a resulting HK$50 million overdraft on Hang Lung Bank's clearing account with it, and the government felt obliged to step in to cover the obligation at the Chartered Bank and to prevent a more serious situation developing.

As a matter of record this was the first time that the Exchange Fund had been mobilised in the capacity of lender of last resort to a bank in the private sector. Usually in the past a Hong Kong bank in difficulties would have been left to find a private sector rescuer or buyer.

On this occasion, however, the Financial Secretary stated that "The Government believes it would be unacceptable, both domestically and internationally, to allow this bank to fail, which would involve considerable loss to depositors .... the depositors' interests override those of shareholder".

In the subsequent days, activity on the banking front, on the currency front, and in other departments of government was feverish. The Secretary for Monetary Affairs took over as chairman of the Hang Lung Bank. Mr. Richard Luce, the British Foreign Office Minister responsible for Hong Kong affairs, was on a busy five-day visit and left on Wednesday September 28th. On Sunday night George Tan, chairman of the high-flying Carrian property group, was arrested. His companies, besieged by creditors, reportedly owed in excess of HK$8 billion to creditors. On the following Wednesday October 5th Governor Sir Edward Youde gave his annual "state of the union" policy address in the Legislative Council, but he made no mention of an impending solution to the HK$ crisis.

That evening he and the Unofficial Members of the Executive Council (i.e. appointees from outside the civil service) flew to London for consultations with the Prime Minister, the Foreign Minister, and the Chancellor of the Exchequer. Meanwhile the Hong Kong dollar which had continued to trade in the 8.40–8.60 range, slipped back to 8.80 and on October 4th the Hang Seng Index of share prices fell below 700 for the first time in the year.

In the week beginning Monday October 3rd Charles Goodhart from the Bank of England and David Peretz from HM Treasury arrived in Hong Kong. They had been invited to review a paper detailing the currency board scheme, and to advise the Financial Secretary on the feasibility and suitability of that scheme. By the end of that week it seemed that the broad outlines of a monetary package had been decided on for the advisers from the Bank of England and Treasury returned home. There only remained the institutional and administrative details to be finalised.

The Governor returned from London over the weekend of October 8–9th. A press statement from Downing Street said that he had had discussions with the Chancellor of the Exchequer, but that the Chancellor had given no currency advice. It was clear from this statement that the monetary package necessary to solve the Hong Kong currency crisis was to be announced by the Hong Kong government alone, and that it was unlikely to involve fixing the Hong Kong dollar to sterling.

These were the events on the public record as participants in the foreign exchanges and money markets waited for the announcement of the government's package.

3. THEORETICAL ELEMENTS OF THE STABILISATION PLAN

At this stage it is necessary to digress from the narrative of the events to discuss some of the theoretical issues underlying the choices facing the monetary authorities at this critical moment. Doubtless few of the dramatis personae — mainly government officials — would have considered the decisions they were taking from the theoretical standpoint that will be outlined below, but irrespective of any rationalisation given at time for the final outcome, to any student of monetary history or comparative monetary systems the intellectual framework within which official decisions had to be made was pre-determined.

For the long term the important problem was to select and define a monetary standard for Hong Kong. For the short term there was the problem of transition from existing arrangements to any new system; whether to adopt full or partial convertibility, the optimum currency on which to base Hong Kong's new monetary standard, and the precise level to be chosen for the new fixed exchange rate.

(A) The Choice of Monetary Standard

The properties of an optimal monetary standard are (i) that it should cost the society a minimal amount of resources to produce, thereby maximising the amount of resources available for other, non-monetary purposes, and (ii) that it should perform essential functions of money, acting both as an efficient medium of exchange and as stable store of value.

From the earliest days of the British occupation of Hong Kong, silver was the de facto commodity standard although it was not until 1869 that the colonial government officially acknowledged the use of silver as legal tender. Since silver was a metal with other non-monetary uses, it cost the community a substantial amount to maintain the physical commodity as money. Consequently after the appearance of banks in Hong Kong, representative paper money began to be issued in exchange for and circulate in place of silver coins and bullion so that gradually silver ceased to be the day-to-day medium of circulation. However, it was not silver's properties as a physical commodity which ultimately caused its demise as the monetary standard of China and Hong Kong. It was as a stable store of value that silver ultimately failed, for when the US Treasury quadrupled the US dollar price of silver in 1934 (from 25 cents to $1.29 per oz.), the external exchange rate of China and Hong Kong was in effect revalued upward by some 400%. This produced a drastic deflation as silver poured out and the local money supplies contracted. In response, China and Hong Kong abandoned the silver standard, with China nominally adopting a foreign exchange standard but in reality going on to a pure paper standard (which ultimately degenerated into hyperinflation), and Hong Kong going on to the sterling exchange standard.

The mechanics of shifting from a commodity (silver) standard to a foreign currency (sterling) exchange standard were surprisingly simple. Under the silver standard the three note-issuing banks had held silver coin or bullion in their vaults against every banknote issued. In 1935 the government took over the silver reserves of the banks, issuing the banks in exchange with "Certificates of Indebtedness" representing indebtedness of a new government institution, the Exchange Fund, to the note-issuing banks. The banks now held the non-interest bearing Certificates of Indebtedness (or CIs), which were denominated in HK$, as assets corresponding to their HK$ note issue instead of silver. The Exchange Fund in turn sold the silver and invested the proceeds in sterling securities, creating for the government a steady stream of income or seignorage which the banks had previously not enjoyed. In sum the government had captured most of the benefits of the note issue (i.e. the seignorage), but avoided the costs by effectively sub-contracting the design, engraving and printing of the notes themselves to the three note-issuing banks.

From 1935 onwards the banks were required to pay sterling to the Exchange Fund for new Certificates of Indebtedness (CIs), which authorised the bank in question to issue new Hong Kong dollar banknotes. The CIs were denominated in Hong Kong dollars, and priced at 1s.3d. (one shilling and three pence) per Hong Kong dollar.

By defining the Hong Kong dollar in sterling and allowing free convertibility (i.e. issue and redemption at fixed price) by the note-issuing banks, the Hong Kong government was in effect selecting sterling as its monetary standard. Also, by transferring from the silver standard to this type of fiat money standard the government secured for the community the two benefits of a desirable monetary standard: (a) that production and transaction costs were minimised, and (b) that, because the value of sterling could be expected to be reasonably stable over time, the value of the Hong Kong dollar (expressed in terms of general purchasing power) could also be expected to remain stable.

In 1972 the Hong Kong dollar was unhitched from sterling and pegged to, or more strictly defined in terms of, the US dollar at HK$5.65 per US$1.00. In principle the Hong Kong dollar ought to have remained as steady against the US dollar as it had traditionally been against sterling. However, partly as a result of certain guarantees which the Hong Kong authorities had made to the note-issuing banks in connection with the US$ value of their sterling assets and the resultant costs this was imposing on the Exchange Fund, and partly as a result of departing from the practice of accepting exclusively foreign currency at a fixed price against issues of Certificates of Indebtedness, the basic soundness of Hong Kong's monetary standard was eroded.

Initially these changes to the monetary standard were concealed by the sharp deflation which Hong Kong had undergone in 1973–74, and the consequent strength of Hong Kong dollar after the currency was floated in November 1974. However, as the subsequent economic recovery developed the new forces regulating the rate of monetary expansion gradually got the upper hand and from 1977 onwards the currency began to decline in value on the foreign exchange market. From time to time the raising of interest rates by the local bank cartel successfully stopped the slide, but this mechanism gradually became less effective, and in any case could only hope to succeed so long as returns on assets Hong Kong were perceived to be "normal" and nominal interest rates were kept roughly in line with interest rates abroad, particularly in the USA. However, the political events of 1982–83 finally destroyed that "normality", precipitating the collapse of the Hong Kong dollar in September 1983.

A basic problem in restoring a sound monetary standard in Hong Kong in September/October 1983 was the lack of familiarity, among those closely involved, with the mechanisms and strengths of earlier monetary standards. Those involved in the discussions at a technical level had either been in junior positions in the pre-1972 era (if they had been in Hong Kong), or they had come from monetary systems with central banks which had in the past decade moved away from fixed exchange rates towards discretionary control of the money supply. Accordingly there was little institutional memory of the old system, and even among those who were familiar with it there was tendency to believe that somehow the existence of the Sterling Area, the prevalence of foreign exchange controls, and the generally fixed parities of the Bretton Woods system were all somehow necessary features of the old colonial currency system. Even a modicum of knowledge of monetary systems in the 19th century or in the pre-World War II period would have shown these beliefs to have been false, but such details of monetary theory and history were simply not part of the common store of knowledge or experience.

Consequently, although the switch from a floating exchange rate system to the convertible banknote system which was finally adopted turned out to be remarkably simple and relatively painless, the intellectual leap required to recognise the deficiencies of the prevailing status quo and to be willing to accept the "new" system was probably a far greater obstacle to the introduction of the new scheme than the practical difficulties of implementing any operational aspects of the new scheme. Understandably, Hong Kong's government officials would have been reluctant to take such a leap in the dark.

The scheme that was finally chosen is reasonably satisfactory when measured against the criteria for an optimal monetary standard. First, a fiat money system requires a minimal quantity of resources, and yet the interest earned on the foreign currency assets which correspond to the issue of currency notes is retained as seignorage by the government. Second, the HK$ currency continues to act as an efficient medium of exchange, and, provided that US monetary policy is conducted in a non-inflationary manner, the HK$ will remain a stable store of value.

In retrospect it is relatively simple to see the choices Hong Kong faced in selecting a monetary standard. However, as in many scientific or theoretical problems the human and political aspects of the choice no doubt assumed a seemingly dominant role at the time. But at a theoretical level the truth was that the authorities had very little choice: they had to select a monetary standard which was compatible with an automatic or non-discretionary monetary system and this effectively meant they had to choose some foreign currency (or currencies) as the monetary standard for Hong Kong. The areas of discretion concerned the degree of convertibility, the choice of currency (or currencies), and the actual level of the exchange rate.

(B) Partial Convertibility or Full Convertibility

An awkward problem for the authorities throughout the HK$ crisis was the widely held view that the Hong Kong government had virtually no capability to fix the exchange rate at any level. In no small degree the government had itself engendered such doubts, for in the years preceding the Hong Kong dollar crisis of September 1983 numerous senior government officials had repeatedly stated that it was technically impossible or at least undesirable in a world of floating exchange rates to fix the value of the Hong Kong dollar to any other currency. This assertion was repeated on several occasions as the slide of the Hong Kong dollar accelerated through the summer.

Given the pervasive view that fixing the exchange rate was not feasible, it was not unnatural for government officials to be concerned that if a rate for the Hong Kong dollar was guaranteed, it might either precipitate a massive conversion of Hong Kong dollar deposits into foreign currency, and/or it would somehow drain the official reserves and even require temporary facilities from the Bank of England or elsewhere. If banks were suddenly to see their HK$ deposits converted to foreign currency on a large scale there was a feeling that this would set off an intense credit squeeze in the Hong Kong dollar money markets. A frequently repeated fear was that this might force banks to liquidate loans, leading to a multiple contraction of credit.

There were two possible solutions to these anxieties: either (a) to adopt a stabilisation plan offering full convertibility which was so sweeping in its extent and so reassuring to the public that there could be no possible doubt of the government's intention to fix the exchange rate, or (b) strictly to limit the government's actions to guaranteeing the currency component of the money supply — in effect only offering partial convertibility — and to force the burden of economic adjustment to the new rate directly on to the private sector.

The first plan, also put forward by the editor of AMM, would incidentally have avoided the need for any credit squeeze by instantly making all Hong Kong dollars — currency and deposits — fully convertible at a fixed price into US dollars by offering this convertibility to every member of the Hong Kong public. Logistically this plan was demanding, requiring large quantities of foreign currency banknotes to be flown into Hong Kong and prepared for distribution at bank branches throughout the territory, but it would have solved the crisis in the classical style by putting the reserves of the system behind the promise of convertibility at the fixed price. (See Appendix 6.6, pp. 165–167, for the actual plan, as submitted.) The presumption underlying this plan was similar to the classical presumption applied in rescuing an individual bank from a bank run — namely, that the right way to deal with a run was to pay out cash currency until confidence returned and the run stopped.

In the case of Hong Kong in September 1983 it was not simply a run on one bank, but a run on the system as a whole. The implication was that the reserves of the system (i.e. the official foreign currency reserves) needed to be mobilised. Just as in a classical bank run it eventually becomes clear to those who have withdrawn cash that they are foregoing interest on their deposits and that their large holdings of cash are in themselves a considerable risk, causing money to flow back into the banking system, so it is for the case of a run on the system. Provided sufficient reserves can be paid out to anxious depositors, there eventually comes a point when the perceived need to convert deposits into reserves evaporates. In the case of Hong Kong the reserves were foreign currency so AMM's short term stabilisation plan proposed that the authorities prepare to meet any conceivable demand by flying in large quantities of foreign banknotes. In the past such a firm demonstration by the authorities was enough to end the panic, and in one case (in 1965) the packages of foreign banknotes were returned to London unopened.

Aside from offering an effective method of stopping the run on the currency, there was another argument in favour of adopting the emergency short-term stabilisation programme. This was that the provision of lender of last resort facilities by the Exchange Fund would have avoided the need for any sharp rise in interest rates, and hence avoided any damaging credit squeeze or any multiple contraction effects from conversion of HK$ deposits into foreign currency. On the other hand this kind of plan would have required extensive administrative preparations both for the distribution foreign currency at bank branches in Hong Kong, and for the temporary pledging of suitable commercial bank assets with the Exchange Fund against advances of foreign currency.

The second course of action ran the risk that it might precipitate a tight credit squeeze on an already weakened economy with a battered property sector and an illiquid banking sector, but it entailed no major logistical operation involving planeloads of banknotes. There can be no doubt that everyone concerned was acutely aware of the risks in this latter option. From an analytical standpoint the extent of the resultant credit squeeze depended partly on the degree of public confidence in the likely success of the new measures (as this would have determined the size of the capital outflows), and partly on the level at which the new exchange rate was set (since a greater depreciation of the Hong Kong dollar would have enhanced the economy's competitiveness and any subsequent trade or current account surplus — and conversely).

The final outcome was that classical orthodoxy was set aside and the less dramatic but economically more risky solution was adopted. In effect, full convertibility was rejected in favour of partial convertibility.

(C) The Choice of Currency

Assuming that for the long term a plan along the lines of AMM's Scheme 2B was adopted, from a purely technical point of view it would not have mattered which currency had been chosen as the unit in which to define Hong Kong's monetary standard. Without prejudice to the operation of the scheme it would have been possible to define the Hong Kong dollar in terms of Sterling, the US Dollar, the Yen, or DM, or any other convertible foreign currency. The important technical consideration ought to have been that the monetary reserves of the Exchange Fund could be held in that currency, and the licensed banks should be able to obtain that currency without difficulty whenever they required new banknotes to meet the public needs. In practice this would have restricted the choice to one of the major trading currencies of the world.

Another set of possibilities was that the Hong Kong dollar could have been defined in terms of an artificial currency such as the SDR which consists of fixed amounts individual currencies (i.e. the fiat money equivalent of a symmetallic standard), or a basket of currencies such as a trade-weighted index of other currencies. The advantage of choosing a composite monetary standard of this type was that instead of the Hong Kong economy being closely tied to the fluctuations of one particular economy it would be linked more broadly to the average trend in the major economies whose currencies comprised the basket, and hence to the global business cycle. The disadvantage of choosing this type of monetary standard was the problem of credibility for man-in-the-street. A composite currency would have been much more difficult to understand, and in the early days of the new scheme public confidence was essential to success in avoiding an intense credit squeeze.

However, more important than these technical considerations was the political dimension to the choice of currency. If sterling were chosen it might have seemed to Peking that Britain was continuing to demonstrate a colonialist attitude towards the Hong Kong and this could have affected the British government's negotiating position at the Peking talks. The yen would have been a good choice on economic grounds since Japan's inflation rate is low, Japan is the dominant economy of the East Asian Pacific rim, and Japan is Hong Kong's third largest trading partner, but the memory of the Japanese occupation of Hong Kong and the long rivalry between the Chinese and the Japanese would have made the yen an unpopular choice on political grounds. The US dollar, on the other hand, was attractive on both technical and political grounds. Economically the USA is Hong Kong's largest trading partner, the US dollar is the dominant international trading currency, US inflation was currently low and the US economy is the primary force in the global business cycle. By tying Hong Kong's currency to the US dollar the authorities were simply recognising these realities. Politically the US dollar was a neutral currency so far as London and Peking were concerned, and by linking the Hong Kong currency to the US dollar the British negotiators in Peking could expect the Chinese to react favourably to the proposition that the Hong Kong dollar was now effectively a US dollar with a different denomination.

(D) The Choice of Exchange Rate

In the last few days before the Hong Kong government announced the currency stabilisation measures the exchange rate for the Hong Kong dollar was trading around HK$8.30–8.40 against its American counterpart. In selecting an appropriate exchange rate, there were three possible courses of action:

      (a)   to devalue the exchange rate by a further margin

or   (b)   to leave the rate at current market levels

or   (c)   to revalue upwards in an attempt to put the clock back to the pre-crisis period.

An outright devaluation by a further margin of, say, 20% from HK$8.40 to HK$10.50 (i.e. from US$0.11905 to US$0.09524) would have immediately raised the HK$ price of imported goods, and as those prices percolated through the economy there would have been a once-for-all increase in the overall price level. Because the devaluation would have taken more time to filter through to such prices as labour or rents it might have seemed that such a devaluation would permanently raise the inflation rate (i.e. the on-going rate of change of prices), but these price changes should be considered as part of the once-for-all adjustment to the devaluation. With a lower US$ price for HK$, Hong Kong goods and services would have had a large competitive advantage, which would have generated a substantial improvement on the external accounts. Under a fixed exchange rate this would have led to a rapid increase in the domestic money supply, which would have allowed domestic prices such as wages and rents to rise. However, once equilibrium had been achieved (i.e. rough equality of prices in Hong Kong and the US at the fixed exchange rate), the overall rate of price change in Hong Kong would be determined by overall price changes in the US. The disadvantage of devaluation was therefore that it would immediately have produced this adverse once-for-all domestic price change, but against that it would have had the advantage of producing a balance of payments surplus and hence a monetary expansion which, in the short term, would have helped to reliquify the economy.

Setting the official level for the new exchange rate at the prevailing market rate would have had two possible advantages. First it would have meant minimising the extent of price adjustments throughout the economy, and second it could be argued that the existing market rate was the rate most likely to inspire public confidence. However it could equally well be argued that since the depreciation in the preceding weeks had not yet percolated through to all prices in the economy, accepting the current market level as a permanent level was defeatist. Why not take the opportunity to roll back inflation by setting the rate at a higher, stronger level against the US$?

The argument for revaluation is the exact converse of the argument for devaluation above. In brief, the argument in favour of upward revaluation was that it would bring about a once-for-all decline in the domestic price level, but the cost of this would have been a balance of payments position which would have produced a smaller increase in money supply, and hence a temporarily tighter domestic liquidity situation.

The precise level chosen for the exchange rate was not important for the *long-term* adjustment of the economy. Given the mechanism in Scheme 2B whereby the money supply would adjust automatically to the balance of payments, no matter what level of exchange rate was actually chosen (within limits) the economy and the domestic price level would *eventually* have adjusted to the new rate. However the level chosen for the exchange rate would clearly have affected the economy and the price level in the *short run* as implied by the analysis in the preceding paragraphs. In the end the choice of exchange rate was not a matter of precise economic calculation; as the Financial Secretary said answer to a question after setting the new rate, it was a matter of "acute personal judgement".

4. INSTITUTIONAL ARRANGEMENTS OF THE NEW SCHEME

Under the new monetary arrangements announced on October 15th the Exchange Fund issues and redeems Certificates of Indebtedness to the two note-issuing banks at the fixed rate of HK$7.80 per US$. The two note-issuing banks have agreed to sell and re-purchase HK$ banknotes at this same rate with all other licensed banks in Hong Kong in effect acting as agents for the Exchange Fund. The government has not made the fixed 7.80 conversion facility available to the non-bank public, and has made no guarantees in respect of the foreign currency price of deposits or cash held by the public which are free to trade at market rates.

These arrangements meet the two requirements of an automatic, non-discretionary fixed exchange rate system specified in "How to Rescue the Hong Kong Dollar: Three Practical Proposals" (Chapter 5) namely

(1) that whatever serves as base money should be available in unlimited amounts at a stated price in foreign currency terms, and that it should be redeemable on similar terms in indefinite quantities, and

(2) convertibility or interchangeability between base money and the deposit money issued by the banks.

The mechanism thus established is basically the same as an old-fashioned gold or silver standard, except that Hong Kong uses the US dollar as its monetary standard in place of a precious metal, and the non-bank public does not have direct access to convertibility at the official parity as under the classical gold standard. Under this system there are two main forces tending to produce market rates of exchange for the Hong Kong dollar close to the official 7.80 rate for Certificates of Indebtedness. (There is a third mechanism, known as the goods arbitrage approach or the law of one price level, but here we shall only deal with the narrower monetary aspects of the adjustment mechanism.)

First, licensed banks are able to arbitrage between the free market rate for Hong Kong dollars or US dollars and the Exchange Fund's rate for Certificates of Indebtedness, buying in the cheaper market and selling in the dearer market. This kind of arbitrage will continue until the difference between the returns from holding deposits (making loans) and the returns from holding cash in either market is equal to the transaction costs of these operations. Deviations between the official rate and the free market rate are thus comparable to deviations between the official parity for gold and its free market price under the gold standard, with the upper and lower bounds of the free market given by the so-called gold points.

The incentive for banks to sell Hong Kong dollar banknotes (or CIs) to the Exchange Fund through this kind of arbitrage only exists when the free market rate for HK$ is at a discount to the official rate (e.g. at 7.82, 7.83 etc.). Sales or redemptions of HK$ banknotes to the Exchange Fund by the banks in these circumstances will tend to reduce the banks' cash-to-deposit ratio, causing them to restrict their lending in HK$ funds, tightening liquidity in the system and raising interest rates. If such a squeeze were to continue it would in time lead to reduced lending and slower money supply growth.

Since the HK$ rate in the free market will only be at a discount when there is an overall balance of payments deficit (e.g. due to an increased capital outflow, or due to a deterioration in the current account), this type of arbitrage will tend to restrict the money supply and raise interest rates. Both of these effects will bring the free market rate for Hong Kong dollars back towards the official parity.

A converse set of statements applies to the case of the incentive for banks to purchase Hong Kong dollar banknotes (or CIs) from the Exchange Fund. However, since banknotes are a non-earning asset for the banks, banks will tend to expand their lending when the Hong Kong dollar is at a premium to the US dollar rather than maintain non-earning cash balances. Consequently when the HK$ is at a premium to the US$ this will be consistent with monetary expansion, which in due course will tend to produce balance of payments effects which will eliminate the premium on the Hong Kong dollar.

The second element of the mechanism tending to keep the free market rate close to the official parity results from competition among the banks. Since bank customers are free to convert Hong Kong dollar deposits into cash at any time, they can, by exercising that right, shop around among the banks for the most favourable HK$/US$ rate for their HK$ banknotes. Theoretically it should be possible for a customer with a large quantity of banknotes to negotiate a price for his banknotes very close to the official parity of 7.80. It is unlikely that this type of transaction will need to occur, but the mere expectation that it could occur will be sufficient to keep the free market rate for banknotes close to the official parity for Certificates of Indebtedness. Banks which offer unfavourable rates can expect to lose customer deposits and lose market share. Hence the importance of the convertibility provision in (2) above, and the importance of free competition among the licensed banks.

There are two features of the new scheme as implemented from October 17th which differ from the proposals set out in AMM's Scheme 2B. First, in our proposals it was suggested (Ch. 5, Scheme 2B, (b) "The Role of Market Forces in the Adjustment Mechanism") that all banks should have direct access to the official rate for CIs, and should be able to sell banknotes direct to the Exchange Fund instead of to the two note-issuing banks. In the scheme as implemented the two note-issuing banks are in effect appointed agents of the Exchange Fund, and all other banks must deal with them, not with the authorities. Given the decision of the authorities not to deal with all banks and the requirement that the note-issuing banks pass on the 7.80 parity to all other licensed banks, the two note-issuing banks were left in the position that other banks would be able to buy or sell US$ at 7.80 or withdraw HK$ cash against HK$ demand deposits with the Hongkong and Shanghai Bank or Chartered Bank. In the event of a sudden large movement of the free market rate, other banks could rapidly adjust their positions at the two note-issuing banks, and all of the strain of adjustment in the system would fall on the two note-issuers. Presumably to avoid this problem the system has been set up so that other banks are obliged to pay US$ for *all* purchases of HK$ banknotes (i.e. they may not draw on their Hong Kong dollar demand deposit accounts at the note-issuing banks for purchases of banknotes), and conversely for *all* redemptions of HK$ banknotes the note-issuing banks will pay US$. Thus in effect all banks are now note-issuing banks in the sense that every new banknote the banks obtain has been paid for by them at the Exchange Fund with US$.

A second important difference between the scheme as implemented and the proposals put forward by AMM is the Hong Kong authorities' decision not to abolish the Interest Rate Agreement of the Hong Kong Association of Banks (HKAB). The failure to abolish the interest rate cartel means that the overall structure of interest rates in Hong Kong adjusts imperfectly to changes in interest rates abroad, or to changes in the supply and demand for credit in Hong Kong, or to changes in perceived rates of return in Hong Kong. Insofar as there are some interest rates which are free (e.g. the interbank and wholesale rates applicable on deposits in excess of HK$500,000) and some which are administered by the cartel, the whole burden of adjustment will temporarily be forced on to the free market interest rates, making those rates act as a kind of safety valve (at least until cartel rates are altered), and almost certainly causing free market rates to be more volatile than they would normally be if there was no interest rate cartel. In the absence of the Interest Rate Agreement the whole structure of rates would adjust slowly and more gradually than is likely as long as the Agreement remains in effect.

*   *   *   *   *

The following pages present the key documents of the Hong Kong dollar stabilisation scheme. Appendix 6.1 gives the official text of the statement by Sir John Bremridge, Financial Secretary, announcing the fixing of the HK$ rate for Certificates of Indebtedness at HK$7.80 per US$. Appendices 6.2–6.5 present the formal notification from the Monetary Affairs Branch to the banks, together with some of the messages between the participating banks outlining the procedures for implementing the new arrangements. Appendix 6.6 records the short term stabilisation plan proposed by the author which would have provided for full convertibility of the Hong Kong dollar.

APPENDIX 6.1

Official Text of the Hong Kong Monetary Stabilisation Scheme
as Announced by Sir John Bremridge

Noon, 15 October 1983

Statement by Financial Secretary

I want to tell you about two steps which the Government is taking now to stabilise the exchange rate of the Hong Kong dollar.

2. First let me give you some background. For 37 years from 1935 to July 1972 the Hong Kong dollar was pegged to sterling. In those days the sterling area existed and for most of that period the international monetary system was characterised by fixed exchange rates. From 1972 to November 1974 the Hong Kong dollar was pegged to the US dollar. Since 1974 Hong Kong in common with other major market economies has had a freely floating exchange rate. This floating system has served us well. It has given us a measure of insulation from the ups and downs of other economies, and under it Hong Kong has recorded very high rates of economic growth. Living standards have risen accordingly.

3. Towards the end of last year the exchange rate started markedly to weaken, reflecting amongst other factors uncertainties about Hong Kong's future.

4. Before the government announced three weeks ago that it was considering proposals to stabilise the exchange rate, currency depreciation was tending increasingly to feed on itself in an unstable and irrational manner. This depreciation was not justified by either current economic developments or future prospects. The economy has rebounded and is doing very well. There is little unemployment and exports are booming. Hong Kong has substantial foreign currency reserves, a generally liquid banking system and virtually no Government debt.

5. The Government has been concerned by the falling exchange rate and has done everything in reason, within the established framework, to attempt to stabilise it. These efforts have achieved only limited success.

6. The circumstances of Hong Kong preclude exchange control. After a thorough examination of realistic options, we have now decided to alter the framework within which the exchange rate is determined. With effect from Monday 17th October, the two note-issuing banks will pay the Government's Exchange Fund for additional Certificates of Indebtedness, which they are required to hold as backing for any increase in their note issues, in foreign exchange at a fixed rate of HK$7.80 equals US$1.

7. From the same date, when notes are withdrawn from circulation and the note-issuing banks surrender Certificates of Indebtedness the Exchange

Fund will pay them the equivalent foreign exchange at the same fixed rate. It is our intention to hold this rate unchanged.

8.   The rates of exchange which a bank customer will obtain, whether exchanging bank notes or making any other foreign currency transactions, will continue to be determined by market forces, but will in practice be close to the fixed rate of HK$7.80 equals US$1.00. This will be the case because from next Monday market forces will operate against the background of the fixed rate for Certificates of Indebtedness. I must emphasise that these new arrangements will mean business as usual between banks and their customers at stabilised rates.

9.   You will ask about the implications for the economy of stabilizing the exchange rate in this way. In the short term there may be some upward pressures on Hong Kong dollar interest rates. Once the stability of the exchange rate becomes evident and accepted, interest rates should fall below present levels. Looking further ahead changes in the exchange rate will no longer be an element in our economy's adjustment process. Factors such as interest rates and money supply will adjust to balance of payments pressures automatically without Government intervention.

10.   The Government believes that this new arrangement must now be preferred to the freely floating exchange rate system. We cannot run the risk of further spiralling depreciation, with the rampant inflation and distress which that would bring to all our community. A return of confidence in our currency is essential.

11.   I said that I had two measures to announce. The second is this. As from Monday 17th October interest on Hong Kong dollar deposits with financial institutions will no longer be taxed. This means that there will no longer be a tax advantage in holding foreign currency deposits or in holding Hong Kong dollar deposits offshore.

12.   As I said last month, the Government must take account of the possible erosion of profits tax revenue arising from the removal of interest tax. We are still studying this complex issue. In removing interest tax on Hong Kong dollar deposits with financial institutions, we are doing the most that is possible, pending the outcome of our study. I hope to be in a position to propose more lasting reforms in these fields of taxation in the budget next February.

13.   These measures are designed to stabilise the exchange value of the Hong Kong dollar, and thus to provide a climate for growing prosperity with restrained inflation. The Government has confidence in the stabilised exchange rate. So can the people of Hong Kong. Let us now get on with our business.

Government Information Services

15 October 1983

APPENDIX 6.2

Telex Message from Monetary Affairs Branch to Bank CEOs

Multi Address Call

15 October 1983

Urgent Message for Your Chief Executive

From: Secretary for Monetary Affairs, Hong Kong Government

Subject: Government Measures to Stabilise the Exchange Rate: Explanatory Note

----

The Financial Secretary has today announced two steps designed to stabilize the exchange rate of the Hong Kong Dollar. One step is the removal of interest tax on Hong Kong Dollar deposits with financial institutions, the other involves revised arrangements for the issue and redemption of banknotes. This message concerns the latter.

2.   The central element in the new arrangements is that, following agreement between the Government and the two note-issuing banks, Certificates of Indebtedness, which are issued by the Hong Kong Government Exchange Fund to the notes-issuing banks to be held as cover for their note issues, will henceforth be issued and redeemed only against payment in US dollars, at the fixed exchange rate of USD1.00 = HKD7.80. The forces of competition and arbitrage should then ensure, as they do at present, that approximately the same rate of exchange is available on transactions in all types of instrument. In other words, exchange rates quoted in the market for the US dollar will be close to the rate of HKD7.80 fixed for Certificates of Indebtedness.

3.   To assist the smooth and equitable functioning of this arrangement, the note-issuing banks have agreed with the Government that they should provide notes to, and accept them from, other banks on the same basis as they themselves deal with the exchange fund — i.e. against payments in US dollars at the rate of USD1.00 = HKD7.80. The note-issuing banks will be notifying other banks individually of the consequent revisions to their procedures for providing notes and for taking them back.

4.   It should be stressed that the market rate will hold close to the announced rate without any need for increased transactions in bank notes. The mere fact that deposits are convertible (at maturity, where relevant) into notes and that HKD notes are ultimately convertible (via Certificates of Indebtedness) into foreign currency will, assisted by the forces of competition and arbitrage, ensure convertibility between HKD deposits and foreign currency deposits at a rate determined principally by the fixed rate for Certificates of Indebtedness, without any intermediate transactions in notes having to take place.

5.   Neither DTCs nor any other bank customers should expect there to be any change in the manner in which they draw notes from or deposit notes with, banks. The new arrangements do not affect bank customers directly. Customers will merely find that the quoted exchange rate is close to HKD7.80, whether for exchanging notes or for other foreign exchange transactions. As a result of the Government fixing the rate for Certificates of Indebtedness, the exchange rate available to bank customers will also remain stable.

6.   As regards broader implications, essentially the new scheme transfers the impact of any adjustment to balance of payments pressures away from the exchange rate and onto the banking system, and more specifically onto the liquid reserve base of the banks and onto the level of interest rates paid and charged on HK deposits and loans. Thus, for example, a capital inflow may lead to increases in liquidity and lower interest rates, while a capital outflow may give rise to a squeeze on liquidity and higher HKD interest rates, instead of leading, as at present, to depreciation of the currency. In the event of an outflow the impact might be more severe on some banks than on others, and the consequences for other sectors, such as DTCs and corporate or individual borrowers, might be painful. The Government will be monitoring the situation carefully, particularly in its initial stages. The Commissioner of Banking and of Deposit-taking Companies will keep a close watch on the effects of the scheme on individual banks and DTCs. The Government would be prepared to consider action to mitigate any difficulties that might arise in particular cases.

Monetary Affairs Branch
TOD 151226

APPENDIX 6.3

Telexed Announcement from the Hong Kong Association of Banks

Multi Address Call
Deposit Interest Rates

The Hong Kong Association of Banks met this morning and decided to leave the deposit interest rates unchanged. This decision was taken after giving consideration to the announcement by Government of measures to stabilize the exchange rate of the Hong Kong Dollar.

Commenting on these measures the Committee welcomed the decision to abolish the withholding tax on Hong Kong dollar deposits — a measure it has consistently advocated as being necessary to remove the tax advantage in holding foreign currency deposits or in holding Hong Kong dollar deposits offshore.

The Committee fully endorsed the view of Government that the new arrangement to require the note-issuing banks to conduct transactions with the Government's Exchange Fund in regard to Certificates of Indebtedness, at a rate of exchange fixed against the US dollar, is a sensible measure which should restore stability to the exchange market with the minimum of official interference with market forces.

In recognizing that the new arrangements may necessitate more frequent adjustments to interest rates, the Committee deicded to meet in future in the mornings as and when necessary. The practice of meeting on Saturdays to review interest rates and the market situation generally will continue.

In a separate joint announcement the Chartered Bank and the Hongkong and Shanghai Banking Corporation announced that they would be issuing today an information notice to banks explaining the method by which the new arrangements for the issuance and redemption of their notes will be conducted between themselves and other banks. The new procedures will be in place by Monday morning to enable the exchange market to reopen at the normal time without disruption to business.

Chairman
Dated 15 October 1983
TOD 151345

APPENDIX 6.4

Letter from Hongkong and Shanghai Banking Corp. to All Licensed Banks in Hong Kong

15 October 1983

Dear Sir

HONG KONG DOLLAR NOTE ISSUE

You will be aware that the Government has announced that the Exchange Fund will in future issue and redeem Certificates of Indebtedness to the note-issuing banks against US Dollars at a fixed parity which will be set by Government.

The note-issuing banks have agreed that they in their turn will require payment in US Dollars when HK Dollar notes are drawn from their Treasuries and will make payment in US Dollars when HK Dollar notes are deposited. For all such transactions the prevailing parity rate will be used.

It is anticipated that your daily operations may require more than one withdrawal and/or deposit of HK Dollar notes at our Treasuries and we will accordingly aggregate or set off such receipts and deliveries during the day so that only one payment to or from your bank in US Dollars is required. This arrangement will reduce the volume of payments needed in New York, but we reserve the right to suspend the arrangement if it should prove operationally necessary to do so.

To facilitate the day-to-day accounting and to avoid any unnecessary transfer of US Dollar funds where there might be more than one cash transaction in any one day, we have arranged to open a US Dollar Settlement account (to which the number ... has been allocated) in your name in our books. All transactions will, in the first instance, be routed over the account with settlement of the net daily position being effected by you, or us as the case may be, at the end of the day. Settlement of funds due to us can be made in one of the following ways:–

(a) by remittance, for same day value, to the Hong Kong and Shanghai Banking Corporation, New York, for account The Hong Kong and Shanghai Banking Corporation, Hong Kong.

(b) by arranging for the purchase of US dollars for same day delivery from our dealers who can be contacted on telephone no. 5-263171 for a rate quotation. The cost of the purchase will be debited to your Hong Kong dollar current account or you may provide us with your Cashier Order.

or

(c) by arranging an overnight US dollar overdraft facility on which interest will be charged at the prevailing rate.

Settlement for any balance due to you will be effected by us to your nominated bank in the United States of America, or should you wish, you may contact our dealers on telephone no. 5-263171 who will quote a rate for the purchase from you of the US Dollars, the proceeds then being applied to the credit of your HK Dollar account in our books.

To ensure that settlements are effected smoothly in New York, we should be grateful if you would advise us as a matter of urgency details of your settlement account in New York, the name and ABA number of your bankers and the relative CHIPS UID number. In the interests of simplicity, only one account should be used for both payments and receipts of US dollars. Details of our account in New York are as follows:– (…)

We attach specimens of letters which we would request your staff to use with effect from 17 October 1983 for the withdrawal and deposit of HK dollar notes. The letters must be signed by duly authorised signatories and delivered to the Bank in duplicate at the time of effecting HK dollar cash transactions.

We shall be grateful if you will confirm your agreement to the opening of the US Dollar Settlement Account in your name in our books by providing us with a resolution to that effect, at the same time providing us with the names and specimen signatures of your authorised signatories for the account.

We trust that this explains the procedures to be followed and should be grateful if you would request your staff to contact our Miss Doris Leung on 5-2672260 if you have any queries.

Yours faithfully,

H.W. Paterson
Assistant Manager
Foreign Exchange and Treasury

APPENDIX 6.5

Standard Letters Issued by HSBC for Use by
Other Licensed Banks Withdrawing or Depositing Banknotes

The Manager
The Hongkong and Shanghai Banking Corporation
Main Treasury
Hong Kong

Dear Sir

Withdrawal of Cash

Please deliver to our authorised representative the sum of HKD _____ (Hong Kong Dollars _____) in reimbursement for which we hereby authorise you to debit our US Dollar Settlement Account No. _____ in your books with USD _____ being the equivalent at the rate of HKD _____ as laid down by Government.

In cover of the debit to our account

(a)   we will arrange to remit USD _____ to The Hongkong and Shanghai Banking Corporation, New York, for your account value today through our designated correspondent bank.

or

(b)   we have arranged a US Dollar purchase contract with your dealers for credit our account value today.

Yours faithfully

The Manager
The Hongkong and Shanghai Banking Corporation
Main Treasury
Hong Kong

Dear Sir

Deposit of Cash

We deliver to you herewith HKD_____ (Hong Kong Dollars_____) and would request to credit our US Dollar Settlement Account No._____with you with USD_____ being equivalent at HKD_____ to USD1.00 as laid down by Government.

In settlement of the credit to our account

(a)   remit the proceeds to our account in New York in accordance with our standing instructions.

or

(b)   we have arranged a US Dollar sale contract with your dealers for debit to our Dollar Settlement Account No. _____, value today. The proceeds should be credited to our Current Account No._____ in your books.

Yours faithfully

APPENDIX 6.6

Essential Elements of a Monetary Stabilisation Programme for Hong Kong

 **ASIAN MONETARY MONITOR LIMITED**

Hong Kong
September 26th 1983

Essential Elements of a Monetary Stabilisation Programme for Hong Kong

Summary

(1) Convertibility of the HK$ at a fixed rate in sterling[1] combined with a strong political statement that Britain[2] is backing the prosperity of the people of Hong Kong.

(2) Demonstrate the convertibility of the currency by flying in sterling and US dollar banknotes.

(3) Explain how the mechanics of convertibility will operate.

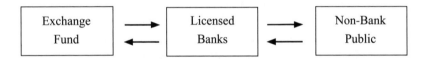

(4) Deal with the implications for banks' balance sheets: the exchange fund as lender of last resort.

(5) Ensure that the automatic adjustment mechanism will work smoothly in the future.

---

1. Or US$, or SDRs, or any other basket of currencies.
2. Or the Government of Hong Kong, or both Governments together. (Similar alternative options apply to statements on the following pages.)

ASIAN MONETARY MONITOR LIMITED

Essential Elements of a Monetary Stabilisation
Programme for Hong Kong

A simultaneous announcement is required from (1) HM Government in Britain on behalf of the Cabinet and the Bank of England and (2) the Governor of Hong Kong on behalf of the Governor-in-Council and the Monetary Affairs Branch to the effect that:

(1)   The Government of Hong Kong and the Exchange Fund, together with the British Government and the Bank of England stand behind the Hong Kong dollar and the people of Hong Kong. As from (date, time) they will guarantee the convertibility of Hong Kong dollar banknotes into sterling at a fixed rate of ___ (or approximately US$___). The available resources of the Exchange Fund and the Hong Kong Government together exceed (3?) times the total Hong Kong dollar banknote issue, and in addition the Bank of England stands ready to make further resources available.[3]

(2)   Arrangements have already been made with both the Bank of England in London and the Federal Reserve Board in Washington to fly sufficient British sterling banknotes and US Federal Reserves Notes to Hong Kong to meet any conceivable demands. Aeroplanes carrying those banknotes are already on their way to Hong Kong.

   (The arrival of the banknotes at Kai Tak Airport should be staged as a news-event. These measures will demonstrate the credibility of the public announcement and help to restore public confidence as early as possible.)

(3)   The convertibility of Hong Kong dollar banknotes into sterling means that any individual may go to his bank and obtain sterling (or US$ foreign currency notes) against Hong Kong dollar banknotes at the fixed rate. These conversion facilities will be provided by all Licensed Banks, and in turn all Licensed Banks will be granted access to the Exchange Fund for the purpose of redeeming HK$ banknotes under special orders to be incorporated in legislative form by amendment to the Exchange Fund Ordinance.

(4)   To ensure that Licensed Banks will have ample sterling or equivalent foreign exchange to meet the needs of their depositors, the Exchange Fund will stand ready to provide such foreign exchange to any Licensed Bank on the security of either Hong Kong dollar assets or foreign currency assets equal in value to 120% of the amount of foreign currency required by each bank.

---

3.   N.B. It is inconceivable that these facilities would actually be required.

(This enables banks to shift their portfolios as between Hong Kong dollar assets and liabilities and foreign currency assets and liabilities. From the standpoint of the Hong Kong Government, however, it will demonstrate publicly that sterling and Hong Kong dollars are each as good as the other.)

(5) Henceforward all issues of Hong Kong dollar banknotes will be authorised only against payment by the two note-issuing banks of sterling or other equivalent convertible currencies at the accounts of the Exchange Fund in London and New York. The Hong Kong dollar always has been and will remain fully backed by foreign currencies. In the past decade the Hong Kong dollar has not been fixed to other currencies and this has recently given rise to undue anxiety both in the business community and among the ordinary people of Hong Kong. By fixing the price of the Hong Kong dollar in sterling we will remove that anxiety once and for all.

I believe that, taken together and announced with appropriate political statements about the commitment of the British Government to the prosperity of Hong Kong, these measures would be sufficient both to stop the temporary crisis, and to put Hong Kong's monetary system firmly back on the rails after a decade of drift.

Signed,

John G. Greenwood
Economist, G.T. Management (Asia) Ltd.
JGG/i1
25/9/83.

CHAPTER 7

THE OPERATION OF THE
NEW EXCHANGE RATE MECHANISM

January–February 1984

By late January 1984, three months from the implementation of the new currency board in October 1983, the linked rate system for the HK$ had settled down and appeared to outsiders to be working tolerably well. The spot exchange rate was holding close to the official parity of HK$7.80, HK$ interest rates had fallen below those for US$, and renewed confidence in Hong Kong was shown by a resurgence in the demand for HK$-denominated money supply. It was therefore appropriate to step back and examine more deeply how the new mechanisms were working, and to examine some possible scenarios for the longer-term adjustment of the Hong Kong economy under a currency board.

Viewed from the perspective of the gold or silver standard, a currency board is a modern form of commodity standard that uses an external anchor currency instead of a commodity as its "standard". This article uses that idea to explain how the re-introduced currency arrangements were working. Thus in the box on pp. 174–175 it adopts the terminology of "internal and external drains" from the gold standard era to discuss the kind of adjustments that the revised HK currency system might make in the wake of the currency stabilisation in 1983.

In reality the free market exchange rate was being kept in line with the HK$7.80 official parity for Certificates of Indebtedness by judicious intervention from the Hong Kong authorities or by the Hongkong and Shanghai Bank as the manager of the clearing system. In retrospect the AMM article probably makes too much of the possibility for cash arbitrage (analogous with the shipment of gold between financial centres when exchange rates moved outside the so-called gold points under the gold standard), but has insights into how the wider aspects of the automatic adjustment mechanism operated. For example, the sections on interest rate determination, monetary growth and the behaviour of the economy under optimistic and pessimistic scenarios are all valid even without the core assumption that the exchange rate was being brought into line automatically. Once committed to a fixed exchange rate, it was important to understand how the Hong Kong economy would operate in the future. For example, the paragraph on the pessimistic scenario contains a plausible forecast (p. 180) of what might happen in Hong Kong after 1997. It was not until the Asian Financial Crisis of 1997–98 that the full extent of the problems of operating the new system was really exposed.

A S I A N   M O N E T A R Y   M O N I T O R
Vol. 8 No. 1 January–February 1984

When the new system for issuing Hong Kong dollar banknotes was implemented from Monday, October 17th 1983 there was a widespread lack of understanding about how the scheme would operate to stabilise the exchange rate for the Hong Kong currency, and consequently a high degree of scepticism that the new official exchange rate of HK$7.80 per US dollar could be maintained for very long. Also, because the HK$7.80 rate was considerably above the market rates of 8.30–40 that had been prevalent on Friday, October 14th, the implementation of the new scheme seemed to provide a heaven-sent opportunity to sell Hong Kong dollars and obtain US dollars while the new parity lasted. Now that the scheme has been in operation for several months and the sceptics who sold Hong Kong dollars in October have been confounded, it is appropriate to explain why the system is so resilient, and to examine the operation of the scheme with respect to (a) the behaviour of interest rates in the Hong Kong dollar money market, (b) the behaviour of the money supply since the implementation of the new scheme, and (c) the likely behaviour of the monetary and other nominal variables under alternative assumptions about the real economy.

(A) THE BEHAVIOUR OF INTEREST RATES UNDER THE NEW MECHANISM

The monetary arrangements set up in October 1983 established a fixed parity between the Certificates of Indebtedness issued to the note-issuing banks as cover for their banknote issue, and the US dollar. Effectively this means that units of Hong Kong's monetary base are simply different denominations of the US dollar, because the government guarantees their convertibility into US dollars at the fixed price. As long as the authorities have sufficient foreign currency reserves to cover the entire HK$ note issue, convertibility is assured.

Given the equivalence of Hong Kong dollars and US dollars at the official parity — and this depends on the assumption that the parity will not be altered — lenders and borrowers of credit in these two currencies ought to be indifferent between the two. Lenders will therefore try to lend in the currency offering higher interest rates, and borrowers will try to borrow in the currency offering lower interest rates. Also, arbitrageurs will borrow in the country with lower rates and lend in the country with higher rates. By these processes money market interest rates for various maturities in each country will tend to equality in the long term. In the short term, two sets of factors can interfere with the equality of interest rates: short term balance of payments disequilibria and short-term variations in the supply and demand for credit. In the long term the mechanism is self-correcting so that interest rate differentials will be eliminated, but in the short term both can produce significant interest rate differentials particularly for short term interest rates.

As a way of studying the recent experience of Hong Kong since the introduction of a fixed parity for Certificates of Indebtedness (i.e. HK$ banknotes at one remove), it is useful to consider the case of (a) an overall balance of payments deficit due to capital outflows, and (b) a reduction in the supply of credit or loanable funds due to large scale conversions of deposits into currency by the non-bank public (see box on pp. 174–175.) These correspond to the two "tests" to which the classical gold standard was subject, namely the *external drain* and the *internal drain*.

The new Hong Kong monetary system which was launched on October 17th 1983 has already been "tested" by both types of drain, and in each case the disruption or disequilibrium has been overcome within a few days. This is a tribute both to the underlying strength of the new mechanism, and to the efficiency of Hong Kong's money and foreign exchange markets.

An example of the external drain occurred immediately after the new scheme was implemented. Since the free market exchange rate for the US dollar had been around HK$8.30–40 in the few days preceding the setting of the new parity at HK$7.80, and since there was almost universal scepticism that the government could fix the exchange rate at any level and hold it there in the face of huge capital outflows, the new rate of HK$7.80 seemed like a splendid opportunity to cash in Hong Kong dollars and obtain US dollars at a particularly favourable rate (which surely would not last ...). Consequently there was considerable selling of Hong Kong dollars, so that although the leading banks had started out with quotations of HK$7.7950–7.8050, the free market rate soon tumbled to around HK$7.95. As explained in the box (pp. 174–175) this induced some banks to redeem HK$ cash currency, while others, wary of their liquidity positions as their deposits were run down, had to borrow short term funds in the HK$ money market, pushing short term interest rates up sharply. At one stage overnight rates hit 42%. One month deposit rates went to 25% or thereabouts, while three-month deposit rates rose to almost 20%. As shown Chart 7.1, however, it took only 4 or 5 trading days for HK$ interest rates in the overnight markets to return to the same level as overnight LIBOR rates, and within 10 trading days Hong Kong dollar overnight rates were substantially below equivalent US dollar rates. Basically the attraction of interest rates in excess of 20% in a currency which was now fixed to and therefore equivalent to US dollars was too good an opportunity to miss, so those who understood the new mechanism borrowed US dollars to lend in Hong Kong, thus helping to bring the HK$ exchange rate back towards parity and reducing the interest rate differential in the two currencies.

The next significant episode — at Christmas time — provided a clear example of the mechanism of the internal drain at work. Chart 7.1 shows how first of all overnight rates began to rise as deposits were converted to cash currency ahead of the four-day Christmas holiday. The rise in HK$ interest rates led to a strengthening of the Hong Kong dollar against the US dollar, and a decisive move from below parity to above parity. Basically what was happening was that the total money supply remained unchanged, but its composition changed so that cash currency increased by approximately HK$920 million in the week ending December 24th. This implied an increase of about 7% in the cash currency held by the non-bank public, and a correspondingly smaller percentage decrease in the total

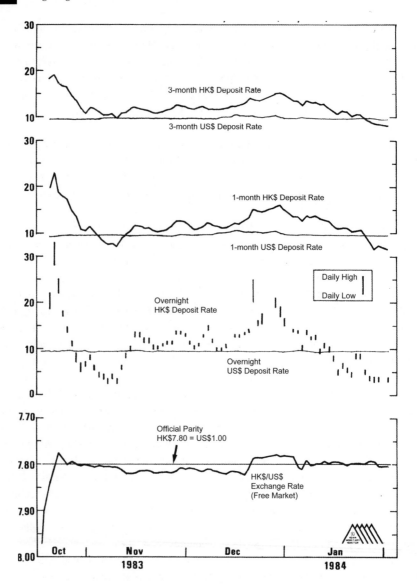

Chart 7.1   HK$/US$ Exchange Rate and Interest Rate Differentials (17 October 1983–31 January 1984) (Daily data)

volume of HK$ deposits. Since the supply of loanable funds was reduced, interest rates had to rise to restore equilibrium in the credit markets. This time overnight interest rates peaked at just over 30% but term rates did not rise nearly so high. Immediately after Christmas and New Year the demand for HK$ cash currency subsided, the supply of loanable funds was increased, and the upward pressure on interest rates in the money markets relaxed, so that the free market exchange rate for Hong Kong dollars returned from a premium to a level very close to the parity (see Chart 7.1). Once again longer term deposit interest rates gradually returned to the levels of US interest rates.

To summarise, the new Hong Kong monetary arrangements have now been put to the test of both an external drain and an internal drain. In a purely technical sense there is no other "test" to which the system can be subjected. In the event of a capital flight, Hong Kong will see a repeat of the October episode; in the event of a conversion of HK$ deposits into HK$ currency Hong Kong will see a repeat of the Christmas and New Year episode. In practical terms, however, the severity of future episodes in each case could be significantly greater, particularly in the case of a run on one or more banks. While this would raise short-term interest rates further and hence increase the incentives for banks and other arbitrageurs to bring funds in and restore equilibrium, it could also expose the system to fears that claims on the Hong Kong banks were not safe. A prolonged episode of this kind would severely test the adaptive capacity of the Hong Kong economy to deflationary conditions. It is essential if the automatic mechanism is to work well in the future

(i)   that market participants be 100% convinced that the government has no intention whatsoever of changing the fixed parity,

(ii) that international capital flows continue to be allowed complete freedom of movement, and

(iii) that claims on Hong Kong banks continue to be regarded as reasonably secure.

Widespread doubt on any of these scores could be fatal to the operation of the self-correcting mechanism.

From this standpoint it was a pity that the Financial Secretary indicated at the press conference following the announcement of the new scheme on October 15th that there was some possibility of the exchange rate being revalued upwards against the US$, but not downwards, and that if the US$ became volatile there was a possibility of switching the fixed parity from the US$ to a basket of currencies. Comforting though it might have seemed at the time to have said this, it has proved more destabilising than stabilising to the foreign exchange and money markets. In particular, from late January 1984 there was a growing and widely held expectation that in the 1984 Budget Speech scheduled for 29th February the Financial Secretary would announce some upward revaluation. As a result there was a flood of "hot money" deposited in Hong Kong during January and February. (Actually, this is metaphorical language. What really happened was that the demand for Hong Kong dollars was such that even with HK$ interest rates substantially lower than equivalent US$ rates, the Hong Kong dollar remained firmly at parity, and the low level of interest rates in Hong Kong — if continued — would have been consistent with increased bank lending and hence a faster growth of the money supply.) This kind of instability in interest rates is quite unnecessary, and insofar as it is a direct result of misplaced expectations it would be desirable for the authorities to reaffirm their official policy not to alter the fixed parity, and perhaps even to emphasise that since the Hong Kong dollar parity does not require official intervention to support it, there can be no close parallel drawn between central bankers who make such assertions only to have to give way to the pressure of market forces, and the Hong Kong situation where the parity it itself maintained by market forces.

HOW THE SELF-CORRECTING MECHANISM OPERATES UNDER THE NEW EXCHANGE RATE MECHANISM

The External Drain

(1) An external drain occurs when there is a widespread conversion of Hong Kong dollars (deposits or currency) into foreign currency associated with an overall balance of payments deficit. To simplify we shall follow the process through the books of the banks for a single transaction representing total net outflows.

(2) Suppose that Customer X with substantial HK$ deposits at Bank A sells HK$ for US$, and that the HK$ are purchased by Customer Y, who maintains his account at Bank B. Customer X's HK$ account is debited and he receives a US$ draft (or credit to a US$ account) equivalent to the HK$ amount sold at the free market rate of exchange, less any commissions or other charges. Initially the HK$ funds are transferred from Customer X's account to the clearing account of Bank A, and a cheque drawn on that account is issued to Bank B.

(3) To settle, Bank A's clearing account is debited and Bank B's clearing account is credited, and subsequently Customer Y's account at Bank B is credited in HK$.

(4) For the banking system as a whole there is at this point no change in the quantity of HK$ deposits, but the increased demand for US$ or the downward shift in demand for HK$ relative to US$ evident in the sale of HK$ for US$, will have pushed the free market rate for HK$ away from the 7.80 parity towards 7.81, 7.82 or 7.83. Depending on the relative demand for HK$ and US$ and therefore how far the HK$ falls against the US$, there will at some stage be an incentive for banks with HK$ cash currency balances to sell US$ for HK$ at the free market rate (say 7.8350), and then take HK$ banknotes to the note-issuing banks for redemption by the Exchange fund at the official rate of 7.80, pocketing the difference between the market rate and the official rate (i.e. HK$0.035 or 3.5 cents per US$).

(5) The sale of HK$ banknotes to the Exchange Fund reduces the amount of HK$ cash currency in the system, and makes it likely that one or more other banks will be short of cash currency or short term liquid funds relative to their deposit liabilities. To alleviate this shortage and ensure they have funds readily available, these banks will initially borrow short-term HK$ funds in the overnight market to top up their clearing accounts

(or they must sell US$ to the Exchange Fund to obtain HK$ cash). The new borrowing in the HK$ overnight market will drive up HK$ interest rates, and through arbitrage in the local money market (borrowing longer term to lend at short term) and in the forward foreign exchange market (borrowing US$ funds to lend in HK$), the rise in overnight rates will be transmitted to the whole spectrum of interest rates in Hong Kong.

(6) Higher interest rates in Hong Kong will reduce the amount of profitable lending opportunities for banks, this will slow down credit-creation, and as a result deposit growth will slow down. In this way the money supply declines or slows down in the aftermath of a net balance of payments deficit or external drain.

The Internal Drain

(1) An internal drain occurs when there is a widespread conversion by bank customers of HK$ deposits to HK$ cash currency. This could occur for purely seasonal reasons (e.g. at Christmas or at Chinese New Year), or because of a run on a bank, or in the case of a generalised banking panic.

(2) The withdrawal of deposits in the form of cash causes an equal depletion of both bank deposits and banks' cash balances. This will adversely affect banks' previous cash-to-deposit ratios; alternatively banks' loans and investments will have risen in relation to their deposits. Banks will now seek to restore their cash-to-deposit ratios, and they will be more reluctant to make new loans.

(3) To restore their HK$ cash positions, banks must sell US$ to the Exchange Fund and obtain HK$ banknotes. If they do not have free US$ balances the banks will have to borrow them in the free market, and then sell the borrowed US$ for HK$, which will tend to raise the value of the HK$ relative to the US$.

(4) Meanwhile the shortage of HK$ cash in bank portfolios will induce in some banks the same response as in the case of the external drain: an upward shift in demand for overnight interbank funds to replace the reduction in loanable funds, and a consequent rise in interbank interest rates. By the same mechanisms as in the external drain, these higher rates will be transmitted to the whole spectrum of interest rates in Hong Kong.

(5) As in the case of the external drain higher interest rates will lead to less credit-creation and slower monetary growth. In this way an internal drain produces a contractionary or deflationary effect on the monetary system.

Aside from uncertainty about the future official parity of the Hong Kong dollar, the remaining factor making for volatility in HK$ interest rates has been the continued existence of the Interest Rate Agreement of the Hong Kong Association of Banks (HKAB). So long as deposit interest rates for a wide sector of the market continue to react insensitively to changes in supply and demand (see Chapter 6, p. 155), any imbalances must be absorbed by that part of the credit market which is not subject to the cartel. The insensitivity of cartel rates to market forces is enhanced by the wide margins between deposit interest rates and prime or best lending rates within the cartel. These margins are very substantially wider than free market margins, so even allowing for the cost of administering small-sized deposits, these margins offer prima facie evidence of the inefficiency fostered by the banking cartel. Abolition of the cartel would mean not only higher rates for depositors and lower rates for borrowers, but, in all probability, more stable interest rates throughout the Hong Kong financial system under any given set of circumstances.

(B) MONETARY GROWTH UNDER THE NEW MECHANISM

Since the announcement of the Hong Kong dollar stabilisation plan in October last year the HK$-denominated money supply (in particular the time deposit component of HK$$M_3$) has grown at an extraordinary rate, sometimes by as much as 5% or 6% per month. Over the period October–February the annualised growth rate of HK$$M_3$ was 82.3% p.a. Meanwhile total M_3 which includes foreign currency deposits has grown at 41.0% p.a., with the foreign currency component growing at 3.9% p.a. (see Chart 7.2.).

These exceptional monetary growth rates can only be a temporary phenomenon. They represent part of the transition process following the currency stabilisation scheme to a new, long run equilibrium growth rate for the Hong Kong dollar money supply. In the first place the new official parity of HK$7.80 per US dollar almost certainly undervalued the Hong Kong dollar, and has helped to generate an exceptionally strong trading performance by Hong Kong exporters in the months since the stabilisation scheme was implemented. In the period October–February the growth of domestic exports over the same period a year earlier was no less than 42.7% in Hong Kong dollar terms. Of this, 23.1% is due to the depreciation of the Hong Kong currency, which suggests that this performance cannot continue beyond next September. But the real key to the strong trading performance is competitiveness, which derives from the fact that domestic prices have not yet fully reflected the depreciation of the local currency. It is even possible that Hong Kong has experienced an overall balance of payments surplus since the new currency mechanism settled down, thus enabling the HK$ money supply to grow rapidly. If this situation were to persist the rapid growth in Hong Kong's monetary aggregates would ultimately be reflected in higher prices in the Hong Kong economy, thus eroding the extra competitive edge gained by the sudden depreciation of the currency in September/October 1983. Once Hong Kong's international competitiveness has returned to "normal" levels the balance of payments will no longer experience the surpluses it

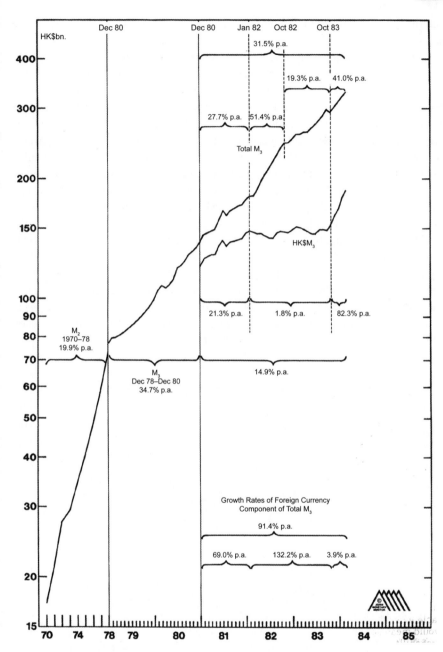

Chart 7.2 Growth of HK$ M_3 and Total M_3

Note: The growth rate of foreign currency deposits is expressed in HK$ terms, and is therefore significantly affected by the depreciation of the HK$ over the whole period since December 1980 when separate data first became available. For example, expressed in US$ terms the growth rate of the foreign currency component of Total M_3 since Dec. 1980 is 67.8% p.a.

has (possibly) experienced in recent months, and monetary growth will resume a more normal path.

Second, the resumption of rapid HK$-denominated monetary growth reflects in part, we suspect, a statistical quirk produced by the past growth of swap deposits. During the period from February 1982 to October 1983 foreign currency deposits at banks in Hong Kong were exempt from a 10% withholding tax on interest to which Hong Kong dollar deposits were liable. In addition, because small-sized Hong Kong dollar deposits were subject to the Interest Rate Agreement of the HKAB, it was profitable for depositors to "swap" HK$ deposits into US$ deposits and thus avoid both the interest withholding tax and the interest rate ceilings of the HKAB cartel. From a statistical point of view it seems that these deposits were reported as foreign currency deposits, even though the depositor still ended up holding HK$, and this is part of the explanation for the slow growth rate of HK$M₃ in the period from early 1982 until October 1983. With the abolition of the residual 10% withholding tax on HK$ deposit interest payments, and the stabilisation of the HK$/US$ exchange rate there is now little incentive to switch to US$ deposits, and accordingly many Hong Kong holders of such swap deposits have been reported as unwinding their positions. One supporting strand of evidence suggesting that the rapid growth of HK$M₃ is likely to be a temporary phenomenon is that loan demand in Hong Kong remains extremely weak (see Chart 7.3) so that the apparent monetary growth has not been associated with new credit creation.

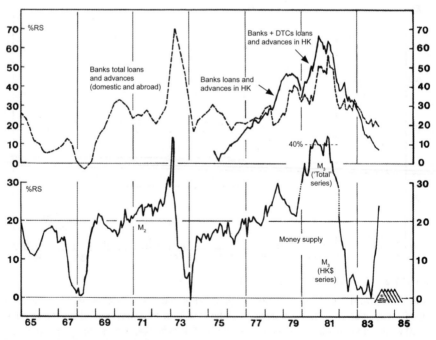

Chart 7.3 Money and Credit Growth

This upsurge in HKM_3$, however, is probably better viewed as part of the general revival of a willingness to hold Hong Kong dollar assets following the currency stabilisation scheme. While the exchange rate was still floating, and particularly in August and September 1983 there was wholesale dumping of all types of Hong Kong dollar assets — property, businesses, equities and currency. Once the currency was stabilised, that whole process gradually went into reverse, and the build-up of HK$-denominated money supply can be viewed, from the demand side, as a resumption of the public's willingness to hold real money balances in Hong Kong dollars again. From this perspective the question to answer is, how far should we expect holders of HK$ money balances to wish to restore their holdings of HK$ deposits and currency? If we could estimate their required transactions balances for any given past level of income, it might be possible to make some kind of estimate, based on current income levels, of the amount of money balances we should expect Hong Kong people to hold now that the disincentives to holding HK$ balances have been removed. Once Hong Kong dollar balances in deposits and currency had returned to these levels we could say that the transition period following the implementation of the new exchange rate mechanism was nearly over. (It would still be necessary for price levels to adjust to the new level of money balances, and only after that adjustment was accomplished could one say that the transition was completed.)

For the long term Hong Kong's monetary growth rate will adjust to whatever is consistent with an overall balance of payments equilibrium, which in turn will depend upon such factors as the growth rate of the economy, the desired holdings of HK$ money balances, and the overall level of prices in Hong Kong. We now turn to a brief consideration of these factors under alternative assumptions about the performance of the Hong Kong economy.

(C) BEHAVIOUR OF MONETARY AND OTHER VARIABLE UNDER ALTERNATIVE ASSUMPTIONS ABOUT THE REAL ECONOMY

In two economies whose currencies are linked together by a fixed parity which is expected to remain fixed at a constant rate, interest rates and price levels must tend to equality in the long term in some aggregate sense. This is simply an application of the law known as the law of one price which predicts that in any one currency area the price of identical goods and services will tend to equality, allowing only for differences in transportation costs. If this holds in a single currency area, it will also be true for two currency areas whose currencies are permanently fixed at a rigid parity, because this will mean that one currency is essentially a different denomination of the other. This was very clear under the gold exchange standard where all major currencies were defined in terms of a fixed weight and fineness of gold, but it is equally applicable to fiat currencies such as the US$ and the HK$ today.

However, although this is true for prices (and interest rates are merely a price — the price of credit), it is not necessarily true for the quantity of money. For two very similar countries with a roughly equal income level and growth rate, and a similar level of financial sophistication, it could be true that identical monetary growth rates would maintain balance of payments equilibrium in the long run, but for two economies as different as Hong Kong and the United States this is most unlikely to be true. In fact the rate of growth of the quantity of money in each economy must accommodate the possibility of different real growth rates (i.e. differing requirements for transactions balances), differing desires for the accumulation of money balance relative to income (i.e. different income elasticities of demand for money balances), and yet still produce equilibrium in the balance of payments if the fixed parity is to remain intact.

For ease of exposition we shall consider two alternative scenarios which assume a constant growth rate in the United States with (1) a slow-growing or stagnant Hong Kong economy or with (2) a rapidly growing and prosperous Hong Kong economy.

The first scenario assumes a generally pessimistic outlook for Hong Kong after 1997. Real capital expenditures might be halved, but remain sufficient to maintain and expand the existing capital stock, and consequently the economic growth rate could gradually decline to a rate of (say) 3.5% p.a., equal to the long term real growth rate of the USA. In order to maintain the price level in Hong Kong at a level which is consistent with equilibrium in the balance of payments it will be necessary for the money supply to grow at roughly the same rate as the money supply in the United States, adjusted for the differential demand for money balances in each country. In the early phases of such a transformation of the Hong Kong economy there might be considerable capital outflows as investment opportunities abroad appeared more favourable than the returns available in Hong Kong. If, temporarily, these capital outflows were to produce an overall balance of payments deficit and a short-term downturn in Hong Kong's money supply, in time the overall price level (including wages) in Hong Kong would adjust to a level somewhat lower than overall prices in the USA. This would give Hong Kong exporters a competitive advantage, enabling Hong Kong to generate a balance of trade and current account surplus sufficient to finance the deficit on capital account. (An important question for Hong Kong is how long would this adjustment process take, and what would be the interim consequences prior to the current account surplus being generated?)

The second scenario assumes a generally optimistic outlook for Hong Kong after 1997. We could assume that capital expenditures would resume their past buoyancy, and that consequently the economic growth rate would continue at something close to the double digit rates it has achieved in the recent past. In order to maintain the price level in Hong Kong at a level consistent with balance of payments equilibrium under these circumstances it will be necessary for the quantity of money to grow much more rapidly than the money supply in the United States, because not only would transactions requirements in Hong Kong be growing much more rapidly, but also one could predict from past experience that the growth in demand for money balances was such that an additional 3–4% p.a. would be required. Thus, under this kind of scenario and assuming a 9% real growth rate in Hong Kong and a 5% inflation rate in the United States, Hong Kong would require an average money growth rate of around 18% p.a. (9% plus 5% plus 4%) to maintain rough equality of prices with the USA.

Under both scenarios the money supply adjusts automatically and without government intervention as a consequence of a combination of factors: the balance of payments position, the demand for transactions balances and other incremental demand for money balances, and the relative inflation rates in Hong Kong and the United States. The new monetary system in Hong Kong thus provides a well-tried mechanism which is capable of accommodating either buoyant or stagnant economic conditions. Because it operates through maintaining balance of payments equilibrium, and because Hong Kong is such an open economy, the mechanism will ensure that the monetary system adjusts rapidly to the needs of the economy. The strength of the mechanism is that it is automatic and impartial to the problems of particular sectors, and it therefore avoids the value judgments as between certain types of industry or employee which other discretionary mechanisms would almost certainly imply. In the uncertain years that lie ahead it is our view that Hong Kong people should have the maximum opportunity to arrange their assets and property as they see best. In this sense the new monetary system is fully compatible with the preservation of the prosperity and stability of the people of Hong Kong.

CHAPTER **8**

WHY THE HK$/US$ LINKED RATE SYSTEM SHOULD NOT BE CHANGED

November–December 1984

This article presents an analytical view of the benefits and costs of the move to a fixed exchange rate in October 1983, and then deals with three alternative proposals intended to solve Hong Kong's monetary problems. Implicitly the point is that no system is perfect — there are costs and benefits in any monetary system. One box discusses partial convertibility versus full convertibility (on pp. 188–190), and another offers an early critique of the interest rate agreement (pp. 192–194) as it operated at that time. The interest rate discussion follows on from the statement in the final paragraph of Chapter 6 that had argued for abolition of the interest rate agreement, and represents an early statement of the case for deregulating interest rates in Hong Kong, a policy that was finally carried out in the years 1999–2002.

The appendices (pp. 195–202) provide eleven different supply-demand diagrams and brief text explaining the analytics of the linked exchange rate system. This section is aimed at students. More general readers may choose to skip the application of supply/demand diagrams to the Hong Kong monetary system.

A S I A N   M O N E T A R Y   M O N I T O R
Vol. 8 No. 6 November–December 1984

Following the signing of the Joint Sino-British Agreement on the Future of Hong Kong (in September 1984), there have been several suggestions that it is time to reconsider the linked rate system for the HK$ which was introduced in October 1983. An implicit theme of bankers and other commentators who propose altering the linked rate is that the system was introduced at a time of crisis, and, since the crisis has now passed, the system has outlived its usefulness. This paper will consider first the economic benefits which the linked rate system for the HK$ dollar has brought to the people of Hong Kong, and second the three principal proposals which have been made to amend or replace the current system.

The restoration of sound currency arrangements for Hong Kong has meant that the HK$ can once again be relied on as a stable store of value and it can act as an efficient medium of exchange. The benefits which the stabilisation of the local currency has brought can be characterised in general terms in several ways: a reduction in uncertainty or information costs, lower transaction costs, and the elimination of arbitrary transfers between debtors and creditors (borrowers and lenders) due to unforeseen inflation. More specifically, three obvious benefits have been achieved:

- The first major benefit is the reduction in inflation resulting from the stabilisation of the currency. The inflation rate in Hong Kong has been much lower than it might otherwise have been in the wake of the currency panic of September 1983. At that time the year-to-year increase in consumer prices was close to 10%, though for a few days during the currency collapse there were signs of an incipient hyperinflation. Since the crisis the inflation rate in Hong Kong has declined markedly, and is gradually converging towards the inflation rate of the United States. (Taking a simple average of the three Consumer Price Indices, prices in Hong Kong have risen only 4.6% in the year since October 1983, while consumer prices in the USA have risen 4.2% over the same period.) For the Hong Kong consumer the purchasing power of the dollar in his pocket has been more stable in the past year than in any of the preceding seven years (since 1977). For the businessman, the attainment of price stability has meant a much more stable environment for costs which has assisted in planning for the future.

- Second, because the vast majority of Hong Kong's trade is priced in US$ and the HK$/US$ rate has been stable within very narrow limits since October 1983, every exporter and importer, every corporate treasurer, and hence every employee of all the companies involved in import/export trade have benefited from the linked rate for the HK$.

- Third, the ordinary man-in-the-street who holds his savings in Hong Kong banks or deposit-taking companies has benefited because, in contrast to the situation prevailing in Hong Kong before the introduction of the linked rate system, he now obtains a rate of interest which is higher than the annual rate of inflation.

There is growing evidence from a variety of economic studies that the provision of competitive real returns to savers improves the allocation of resources, encourages investment and discourages wasteful speculation in assets which are primarily hedges against inflation. In linking the HK$ to the US$ and thereby bringing free market HK$ interest rates closely into line with US$ interest rates, many of the benefits of recent financial innovation and financial deregulation in the United States have been brought to Hong Kong at a stroke.

These benefits are very large and substantial. They have accrued, directly or indirectly, to virtually every individual in Hong Kong. At the same time there have also been costs under the new linked rate system, but these costs are either the unavoidable side effects of political uncertainty, or the consequences of certain technical features of the linked rate system which could in fact be alleviated.

One undoubted cost has been the greater variability of short-term interest rates under the linked rate system. Under the current mechanism political uncertainty can lead to a capital outflow (i.e. an external drain), which produces higher interest rates in the first instance as a step towards reducing the money supply. (See Chapter 7, "How the Self-Correcting Mechanism Operates under the New Exchange Rate Mechanism", pp. 174–175.) However, this greater variability of interest rates has to be considered against the alternative. Given the political uncertainties and the associated capital outflows which have confronted Hong Kong over the past two years, and which will no doubt recur from time to time in the future, the choice facing the Hong Kong authorities was between the floating rate system which was acutely vulnerable to adverse changes in sentiment and exposed every holder of HK$ to the risk of currency depreciation, and the linked rate system which has proved capable of absorbing every disturbance to date in short term movements of interest rates, usually returning to equilibrium after a period of a few days.

Under a floating exchange rate system with no central bank there can be little doubt that Hong Kong would have been subject to a higher degree of volatility in its exchange rate and hence in its domestic price level than has actually occurred since October 1983. Under the linked rate system, by contrast, the exchange rate and the domestic price level remain largely stable, and those who are willing to hold HK$ at times of political anxiety get rewarded with high rates of interest, while those who deliberately establish HK$ liability positions (i.e. those who seek to benefit from a depreciation of the HK$) are penalised by having to pay high interest rates. In other words, those who back Hong Kong and its currency are being rewarded while those who bet against it are penalised.

Also, under the floating rate system any increase in political anxieties produced benefits which accrued only to those who maintained net short positions in HK$, while the "costs" of the political disturbances affected everyone in Hong Kong through currency depreciation and inflation. In contrast, under the linked rate system the benefits of a stable currency and low inflation accrue to the whole community and the "costs" only affect a narrow cross-section of the population.

Another alleged cost of the linked rate system comes from the deviations between the free market rate for the HK$ and the official parity. However, this is not so much a cost for the community as a whole but rather a redistribution of the costs and benefits of operating the system among the banks, DTCs, companies, individuals and the government (to the extent that the government intervenes to manipulate interest rates or the exchange rate).

The basic reason for the deviations between the free market rate for the HK$ and the official parity is that the Hong Kong government decided to adopt a system of partial or limited convertibility rather than a system of full convertibility. (See Chapter 6, "The Stabilisation of the Hong Kong Dollar", Section 3 (b), pp. 149–151, and box on pp. 188–191.) Under a system of partial convertibility (i.e. offering convertibility of HK$ banknotes to US$ at 7.80 *only to banks*) the cash arbitrage process is greatly inhibited, and in addition the smooth functioning of the system is forced to depend not on the deposit-to-currency ratio of the public, which historically has been highly stable, but on the rather more variable ratio of deposits-to-vault-cash held by the banks (see Chart 8.2). If convertibility at 7.80 was made available to everyone who held HK$ banknotes and not just the banks, then the divergence between the free market rate for HK$ and the official parity would, allowing for transactions costs of different types of money, be minimal. Moreover, the volatility of short-term interest rates under a system of full convertibility would tend to be less than under present arrangements because adjustments to the money supply would be quicker, and therefore deviations away from an equilibrium level of the money supply would occur less frequently.

Summarising the argument so far, the benefits of the present system to the community as a whole far outweigh the costs of the technical defects of the system, which in turn suggests a prima facie case in favour of retaining the present system rather than introducing any changes.

Turning to the three principal proposals which have from time to time been made to change the linked rate system, aside from the general arguments cited above in favour of the new mechanism, there are objections in principle to each specific proposal, and hence good grounds for not adopting the proposed reform.

First, there are those who believe the linked rate mechanism should be abandoned and the Hong Kong currency should be allowed to float. Those who make this proposal do not appear to understand that the linked rate system was introduced not simply to deal with the crisis situation of September 1983, but also to deal with some of the deeper problems which had troubled Hong Kong's monetary system since the early 1970s. The immediate problem at the time of the currency panic in September 1983 was that the Hong Kong government could not counteract currency flight by tightening the money supply, raising interest rates, and attracting funds back to Hong Kong. This was symptomatic of the underlying problem of the lack of monetary control which had plagued the system during the decade of floating exchange rates (1974–1983). For example, in the period 1978–1981 Hong Kong suffered extremely rapid rates of bank credit expansion (over 60%) and money supply growth (over 40%). As a result property prices and rents spiralled, the currency weakened, and generalised inflation took a firm hold. Conversely in 1982 and 1983 money supply and bank credit growth slumped. The downturn in business activity, even before the Sino-British negotiations in Peking started, was very severe, and as a result there were numerous problems in the property sector, among the deposit-taking companies, among commodity traders and in other sectors of the economy.

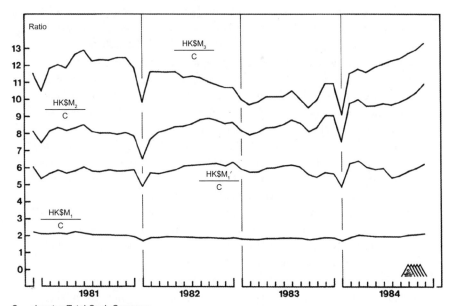

C   denotes Total Cash Currency
M_1' equals sum of Demand Deposits, savings deposits and cash held by public

Chart 8.1   The Monetary Multipliers

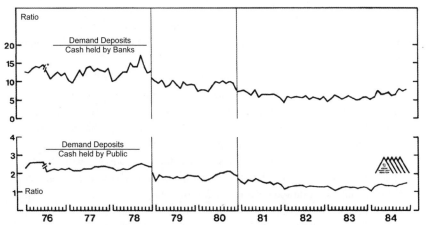

*   Deposits at 7 days notice or less previously included under demand deposits are now included under time deposits.

Chart 8.2   The Monetary Determinant Ratios (for HK$$M_1$)

PARTIAL CONVERTIBILITY VERSUS FULL CONVERTIBILITY

The linked rate system for the HK$ is similar in some respects to the classical gold standard mechanism, or to the silver standard mechanism which operated in Hong Kong until 1935. The essential feature of the gold and silver standard systems, and of the Hong Kong system, is the *convertibility* of the local currency unit (pounds, US dollars, or Hong Kong dollars) *into a fixed quantity* of gold, silver or — in the case of Hong Kong today — US dollars.

However, whereas under the old gold and silver standards the right of convertibility at the official parity was available to every holder of the local currency, under Hong Kong's present system it is only the banks which enjoy the right of convertibility at the official parity. In order to obtain new banknotes every non-note-issuing bank must pay to the note-issuing banks US$1.00 for every HK$7.80, and when redeeming banknotes each non-note-issuing bank will obtain US$ at the same rate. The two note-issuing banks, Hongkong and Shanghai Banking Corp. and the Chartered Bank, in turn must pay US$ at the same rate to the Exchange Fund to obtain Certificates of Indebtedness against which they are entitled to issue new banknotes, and these are again redeemable at the same rate. In this way the two note-issuing banks effectively act as agents for the Exchange Fund, enabling all banks to have access to convertibility at the official parity.

However, the man-in-the-street must deal at the best terms he can obtain from the banks, which typically involves some margin to cover banks' holding and handling costs, commission etc. Thus, for the man-in-the-street convertibility is partial and indirect; unlike the banks he cannot go to the government and obtain US$1.00 for his HK$7.80 or vice versa. The banks enjoy full convertibility; the public must make do with partial convertibility or convertibility at one remove.

How does this feature affect the operation of the convertible currency mechanism and, in particular, the process of monetary expansion and contraction?

First, it means that deviations of the free market rate for HK$/US$ from the official parity will tend to be greater than they would be if individuals had the right of access to the official 7.80 parity for banknotes. This is because, if everyone could obtain HK$7.80 per US$1.00, deviations of the free market rate would be limited to the transaction costs incurred by individuals having to (i) convert HK$ deposits to banknotes, (ii) take the banknotes to a teller's desk operated by the Exchange Fund, (iii) redeposit the US$ received, together with (iv) any costs due the inconvenience of holding US$ in place of HK$. Conversely, if all individuals had the right of convertibility of banknotes at the official 7.80 parity, no foreign exchange dealer at a bank or DTC or money changer's shop could set his prices for HK$/US$ outside the narrow limits implied by the transaction costs of steps (i)–(iv) above without losing business to those whose prices were more competitive. Of course the prices for cash, deposits and travellers' cheques would each be slightly different, reflecting their differential handling costs, but all would vary within the limits set by competition among dealers.

Second, in the event of a sudden shift in the balance of payments, e.g. due to a capital outflow, it seems probable that the free market rate for HK$/US$ would alter less under a system of full convertibility than under the present system of partial convertibility. Under the present system radical adverse shifts in the balance of payments cause the HK$/US$ rate to move sharply as buyers of US$ are willing to pay well in excess of HK$7.80 to be relieved of the risk of holding HK$. The only countervailing force — at least in the first instance — is the willingness of banks to buy HK$ deposit funds for their own account, then collect together HK$ banknotes and redeem these for US$ with the Exchange Fund, i.e. to conduct *cash arbitrage*. However, unless a bank has excess HK$ cash currency in relation to its desired deposit-to-vault-cash ratio it is taking a considerable risk in redeeming HK$ because it runs the risk of being caught short of HK$ cash with which to meet withdrawals of HK$ deposits. Yet until this redemption of notes occurs there is no contraction in the quantity of base money, and hence no pressure from this source for a reduction in the money supply.

Third, due to this impediment the system depends more on funds arbitrage than cash arbitrage. In the event of substantial sales of HK$ for US$ by the non-bank public there will be a shortage of spot HK$ funds in the interbank market, putting pressure on the clearing accounts of individual banks which will then be obliged to borrow short-term HK$ funds, forcing up interest rates. It is only at this stage, once HK$ interbank deposit interest rates have risen sharply, that the incentive for *funds arbitrage* (i.e. in this case borrowing US$ to lend in HK$) by banks or the non-bank public occurs. In other words, under the system of partial convertibility funds arbitrage may be delayed until after there has been a substantial sale of HK$ (i.e. a substantial external drain).

Under a system of full convertibility both the banks and the non-bank public could convert HK$ banknotes to US$ (and vice versa) at the official 7.80 parity. As explained above, full convertibility would greatly increase the competitive pressure on dealers to set rates close to the official parity. In addition, given a sudden adverse shift in the balance of payments which caused the HK$ to weaken (i.e. the HK$ price of US$ to rise), the process of cash arbitrage would start much sooner, raising the whole spectrum of deposit interest rates slightly, but provoking funds arbitrage transaction immediately. The public, as final wealth-holders, would find it advantageous to exploit any difference between the free market rate and the official parity, whereas banks, as intermediaries, will tend only to hold such HK$ banknotes as necessary to meet the needs of depositors and will seldom hold excess HK$ banknotes collectively unless there has been an unanticipated downward shift in the demand for HK$ deposits. (Even in this case banks may prefer to wait until they perceive the reduced demand for HK$ deposits to be permanent before redeeming their excess holdings of HK$ cash in order to adjust their deposit-to-vault-cash ratios down to their desired or optimal level.)

To summarise, under the system of partial convertibility the incentive for cash arbitrage by banks is relatively weak since there are many complex factors entering banks' profit maximisation function, whereas under a system of full convertibility the incentive for individuals to conduct cash arbitrage is relatively straightforward. Moreover, funds arbitrage under partial convertibility will only be stimulated once a substantial shortage of funds has developed in the interbank market, whereas under a system of full convertibility there need be no such delayed reaction. We may hypothesize that it is the shortcomings of the system of partial convertibility which account for the occasional sharp deviations of the free market rate away from the official parity. Theory suggests that such deviations would be considerably reduced under a system of full convertibility.

These extremes of boom and bust were largely a consequence of a monetary system in which the process of bank credit and money creation were independent of the process of external adjustment. Since the foreign exchange rate could adjust to the internal price level or the price level could adjust to the external foreign exchange rate, changes in the exchange rate or the domestic price level could be initiated independently. The exchange rate was vulnerable to sudden shifts in capital flows, whilst the growth of the money supply was mainly determined by the willingness of the banks to create new credit. The money supply, in short, was not subject to any external discipline.

The new currency arrangements of October 1983 make it very clear that in future Hong Kong's monetary growth will be closely linked to the performance of the balance of payments on current and capital account. Thus the linked rate system for the HK$ not only solved the problem of the panic in September 1983, but it also solved the underlying problem of monetary control in Hong Kong. This is a most important reason why the linked rate system should not be abandoned now.

A second proposal, which is sometimes made, is not that the *mechanism* should be changed, but that the *rate* against the US$ should be changed. At the time of the original announcement of the linked rate system on October 15th, 1983, the Financial Secretary said that he would not contemplate moving the rate downwards (i.e. devaluing), and this has been repeated subsequently. However, a common anxiety today is that the US$ might fall sharply, perhaps by 20% or 30% on a trade-weighted basis, and that under these circumstances the HK$ would effectively depreciate against most major currencies. A related fear is that this might set off inflation in Hong Kong.

There is little doubt that these anxieties are exaggerated. Moreover, so long as the US monetary authorities pursue sensible money growth policies there is no serious likelihood of a collapse of the US$ or of a serious outbreak of inflation in the US. Since Hong Kong's inflation rate is tied to the inflation rate in the USA through the linked rate system, even a fall in the external exchange rate of the US$ does not automatically spell inflation for Hong Kong. More importantly, if the HK$ were to be revalued, the sole effect would be a once-for-all change in Hong Kong's price *level* but, after a transitional period, Hong Kong would revert to the same inflation *rate* so long as the HK$ continued to be linked to the US$. (See Appendix 8.4, pp. 200–202.) In other words, a revaluation simply imposes significant adjustment costs on the economy for no permanent gain in the underlying inflation rate. Further, the success of the linked rate mechanism depends on the willingness of banks and others in the private sector to conduct cash arbitrage or funds arbitrage transactions which are predicated on their confidence that the official parity will be maintained. Once that confidence is jeopardised by shifting the rate, the viability of the mechanism will be undermined. Therefore a revaluation of this kind would be unwise and unhelpful.

The third and final proposal which has been made by several commentators is to link the HK$ to a basket of currencies, such as the SDR, or to some abstract index of other currencies, rather than simply to the US$. This is a proposal which has some *intellectual* merit, and indeed it is one which was advanced in Asian Monetary Monitor as far back as 1979. (See "Proposals for a Reform of the Hong Kong Monetary System" AMM, Mar.–Apr. 1979). However in the political and institutional circumstances of Hong Kong today, the proposal has some significant *practical* drawbacks.

First, the proposal is only applicable in a system where there is a central bank or monetary authority which sets the exchange rate and then actively intervenes to control the supply of base money so as to enforce its chosen rate. In Hong Kong's institutional framework where the monetary authority is a passive supplier of currency only, not bank reserves, linking the HK$ to a basket of currencies would require that the linked rate expressed in US$ be altered virtually on a daily basis, and this would not only be disruptive to the cash arbitrage process of the banks, but also conducive to unproductive speculation by the public. Fixing the currency to a basket of other currencies is feasible in a discretionary system with a central bank, but it is doubtful if it is appropriate in an automatic system which, like Hong Kong's, relies on private sector arbitrage for effective stabilization.

Second, and more important, given the way the linked rate system was set up (i.e. with partial convertibility rather than full convertibility) the mechanism depends more on interest rate or funds arbitrage than cash arbitrage. While funds arbitrage is straightforward when the currency is linked to one currency, it is a different matter when the currency is linked to a basket. Funds arbitrage under a fixed rate system is simple because it is easy to see when interest rate differentials between two countries arise, and, so long as people are convinced that the fixed parity will be maintained, there is ample incentive to move funds from one area to the other and thereby restore equality of interest rates in the two currency areas. However, under a basket arrangement where the local currency is not tied to any one single currency it is not clear what the equilibrium market interest rate in the domestic currency area should be, and therefore there will

THE INTEREST RATE AGREEMENT — WHO BENEFITS?

The Interest Rate Agreement (IRA) limits the interest rates payable on time and savings deposits under HK$500,000 (approx. US$64,000) at licensed banks in Hong Kong to rates set by the Hong Kong Association of Banks (HKAB). These rates are substantially below those offered to large depositors at free market rates. This means that some of the benefits of the linked rate system are denied to the small, retail depositors, though competition among the banks and the growth of personal incomes in Hong Kong can be expected gradually to erode the market share of deposits covered by the Interest Rate Agreement.

Arguments in favour of maintaining the Interest Rate Agreement are normally cast in terms of a barely disguised protectionism. The official view is that free competition for deposits would undermine the stability of the banking system by threatening the profitability of the smaller, local banks, and thereby ultimately harm depositors. In reality banks seldom fail because they bid competitively for depositors' funds; normally they fail on account of mistakes in lending policy, such as maturity mismatching or excessive concentration in one sector, or they fail due to mismanagement or fraud.

The official view makes too little of the benefits that would accrue to the economy as a whole from abolition of the Agreement. A distinction needs to be made between the desirability of some form of protection for depositors and the alleged need for "stability of the banking sector". There is a legitimate case for depositor protection through tighter prudential ratios, through stricter supervision, or through some form of compulsory insurance, but depositor protection should not extend to an officially sanctioned structural rigidity or protection of the status quo in the banking sector. Just as consumers have benefited from the recent (1984) price war and the resulting structural shake-out among the supermarkets in Hong Kong, depositors would benefit from more competitive deposit interest rates and some restructuring among the banks.

Abolition of the HKAB Interest Rate Agreement would oblige licensed banks' deposit interest rates to move towards their competitive, free market equilibrium levels. This would lead to greater financial intermediation between savers/depositors and investors/borrowers, increasing the incentives to save through higher returns to savers, and at the same time raising the average efficiency of investment. This is because higher real rates would deter borrowers with low-yielding investment projects. Since savings are suboptimal when interest rates are artificially restricted, these benefits would be enhanced if interest rates were allowed to rise to free market equilibrium levels.

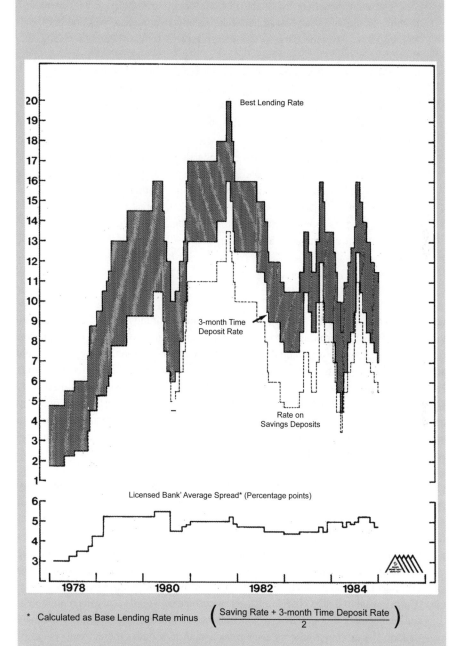

Chart 8.3   Bank Spreads under the Interest Rate Agreement

The main beneficiaries of the IRA are bank shareholders who benefit from the artificially wide spread between retail deposit interest rates and bank lending rates. Accurate data on the overall cost of funds to banks in Hong Kong and average lending rates are not available, but an indication of the spread due to the IRA is the difference between the HSBC's Best Lending Rate and an average of the Savings Deposit Rate and the rate on 3-month Time Deposits, both of which are set by the Interest Rate Agreement (see Chart 8.3). Over the period 1978–84 this spread has averaged 4.69 percentage points on a time-weighted basis.

Supposing HK$ deposits subject to the IRA amount to HK$90 billion — i.e. all of the savings deposits and half of the time deposits at banks in HK$ — reduction of the banks' spread by one percentage point would benefit depositors by HK$900 million, and in addition the increased pressure on banks' margins would compel an improvement in the allocation of bank resources to the advantage of all bank customers.

be greater hesitation on the part of arbitrageurs to borrow funds in one centre and lend to another. (Basically arbitrageurs in this position are taking on both an exchange rate risk and an interest rate differential risk.) Thus moving to a basket arrangement would actually inhibit the funds arbitrage process, whereas to maximise the efficiency of Hong Kong's linked rate system the arbitrage process needs to be enhanced, not limited.

In conclusion, it should be clear that Hong Kong's linked rate system is not perfect, and as suggested it could be improved by moving from a system of partial convertibility to a system of full convertibility. However, it would not be improved by any of the three specific proposals examined above.

To summarise:

(1) The proposal to return to a floating exchange rate implies abandoning monetary control, and it would also expose the HK$ to a possible repetition of the crisis of September 1983.

(2) The proposal to revalue the exchange rate against the US$ implies the imposition of adjustment costs in exchange for no permanent benefit, and by undermining confidence in the fixed parity it would undermine the future operation of the arbitrage process on which the automatic adjustment mechanism depends.

(3) The proposal to fix the HK$ to a basket of currencies would satisfy the requirement for monetary control, but it would undermine the operation of the system by making the arbitrage process even weaker than it is under the current system of partial convertibility.

In the absence of other serious proposals, therefore, it follows that the linked rate system for the HK$ would be best retained both in its present from (i.e. linked solely to the US$) and at the present rate of HK$7.80.

APPENDIX 8.1

Simple Analytics of the HK$/US$ Linked Rate System

Under the linked rate system the *price* of money is controlled, not the quantity.

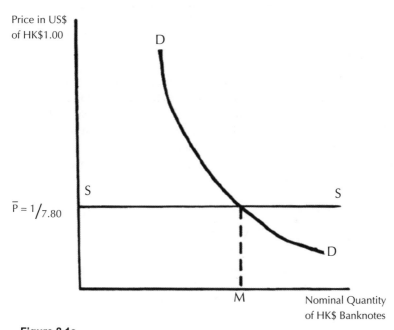

Figure 8.1a

Under the linked rate system for the HK$ the price of HK$ banknotes is set at US$1.00 = HK$7.8 or HK$1.00 = US$1/7.80 (= 12.8205 cents) on the vertical axis, shown by the horizontal supply curve, SS. The perfectly elastic supply curve reflects the willingness of the Hong Kong authorities to issue or redeem any number of Certificates of Indebtedness (equivalent to HK$ banknotes) at the fixed price in US$. The quantity of HK$ banknotes demanded depends on the slope and position of the demand for HK$ banknotes, DD. The intersection of SS and DD gives the nominal quantity of HK$ banknotes demanded, M. Since banknotes are convertible into HK$ deposits and vice-versa the price of deposit money in US$ cannot deviate far from the official parity for banknotes.

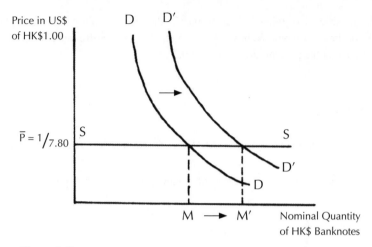

Figure 8.1b

Under the linked rate system for the HK$, changes in the quantity of money result from shifts in the demand for money. Since the Hong Kong authorities supply HK$ banknotes passively at the fixed price of HK$1 = US$1/7.80, if demand shifts to the right (DD to D'D') the quantity of banknotes demanded will increase from M to M'. Such increases in the money supply could continue so long as they were consistent with equilibrium in Hong Kong's overall international balance of payments (i.e. on combined current and capital account).

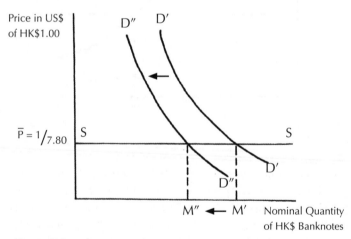

Figure 8.1c

Alternatively, if the demand for the HK$ banknotes declines (shifts to the left) from D'D' to D"D", the quantity of HK$ banknotes falls from M' to M". (The mechanism for this kind of contraction is explained in Chapter 7, pp. 174–175.) As long as the exchange rate is fixed, the money supply and the internal price level will adjust automatically until there is equilibrium in the balance of payments at the fixed exchange rate.

APPENDIX 8.2

Simple Analytics of Monetary Base Control

Under monetary base control the quantity of base money is controlled, not the price.

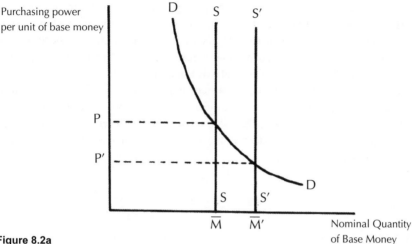

Figure 8.2a

Increasing the quantity of base money from $\overline{M}$ to $\overline{M}'$ with the demand for money DD unchanged reduces the purchasing power (or value or foreign exchange price) of each nominal unit of money from P to P'. Conversely, reducing the quantity of base money from $\overline{M}'$ to $\overline{M}$ with demand DD unchanged raises the purchasing power of each nominal unit of base money from P' to P.

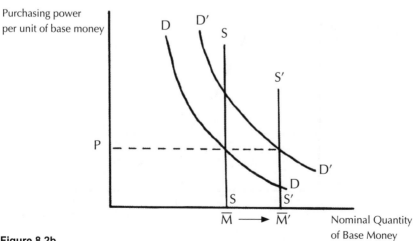

Figure 8.2b

As productivity increases and real incomes rise, the demand for money also increases. Hence in a conventional monetary system with a central bank which can control the money supply (or base money) at its own discretion, the monetary authorities deliberately adjust the quantity of money in response to shifts in money demand, usually aiming to keep the purchasing power of money (measured in terms of the domestic price level or as the external exchange rate) roughly stable. For example, in Chart 8.2b, with demand DD, the quantity supplied is $\overline{M}$. Now suppose the demand for money increases (shifts to the right) to D'D' over the next twelve months. The central bank will try to anticipate the increase in demand for money over the year by steadily increasing the quantity of money to $\overline{M}'$, at which level the purchasing power of money (i.e. price level or exchange rate) P, shown on the vertical axis is unchanged.

Under the linked rate system the monetary authority only supplies part of the total money supply — namely, base money. However, as long as deposit money is convertible into base money and vice-versa, the value or purchasing power of each unit of the monetary base and each unit of deposit money should tend to equality under currency board or central bank systems.

APPENDIX 8.3

The Effect of Floating the HK$

Since Hong Kong has no central bank to control the *quantity* of base money, abandoning the linked rate system and refloating the Hong Kong dollar would imply moving to a system in which neither the price nor the quantity of Hong Kong dollars was controlled.

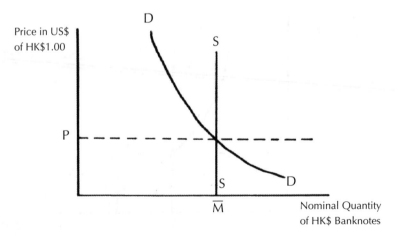

Figure 8.3a

If the official 7.80 parity for HK$ banknotes were to be abolished and the currency were to be floated the quantity of money supplied need no longer be consistent with equilibrium in the international balance of payments at 7.80 (as in Figures 8.1b and 8.1c). Assuming the Hong Kong authorities continued to allow HK$ banknotes to be issued passively, the demand for banknotes would be dependent upon the amount the public and the banks chose to hold in relation to the volume of deposits. Deposits in turn are related to the amount of bank credit, and therefore the proximate determinant of the money supply would be the interest rate set by the banks' interest rate cartel. But there is no intrinsic reason why the banks should set interest rates at a level consistent with balance of payments equilibrium.

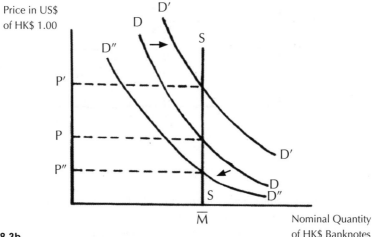

Figure 8.3b

Now assume the money supply is fixed in the short term ($\overline{M}$). Supposing there was a sudden shift in the demand for HK$ due to a change in perceptions about the political future of Hong Kong, or due to other factors, how would the exchange rate behave?

With a rightward shift in the demand for HK$ from DD to D'D', there would be an upward movement in the purchasing power of the HK$, and also in the exchange rate from P to P'. Conversely, in the event of a leftward shift in the demand for HK$ to D"D" the purchasing power and/or exchange rate would depreciate to P". This is essentially what happened in the HK$ currency crisis of September 1983. Thus refloating the Hong Kong currency without first establishing a central bank to control the quantity of base money would mean that, even with no change in the quantity of money, the HK$ would become vulnerable to the kind of sharp depreciation which occurred in September 1983.

APPENDIX 8.4

Effects of a Revaluation of the HK$ under the Linked Rate Mechanism

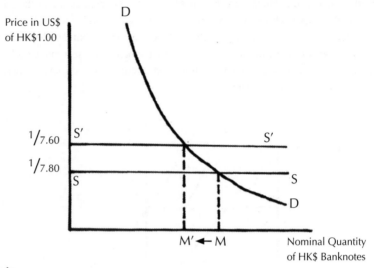

Figure 8.4a

Figure 8.4a shows the adjustment of the quantity of HK$ to an upward revaluation of the supply price of HK$ from HK$7.80 to HK$7.60 per US$ (or a change in the US$ price of HK$1.00 from US$1/7.80 to US$1/7.60). The supply of money, SS, shifts to S'S', but the supply curve is still horizontal (i.e. perfectly elastic) at the new exchange rate (7.60). The money supply, M, adjusts downwards to M' (moving to the left on the horizontal axis), reflecting a movement along the demand curve for money (DD).

Figure 8.4b shows the effect of the revaluation on the real value of each nominal unit of HK$ money (or its equivalent, the inverse of the overall price level). Since the money supply shifts from M to M', the value of a nominal unit of money increases from A to B, i.e. the price level declines. This is a once-for-all change in response to the revaluation, but it tells us nothing about how the price level in Hong Kong behaves over a long period in relation to prices in the USA. For that we must turn to Figures 8.4c and 8.4d.

All figures so far have been confined to static analysis. In Figures 8.4c and 8.4d we introduce time on the horizontal axis, and the analysis shifts to dynamics.

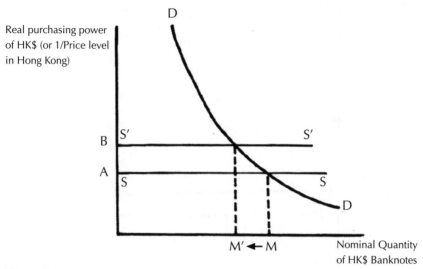

Figure 8.4b

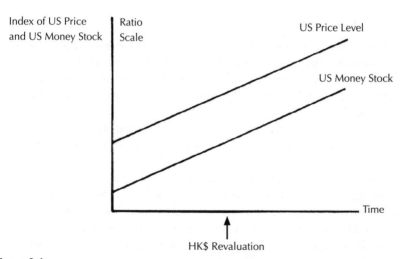

Figure 8.4c

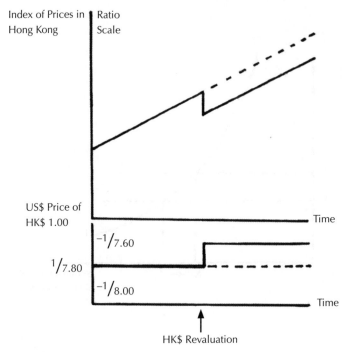

Figure 8.4d

The US money stock is assumed to be rising at a constant rate, and prices in the US are also assumed to be rising at a constant rate, i.e. the US economy is in a steady-state equilibrium (Figure 8.4c). At a certain point in time the HK$ is revalued, but there is no change in the rate of US monetary growth and accordingly no change in the rate of inflation in the US.

In Hong Kong prices are rising at a constant rate roughly equal to the rate of increase of prices in the USA prior to the revaluation of the HK$. Upon revaluation the price level in Hong Kong (which is the inverse of the purchasing power of the HK$) makes a once-for-all downward shift, consistent with that in Figures 8.4a and 8.4b.

However, since Hong Kong's international payments must balance at a price level which is consistent with US prices at the new exchange rate of 7.60, Hong Kong's money supply must adjust in future to keep Hong Kong prices in line with US prices as before. Therefore, following the once-for-all correction (which may in practice be spread over some transitional period of time), Hong Kong prices start to rise again in line with US prices at the same rate as previously (Figure 8.4d).

CHAPTER 9

ADJUSTING TO THE LINK

July–August 1985

This article, written two years after the linked rate had been established, attempted to provide an overview of how the economy was adjusting to the new framework. Section 1 addresses the adjustment of prices in Hong Kong relative to prices in the US and the OECD as a whole. Section 1 makes the claim that within about 18 months most of the price adjustment to the new exchange rate had been achieved. Interestingly, in view of the divergence of CPI inflation in Hong Kong and the US that came later, the discussion omits any mention of the Balassa-Samuelson effect, the proposition that, in an economy where productivity is rising more rapidly than in the economy to whose currency it is pegged, non-traded goods and service prices can rise more rapidly than in the anchor currency country without the economy losing competitiveness. This phenomenon had operated in Japan between 1949 and 1971 while the yen was pegged to the US dollar (see Chapter 4, pp. 83–89), and in Hong Kong in the 1950s and 1960s. To the extent that China keeps its currency on a fixed or quasi-fixed exchange rate vis-à-vis the US$ today, it would be applicable to a comparison of prices in China with prices in the US.

Section 2 discusses the how Hong Kong's balance of payments was adjusting (based on rather little data), but it makes the politically controversial point that larger current account surpluses in the wake of the currency stabilization were almost certainly accompanied by greater capital outflows. Section 3 discusses changes in the money markets, specifically how and to what degree interest rates in Hong Kong and the US were converging. Finally section 4 discusses the increases in the money multipliers as a result of the increase in confidence following the stabilisation of the currency in October 1983.

At this stage there is a general sense that the currency board mechanism is settling down well and performing to expectation. Three years later (by 1988) this sense of satisfaction was starting to be eroded, and was replaced with a growing sense that the system was not quite working properly.

A S I A N   M O N E T A R Y   M O N I T O R
Vol. 9   No. 4   July–August 1985

Following the switch in Hong Kong's monetary system from a floating exchange rate to a fixed exchange mechanism in October 1983, major changes have occurred in the behaviour of a whole range of nominal economic indicators. To review those changes this article considers the adjustment of Hong Kong's economy to the new US dollar linked exchange rate in four areas: the adjustment of domestic prices to prices in the USA, the changes in Hong Kong's external balance of payments, developments in Hong Kong's credit and capital markets, and how the monetary multipliers which affect the behaviour of the Hong Kong dollar money supply have moved since October 1983.

1. ADJUSTMENT OF THE DOMESTIC PRICE LEVEL TO US PRICES

The linking of the Hong Kong dollar to the US dollar at an official parity of HK$7.80 = US$1.00 for banknotes fixes the value of money in Hong Kong in two complementary ways. First, it sets the external purchasing power of the Hong Kong currency. The free market exchange rate for the US$ in Hong Kong fluctuates in a narrow range around HK$7.80, so that the external purchasing power of the Hong Kong currency remains very stable in relation to the US$. Of course the value of the US$ may fluctuate against other currencies, and the value of the Hong Kong dollar will alter accordingly. (In just the same way, the value of all silver standard currencies altered in value in relation to gold standard currencies when the world operated with two metallic standards.) Second, and more importantly, the linked rate system ties the domestic purchasing power of the Hong Kong dollar to the domestic purchasing power of the US dollar. Domestic purchasing power means the average purchasing power of a unit of currency spread over all goods and services. A measure of the current price of all goods and services is provided by the price index for the GDP, or the GDP deflator. The purchasing power of the currency is therefore equivalent to the inverse of the overall price level so that as domestic prices rise the general purchasing power of the currency falls, and as domestic prices fall the general purchasing power of the currency rises.

In Hong Kong the gross domestic product (GDP) and its deflator are calculated only annually and one must make do with a consumer price index for measurements over shorter periods. Consumer spending accounts for about 65% of Hong Kong's GDP, so the CPI is the closest proxy for the GDP deflator. From the argument above it follows that, under the linked rate system for the HK$, the level of consumer prices in Hong Kong should move roughly in line with the level of consumer prices in the USA over time, allowing for differences in the composition of the US and Hong Kong indices. Chart 9.1 shows what has happened to relative prices in Hong Kong and the USA in the last three and a half years under the floating exchange rate and in the period since the introduction of the linked rate system for the HK$ in October 1983. As shown in the

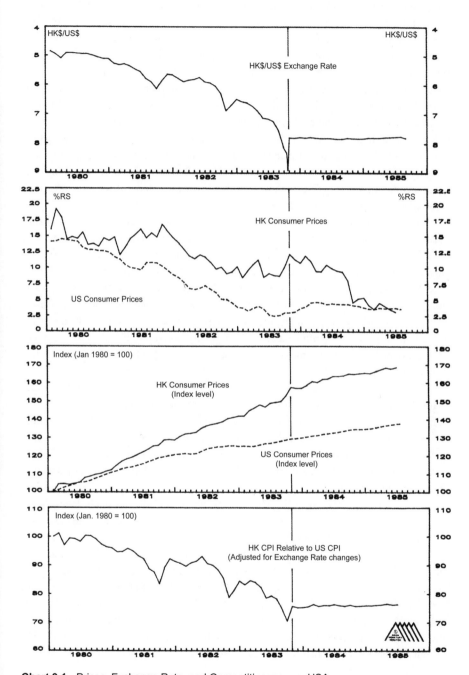

Chart 9.1 Prices, Exchange Rate, and Competitiveness vs. USA

top panel, the Hong Kong dollar depreciated steadily from around HK$5 = US$1.00 to around HK$6 in mid-1982, whereupon, following Mrs. Thatcher's visit to Peking in September 1982 the Hong Kong dollar plunged, recovered temporarily, and then fell at an accclerating pace until September 1983. Since Hong Kong's imports amount to somewhere around 80–90% of GDP, the translation of import prices into the general consumer price level is very rapid. Thus instead of rising more slowly as US prices did in 1981–82, Hong Kong prices continued to rise at double-digit rates through mid-1982, as illustrated in the second panel of Chart 9.1, reflecting the continued rapid rise of the index level in the third panel of the same chart. Adjusting Hong Kong's higher rate of price rise for changes in the exchange rate against the US$, it is nevertheless clear that the depreciation in the exchange rate up to mid-1982 was sufficient to maintain Hong Kong's competitiveness. This is shown by the downward slope of the exchange rate-adjusted relative price line in the bottom panel.

Once the linked rate was introduced in October 1983, however, a dramatic change occurred in all three measures. The year-on-year rate of change remained around 10% until October 1984, but then as the effect of pre-October 1983 price increases was removed the year-to-year change declined steeply, so that between September 1984 and June 1985 the average year-on-year increase for the three consumer price indices in Hong Kong fell from 8.0% to just 3.1%. It is evident that the level of prices (in the third panel) stabilised very quickly after the pegging or fixing of the Hong Kong dollar. In the bottom panel this is illustrated by the virtually horizontal line for relative prices since October 1983 i.e. consumer prices in Hong Kong and the USA have moved in line together since October 1983.

Chart 9.2 shows the same set of comparisons but this time for Hong Kong prices relative to the average level of prices or inflation in the OECD. Here again prices in Hong Kong generally rose faster than prices in OECD countries (see the two middle panels), but this was offset by the depreciation of the Hong Kong dollar against a basket of other currencies (top panel), meaning that on average the competitiveness of Hong Kong was not much affected until mid-1982 (bottom panel) when the currency began to slide much more rapidly.

The sharp depreciation of the Hong Kong dollar in 1982–83 made Hong Kong much more competitive than its main trading partners, and helped to stimulate the export led boom of 1983–84. Allowing for Hong Kong's higher rate of inflation the gain in competitiveness between 1982 Q3 and 1983 Q3 was about 16%. Once the currency had been linked to the US$, however, Hong Kong's competitiveness became subject to the level of the US$, and as the US$ appreciated through 1984 and up to March 1985 Hong Kong lost the competitive edge it had gained through currency depreciation in 1982–83. In the period January–June 1985 the index of Hong Kong's competitiveness relative to OECD countries averaged 95.2, up some 17.8% from its level of 80.8 in October 1983, and only some 3% lower than its average level of 98.3 in the period January 1980 to September 1982.

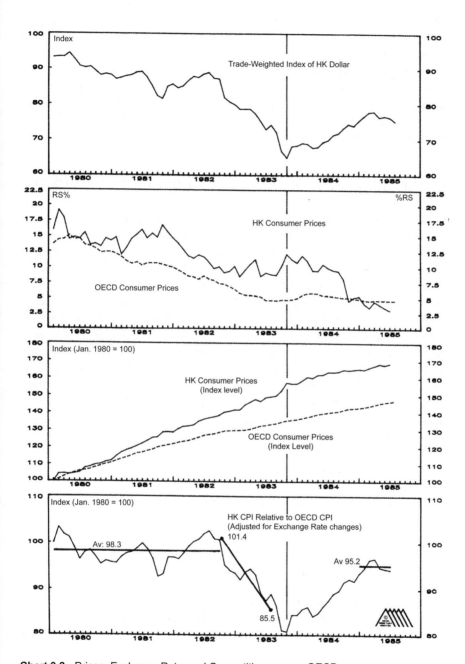

Chart 9.2 Prices, Exchange Rate, and Competitiveness vs. OECD

To summarise, Hong Kong's adjustment in terms of its domestic price level to the new linked exchange rate system appears to have been largely completed by early 1985. On a bilateral basis vis-a-vis the USA the year-to-year increase in consumer prices in Hong Kong had fallen below the equivalent measure for the USA, and the level of prices in Hong Kong was moving almost exactly in line with prices in the US as one would expect from the theory of purchasing power parity; and on a multilateral basis, comparing Hong Kong with other countries in the OECD, the temporary gains in competitiveness due to the sudden depreciation of the Hong Kong dollar in 1982–83 had been almost entirely given up by early 1985.

2.   THE ADJUSTMENT OF THE EXTERNAL BALANCE OF PAYMENTS

Another aspect of the adjustment of the Hong Kong economy to the linked rate system concerns the changes in Hong Kong's overall balance of payments. As shown in Chart 9.3 which covers the period 1975–1984, the traditional pattern for Hong Kong's external transactions is that the territory operated a balance of trade deficit which was partially offset by a generally positive balance on the remainder of the current account, with the result that the general shape of the current balance (in the second panel) resembles that of the trade balance. Unfortunately the measured current account balance for Hong Kong is not a complete statement corresponding to the generally accepted definition of the current account since several financial transaction components are excluded (viz. net interest and dividend receipts or payments of residents, and net transfers). In the absence of these data one can only say that since net official and private capital flows together must balance the current account, the implied capital flows (inclusive of the items omitted from the measured current balance) must be whatever is necessary to achieve equilibrium in the overall balance of payments. The basic equation is:

> Current Balance + Capital Balance = 0

or,

> (Visible Trade Balance + Invisible Balance + Transfers) +
> (Official and Private Capital Balance) = 0

The measured components for Hong Kong are:
> Visible Trade Balance + Certain Services = "Current Balance"

The components which are not measured are:
> Private and Official Capital Balance + Transfers + Other Invisibles
> = "Implied Capital Balance"

As shown in Chart 9.3, there was a dramatic improvement in Hong Kong's trade and measured "current" balance in 1984, resulting in a measured surplus of HK$12 billion on "current" account. The counterpart of the current surplus, however, must have been an equivalent negative figure on capital account, shown in Chart 9.3 in the Implied Capital Balance.

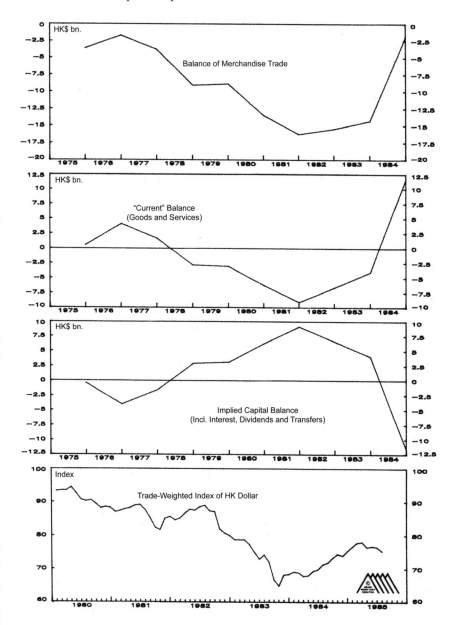

Chart 9.3 Balance of Payments

During late 1982 and through to September 1983 there was almost certainly a net capital outflow from Hong Kong-residents. After the linking of the Hong Kong dollar to the US$ in October 1983, some residents would have repatriated funds held overseas partly because of a return of confidence, and partly because of the high real interest rates newly available on Hong Kong dollars due to the linked rate system. Once the Sino-British Agreement on the future of Hong Kong was announced and initialed in September 1984, there was probably some further repatriation of funds by residents, and non-residents also began to move funds back into Hong Kong. However, it would be entirely rational for residents to wish to export capital from Hong Kong while non-residents might simultaneously wish to increase their investments in Hong Kong. The overall capital flow would depend upon the net balance between residents and non-residents.

Supposing Hong Kong residents (including corporate entities, government etc.) saved 15% of their gross income, or 15% of GDP i.e. about HK$37.5 billion in 1984 (this represents about HK$6,800 per capita). If 5% of gross incomes were placed overseas as an insurance policy or as some kind of nest-egg for future consumption, i.e. about HK$12.5 billion p.a., what would happen to investment In Hong Kong? On the surface it would appear to fall from HK$37.5 billion to around HK$25 billion, but the actual final figure will depend on the net inflows from non-residents. As direct investment in Hong Kong in 1984 amounted to some HK$11.5 billion, it seems reasonable to assume that the inflow for portfolio investment and in the form of bank loans etc. could be substantially greater. As a rough estimate, therefore, the estimate of a reduction in the overall capital inflows in 1983 and a shift to a net capital outflow in 1984 as shown in Chart 9.3 is by no means inconceivable. There has clearly been a radical shift in Hong Kong's trade and current accounts as measured; the counterpart to these shifts on current account suggests a reduction in the capital inflow, and perhaps even an overall capital outflow. This follows from the simple arithmetic of the balance of payments: the greater the surpluses on current account, the greater must be the deficits on capital account.

3.   THE ADJUSTMENT OF HONG KONG'S CREDIT AND CAPITAL MARKETS

Under the floating exchange rate regime in Hong Kong between November 1974 and October 1983, the level of interest rates in Hong Kong was, to a significant degree, independent of interest rates overseas. With the implementation of the linked exchange rate system for the Hong Kong dollar, the Hong Kong currency became effectively unified with the US dollar, being defined as a different denomination of the US currency. In the same way the Hong Kong credit markets are now in effect an extension of the US credit market in the sense that Hong Kong borrowers and lenders can select from the available opportunities offered by both markets while taking very little exchange risk. If borrowers find it cheaper to borrow in Hong Kong dollars and lenders find it more profitable to lend in US dollars, these differences will in the theory be exploited until the difference between the two markets is reduced to little more than the transaction cost of moving funds from one market to the other.

In practice the cost of credit (or the returns available on loanable funds) in the US dollar market differs substantially from rates available in the short term market in Hong Kong. This is partly because the two currencies are not viewed as perfect substitutes and therefore the costs of switching between the two are in reality quite high. For example in Hong Kong there is no facility for clearing US dollar cheques, and therefore local banks do not offer US$ demand deposits with facilities for writing cheques drawn in Hong Kong. The US dollar cannot be used as a true transactions medium in Hong Kong; it can only be used as a store of value in the form of a savings or other term deposit. For the large-sized firm or other institutional depositors who may maintain US$ checking accounts in New York or elsewhere switching between the two currencies to find the better yield may not be very costly, but for the ordinary individual the cost in terms of liquidity foregone is substantial.

Also, the equalisation of interest rates in the two currencies requires that the money supply in Hong Kong adjusts to the equilibrium size appropriate to interest rate parity. However, the linked rate system was set up in such a way that only the banks are able to exchange HK$ banknotes for US dollars at the official rate with the Exchange Fund. As explained in a previous issue of AMM, banks have limited incentive to conduct these cash arbitrage transactions because their demand for cash is a derivative demand: to satisfy the need to meet withdrawals of deposits. The level of deposits in turn is not rapidly altered when, for example, depositors want to shift from Hong Kong dollars to US dollars because for every seller of Hong Kong dollars there must be a buyer of Hong Kong dollars. This means that in the event of an external drain (i.e. a demand for foreign currency as opposed to a demand for domestic cash currency) the pressure for contraction of the money supply and hence the adjustment of interest rates is much weaker than it would be if private individuals or firms were able to redeem Hong Kong currency directly at the Exchange Fund's official parity.

In short, due to the system of partial rather than full convertibility (i.e. only banks having the right of access to the Exchange Fund's official rate, not all individuals), the adjustments to Hong Kong's money supply are slower and more imperfect than they should be. Hence, supposing the demand for credit in Hong Kong is weaker than in the US, the supply of loanable funds in Hong Kong is not reduced as quickly as it should be to restore interest rate equality between the two markets. For this reason Hong Kong's interest rates can and do continue to diverge from US levels for sustained periods. Nevertheless, the mechanism does appear to work sufficiently well that the general tendency is for Hong Kong interest rates to fluctuate around US interest rates of equivalent term over periods of a few months, as illustrated in Chart 9.4. This conclusion is necessarily tentative and may need modification after a longer trial of the linked rate system.

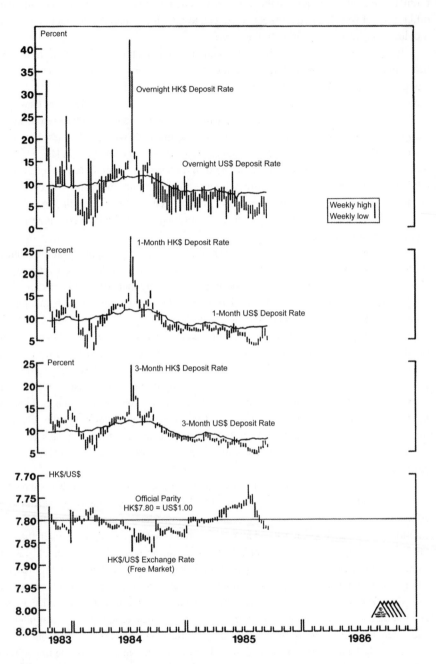

Chart 9.4   HK\$–US\$ Interest Rate Differentials and Foreign Exchange Rate vs. Official Parity

One development in Hong Kong's credit or capital markets which deserves mention here is the recent evolution of a long-term fixed interest market, which is a direct result of the linked exchange rate mechanism. Prior to the linked rate system there was no real standard of reference for long term borrowers in Hong Kong, and the only debt issues in this area were government or government-guaranteed corporations. Since these issues were occasional and spasmodic at best there was no choice of maturities available to the investor, and no meaningful yield curve existed. With the implementation of the linked rate system borrowers have for the first time been able to use yield curves from the US market as a standard of reference, and during the period January to August 1985 there have accordingly been a series of long term debt issues amounting to HK$2.9 billion, marking a major new development of the Hong Kong capital market.

4. BEHAVIOUR OF THE MONETARY MULTIPLIERS

Under the linked rate mechanism for the Hong Kong dollar, the price of each nominal unit of Hong Kong currency is set by the authorities. The quantity of base money is, however, free to vary according to the amount demanded at that price by the banks and by the non-bank public. Since banks in Hong Kong do not hold reserve deposits with the monetary authorities, the quantity of base money is quite simply the amount of banknotes and subsidiary coin in the hands of the banks and the non-bank public, or the total currency issued. The total quantity of money, defined as deposits and currency in the hands of the non-bank public, is related to the total currency by a ratio known as the monetary multiplier.

$$M = m.C \text{ and } m = M/C$$

where M is the money supply, m is the multiplier, and C is the total currency issued.

Chart 9.5 shows the monetary multiplier for various definitions of the Hong Kong dollar money supply. The multiplier for HK\$M$_1$ has been very steady over the period since 1981, showing only fractional declines around January/February each year, associated with the conversion of deposits to currency at Chinese New Year. Other multipliers for wider definitions of money show the downward spike much more strongly than the multiplier for HK\$M$_1$, implying a greater proportionate drawing down of savings and time deposit accounts for conversion to cash at this time of year. In most years the Chinese New Year phenomenon shows up as a sharp downward spike in January or February. In 1983 the decline was spread over January, February and March as a rounded curve. Later in the same year there was another decline associated with the currency crisis of August–October. Probably there was both a reduction in the quantity of Hong Kong dollar deposits as the capital flight gained momentum, and some hoarding of currency out of concern that if the crisis were prolonged banks could well be closed whereas payments could still be made with cash currency. Immediately after the linking of the Hong Kong dollar to the US dollar there was a recovery in the multipliers, suggesting that such precautions were rapidly reversed as people returned to their previous modes of behaviour.

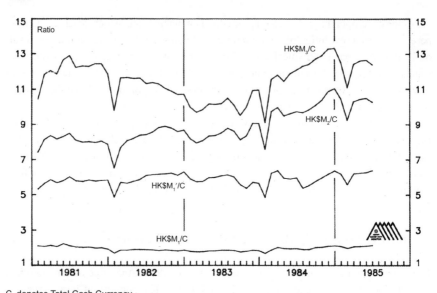

C denotes Total Cash Currency
HK$M₁′ equals sum of HK$ components of Demand Deposits, Savings Deposits and Cash held by public

Chart 9.5   The Monetary Multipliers

However it seems clear that multipliers for HKM_2$ and HKM_3$ have risen in the aftermath of the linking of the Hong Kong dollar to the US dollar. Once confidence in the stability of the local currency was restored, there was a resurgence in the general willingness to hold Hong Kong dollar assets, including deposits, whereas the need for cash for transactions purposes did not alter significantly. This could account for some rise in the HKM_2$ and HKM_3$ multipliers, but one is bound to ask why the multipliers for HKM_1$ and HKM_1$′ have not risen as much. An obvious explanation is that since the introduction of the linked rate scheme, money market deposit interest rates, particularly on large time deposits, and on deposits at deposit taking companies (in HKM_2$ and HKM_3$ respectively) have been higher in real terms than under the floating rate system for the Hong Kong dollar. This alone has provided an incentive to hold a greater relative quantity of such deposits relative to holdings of cash currency. On the other hand, demand deposits in HKM_1$ are non-interest bearing, and have remained so subsequent to the introduction of the linked rate system so that there has been no new or additional incentive to hold more demand deposits relative to currency. The savings deposits included in HKM_1$′, however, are largely retail and subject to the deposit interest rate agreement of the Hong Kong Association of Banks, an arrangement which results in lower rates for small depositors than they would obtain under a free market mechanism. Thus although even the level of real rates on savings deposits has been generally more favourable than under the old regime, nevertheless the increase has not been sufficient to raise the HKM_1$′/C ratio nearly as much as the broader ratios. This is clear evidence that the interest rate agreement discriminates against small depositors.

The rise in the HKM_2$ multiplier can be broken down into two contributing elements: a rise in the deposit-to-cash ratio of the non-bank public, and a rise in the banks' deposit-to-cash ratio, as shown in Chart 9.6. The rise in the ratio of deposits-to-cash held by the non bank public almost certainly reflects the same two phenomena mentioned earlier — the renewed willingness of the non bank public to hold HK$-denominated claims on the banks following the pegging of the Hong Kong dollar to the US dollar, and the attraction of Hong Kong dollar time deposits paying positive real rates of interest on a consistent basis in line with US dollar deposits following the implementation of the linked rate system. The rise in the deposit-to-cash ratio of the banks since October 1983 reflects the same phenomena, the key point being that banks need to hold smaller amounts of cash against time deposits than against demand deposits, and this has allowed their overall deposit-to-cash ratio to rise.

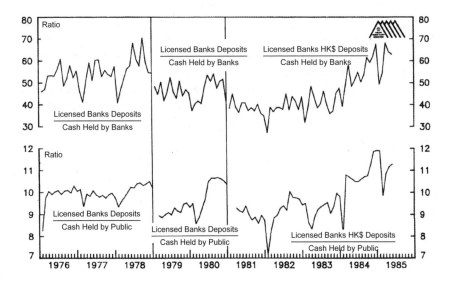

Chart 9.6 Monetary Determinant Ratios (for HKM_2$)

FORECAST

Hong Kong's domestic prices have now adjusted under the linked rate system to price levels prevailing in the US in the sense of attaining levels which are compatible with equilibrium in the balance of payments. In future the overall price level in Hong Kong will fluctuate around the price level in the US, keeping Hong Kong's economy roughly competitive with the US at the given exchange rate. Differences in inflation rates will surely emerge over the short to medium term, but over time these will be small (where they are not due to different composition of the indices under comparison). A dramatic illustration of the reduction in Hong Kong's inflation rate will be a sharp deceleration in the GDP deflator from 9.8% in 1982 to perhaps 5% in 1985. On the balance of payments front Hong Kong may continue to enjoy trade and current account surpluses, but this should be interpreted cautiously since the counterpart of a large current account surplus must be a net capital outflow.

Interest rates in Hong Kong's credit markets continue to diverge from the levels of equivalent maturity instruments in the US dollar markets. The reason is that the cost of switching from Hong Kong dollars to US dollars while retaining the same degree of liquidity is substantial for small sums. Another factor keeping Hong Kong dollar and US dollar interest rates apart is the restriction on convertibility at the official parity to the licensed banks only, which results in very limited cash arbitrage transactions and hence a slow adjustment of Hong Kong's money supply to its equilibrium level. These divergences must be expected to continue, even in the absence of political shocks, as long as the mechanism is maintained in its current form.

Finally the implementation of the linked rate system has resulted in some predictable changes for Hong Kong's monetary multipliers. Over time the multipliers for the broad aggregates can be expected to rise as Hong Kong people increase their holdings of interest bearing financial assets relative to cash currency, while the multipliers for the narrower aggregates should remain roughly constant unless there are technological changes which radically affect the amount of cash which banks or the non-bank public need to hold in relation to transactions-type deposits.

CHAPTER **10**

NEGATIVE INTEREST RATES
A Comparison of the Hong Kong and Swiss Schemes
January–February 1988

It was not only the contributors to AMM who worried about the performance of the restored currency board mechanism. The authorities were clearly troubled by some elements of the new system. Although broader performance measures of the economy such as economic growth and inflation were satisfactory, in the foreign exchange market the system was not producing an exchange rate that was either stable enough or close enough to the official HK$7.80 parity to be able to leave things entirely to market forces.

In 1986–87, partly due to the variability of the spot rate for the HK$/US$ relative to the official parity, and partly due to persistent weakness of the US$, there were periodic, unsettling speculative flows into Hong Kong in anticipation of a possible upward revaluation of the currency. One response of the authorities was to prepare legislation that would deter such inflows by imposing negative interest rates — effectively charging customers for maintaining large HK$ deposits. In fact the measures were never implemented, but the fact that such legislation was put in place shows that the authorities were not prepared to take the risk that increasingly large inflows of capital could be dealt with by means of automatic adjustment via market forces. The mechanism needed supplementing.

Two aspects of the negative interest rates scheme are interesting. First, the Swiss authorities had imposed a similar scheme when the Swiss franc had been under upward pressure in 1977–78, so AMM's comparison of the two schemes is useful. It would appear from these two cases that small, open economies with sound monetary arrangements are vulnerable to unwelcome speculative inflows whenever the currency to which they are pegged experiences a prolonged episode of weakness. The implication is that there must be enough flexibility in the smaller economy to absorb such pressures if the inflows are not to be permanently disruptive. Second, this was an interim attempt to deal with some of the side-effects of speculative pressure on the HK$ before the introduction of the new "accounting arrangements" in July 1988 that gave the authorities more direct control over the money markets and more influence on the spot rate (whether it was stronger or weaker than the parity). As with some of the other steps along the way towards the 1998 reforms, the negative interest rate scheme was significant but ultimately of second-order importance in the restoration of credibility in Hong Kong's currency board.

A S I A N   M O N E T A R Y   M O N I T O R
Vol. 12   No. 1   January–February 1988

1. NEGATIVE INTEREST RATES — THE HONG KONG SCHEME

Concerned at the continued speculation on an upward revaluation of the Hong Kong dollar, the Hong Kong authorities have devised and announced a scheme to impose charges on certain credit balances at banks in Hong Kong. As announced so far the scheme has two parts:

(i) a charge payable to the Exchange Fund on incremental balances (relative to a base date) of licensed banks on credit balances at the Clearing House, and

(ii) a charge on customers' credit balances at licensed banks in Hong Kong dollars.

The first part of the scheme was announced on Saturday, December 19th 1987, by the Committee of the Hong Kong Association of Banks. A new rule known as the "Specified Rate Rule" was introduced "as to the conduct of the business of banking by the authority vested in the Laws of Hong Kong, the Hong Kong Association of Banks Ordinance Chapter 364 Part IV Para 12." The press release went on to give the text of the new "specified rate rule" as follows:

"1. In these supplementary rules expressions and terms which are defined in the rules relating to the Clearing House (dated 29th March 1982) as amended shall have the same meaning when used in these supplementary rules.

2. (a) Each settlement bank (including the management bank in its function as a settlement bank for the purposes of this rule) shall promptly on the business day following the completion of settlement for each day upon which the specified rate is other than zero deliver to the Management Bank a reconciliation statement showing how its balance with the Management Bank is comprised as between (1) balances with that Settlement Bank of each member bank clearing through it and (2) the balance attributable to its own business, provided that in the case of the Management Bank the reconciliation statement shall only show the balances of member banks clearing through it. At the same time each settlement bank shall debit to the account of each such member bank an amount of interest calculated at the rate set out in rule 4 below in respect of such member bank's balance with it and deliver such amounts to the Management Bank together (in case of each Settlement Bank other than the Management Bank) with a similar amount of interest in respect of that part of the balance with the Management Bank (as shown in the reconciliation statement) as is attributable to its own business.

(b)   If the net clearing balance at the completion of settlement on any day upon which the specified rate is other than zero is less than the net clearing balance on the last preceding day upon which the specified rate was zero, the Management Bank shall be charged interest at the rate set out in rule 4 below upon the amount of the difference between such net clearing balances.

For the purposes of this rule the net clearing balance shall be the sum of the balances of the settlement banks with the Management bank and of the member banks which clear through it.

3.   The Management Bank shall promptly pay all amounts of interest charged pursuant to these rules to the Financial Secretary as Controller of the Exchange Fund.

4.   Interest rates for the purposes of these rules shall be calculated on a daily basis by reference to an annual interest rate ("the specified rate"). This rate and the applicable system of charging as set out below will be determined from time to time by the Committee after consultation with the Financial Secretary.

System A
(A) On the amount of any credit balance between $10 million and $25 million inclusive the specified rate shall apply.
(B) On the amount of any credit balance above $25 million and not exceeding $100 million four times the specified rate shall apply.
(C) On the amount of any credit balances above $100 million and not exceeding $200 million eight times the specified rate shall apply.
(D) On the amount of any credit balances in excess of $200 million sixteen times the specified rate shall apply.

System B
On the amount of any credit balances in excess of $25 million the specified rate shall apply."

The new rules were adopted by the Hong Kong Association of Banks at their meeting on Saturday, 19th December. Commenting on the provision for the charging of interest on credit balances held overnight at the Clearing House, the Chairman of the Hong Kong Association of Banks, Mr. John MacKenzie, said, "The Hong Kong Association of Banks has introduced this new rule, after consultation with the Financial Secretary, to provide a mechanism for collecting interest on excessive credit balances, and in response to the continued speculation regarding the HK$/US$ link rate.

"Government has repeatedly affirmed that the link rate of 7.80 HKD will not be changed and by these categorical assurances has given fair and explicit notice of its intentions.

"Nevertheless speculation continues and is a thorough nuisance to the conduct of non-speculative business, to genuine commercial activity, and has substantially reduced the income of savers, of the man in the street.

"We now have this mechanism in place and in case of need it will be used to eliminate or reduce speculation by charging punitive rates of interest on excessive credit balances. These punitive rates will be charged to the banks but will be passed on by the banks to their customers including overseas banks, financial institutions and corporations. By virtue of paragraphs 2(a) and (b) all banks including the Management Bank will be charged. If the rule were to be activated in present circumstances the specified rate, under System A might well be 5.5% per annum in which case the charge to a bank on balances of over HK$200 millions in its clearing account would be 88% per annum. It could of course be higher or lower, depending upon the chosen figure for the specified rate, and under System B the chosen rate would again be whatever rate the Association after discussion with the Financial Secretary considered necessary to achieve the objective of the rule. Banks are at liberty to pass on the charge at a higher rate should they feel this to be warranted. To the extent that any banks are holding speculative long Hong Kong dollar positions for their own account the charge would properly be for their own account.

"The Association has decided that all funds collected under this new rule from the Management and Settlement banks will be paid over to Government by the Management Bank of the Clearing House.

"I would stress that for the moment the specified rate is zero % per annum. The punitive charge will commence if and when a change to the specified rate is announced.

"The application of this measure will be seen as stringent and unpopular in some quarters. However, the Hong Kong Association of Banks feels it has a duty to intervene if there is a threat of damage to genuine business activity on which the community relies for its livelihood — and is not prepared to allow this damage to continue unabated.

"We have seen all too recently the consequences of overheated speculation. This rule has been adopted in what the Hong Kong Association of Banks sees as the wider public interest."

The second part of the scheme known as the Deposit Charge Rule concerns the passing on of these charges to customers, and is best explained by reference to the letters which individual licensed banks have recently sent out to their customers warning them that certain credit balances in excess of HK$1 million could be liable to charges should the first part of the scheme be implemented.

The consequences of negative interest rates for the Hong Kong banking system can be analysed from the standpoint of the impact it will have on the behaviour of (a) the licensed banks, and (b) the non-bank public.

Since the "specified rate" will apply to incremental credit balances of licensed banks at the Clearing House, the banks will have a powerful incentive to try to minimise their clearing balances. The easiest way for a bank to reduce its clearing balances is to increase its lending to the maximum possible capacity. This means that if banks expect that the "specified rate" scheme is to be imposed in the near future they will take every step possible to find new customers, to extend their mortgage lending, to extend their lending to traders, industrialists and investors, and they may also attempt to draw down their clearing balances by making investments in commercial paper, CDs and other marketable instruments. The net effect of increasing their lending and other investments in this way will be to expand correspondingly their deposits, and as a consequence the overall money supply in Hong Kong, i.e. HK$ M_3, will accelerate.

In addition to attempting to avoid having large positive clearing balances, the banks also have to face the problem of how to pass on the "specified rate" charges to their customers. On any one day a large bank in Hong Kong has many thousands of items processed through its clearing account and it is therefore impossible to determine on any fair basis, which particular transaction or transactions were responsible for the bank's clearing balance having increased. Because of the difficulty of passing on these charges the Hong Kong Association of Banks has devised a scheme whereby deposits in excess of HK$1 million may be subject to penalty charges during periods when charges on credit balances at the Clearing House are effective. This rule is clearly highly discriminatory and there have been numerous requests by different groups such as pension funds, charitable trusts and other bona fide holders of Hong Kong dollars for exemption from this provision. Some smaller banks will be very reluctant to impose these charges on their customers and we can expect a variety of subterfuges in order to avoid customers having to suffer these penalties.

Of course, individuals and corporations may attempt to hold cash instead of deposits but this is likely to be discouraged by the banks and, in any case, holding cash currency runs serious security risks. Therefore the main response of individuals and corporations is likely to be that they will attempt to hold assets in Hong Kong other than bank deposits which would be liable to the penalty charges.

The net effect of these reactions by banks and individuals will be to accelerate the transmission of speculative capital flows from temporary inflows into permanent increases in the Hong Kong dollar money supply via more rapid growth of bank lending, and to create a preference for assets which are not bank deposits — such as equity shares, CDs, commercial paper and cash, i.e. a decline in the demand for deposit money relative to other HK$ assets. Assuming there is no revaluation of the Hong Kong dollar, then as a result of faster money supply growth the domestic price level can be expected to rise more rapidly than otherwise. In the final analysis therefore the Hong Kong economy would "adjust" to the speculative capital inflow by a rise in domestic prices rather than through a change in the external value of the currency. By raising the internal price level through inflation, this kind of adjustment would undermine Hong Kong's export competitiveness and over time Hong Kong's overall trade position could be expected to deteriorate somewhat as exports slowed in response to higher wages and other domestic costs, and imports accelerated.

2. NEGATIVE INTEREST RATES — THE SWISS EXPERIENCE

In the post war period Switzerland, unlike Hong Kong, has maintained foreign exchange controls which required commercial banks to differentiate between resident and non-resident account holders in Swiss Francs. In the period 1964–66 a ban was imposed on the payment of any interest on such non-resident deposits in Swiss Francs. The same framework was revived from 4th July 1972, this time with a provision for a tax to be imposed on any increment in those deposits in Swiss Francs held by non-residents. Initially the charge was set at 2% per quarter. From 1st October 1973 the penalty fee was suspended, only to be re-imposed from 20th November 1974 at a rate of 3% per quarter — as usual, on any increment. From 22nd January 1975 the rate of tax was increased to its maximum level of 10% per quarter. After the Swiss Franc had peaked in November 1978 the speculative pressure abated and one year later, on 1st November 1979, the tax rate on non-resident deposits in Swiss Francs was lowered to 2.5 per cent per quarter. As from 1st December 1979 the tax rate was suspended (i.e. reduced to zero), and as from 20th February 1980 the whole scheme was finally abolished.

In addition to the tax charges against credit balances held in Swiss Francs by non-resident depositors, the Swiss authorities found it necessary to take various other legislative actions in order to prevent individuals and corporate depositors from exploiting some of the more obvious loopholes. For example, between 14th April 1976 and 20th April 1977 a limit was imposed on the importation of foreign banknotes, restricting each individual to the equivalent of SF 20,000. This particular restriction was aimed at Italians, but in 1978 a more general step was taken when the Federal Post Office administration made an informal agreement with the Swiss National Bank not to accept large non-resident accounts in Swiss Francs — i.e. not more than SF 100,000 in cash accounts in Switzerland.

According to the International Currency Review Swiss commercial banks were prohibited from placing Swiss Franc denominated bank notes in safe deposit boxes rented by non-residents, and in addition, Swiss banks were not permitted to keep cashier's cheques on file with large denominations drawn in their name to the order of foreign clients. Finally, Swiss commercial banks were threatened with the requirement to open foreign currency accounts at fixed rates of exchange. (We have not been able to verify these three supplementary restrictions with the Swiss National Bank, but they would appear to be consistent with the general tenor of restrictions imposed at the time). This list of administrative provisions indicates how difficult it was for Switzerland — which at the time was relatively open economy with a relatively free financial system — to prevent foreigners speculating on a revaluation of the Swiss franc by means of penalties on supposedly speculative transactions. Much more important in restoring stability to the Swiss monetary system and reducing foreign speculative pressure were the measures taken at a macro-economic level to deflect speculation away from the Swiss currency and onto the Deutschemark.

The years 1977–78 witnessed a period of dramatic US dollar weakness, which precipitated a general flight from US dollars into commodities, precious metals, real

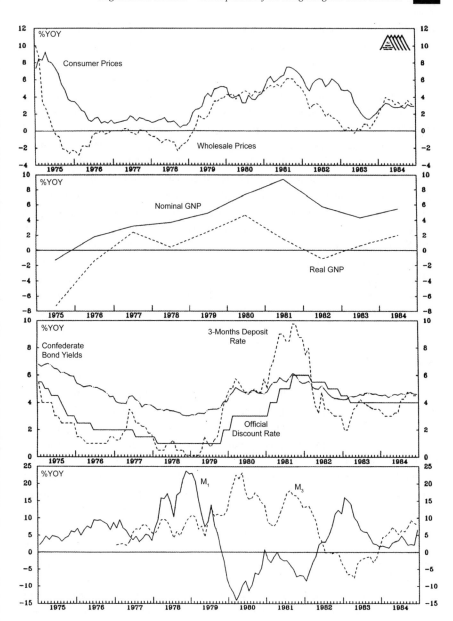

Chart 10.1 Money, Interest Rates, Output, and Prices in Switzerland, 1975–84

estate, and into other "hard" currencies, in particular the Swiss Franc. Initially the Swiss authorities allowed their currency to appreciate from SF 2.42 per US dollar at the end of December 1976 to SF 1.98 by the end of 1977, and then to an ultimate peak of SF 1.46 in November 1978. However, during 1978 the upward pressure on the Swiss franc became very acute, requiring the Swiss National Bank to intervene heavily in the foreign exchange market, buying US dollars and selling (i.e. creating) Swiss francs. The net result (see Chart 10.1) was a sharp acceleration in the Swiss M_1 money supply, from 4% year-on-year in the final quarter of 1977 to 22% in the final quarter of 1978, clearly violating the Swiss National Banks' target for monetary growth. Inflation, which had been below 2% per annum in 1977–78, was not an immediate concern, but the Swiss authorities were well aware of the lagged impact of money growth on domestic price changes. Accordingly they were extremely anxious on the one hand to prevent the money supply growing too rapidly, while on the other hand they were determined not to allow the Swiss franc to rise so much that it threatened the survival of many of Switzerland's export-oriented companies. The way this dilemma was ultimately resolved was by suspending the Swiss National Banks' monetary aggregate targets from 1st October 1978 (and through 1979), and by pegging the Swiss franc to the Deutschemark in the range SF 0.80–0.90 per DM 1, thus deflecting speculative pressure from the Swiss franc to the Deutschemark, and hence on to the EMS as a whole. This policy was successful in the sense that Switzerland was able to restore monetary targeting in 1980, but it is not clear what would have happened if the US dollar had not troughed in November 1978 and subsequently strengthened against all European currencies and the Japanese yen.

CONCLUSION

The Swiss experience shows that negative interest rates were not, on their own, a satisfactory defence against foreign speculators. But the Swiss authorities began from a different starting point compared to the Hong Kong authorities. In Hong Kong in 1987–88 the problem has been to convince speculators that the official HK$/US$ rate of 7.80 would not be altered; in Switzerland in 1977–78 the problem was to convince speculators that the Swiss Franc would not rise more against the US$ than the Deutschemark. Ultimately this was only accomplished by Switzerland abandoning her domestic monetary aggregate targets, and pegging the currency explicitly to the DM. Soon after the announcement and implementation of these macro-economic measures the upward pressure on the Swiss Franc eased (in November 1978), and the US$ bottomed, with the result that the need for punitive charges on non-resident Swiss Franc depositors quickly evaporated.

In the case of Hong Kong it should already be clear that the macroeconomic framework for maintaining a pegged and unchanged exchange rate is already in place: the authorities have no monetary target nor any interest rate constraint to be concerned about. The real problem, it would seem, is not any question about the determination of the authorities to maintain the current 7.80 parity for the Hong Kong dollar, but the tendency for small deviations in the free market rate to encourage speculators to believe in the possibility of a greater adjustment to the official parity — however remote — and hence to make large scale speculative purchases of Hong Kong dollars. We believe the best approach to this problem is to improve the operation of the linked rate system by tightening up the cash arbitrage, thereby reducing deviations of the free market rate from the official parity, rather that superimposing an additional framework of ad hoc rules and procedures designed to deal with the symptoms arising form the current imperfections in the system. Better to perfect the system than to pile additional weapons on to an imperfect mechanism.

CHAPTER 11

INTERVENTION REPLACES ARBITRAGE
The July Package of Monetary Measures
July–August 1988

The July 1988 package of new accounting arrangements for the Hong Kong monetary system represented the first major change in the design of the system since 1983. These measures were the official response to some of the defects in the original template as set out in AMM, but they also set a new direction. In the early years after 1983 the authorities and the Hongkong and Shanghai Banking Corporation (HSBC) had cooperated in intervening to support the HK$ market exchange rate, but if the design of the system had been adequate in the first place, such intervention should not have been necessary. In retrospect AMM had paid insufficient attention to one of the key problems that the July package sought to address — namely the potential leakage of funds into the system from the inter-bank clearing arrangements. In effect the AMM design had concentrated on only one element of the monetary base, namely the banknote issue and its backing. As mentioned earlier, this was based on the idea, derived from the operation of gold and silver specie standards, that if banknotes and deposits were interchangeable, then market arbitrage could be relied upon to bring the convertibility rate for banknotes and the exchange rate for wholesale funds into line. In practice this never happened, and the July 1988 package of measures was the first step to tackling this problem by moving in a different direction.

Looking back on these events from the perspective of 2006 one can see that the new direction implied, but not articulated, by the July 1988 measures was to start to extend gradually the authorities' control over all the elements in the monetary base, not simply the currency issue. Only then would any tightening or easing, whether market-induced or deliberately induced by the authorities, be transmitted to all parts of the system in such a way that interest rate movements reinforced the tendency of the market exchange rate to appreciate or depreciate. It was obvious (as pointed out in Chapter 5) that Hong Kong's banks did not maintain reserves at the monetary authority, but the fact that Hong Kong's banks had maintained a private clearing and settlement system obscured the fact that the ultimate settlement bank (HSBC) in fact had the power to operate like a central bank in the sense of granting credit to any bank in the system that might become overdrawn on its settlement account. Such credits were equivalent to the creation of high-powered or base money, and therefore undermined the ability of either the authorities or any auto-pilot mechanism in the currency board to exercise monetary control.

It is important that students of the Hong Kong monetary system understand the significance of this shift, and see that this was a first logical step on the way to the "seven technical measures" of September1998 that finally made the system much more robust. The text provides a full explanation of the new measures (pp. 229–236), including two pages of T-form balance sheets setting out the mechanics of the new arrangements, together with a key historical document (the press release announcing the new measures and their effect) as an appendix (pp. 242–247). At the end of the article there is some mild criticism (pp. 238–239 and 241) of the measures, though it is more suspicion of the authorities' motives than any view that the measures would not work. The central contribution of the article is a detailed explanation of how any mandated changes in the size of the account to be held by HSBC at the Exchange Fund would enable interest rates to support desired changes in the market exchange rate. This mechanism remained the core of the system from July 1988 until December 1996 when a new clearing system (real-time gross settlement, or RTGS) was introduced, and all licensed banks were required to maintain clearing accounts with the Exchange Fund or the Hong Kong Monetary Authority (HKMA) as it became known following its merger with the Office of the Commissioner of Banking in April 1993.

A S I A N   M O N E T A R Y   M O N I T O R
Vol. 12 No. 4 July–August 1988

INTRODUCTION

On Friday 15th July, the Hong Kong Government announced some radical changes to Hong Kong's monetary system to be made effective from Monday 18th July. Their introduction represents a major change in the role of the Exchange Fund on the one hand and the role of the Hongkong and Shanghai Banking Corporation (HSBC) on the other. The changes convert the Exchange Fund from a passive issuer of currency in the style of a traditional colonial currency board to a potentially active force in the money and foreign exchange markets since they provide to the Exchange Fund some critical new elements in its balance sheet which together constitute the essentials of a central bank.

    With respect to the operation of the monetary system, the changes herald a shift from dependence upon private sector arbitrage to dependence upon official intervention as a device for ensuring stability of Hong Kong's exchange rate. So far as the role of the HSBC is concerned, some of the privileges which it previously enjoyed have been removed but the changes still leave HSBC an important role as agent of the Government in certain specific respects.

    On the whole, the linked rate system was operating reasonably well with deviations of the free market exchange rate from the official HK\$7.80 = US\$1.00 parity generally being contained within a band of 1% on either side of the 7.8 rate. Unfortunately, the variability in the free market rate tended to prompt occasional speculation that Hong Kong's official parity might be altered. This in turn led to some wide fluctuations in Hong Kong's short term interest rates. Analytically, there were two ways to deal with this problem. In an earlier issue of AMM (Jan.–Feb. 1988, Vol. 12 No. 1: "How to Tighten Up the Linked Rate Mechanism") we advocated improving the arbitrage mechanism, for example by making the official 7.80 parity available to the non-bank public for the purchase and sale of banknotes, or by making bank notes convertible into clearing account deposits of the banks and vice versa. An alternative approach was for the Exchange Fund to intervene more effectively in the foreign exchange and money markets. To make that intervention effective it would have been necessary to make a number of changes to the balance sheet of the Exchange Fund in order to enable it to act like a central bank. This is in fact what has now been done.

In terms of results, we expect that the new arrangements will be highly effective in reducing the deviation of the free market exchange rate from the official parity, but it is doubtful if under these arrangements it is appropriate to continue to describe Hong Kong's exchange rate mechanism as a linked rate. Private arbitrage may still play a role, but if intervention takes over as the primary means of minimising the gap between the free market rate and the parity, the system is more accurately described as a pegged rate rather than a linked rate.

CHANGES INTRODUCED BY THE NEW ACCOUNTING ARRANGEMENTS

The new arrangements have been billed as mere changes in the "accounting arrangements" between the Exchange Fund and the HSBC. In reality they are more significant and fundamental than this. In order to see why the change in the arrangements marks a decisive departure from the past, it is necessary to set out the changes in some detail.

The first change is the creation on 18th July at the Exchange Fund of a Hong Kong dollar account for HSBC which is a liability of the Exchange Fund. One of the unique features of Hong Kong's banking system from 1935 until July 1988 was that the Exchange Fund had always been a customer of the banking system, holding Hong Kong dollar deposits (as an asset) at HSBC and at other banks. This was in contrast to the typical arrangement in other banking systems where private banks hold deposit liabilities at a central bank. According to the Government's press release (see Appendix 11.1) HSBC will now maintain a Hong Kong dollar account ("The Account") with the Exchange Fund, and it will be required to maintain a balance in that account no less than the net clearing balance (NCB) of the rest of the banking system (see items 7a and b in the appendix). To see the significance of this it is important to understand how the clearing system operates in Hong Kong. The clearing house in Hong Kong is not an independent entity. It exists, so to speak, within the HSBC. Including HSBC there are ten Settlement Banks, and all other banks (sub-settlement banks) must maintain an account with one of the Settlement Banks. Since the clearing house operates as an adjunct to

HSBC and HSBC is also the Manager of the clearing house, net credit balances of the Settlement Banks at the clearing house are held as non-interest bearing deposits at HSBC, and net debit balances of Settlement Banks are treated as overdrafts with HSBC, attracting interest charges at the best lending rate plus some margin. In an independent clearing house, by contrast, the manager would have placed any net clearing balances on deposit at competitive rates in the interbank market, using the income to offset its operating costs.

In the new scheme no interest will be paid to HSBC on its credit balances in The Account. However, if the balance in the account falls short of the NCB, HSBC will be obliged to pay interest on the shortfall to the Exchange Fund, and similarly if NCB is in overall debit. In addition the rates of interest payable by HSBC will be the higher of BLR (Best Lending Rate) or HIBOR (Hong Kong Interbank Offered Rate).

Basically these provisions deprive HSBC of the free use, which it previously enjoyed, of the net clearing house credit balances of other banks. They also create a financial incentive for HSBC to meet its new obligation to maintain a balance in The Account equal to the net clearing balance of the rest of the banking system. This means HSBC is now in the same position vis-a-vis the clearing house as other banks. In effect, The Account creates a kind of clearing account for HSBC, which can be credited or debited at the whim of the Exchange Fund.

Finally, the creation of The Account will enable the Exchange Fund to conduct intervention in the foreign exchange market or open market operations in the domestic money market in a way which overcomes the deficiencies which were apparent under the old structure and which were a material cause of the currency crisis of 1983 (see Chapter 2, especially pp. 30–31). The reason is that HSBC's quasi-central banking power derived not so much from its note-issuing privileges as from the fact that most banks maintained an account with HSBC (or with another bank which in turn cleared with HSBC), just as in a central banking system all banks are usually obliged to maintain an account with the central bank. This unique structure meant that HSBC could — within limits — regulate the interbank market in much the same way as a central bank could, extending credit to or withholding credit from other banks in a discretionary manner. The transfer of NCBs to the Exchange Fund not only means HSBC is deprived of the use of the clearing balances, but it also means that HSBC cannot now extend credits to other banks without simultaneously increasing the size of balance that it must maintain at the Exchange Fund. This is because every interbank loan that HSBC makes automatically increases NCBs by an equivalent amount. Furthermore, the Exchange Fund now has on its balance sheet a liability whose size it can determine from day to day by means of transactions with HSBC (or other banks). In summary, the new account for HSBC at the Exchange Fund amounts to the provision of a central banking facility or reserve account at the Exchange Fund which will enable it — should the authorities choose to use The Account actively — to regulate the level of short term interest rates, to influence the amount of money in the inter-bank market, and more broadly to adjust the overall level of money supply in the economy.

The balance sheets of the Exchange Fund before and after the introduction of The Account are set out in the box on pp. 232–233, together with the balance sheet of a typical central bank.

The second set of changes introduced by the new arrangements involves the creation of a new account at the Exchange Fund for the Treasury. Like the new account of HSBC at the Exchange Fund, the new account for the Treasury is also a liability item on the Exchange Fund's balance sheet. The details of the Treasury's new account are set out in the appendix and in the T-form diagrams on p. 233, but a simplified summary would be that just as the Government in other monetary systems is able to affect the money supply by transferring deposits from the commercial banking system to the central bank (or vice versa), so in Hong Kong's new system the Government will be able to contract or expand liquidity in the system by transferring money balances from the licensed banks to the Exchange Fund and vice versa.

Having set out the key changes which have been introduced by the new "accounting arrangements" it is worthwhile to compare the structure of the Exchange Fund's liabilities with the structure of a conventional central bank. There are in fact very few significant differences from an analytical standpoint.

1. **Certificates of Indebtedness.** These are issued to HSBC and Standard Chartered Bank by the Exchange Fund and represent the value of the authorised HK$ note issue. As with banknotes in central banking systems, HK$ banknotes (and therefore CIs) are issued in response to demand from the banks who in turn are responding to demand from their customers. This part of the Exchange Fund's balance sheet is essentially no different from the note issue component of a central bank's balance sheet.

2. **"The Account" of HSBC at the Exchange Fund.** This corresponds closely to the reserve or settlement accounts of commercial banks at a central bank. Whereas in central banking systems all commercial banks typically maintain an account at the central bank, in the Hong Kong system only the HSBC maintains an account at the Exchange Fund. However, since the Exchange Fund uses HSBC as an agent for settling its transactions with other banks there are no differences in practice between the impact of operations of conventional central banks on the reserve or settlement accounts of commercial banks. The critical question is how active the Exchange Fund is going to be in manipulating The Account.

3. **The Treasury's account at the Exchange Fund.** This is precisely comparable with the accounts which many central governments maintain with their central banks. Moreover, just as in other central banking systems governments maintain deposit balances *both* with the commercial banks *and* with the central bank, so under Hong Kong's new arrangements the Treasury will maintain accounts both at the licensed banks and with the Exchange Fund.

4. **Debt certificates.** Since the late 1970s, the Exchange Fund has managed the majority of the fiscal balances of the Hong Kong Government (i.e. the cumulative fiscal surpluses) and these are represented on the liability side of the balance sheet of the Exchange Fund by Debt Certificates denominated in HK$ and issued to the

SIMPLIFIED BALANCE SHEETS FOR THE EXCHANGE FUND
AND A TYPICAL CENTRAL BANK

Part 1: "The Account" of HSBC at the Exchange Fund

Before July 18, 1988 the essential features of the Exchange Fund were:

Exchange Fund

Assets	Liabilities
Foreign Exchange Reserves (FA)	Certificates of Indebtedness (= HK$ Banknotes)
HK$ Deposits at HSBC (DC)	

After July 18, 1988 the essential features are:

Exchange Fund

Assets	Liabilities
Foreign Exchange Reserves (FA)	Certificates of Indebtedness (= HK$ Banknotes)
HK$ Deposits at HSBC (DC)	The Account

A proto-typical central bank's balance sheet consists of:–

Central Bank

Assets	Liabilities
Foreign Assets (FA)	Currency Outstanding
Domestic Credit (DC)	Reserves and/or clearing balances of banks

FA = Foreign Assets   DC = Domestic Credit

In a typical central bank,
Currency + Reserves = Monetary Base

In Hong Kong, after July 18, 1988:
Certificates of Indebtedness + The Account = Monetary Base (B)
and, in this simplified model,

$$FA + DC = B$$

If the Exchange Fund or Central Bank acquires DC while the monetary base B remains unchanged, FA must fall.

**SIMPLIFIED BALANCE SHEETS FOR THE EXCHANGE FUND AND
A TYPICAL CENTRAL BANK**

Part 2: The Treasury's Account at the Exchange Fund

Before July 18, 1988 the essential features of the Exchange Fund including its obligations to the Treasury were:

Exchange Fund

Assets	Liabilities
Foreign Exchange Reserves (FA)	Certificates of Indebtedness (= HK$ Banknotes)
HK$ Deposits at HSBC (DC)	Debt Certificates

Debt Certificates are receipts issued by the Exchange Fund to the Treasury against funds held and managed on behalf of the Treasury.

After July 18, 1988 the essential features, including the new Treasury Account at the Exchange Fund, are:

Exchange Fund

Assets	Liabilities
Foreign Exchange Reserves (FA)	Certificates of Indebtedness (= HK$ Banknotes)
HK$ Deposits at HSBC (DC)	The Account
	Treasury Account
	Debt Certificates

A proto-typical central bank's balance sheet, including the deposits of government at the central bank, consists of:

Central Bank

Assets	Liabilities
Foreign Assets (FA)	Currency Outstanding
Domestic Credit (DC)	Reserves and/or clearing balances of banks
	Treasury Account

FA = Foreign Assets   DC = Domestic Credit

For Hong Kong, after July 18, 1988:

Certificates of indebtedness + The Account = Monetary Base (B)

and B = FA + (DC - Treasury Account - Debt Certificates) - Net Worth

If the Exchange Fund wishes to tighten the money market via the Treasury Account it must reduce the monetary base. To do this it will transfer Treasury funds from the licensed banks to the Treasury Account at the Exchange Fund, debiting The Account of HSBC and crediting Treasury Account. To ease the money market it will conduct the reverse operation.

Treasury, and on the asset side by a mixture of HK$ and foreign currency assets. This part of the Exchange Fund's balance sheet is best viewed as part of the fiscal accounts of the Government and not part of the monetary accounts of the Exchange Fund.

The Exchange Fund's assets differ in composition from those of central banks, but there are no substantive differences from an analytical point of view.

1. **Foreign Assets (including gold).** The Exchange Fund is said to hold a diversified portfolio of assets in foreign currencies and it may even hold some gold. The foreign currency assets, like the foreign assets of central banks elsewhere, probably consist of foreign currency deposits and short, medium and long term government paper such as Treasury bills and bonds. There is absolutely no difference between the position of the Exchange Fund and the position of other central banks with respect to their holdings of gold and foreign exchange except the legal provision in the Exchange Fund Ordinance which effectively requires the Exchange Fund to maintain assets equal to 105% of the sum total of Certificates of Indebtedness outstanding plus the aggregate of borrowings of the Exchange Fund.

2. **Domestic Credit.** In most countries central bank holdings of domestic credit consist of government securities, and private sector credit instruments such as commercial bills and loans to banks. In the case of the Exchange Fund, domestic credit consists almost entirely of loans to (or deposits with) the banking system because (a) there is only one issue of government debt outstanding (HK$1 billion, of 10% coupon debt issued in 1984 and maturing in 1994), which is held largely by banks, and (b) there is only a limited market in commercial paper in Hong Kong. The composition of Exchange Fund holdings of domestic credit differs, therefore, from the composition of domestic credit held by central banks, but its monetary impact would be no different than it would be if it consisted of government debt and commercial paper.

INTERVENTION BY THE EXCHANGE FUND UNDER THE OLD AND NEW STRUCTURE

Until the new changes announced on July 15th, the Exchange Fund was a client of the banking system in Hong Kong, holding Hong Kong dollar deposits at HSBC and other banks in Hong Kong, just like any individual or corporation in the territory. Accordingly, under the old structure when the Exchange Fund intervened in the foreign exchange market to buy or sell Hong Kong dollars, it settled these transactions by debiting or crediting its Hong Kong dollar deposit account at HSBC, and conversely the account of another bank or individual or company would have been correspondingly credited or debited in Hong Kong dollars. In other words when the Exchange Fund intervened, deposits in Hong Kong dollars were transferred from its account to the account of another individual or company in Hong Kong; there was no change in the aggregate size of the deposit liabilities of the banking system. Technically, Exchange Fund intervention was conducted in low powered money as opposed to high powered money, so that there was no multiple expansion or multiple contraction resulting from the Exchange Fund's intervention as there would have been in the case of a normal (unsterilised) central bank intervention (See Chapter 2, pp. 30–31).

Therefore, when the Exchange Fund intervened in the money market in Hong Kong its effectiveness under the old regime was strictly limited. Similarly, when the Exchange Fund borrowed Hong Kong dollars in order to raise interest rates, these Hong Kong dollars were redeposited in the banking system by the Exchange Fund and there was no change in the overall level of interest rates. It was basically this ineffectiveness in the Exchange Fund's intervention operations that led the Government to introduce the July package of measures designed to make its intervention more effective in the future.

Under the new structure when the Exchange Fund intervenes in the foreign exchange market to buy Hong Kong dollars, which it would tend to do when the Hong Kong dollar was weakening against the official parity (i.e. moving towards 7.85 or 7.90), it will in future sell US dollars from its portfolio and buy Hong Kong dollars from one of the banks. Instead of paying Hong Kong dollars out of its deposit account with the Hongkong and Shanghai Bank as in the past, it will in future debit The Account of the HSBC at the Exchange Fund if it bought the Hong Kong dollars from the HSBC, or debit The Account with instructions to HSBC to debit the account of some other bank from which the Exchange Fund bought the Hong Kong dollars. This set of transactions produces a very different result compared to the old-style intervention. The result is a *contraction* in the level of funds available to the inter-bank market, and to the extent that banks regard these funds as reserves, there will be a multiple contraction throughout the Hong Kong banking system. This will tend to push interest rates upwards, thus helping the exchange rate to appreciate back towards the official parity of 7.80.

Conversely, when the Hong Kong dollar is trading at a premium to its parity, e.g. when there is speculation that there might be a revaluation of the Hong Kong dollar and the free market rate is 7.75 or above, the Exchange Fund can now intervene by selling Hong Kong dollars and buying US dollars. Again it will settle this transaction by crediting The Account of the HSBC at the Exchange Fund, which will *increase* the funds available in the interbank market, and will have a multiple expansion effect throughout the banking system. This will tend to push interest rates downwards, thus helping the exchange rate to depreciate back towards the official parity of 7.80.

These transactions are quite different from the Exchange Fund's practice in the past of transferring Hong Kong dollar funds from the Exchange Fund account at HSBC to other parties (or vice-versa). The results of intervention under the July package will be to increase (or decrease) funds both in the inter-bank market and throughout the banking system and as a result interest rates will react more sharply than they have in the past whenever the Hong Kong dollar moved upwards or downwards relative to the official parity.

In summary, the new structure means that Exchange Fund intervention in the foreign exchange market and in the money market will be much more effective in keeping the free market rate for the Hong Kong dollar near to the official parity because its intervention operations will be transmitted more directly to the level of interest rates and hence to the quantity of money in the system as a whole. The problem under the previous regime was that it required a significant deviation of the free market exchange rate from the official parity in order to induce banks to conduct the arbitrage necessary to bring the free market rate back to the parity. Under the new arrangements the Exchange Fund will be able to intervene more rapidly and achieve a greater impact without having to wait for private sector arbitrage to do its work. In short, official intervention has taken the place of private sector arbitrage. There are real risks, however, associated with the new mechanism (see pp. 238–241).

HOW THE HSBC ADJUSTS THE SIZE OF "THE ACCOUNT"

Under the new arrangements, HSBC has undertaken to maintain its account at the Exchange Fund at a level equal to the net clearing balances of the rest of the banking system. This means that on any particular day HSBC can find itself with an excess balance at the Exchange Fund or a shortage of funds at the Exchange Fund. How will it respond in this situation? Let us take the case of HSBC having an excess of funds at The Account. In this case HSBC will wish to either increase the size of NCBs or decrease the size of The Account. There are two ways in which it can do this: either HSBC can buy foreign exchange from other banks which will result in a crediting of Hong Kong dollars to the net clearing balances of other banks, or HSBC can increase its lending activities relative to other banks, which will in time lead to HSBC having negative net clearings at the clearing house, which will increase the size of other banks' NCBs.

The size of The Account is not any determinate number, nor is there any necessary relation between the size of NCBs and the overall money supply. The probability is that in the early stages of the new arrangements the absolute size of The Account will progressively decline as the Hongkong and Shanghai Bank improves its cash management and forecasting techniques so as to minimise the size of its non-earning balances at the Exchange Fund. However, thereafter the level of NCBs or The Account will depend at least as much on the actions of other banks and their customers as on the actions of HSBC and its customers. (In the early days of the new system The Account was HK$ 1.25 billion. It has recently declined to HK$ 880 million).

HOW THE EXCHANGE FUND ADJUSTS THE SIZE OF "THE ACCOUNT"

When the Exchange Fund wishes to increase the size of the account — i.e. increase interbank liquidity and lower interest rates — it has several options available. One option is to purchase foreign exchange from HSBC or from any other bank, in which case it will increase both sides of its balance sheet, adding to its portfolio of foreign exchange on the assets side and crediting The Account in Hong Kong dollars on the liabilities side of its balance sheet. A second option is to make a direct loan to HSBC or

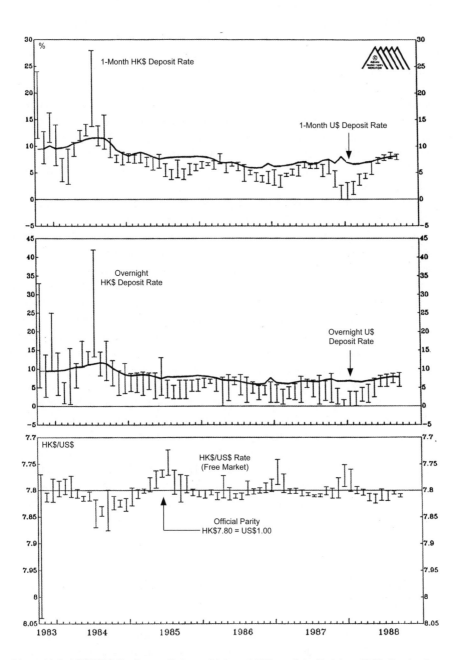

Chart 11.1 HK$/US$ Exchange Rate and Interest Differentials (October 1983–September 1988; Monthly Ranges for HK$ data; Monthly Averages for US$ data)

to another bank in Hong Kong dollars by crediting The Account in Hong Kong dollars. Once again this will lead to an increase in its assets (this time a Hong Kong dollar loan) and a corresponding increase in the size of The Account on the liabilities side of its balance sheet. Third, it could purchase commercial paper, Certificates of Deposit or some other money market instrument denominated in Hong Kong dollars which would also result in an increase in its assets with a corresponding credit to The Account on the liabilities side of its balance sheet. A fourth option is for the Exchange Fund to shift funds from the Treasury's account at the Exchange Fund to the banking system via The Account. In this case the Treasury's account at the Exchange Fund will be debited, and The Account of HSBC at the Exchange Fund will be temporarily credited for the benefit of the Treasury, so that HSBC would in turn credit the account of the Treasury at HSBC (or another bank) with a corresponding amount.

All of these transactions are precisely comparable to the actions of a central bank which wishes to expand the money supply. In Hong Kong's institutional setting the initial result is a lowering of interest rates which will in turn prompt the banks to increase their loans which in turn will result in an increase of the money supply. The new arrangements consequently enable the Exchange Fund to set short term interest rates at whatever level they choose and the money supply will adjust to that level. The stated intention of these measures is to ensure the stability of the 7.80 linked rate system for the Hong Kong dollar, but in reality the new arrangements introduce an element of discretion which will enable the authorities to move the money supply up or down as they choose. This means that Hong Kong's monetary system no longer depends on an automatic adjustment mechanism but will rely ultimately upon the intervention of the authorities to ensure that the money supply and interest rates remain at a level consistent with the 7.80 exchange rate. Given this mechanism it is also true that there is no need to insist that the foreign exchange rate for the Hong Kong dollar remains at 7.80. The argument for persisting with the 7.80 rate indefinitely depended largely on the proposition that private sector interest arbitrage was the key to keeping the free market rate close to the official parity. Since this is no longer the case it can no longer be argued that the 7.80 rate cannot be changed. Now that the Government has the means to enforce any rate that it chooses, the basis for sticking with 7.80 has been eroded. In abandoning automaticity and introducing discretion the Government has undermined the practical necessity of holding the linked rate at 7.80.

ALTERNATIVE OPERATING PROCEDURES UNDER THE NEW ARRANGEMENTS

Given the new apparatus, it is inconceivable that the authorities will not use their new instruments. This raises the question of how the operating rules will be set. Several strategies are possible, but we shall here examine just two likely procedures.

An obvious operating rule would be to set a band on either side of the official parity, say 7.78–7.82. Whenever the free market rate in the HK$–US$ foreign exchange market approaches either limit, the authorities would intervene. As long as the authorities supplied Hong Kong dollars when the market rate threatened to penetrate the 7.78 level, or supplied US dollars when the market rate threatened to penetrate the 7.82 level there would be no problem with this procedure. The Hong Kong dollar-denominated money supply would be encouraged to adjust in line with the exigencies of the balance of payments, expanding when there was strong demand for Hong Kong dollars, and contracting when there was an excess supply of Hong Kong dollars on the foreign exchange market. This procedure would be similar in practice to the operation of the Bretton Woods system of fixed exchange rates which operated between 1944 and 1973.

An alternative operating rule would be to set a target for interest rates. For example, the authorities might try to ensure that overnight, one-week, one-month or three-month Hong Kong dollar money market rates were approximately equal to their US dollar equivalents. This procedure sounds reasonable on first sight, but it assumes that Hong Kong dollar interest rates should be equal to their US dollar or US dollar equivalents, an assumption which is by no means justified except in the long term on the presumption (i) that the 7.80 parity will not be changed and (ii) that the level of the Hong Kong dollar money stock is already at its equilibrium level, and (iii) that interest rate controls, taxes, and other fiscal and administrative factors affecting interest rates in Hong Kong and in the US dollar market are identical — which they are clearly not as long as the Interest Rate Agreement of the Hong Kong Association of Banks exists in Hong Kong. Under interest rate targeting the authorities could easily allow the Hong Kong dollar money supply to expand or contract to the point where the level of money supply was incompatible with maintenance of the fixed parity. For example, a prolonged effort to keep interest rates in Hong Kong below the level they otherwise would be in the absence of intervention would lead to an increase in the money supply, which in time would result in a period of inflation which would undermine equivalence in the Hong Kong price level and the foreign price level at the fixed exchange rate, requiring a realignment of the exchange rate.

Ahead of 1997 such a possibility is not entirely hypothetical. Suppose there is a substantial and sustained capital outflow in the years prior to and even subsequent to the transfer of sovereignty of Hong Kong from Britain to China. What would be the effect on interest rates? The initial effect of a sudden outflow is to raise interest rates in Hong Kong sharply. In time the higher level of interest rates will slow monetary growth, slow nominal spending (including imports), and reduce inflation (or actually bring down wages and the price level). These effects will help to generate a trade or current account surplus which will finance the capital outflow. The longer term effect of the capital outflow on money market interest rates is not clear. They could return to levels approximately equal to US dollar rates, or they could return to levels below rates in US dollar markets if investment expectations about the future are seriously and negatively affected so that the demand for loans remains very weak. These considerations are sufficient to show that a policy of intervention by the Exchange Fund to maintain any particular relative or absolute level of interest rates could have very different effects, dependent upon the prevailing circumstances. In general terms, then, intervention by the authorities to peg

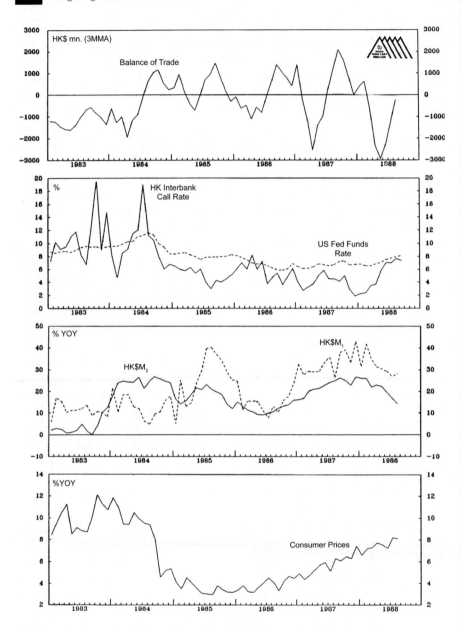

Chart 11.2 Money, Interest Rates, Trade, and Prices

interest rates would be risky and potentially destabilising, while intervention to maintain the free market exchange rate within a narrow band around the fixed parity will have less serious consequences.

However, even intervention to hold the exchange rate has consequences beyond that envisaged in the design of the linked rate system. Under the 1983–1988 regime there was no obligation on the authorities to intervene, so that capital outflows or inflows had to be matched in the (private) foreign exchange market until private sector arbitrage occurred sufficient to offset the initial disturbance. Under the new arrangements from July 1988 the danger is that the monetary authorities will immediately become the counter-party to the inflow or outflow, with the result that the foreign reserves of the Exchange Fund become the first line of defence. In the event of a prolonged and persistent outflow, who can be sure that the authorities will have sufficient reserves to withstand the outflow while at the same time maintaining the foreign exchange backing for the currency? Add to this the possibility that the authorities may also be trying to keep interest rates at some predetermined levels, and it is clear that the new discretionary tools open the system to potentially serious threats which it was not subject to as long as the authorities remained passive.

CONCLUSION

The new arrangements introduced in July by the Hong Kong monetary authorities constitute a major step towards the establishment of a central bank in Hong Kong. In particular the new arrangements give the Monetary Affairs Branch a degree of discretion in the determination of money market trends which it was never intended they should have under the 1983–88 regime. Alternative solutions were possible which would have solved the problems of the linked rate system without giving so much discretion to the authorities. We do not doubt that, used only to a limited degree and in relatively normal circumstances, the new tools will be highly effective in keeping the free market exchange rate for the Hong Kong dollar close to the official parity. The concern arises from the danger that the new instruments will be used more and more frequently and in circumstances where the inflows or (especially) outflows are so significant as to require large-scale intervention which will ultimately put the territory's reserves at risk. Any shift from a system of rules to a system of discretionary intervention must be regarded with circumspection; when that system could be put to the test by very large capital flows it is hard to avoid the conclusion that the new arrangements entail more risks than the previous mechanism.

APPENDIX 11.1

Press Release from Secretary for Monetary Affairs, 15 July 1988

金　融　事　務　司
香港夏慤道十八號
海富中心第二座二十四樓

SECRETARY FOR
MONETARY AFFAIRS OFFICE
24TH FLOOR,
ADMIRALTY CENTRE TOWER II,
18 HARCOURT ROAD.

From: Secretary of Monetary Affairs

To:　Chief Executives of all Licensed Banks

Chairman of the Hong Kong Association Banks

Members of the Exchange Fund Advisory Committee, the Banking Advisory Committee and the Deposit-taking Companies Advisory Committee

Chairman of the Deposit-taking Companies Association

New Accounting Arrangements between the Exchange Fund and the Hongkong and Shanghai Banking Corporation

Introduction

This paper describes new accounting arrangements to be entered into on Monday 18 July 1988, with the approval of the Governor in Council and the agreement of the Hongkong and Shanghai Banking Corporation (HSBC), between the Exchange Fund and HSBC as the Management Bank of the Clearing House of the Hong Kong Association of Banks (HKAB). Members of the Exchange Fund Advisory Committee have been consulted and have unanimously supported the introduction of these new arrangements. The paper also explains how the new accounting arrangements are to be operated.

2.　The purpose of the new accounting arrangements is to enable the Government, through the use of the Exchange Fund, to exercise more effective influence over the availability and price of money in the interbank market and thus to assist it better to maintain exchange rate stability within the framework of the linked exchange rate system. Under the present arrangements, there can be perverse side-effects which reduce the effectiveness of action by Government and HSBC to influence interest rates and the level of liquidity in the interbank market for the purpose of ensuring exchange rate stability.

The Interbank Market

3.   Each licensed bank in Hong Kong maintains an account, either with HSBC, the Management Bank of the Clearing House of HKAB, or with a settlement Bank (as defined in Rules relating to the Clearing House of HKAB) which in turn maintains an account with HSBC, for the purpose of clearing Hong Kong dollar cheques and for settling interbank transactions denominated in Hong Kong dollars. Banks with surplus Hong Kong dollar balances on their clearing accounts lend those funds, through the interbank market, to banks which are short of funds. Deposit-taking companies and large corporate customers also make use of the interbank market, but settlement is effected through their accounts with licensed banks. Interbank interest rates are determined by the forces of supply and demand for funds in that market.

4.   At present, HSBC, as the Management Bank of the clearing House, does not itself have a clearing account. Settlement of Hong Kong dollar transactions between HSBC and other banks are effected through HSBC crediting or debiting, as the case may be, the clearing accounts maintained by these banks or by their settlement Banks with HSBC. The Exchange Fund is a customer of HSBC and of a number of other banks. These existing arrangements have certain consequences on how the supply of money in the interbank market is determined and how interbank interest rates behave. Specifically, the supply of Hong Kong dollars in the interbank market increase and interbank interest rates ease when:

(a)   HSBC buys foreign currency or other assets from another bank, or from customers banking with another bank, with Hong Kong dollars; or

(b)   HSBC lends Hong Kong dollars in the interbank market, or

(c)   a customer of HSBC pays Hong Kong dollars from his account with, or credit facility made available by, HSBC to another person banking with another bank.

Similarly, the supply of Hong Kong dollars in the interbank market decreases and interbank interest rates firm when:

(a)   HSBC sells foreign currency or other assets to another bank, or to customers banking with another bank, for Hong Kong dollars; or

(b)   HSBC borrows Hong Kong dollars in the interbank market; or

(c)   a customer of HSBC accepts Hong Kong dollars for his account with, or for reducing a credit facility made available by, HSBC from another person banking with another bank.

5.   Thus when the Exchange Fund, as a customer of HSBC, carries out foreign exchange and money market operations to stabilize the exchange rate, the effectiveness of such action can stand to be gradually eroded.

6.   To illustrate, consider the case when, for whatever reason, the exchange rate is weakening away from 7.80. Arbitrage between the fixed-rate market for Hong Kong dollar bank notes and the foreign exchange market, or the threat of it, will contribute to containing the deviation from 7.80. At the same time and working in the same direction, the correct monetary policy response must be to keep conditions in the interbank market tight and interbank interest rates high relative to those of the US dollar. This can be achieved by the Exchange Fund selling US dollars for Hong Kong dollars or borrowing Hong Kong dollars, both through HSBC. If, however, other customers of HSBC are at the same time switching out of Hong Kong dollars into US dollars and to the extent that HSBC covers the short US dollar position by recouping the corresponding amount from the foreign exchange market, the tightness in the interbank market will inadvertently be relieved. Other customers of HSBC may also be taking advantage of the high Hong Kong dollar interbank interest rates available by running down HKAB-type deposits with, or drawing down best lending rate (BLR) facilities made available by, HSBC and placing those funds with other banks in the form of deposits which attract interbank interest rates. This again will unhelpfully relieve tightness in the interbank market.

New Accounting Arrangements

7. Such erosion in the effectiveness of foreign exchange and money market operations carried out by the Exchange Fund for the purpose of maintaining exchange rate stability is clearly undesirable. The Government and HSBC have both recognised this for sometime. New accounting arrangements between the Exchange Fund and HSBC, which effectively eliminate this shortcoming, have therefore been developed. The details of the new accounting arrangements are as follows:

(a)   HSBC maintains a Hong Kong dollar account (the "Account") with the Exchange Fund;

(b)   HSBC aims to maintain a balance (the "Balance") in that account no less than the net clearing balance ("NCB") of the rest of the banking system;

(c)   no interest is paid on credit balances in the Account;

(d)   if the Balance falls short of the NCB, HSBC pays interest on the shortfall to the Exchange Fund;

(e)   if NCB is in debit, HSBC pays interest on the debit amount to the Exchange Fund;

(f)   up to a certain amount, the rate of interest payable by HSBC under (d) and (e) is BLR or Hong Kong interbank offered rate (HIBOR), whichever is higher. Beyond that amount, the interest rate payable is 3% over BLR or HIBOR, whichever is higher. In exceptional circumstances, an alternative rate may be determined by the Financial Secretary, after consultation with HSBC;

(g) the Exchange Fund will use the Account, at its discretion, to effect settlement of its Hong Kong dollar transactions with HSBC;

(h) the Exchange Fund will also use the Account, at its discretion, to effect settlement of its Hong Kong dollar transactions with other licensed banks;

(i) in case of (h), the Exchange Fund will either credit or debit the Account and HSBC will correspondingly credit or debit the clearing accounts of banks dealing with the Exchange Fund.

8. Along with these new accounting arrangements between the Exchange Fund and HSBC, the Treasury will also maintain a Hong Kong dollar account with the Exchange Fund where money transferred from the General Revenue to the Exchange Fund in return for interest bearing Debt certificates will be accounted for. This provides an additional mechanism for the Exchange Fund to influence the supply of money in the interbank market.

9. Thus under the new accounting arrangements, the supply of Hong Kong dollars in the interbank market will increase and interbank interest rates will ease when:

(a) the Exchange Fund buys foreign currency with Hong Kong dollars; or

(b) the Exchange Fund lends Hong Kong dollars in the interbank market; or

(c) Debt Certificates are redeemed from the Treasury and the balance in the Treasury's account with the Exchange Fund is reduced.

Similarly, the supply of Hong Kong dollars in the interbank market will decrease and interbank interest rates will firm when:

(a) the Exchange Fund sells foreign currency for Hong Kong dollars; or

(b) the Exchange Fund borrows Hong Kong dollars in the interbank market; or

(c) Debt Certificates are issued to the Treasury and the balance in the Treasury's account with the Exchange Fund is increased.

Practical effects of the new accounting arrangements

10. Under the new accounting arrangements, the Exchange Fund will in effect be the ultimate provider of liquidity to the interbank market. It will be capable of influencing much more effectively the availability and the price of money in the interbank market and in a much better position to maintain exchange rate stability within the framework of the linked exchange rate system.

11. The new accounting arrangements will have no effect on the day to day operation of licensed banks in Hong Kong, other than HSBC. Those which have had, or are likely to have, dealings with the Exchange Fund should, however, be aware that, in addition to the established practice for effecting

Hong Kong dollar settlements with the Exchange Fund as a customer, the Exchange Fund may choose to effect settlement through requesting HSBC to credit or debit, as the case may be, their clearing accounts maintained at HSBC. The Exchange Fund will at the same time credit or debit the Account as appropriate.

12.   Thus when the Exchange Fund sells US$100 million to, say, the Standard Chartered Bank at 7.85, the Hong Kong dollar settlement may be effected through:

(a) the Exchange Fund debiting the Account HK$785 million; and

(b) HSBC debiting Standard Chartered's clearing account with HSBC HK$785 million.

The monetary effects of this transaction will be that, other things being equal, both the Balance and NCB will be reduced by HK$785 million. Interbank interest rates will as a result (and by design) be driven higher, thus giving support to the exchange rate.

13.   Alternatively, in response to the exchange rate being at 7.85, Hong Kong dollars may be transferred from the General Revenue to the Exchange Fund, to the extent that there are surplus General Revenue balances in the banking system. Assuming that HK$500 million is transferred from the General Revenue to the Exchange Fund and the Treasury meets that demand by withdrawing a HK$300 million deposit from the Hang Seng Bank and HK$200 million deposit from the Hang Lung Bank, the Hong Kong dollar settlements will be effected as follows:

(a) the Exchange Fund credit Treasury's account with it by HK$500 million and issues a Debt Certificate of that amount to the Treasury;

(b) the Exchange Fund debits the Account HK$500 million;

(c) HSBC debits Hang Seng Bank's clearing account with itself HK$300 million;

(d) HSBC debits Hang Lung Bank's clearing account with itself HK$200 million;

(e) Hang Seng Bank debits the Treasury's deposit account with itself HK$300 million; and

(f) Hang Lung Bank debits the Treasury's deposit account with itself HK$200 million.

The monetary effects of this transaction will be that, other things being equal, both the Balance and NCB will be reduced by HK$500 million. Interbank interest rates will again be driven higher, giving support to the exchange rate.

14.   The undertaking by HSBC to maintain a balance on the Account no less than the NCB of the rest of the banking system means that it will have in effect created for itself a clearing account. Thus, when HSBC purchases for its customers US dollars with Hong Kong dollars, NCB will increase. So that this will not result in the Balance falling short of NCB, it will be in the interest of HSBC to fund the US dollar purchase by borrowing Hong Kong dollars in the interbank market, in a manner identical to that in which any other licensed bank would currently act. In doing so, the supply of Hong Kong dollars in the interbank market will not be affected.

Market information

15.   Given the monetary effects of Exchange Fund operations under the new accounting arrangements, it will be useful to participants in the foreign exchange and money markets to have access to certain relevant information. Arrangements are being made for the Exchange Fund to publish at appropriate times on each day through the electronic media the Balance at the close of the previous day and the net effect of operations carried out by the Exchange Fund during the day on the Balance. It is hoped that such information will start to be made available in early September. When considered appropriate, other information will also be so published.

16.   Any request for clarification of the matters described in this paper should be addressed to the Deputy Secretary for Monetary Affairs who is in charge of the operation of the Account. He can be reached at 5–290021.

CHAPTER **12**

THE IMPACT OF THE TIANANMEN SQUARE INCIDENT ON HONG KONG'S MONETARY SYSTEM

May–June 1989

This final article from AMM describes the response of the currency board mechanism in Hong Kong, as amended by the new accounting arrangements of July 1988, to the crisis in Beijing surrounding the Tiananmen Square demonstrations of May/June 1989. Using the terminology of Chapter 7, there was both an "internal drain" (in the form of a withdrawal of funds from the Bank of China) and an "external drain" (an outflow of funds through the sale of HK$ for foreign currencies). The article provides detail about how these events impacted the Hong Kong monetary system — the response of the authorities, interest rates, and the spot rate for the HK$/US$ to the internal fund shifts and to the outflow. In some ways this was the most severe test of the resilience of Hong Kong's currency board system since the early days of 1983–84, and it certainly the provides the best-documented case study of a combined "internal drain" and "external drain". By now the automatic self-correcting properties of the currency board mechanism as adopted by Hong Kong in 1983, i.e. the provision for banknote convertibility at HK$7.80 per US$, had been supplemented with the authorities' ability to tighten or ease money market conditions through adjusting the balance that HSBC was required to maintain with the Exchange Fund. The article provides an assessment of how the new, supplemented mechanism operated in the face of this internal and external drain.

As a proponent of the 1983 scheme, I was still dubious about the innovations of July 1988, mainly on the grounds that they could, if improperly administered, lead to discretionary currency and interest rate manipulation. This is clear from the sceptical tone adopted towards the end of the article regarding the additional steps that the Hong Kong monetary authorities were taking in 1989 to improve their techniques for managing the local money market.

With the benefit of hindsight one may say that the attacks on the Hong Kong dollar during the Asian financial crisis in 1997–98 and their damaging side-effects eventually provided proof of the futility of these moves towards greater day-to-day control of the money markets. Having abandoned the idea that deviations of the exchange rate under Hong Kong's currency board arrangements were self-correcting, it would have been logical for the authorities to press ahead with developing alternative mechanisms that ensured (1) some limits to the range of fluctuation for the free market HK$ exchange rate, combined with (2) practical and non-disruptive solutions to speculative inflows or outflows. In the event, Hong Kong had to wait almost a decade (from 1989 until 1998 — see Epilogue) for a comprehensive solution to the problem of combining the assurance of convergence between the market exchange rate and the conversion rate for banknotes on the one hand with day-to-day flexibility in coping with speculative inflows and outflows on the other hand.

A S I A N   M O N E T A R Y   M O N I T O R

Vol. 13 No. 3 May–June, 1989

There are two types of "test" to which the linked rate for the Hong Kong dollar can be subjected. First, there is the internal drain, i.e. the conversion of HK$ deposits into HK$ currency on a large scale and, second there is the external drain, i.e. the conversion of HK$ deposits into foreign currency in substantial amounts. In the early days of June (1989) there was the possibility that the linked rate mechanism could be subjected to both types of test.

On June 5th and 6th in the wake of the Tiananmen incident Hong Kong residents showed their disgust at the conduct of the PRC government by making substantial withdrawals of deposits and cash from the Bank of China and its affiliated banks in Hong Kong. The reduction in deposits at the Bank of China and its sister banks would have caused those banks to experience overdrafts on their balance at the Clearing House. If those overdrafts had become too large, it is quite possible that instead of becoming excessively overdrawn with the Hongkong and Shanghai Banking Corporation (which operates the Clearing House), arrangements could have been made for other banks to have extended loans to the Bank of China group. The withdrawals of cash — the traditional form of the internal drain — from the Bank of China group would have led to the kind of consequences described in Chapter 7 ("The Operation of the New Exchange Rate Mechanism"). Briefly, in this case the Bank of China's loss of cash and hence deposits would have further increased its overdrafts at the Clearing House. In addition, the Bank of China would have been obliged to purchase HK$ banknotes with US$ — possibly drawing on gold or other non Hong Kong dollar foreign currency assets — from one of the two note-issuing banks in Hong Kong in order to satisfy its customers' demand for cash. Since the Bank of China could not have called in its normal loans and advances sufficiently rapidly to meet the cash or deposit drain it would have been forced to borrow additional funds in the money market thus causing interest rates in Hong Kong to rise. As a result overnight interbank rates rose from 10% to 12% between June 5 and 8, about 3% above the overnight LIBOR dollar equivalent for US$ (see Chart 12.1). At the same time the Hong Kong dollar rose to a 2 cent premium (7.78) relative to its parity of 7.80 (see Chart 12.2).

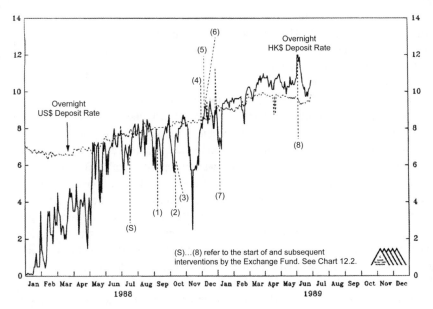

Chart 12.1 Overnight HK$ and US$ Interest Rates

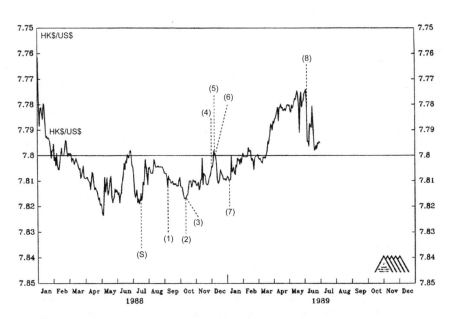

Chart 12.2 HK$/US$ Exchange Rate (January 1988–December 1989)

This mechanism is precisely similar to the chain of events which occurred at Christmas and New Year 1983/84 just after the linked rate system for the Hong Kong dollar was established (see Charts 12.3 and 12.4) when there was a large demand for cash from the public for the first time under the new system. Since banks had failed to anticipate the effects of the cash drain at this time interest rates rose sharply, and the Hong Kong dollar moved up to a premium relative to the parity. In subsequent years the banking system has learned to cope with seasonal cash drains of this kind, but the kind of cash drain which occurred on June 5th and 6th 1989 was clearly unexpected and therefore could not have been anticipated by appropriate portfolio actions.

In the immediate aftermath of the withdrawals of deposits from the Bank of China it was unlikely that the internal drain would cause any serious problems for the linked rate system because funds from the Bank of China were, for the most part, being re-deposited with other banks in Hong Kong, so that the overall HK$ money supply remained largely unchanged. To date there has been no significant evidence of the second type of problem, namely the external drain. However, if the crisis in China had continued or worsened then it is quite possible that there would have been outflows of funds as there were in July 1984 for example. Charts 12.3 and 12.4 show how during that episode the Hong Kong dollar fell to around 7.87 while one month interbank HK$ deposit rates rose to 28%.

The key difference between an internal drain and an external drain can be illustrated by considering what happens to the free market exchange rate under each set of circumstances. In the case of an internal drain, interest rates rise and the free market rate for the HK$ goes to a premium relative to the parity, e.g. 7.75, but in the case of an external drain the HK$ goes to a discount relative to the parity, e.g. 7.85, while again interest rates rise. Throughout most of the recent June 1989 episode the HK$ remained at a premium to the parity which suggests that the internal drain dominated the external drain.

The linked rate system has withstood both kinds of attack — internal and external drains — before, and one can be reasonably confident that it will easily withstand either the internal drain or the external drain, or a combination of the two, in future. Basically, the HK$ is simply a different denomination of the US$, but during episodes of internal or external drain it yields a higher rate of interest than US$.

The only major qualification which needs to be made to all of the statements above is that since July 1988 the Exchange Fund has been operating more like a central bank than a passive colonial currency board. (See Chapter 11 for details of the new arrangements). Between July 1988 and June 1989 there have been eight episodes of intervention by the Exchange Fund using the new machinery, as shown in Table 12.2. The timing of each episode of intervention is also pinpointed by the numbers shown on Charts 12.1 and 12.2. The interventions have either been conducted with the aim of keeping the free market rate for the Hong Kong dollar within some unspecified band on each side of the 7.80 parity, or in some cases to manage money market interest rates. One example of intervention aimed at money market management was the injection and subsequent withdrawal of HK$ 200 million at the time of the Hong Kong Telecom share

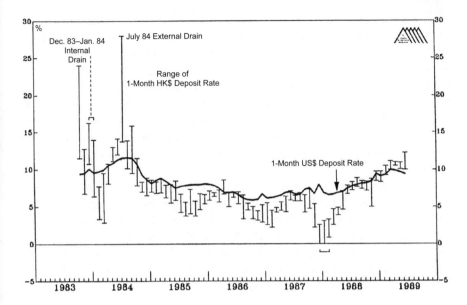

Chart 12.3 HK$ and US$ Interest Rate Differentials

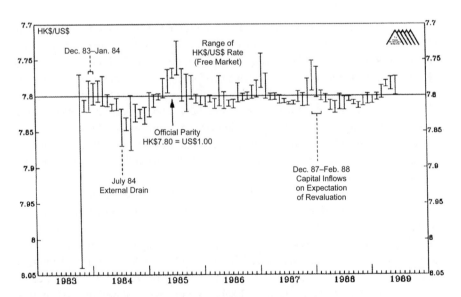

Chart 12.4 HK$/US$ Exchange Rate (December 1983–January 1984)

issue in December 1988. When the Bank of China found itself in difficulties on June 5th and 6th the Hong Kong authorities were quick to intervene again with an injection of funds into the system. This time the injection was HK$194 million. Thus instead of allowing the internal drain or external drain to run their full course, the Hong Kong authorities are regularly intervening to offset the consequences of natural market forces. On the surface the scale of intervention has been quite small, but it should always be remembered that the impact on the banking system as a whole is potentially many times greater than the size of the intervention itself. To gauge the impact one must calculate the monetary multiplier and apply that to the amount of the intervention as shown in Tables 12.1 and 12.2.

When the authorities introduced their "new accounting arrangements" in July 1988, they thereby changed the definition of the monetary base in Hong Kong. Before July the monetary base consisted only of cash currency held by the public and by the banks and deposit-taking companies (DTCs). Since the introduction of the new scheme the monetary base has consisted of cash currency held by the public and by the banks and DTCs plus the amount of funds required to be held to the account of the Hongkong and Shanghai Bank at the Exchange Fund. In symbols:

$$B = C + A$$

where B is the monetary base, C is the total currency issued, and A is the amount of funds in "The Account".

The new monetary multiplier for Hong Kong is HK$M/B = HK$M/(C + A), where HK$M is the relevant definition of the Hong Kong dollar denominated money supply. Data for the new multiplier for HKM_1$ and HKM_3$ are shown in Table 12.1. Roughly speaking, any intervention by the Exchange Fund has a two-fold impact on HKM_1$ and an eleven-fold impact on HKM_3$. This is precisely the same kind of multiple expansion or multiple contraction effect which any central bank's foreign exchange interventions or open market operations have on the domestic money supply of that country. Of course it takes time for this monetary multiplier to have its effect, so that following any intervention it would be a matter of several weeks before the full impact was achieved.

Not content with the degree of intervention achieved so far, the Hong Kong authorities are now planning to introduce Exchange Fund discount bills as a further monetary instrument to assist in their money market management operations. If transactions in the new bills are settled by debits or credits to The Account of the Hongkong and Shanghai Bank at the Exchange Fund then operations by the Exchange Fund in the new bills will have an equally powerful multiple expansion or multiple contraction effect on the banking system as a whole. However, if they are settled by debits and credits to the accounts of the Exchange Fund with the banking system, then they will not have more than a trivial impact on the volume of funds in the system.

Table 12.1 Monetary Multipliers for Hong Kong from July 1988

	$HK\$M_1$	$HK\$M_3$	C	A	Base= A+C	$\dfrac{HK\$M_1}{Base}$	$\dfrac{HK\$M_3}{Base}$
1988							
July	73,188	356,457	30,977	1250	32,227	2.27	11.06
Aug	73,834	355,204	30,899	1250	32,149	2.30	11.05
Sept	75,009	357,261	31,549	1100	32,649	2.30	10.94
Oct	77,725	372,052	31,895	880	32,775	2.37	11.33
Nov	78,698	387,345	32,298	860	33,158	2.37	11.68
Dec	79,257	389,052	34,087	860	34,947	2.37	11.13
1989							
Jan	87,362	401,177	39,975	728	40,703	2.15	9.86
Feb	82,844	400,052	36,415	728	37,143	2.15	9.86
Mar	80,623	401,505	35,766	728	36,494	2.21	11.00
Apr	78,285	408,119	35,300	728	36,028	2.17	11.33
May				728			
June				922			

Notes: Monthend data in HK$ millions

C = Total Cash Currency Issued

A = Level of funds in The Account. For consistency monthend data have been used to calculate the base.

Table 12.2 Record of Interventions by the Exchange Fund since July 1988

		Outstanding Balance of The Account	Scale of Intervention	Approx. Impact on $HK\$M_1$	Approx. Impact on $HK\$M_3$
	1988				
S	July 18	1250			
1.	Sept. 7	1100	−150	−345	−1650
2.	Oct. 11	950	−150	−345	−1650
3.	Oct. 12	880	−70	−160	−775
4.	Nov. 30	860	−20	−50	−235
5.	Dec. 6	1060	+200	+460	+2100
6.	Dec. 7	860	−200	−460	−2100
	1989				
7.	Jan. 5	728	−132	−290	−1390
8.	June 5	922	+194	+445	+2150

Notes: The multiplier is calculated as the average of the HK$ money supply divided by total cash currency plus funds in the Account for the month-end immediately preceding and the month-end immediately after the specified intervention.

Needless to say, with the expansion in Exchange Fund operations goes an expansion in staff, so the Exchange Fund is recruiting dealers for its foreign exchange and money market dealing room. This is to be accompanied by the appointment of recognised dealers or market-makers who will have to meet capital adequacy requirements similar to those in existence for banks and DTCs. With the development of this additional machinery it seems likely that Hong Kong will move to a system of regular discretionary intervention in the domestic money market and/or in the foreign exchange market. Once this is accomplished later this year it will no longer be possible to claim that Hong Kong does not have a central bank. All the important market operations of a central bank — i.e. foreign exchange intervention and domestic open market operations each with a full multiple expansion or multiple contraction effect — will be regularly conducted by the Exchange Fund. The Exchange Fund bills will be liabilities of the Fund rather than liabilities of the government or Treasury. The issue of this short term debt is therefore purely for monetary rather than fiscal purposes, though there is the secondary objective of helping to develop the capital market in Hong Kong.

Not surprisingly, capital market participants such as banks, merchant banks and brokers have reacted enthusiastically to the proposed new bills because it will mean more business for them as well as providing a local benchmark for pricing other Hong Kong dollar denominated issues. However, judged strictly from the standpoint of the conduct of monetary policy, this development will take Hong Kong even further down the path towards full-scale central banking. The only instrument that the Exchange Fund would not have at this stage is a discount window, but since the Exchange Fund has acted on numerous occasions in recent years to rescue banks which might otherwise have failed it is clear that the authorities already act as lender of last resort — discount window or no discount window. Aside from not operating a discount window, the only major functions which the Hong Kong authorities will not be conducting themselves are (1) the operation of the clearing house and (2) the issue of the banknotes.

CONCLUSION

The run on the Hong Kong branches of the Bank of China and its sister banks in the wake of the Tiananmen incident has provided another test of the linked rate system for the Hong Kong dollar. Instead of the anxiety about events in China leading to a serious external drain, as some observers expected, the internal cash drain proved to be the more dominant phenomenon. However, the impact of the internal drain was itself partially offset by an injection of funds into the system by the Exchange Fund using the intervention machinery created in July 1988. These operations are to be supplemented later this year by the introduction of Exchange Fund bills, at which time the authorities will possess effective tools for both domestic money market intervention and foreign exchange market intervention. Both sets of operations will have comparable multiplier effects on the broader monetary system, giving the authorities scope for day-to-day discretionary intervention in the classic style of any central bank. With these developments, it will no longer be possible to say that Hong Kong's monetary system is an automatic, non-discretionary system. Regular operations by the authorities in the domestic money market and in the foreign exchange market will fundamentally alter the character of Hong Kong's monetary system. Whether or not these are desirable changes is largely a value judgment, but given the power to intervene in this way, governments very seldom reverse the process by giving them up. In Chapter 11 we said that "the new arrangements ... constitute a major step towards the establishment of a central bank in Hong Kong". Since that time Hong Kong has taken a few more steps along the same road.

CHAPTER 13

BUILDING RESILIENCE AND AUTOMATICITY, 1983–2005[1]

INTRODUCTION

The selected AMM articles in Chapters 1 to 7 showed how the fundamental flaws in Hong Kong's monetary system in the 1970s and 1980s were identified; brought to the notice of academics, bankers, investors and the Hong Kong authorities; and eventually addressed after the dangerous run on the currency in September 1983. Chapters 8 to 12 traced some of the subsequent debate about why the automatic adjustment mechanism did not appear to be acting as efficiently as had been intended in keeping the free market rate for the Hong Kong dollar at or close to the official parity of HK$7.80 per US$ and the initial steps the authorities took to correct these problems.

In this chapter, section 1 presents a summary and assessment of the initial reforms covered by AMM during the years 1983–89; section 2 reviews the period 1990–98, including developments after AMM ceased publication; and section 3 covers the period 1998–2005, when the mechanism of the currency board was substantially amended following the Asian financial crisis and subsequently fine-tuned. Each section is divided into two halves covering (a) the changes that were relevant to the monetary regime, and (b) an assessment of how the economy behaved under the currency board system in each phase.

1. SUMMARY OF MONETARY REFORMS, 1983–89

(A) Monetary Changes, 1983–89

(i) Problems with Convergence

In the years from the re-adoption of the currency board system in October 1983 until 1989, my approach at AMM had been to focus on the deficiencies of the cash arbitrage

---

1.   This is a slightly revised version of the Epilogue in the previous edition of this book. The discussion of alternative exchange rate arrangements has been shifted to Chapter 14, section 4, and some minor editorial changes have been made.

process. It was preferable, in my judgement, that the system operate automatically rather than that the authorities be continuously intervening in the local money markets or in the foreign exchange market. The authorities, however, were in a better position to observe the limited extent of any such cash arbitrage and had progressively moved to a position where, through interest rate management, they took responsibility for ensuring adequate, albeit limited, convergence between the official rate for banknotes and the wholesale market exchange rate.

In view of the shortcomings of cash arbitrage, and to maintain exchange rate stability, the authorities felt obliged "to influence interbank liquidity and thus short-term interbank interest rates, and [to engage in] direct intervention in the foreign exchange markets" (John Nugee, "A Brief History of the Exchange Fund", *HKMA Quarterly Bulletin*, May 1995). According to this account, HSBC also collaborated with the authorities to carry the burden of any intervention costs.

Since these ad hoc interventions were inherently unsatisfactory in bringing about full exchange rate convergence, the authorities had to accept second-best solutions. To ensure a more consistent and successful outcome for their intervention operations, they relied on three main instruments. First there was the money market borrowing scheme intended to tighten monetary conditions (see Chapter 4, section 3, "The Exchange Fund's Borrowing Scheme: A Twist on Operation Twist", pp. 70–72). Second, to guard against exceptionally large and prolonged inflows, the authorities had developed the negative interest rate scheme in December 1987. (Although this scheme was approved by an ordinance passed by the Legislative Council, it was never actually implemented.) Third, a more decisive break with past practice was accomplished with the "Accounting Arrangements" in July 1988, which made the two previous schemes largely redundant.

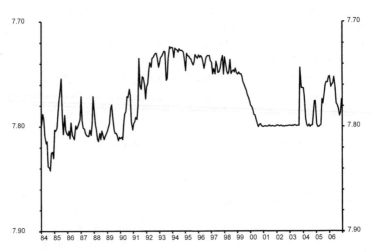

—— HK$/US$ Spot Rate

Chart 13.1 HK$/US$ Spot Rate, 1984–2006 (Source: Datastream, as of 20/3/2007)

(ii) Abandonment of the Simple, Standard Model and the July 1988 Measures

The new Account of HSBC at the Exchange Fund (EF) amounted to a reserve account for the system as a whole and brought short-term money market interest rates (directly) and the wholesale market exchange rate (indirectly) within the control of the authorities. In calm periods the system could be adequately maintained without assistance from the authorities, but in more disturbed times the system was dependent upon intermittent intervention operations by the authorities. However, as we shall see, these new arrangements only addressed one part of Hong Kong's underlying monetary problems — achieving a modicum of convergence. At the same time, they obscured the essential fragility of the system and left it vulnerable to a more concerted attack.

The July 1988 package of measures enabled the authorities to do two things. First, on a short-run basis, by giving them control over money market interest rates the measures enabled any intervention to be backed up by interest rate moves in the corresponding direction. For example, reducing HSBC's balances in The Account at the EF (or at the HKMA after April 1993) by means of EF sales of US$ in the market and debiting the equivalent HK$ amount to The Account of HSBC would reduce the amount of funds in the money market, driving up interest rates, while at the same time tending to strengthen the spot rate for the HK$. Second, on a long-run basis, the authorities could now guide the market to an understanding of what they deemed to be an acceptable range for the spot rate.

In practice, between 1991 and 1998 the acceptable range was not a narrow spread on each side of the official parity (such as HK$7.78–7.82) but more typically a range like HK$7.73–7.75, representing a premium to the fixed parity of 500–700 basis points (see Chart 13.1). In effect, the authorities appeared to use the new mechanism to build a buffer between the spot rate and the official parity, thus providing the Hong Kong dollar with a safety cushion in the event of any unwanted downward lurch due to a bout of speculative selling of the local currency. They had, for a while, abandoned the attempt to achieve convergence between the market exchange rate and the conversion rate for banknotes or Certificates of Indebtedness (CIs).

While the July 1988 package succeeded in enabling the authorities to manage the spot rate far better, my view at the time was that the new arrangements were all stick and no carrot. If the spot rate deviated from the authorities' desired range, the size of HSBC's account at the EF could be increased or decreased by purchases or sales of foreign currency or HK$ money market instruments, effectively increasing or decreasing the monetary base by an equivalent amount. EF adjustments to the size of The Account were now the primary driver of the range for both the spot rate and for money market interest rates. Even if cash arbitrage had been a feasible way to achieve convergence in the past, there was no longer any incentive for the banks to conduct such transactions. The authorities had established the means of achieving full control of the spot rate and money market rates — if they chose to exercise it.

In addition, thanks to the increasing efficiency of the clearing system due to the use of computers, banks were able to operate in the new environment with very low levels of clearing balances. This was entirely without problem so long as buyers and sellers of Hong Kong dollars were roughly matched but could cause problems if there was ever a significant imbalance of sellers over buyers. Thus when there was large-scale selling of the HK$, one bank or a number of banks could find themselves overdrawn on their clearing accounts. Since the rules of the clearing system required banks to maintain positive balances on their clearing accounts, and there was no discounting mechanism available to the banks to enable them to convert securities or bills into funds at the clearing house, the only remedy open to a bank that found itself overdrawn was to bid for funds from other banks in the interbank market. Conversely, when there were large inflows, the interbank market would be flooded with funds, pushing rates down abruptly. Finding a solution to the instability of interest rates and their knock-on effects on the spot rate for the HK$ was to become the major focus of the authorities' attention during the 1990s.

Having established control over interbank liquidity in July 1988, the authorities made some minor legislative changes to achieve the full flexibility of interest rates that might be needed to defend the fixed exchange rate. Chapter 10 described the introduction of negative interest rates, but in addition the Moneylenders Ordinance was amended to eliminate the 60% ceiling on interest rates. The authorities could now raise or lower rates in the money market as far as might be necessary to defend the exchange rate.

(iii) Summary

To summarize, by the end of 1989 the Hong Kong monetary system had been reformed so that the convertibility of banknotes at a fixed rate provided some sort of anchor for the currency, but there was no assurance of convergence between the wholesale market exchange rate and the convertibility rate for banknotes. As a result, the authorities had brought in several measures, primarily The Account of HSBC at the EF, to enable them to steer interest rates in a direction that would assist that convergence. Although AMM continued to argue (mistakenly, in retrospect) for cash arbitrage to be given a greater opportunity to work, the authorities shifted to a different tack. Most of the 1990s was spent developing mechanisms that would (a) give the authorities greater control over money market rates, and (b) enable the banks to resolve any overdrafts or surpluses in their settlement or reserve accounts through a discount window or deposit facility, while providing the requisite instruments to enable the banks to conduct such transactions without the EF being put at risk. The former would achieve adequate convergence, while the latter was intended to prevent sudden, sharp movements in interest rates that could threaten the stability of the system. The system was still far from operating on autopilot.

(B) Business Cycle Developments, 1983–89

(i) Recovery and Mid-Course Correction

The years 1983–89 saw a fairly continuous expansion in business activity, both globally and in Hong Kong. According to the National Bureau of Economic Research (NBER), the US economy began a long expansion from its trough in November 1982, which continued until July 1990. Since Hong Kong was operating a currency board, even if an imperfect one, the broad shape of business cycle developments affecting Hong Kong would necessarily be determined by external influences. Under a currency board, monetary policy is essentially passive, the currency board economy importing interest rate levels, which in turn largely determine monetary conditions in the local economy. This implied that the stimulus to business activity and inflation would come primarily from interest rates in the anchor currency country and/or by the interaction of the US-determined local interest rates with prevailing local business opportunities. When US rates were low, lending opportunities would tend to be greater; when US rates were high, lending opportunities would tend to diminish. Hong Kong would therefore tend to experience business cycle expansions when the US economy was experiencing an upswing, and economic downturns when the US went into recession.

In these years the principal US influences were initially strongly expansionary, as the US Fed funds rate remained at a low 8.0% in 1983–84 (compared with peak levels of 19.0% in 1981), enabling Hong Kong to make a vigorous recovery in 1984, following the currency crisis of the previous year. In fact, the economy had been on a recovery path despite the currency crisis, with exports stimulated in part by the depreciation of the HK dollar during the currency crisis. Real GDP growth recovered from 0.5% (year-on-year) in 1983 Q1 to reach 14.2% in 1984 Q2 (see Chart 13.2).

From early 1984, the Fed started raising rates from 8.0% to 11.75% by August (Chart 13.3), causing the US economy to slow, and this mid-course correction was transmitted directly to Hong Kong. Asset prices which had recovered strongly in late 1983 and early 1984 underwent another downturn, exacerbated by adverse developments in August in the Sino-British talks on the future of Hong Kong. Equally serious for Hong Kong during the US mid-course correction of 1984–85 was the exceptional strength of the US$, boosted by President Reagan's supply-side budget measures and by rising US interest rates. The US currency had been appreciating ever since Reagan won the election in November 1979, the US dollar trade-weighted index peaking in March 1985, 53% above its pre-election level. Despite the prior depreciation of the HK$ during 1983, Hong Kong's greater exposure to international trade together with a relatively minor episode of capital flight in August 1984 (which generated an upward spike in HK$ interest rates) caused Hong Kong's GDP to be much more severely affected than that of the US (which only experienced a mild slowdown). Real GDP in Hong Kong plunged from double-digit growth rates in most of 1984 to –2.6% in 1985 Q2 and Q3 (Chart 13.2), with total exports slowing from a 50% growth rate in early 1984 to zero by mid-1985.

(ii) Secondary Expansion

However, once US interest rates were again on an easing path from October 1984 until the end of 1986, the value of the US$ was again depreciating (especially after the Plaza

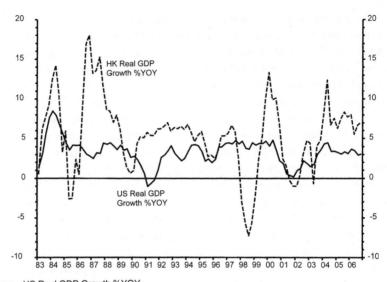

US Real GDP Growth %YOY

HK Real GDP Growth %YOY

Chart 13.2 Hong Kong and US Real GDP Growth (Source: Datastream, as of 20/3/2007)

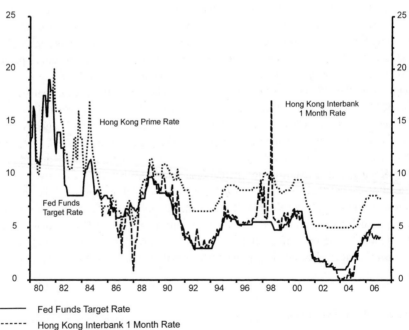

Fed Funds Target Rate

Hong Kong Interbank 1 Month Rate

Hong Kong Prime Rate

Chart 13.3 Hong Kong and US Interest Rates (Source: Datastream, as of 20/3/2007)

Agreement of September 1985), and the hurdle of the Sino-British talks was passed, Hong Kong's economy entered a period of exuberant expansion. Between mid-1986 and the end of 1987 the economy grew at a double-digit rate, averaging an astonishing 14.8% per annum in real terms. Hong Kong's heavy external trade dependence worked strongly in its favour this time, helped by the strong bounce-back from the downturn of 1985.

From early 1987, through most of 1988 and until June 1989 the Fed, under its new chairman, Alan Greenspan, embarked on another tightening phase, the Fed funds rate rising from 6.0% to 9.75% (Chart 13.3). These rates hikes were again transmitted to Hong Kong and were reflected in the stock market crash of October 1987 and an associated crisis in the futures market, as well as in a gradually slowing growth rate. After the October crash, US interest rates were lowered several times, enabling the Hong Kong economy to grow at 8.0% in 1988 (though this deceleration — from 14.8% — should perhaps be regarded as a slowing to Hong Kong's then sustainable growth rate) but subsequently slowing progressively through 1989 to a low of 0.7% in Q4 and 1.0% in 1990 Q1.

Local factors could and did affect structural and sectoral developments in Hong Kong, but this would also be true under any other type of exchange rate arrangement. Thus, for example, these years saw a high level of immigration from mainland China into Hong Kong, and the currency board system was able to accommodate this quite simply by allowing greater expansion of the supply of money in Hong Kong. Hence over the period 1984–89 Hong Kong's broad money supply (M3) averaged 23.3% p.a., far ahead of its US counterpart. As explained in Chapter 8, Hong Kong's currency board regime meant that the supply curve for currency was horizontal, and the authorities were therefore able to supply CIs (effectively banknotes) as long as the note-issuing banks were willing and able to pay US$ at the fixed rate to the EF. Meantime, the banks were willing to lend, as long as the level of US rates was compatible with new lending in Hong Kong.

(iii) The Divergence of Hong Kong and US Inflation

Inflation declined sharply after the 1983 currency stabilization (see Chapter 9). From a year-on-year increase of 11.9% in December 1983 (when the economy was still adjusting to the weakened exchange rate), consumer price inflation fell to 4.0% by December 1984, 2.9% in December 1985, and declined to a trough of 2.3% in May 1986 (Chart 13.4). Thereafter, inflation in Hong Kong began a gradual and extended rise, eventually reaching a peak of 12.6% year-on-year in May 1991. In part, this 10.3 percentage point increase was driven by the upturn in US inflation. Following a short-lived slump in oil prices in 1986, the US CPI increased from an oil-affected low of 1.1% in December 1986 to 6.3% in October and November 1991, an increase of 5.2 percentage points, or close to half the increase in Hong Kong. The other half of the rise in Hong Kong's prices has to be explained by the Balassa-Samuelson effect. Briefly, this is the proposition that non-traded goods prices will rise more rapidly in an economy where productivity is rising more strongly.

Chart 13.4 Hong Kong and US Inflation Rates (Source: Datastream, as of 20/3/2007)

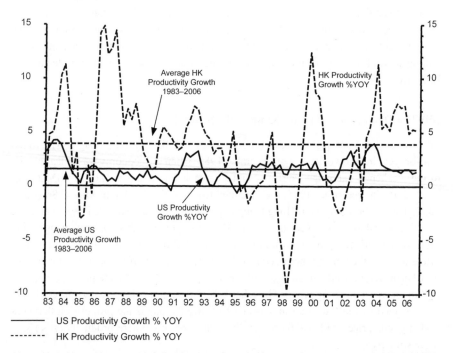

Chart 13.5 Hong Kong and US Productivity Growth (Source: Datastream, as of 20/3/2007)

In Hong Kong over the years 1984–96,[2] productivity was rising at 4.7% p.a., compared with 1.2% p.a. in the US over the same period (both measured as real GDP growth less the growth of the labour force; see Chart 13.5). Consequently, Hong Kong's domestic price level was able to rise more rapidly than the US price level, without Hong Kong losing competitiveness at the fixed exchange rate. The same phenomenon can be observed in the relation between inflation in Japan and the US during the era of the Bretton Woods fixed exchange rate system (see Chapter 4, pp. 83–89, which discusses the convergence and divergence of traded goods prices in both economies).

Perhaps the major problem in the years 1983–89 was not so much the transmission of US business cycle influences to Hong Kong but the severity of upward and downward movements in asset markets and in economic activity. The volatility in the growth rate of Hong Kong over this period relates primarily to the abrupt downturn of real GDP in 1985–86. Would it have been possible for Hong Kong to avoid or moderate the downturn?

First, it could be argued that Hong Kong should have chosen a different type of exchange rate regime, such as a managed or floating rate system. However, it is clear from the debate about the adoption of the basic currency board model in 1983 that these options were not on the table in 1983. Conceivably, such alternative regimes could have been considered and adopted subsequently, but before July 1988, the adoption of a more flexible exchange rate would simply not have been feasible. As Hong Kong's monetary system has evolved, the feasibility of a move to a managed or variable exchange rate has increased, but account has to be taken of the benefits of simplicity and transparency that are associated with currency boards. The trade-off between the benefits and costs of a rigid peg to the US$, along with proposals for an alternative exchange rate regime for the territory are discussed in section 4 of Chapter 14.

Second, it should always be recognized that Hong Kong at this time was unquestionably a rapidly growing economy and that its growth rate was further enhanced by substantial additions to the labour force by immigration from mainland China. Variations in growth tend to be larger in economies with higher average growth rates. The volatility of Hong Kong's real GDP was probably increased by the territory's growing specialization in financial services and property-related industries, but this could not have been avoided without reducing the long-term average growth rate.

2. STEERING WITH INTEREST RATES, 1990–98

Over much of the next decade until 1998, developments in Hong Kong's monetary system were mainly aimed at the creation of a more efficient short-term debt market and the simultaneous development of mechanisms for smoothing out day-to-day imbalances

---

2. Since the non-traded goods price divergence between Hong Kong and the US continued until the onset of the Asian financial crisis in 1997–1998, it is preferable to deal with this whole episode (1983–1996) now rather than revisit it in section 2 (B).

in the interbank market. Although AMM continued to monitor these developments, and a number of articles were written on these issues during these years, the author himself moved from Hong Kong to San Francisco at the end of 1993. My focus on monetary developments in Asia became less intense, and ultimately AMM ceased publication at the end of 1995.

(A) Monetary Changes, 1990–98

Having created a mechanism for managing the money market through The Account of HSBC at the EF, the Hong Kong authorities viewed the next set of priorities as the orderly development of a deeper and more active money market. Hong Kong prided itself on its role as an international financial centre in Asia, but it had always felt handicapped by the fact that, due to continuous budget surpluses and hardly any government borrowing, there was essentially no government debt market in Hong Kong. This would inevitably impose constraints on the range of instruments the EF could deal in when conducting transactions to influence liquidity in the local market via the level of The Account of HSBC, but it also meant that there was no satisfactory array of high-quality debt issues that could serve as a benchmark for market participants. The solution was for the EF to create some liabilities on its own balance sheet and issue these to the market with enough maturities to build a quasi-Hong Kong government yield curve.

(i) Money market Reforms (EFBN and LAF)

The Exchange Fund first extended its reach from the short-term money markets to a broader range of maturities. A spectrum of debt securities was developed, issued as liabilities of the Exchange Fund, and sold to banks and other institutional investors. The Exchange Fund Bills programme (with maturities up to one year) was begun in March 1990, and Notes (with longer maturities) were introduced from March 1993. The motives for this scheme were twofold: to promote the development of Hong Kong's debt markets by providing an official benchmark as a reference for investors and borrowers, and to provide the banks with very liquid, high-quality securities that would enable them to better manage their balance sheet positions. In addition, the creation of the Exchange Fund Bills & Notes (EFBN) market would enable the authorities to conduct open market operations in their own paper, saving interest costs because the yield on EFBN instruments was typically lower than equivalent-maturity HIBOR rates, and avoiding any credit risk because the EFBN were the authorities' own liabilities. From the beginning, EFBN issues were very well received by the market, especially by the banks, which often owned as much as 70%–80% of all outstanding issues.

Second, the authorities introduced the Liquidity Adjustment Facility (LAF) in June 1992, to provide banks with discounting and limited overnight deposit facilities. The facility was limited because the LAF bid-and-offer rates effectively set a floor and ceiling for overnight interbank rates. In normal times the banks were able to make late adjustments to their clearing accounts either by borrowing funds overnight at the offer rate, in the form of repurchase agreements collateralized by eligible securities, or by placing funds overnight with the EF at the bid rate. If rates moved outside the bid-and-offer bands, then banks would have to lend or borrow as best they could with other counterparties in the banking system. The benefit to the banks in adjusting their end-of-day positions was clear, but the authorities were also able to influence short-term rates directly by varying the LAF bid-and-offer rates. Initially the operating tactics in the interbank market were focused on the volume of liquidity, but following the establishment of the Hong Kong Monetary Authority (HKMA) in April 1993,[3] the target was amended to the level of the interbank rate. Following the shift of target in March 1994, this approach appeared to be successful in reducing day-to-day volatility in the interbank market and led to a gradual convergence between the overnight HIBOR and the LAF Offer rate.

(ii) Expanded Role of the Exchange Fund and Reconciliation with the Monetary Rule

Strictly speaking, all these debt market innovations were separate from the monetary regime in the sense that they did not impinge on the requirement that note-issuing banks had to pay US$ for the CIs that authorized them to issue HK$ banknotes, and were entitled to receive US$ upon redemption. This part of the monetary base remained unaffected. However, the creation of The Account of HSBC at the EF and the introduction of EFBNs fundamentally changed the composition of the monetary base and ultimately the role of the EF.

The Accounting Arrangements established in July 1988 made the size of the net clearing balance of the banking system at HSBC subject to the directives of the EF, an arrangement that was backed up with interest rate penalties in the event of a divergence. The EF was now in the position of any other central bank, able to influence the volume of funds in commercial banks' clearing accounts, albeit at one remove through the intermediary of the HSBC Account. When real-time gross settlement (RTGS) for interbank clearing and settlement was introduced in December 1996, all licensed banks were required to maintain clearing balances with the authorities instead of clearing through a commercial bank. The combined total of clearing balances became known as the Aggregate Balance. This formally brought Hong Kong's hitherto unusual arrangements into line with normal practice elsewhere, enabling the authorities to

---

3. The creation of the Hong Kong Monetary Authority in April 1993 brought together the Exchange Fund, which had been responsible for the conduct of monetary policy under the Monetary Affairs Branch, and the Office of the Banking Commissioner, which had been responsible for prudential supervision of the licensed banks and deposit-taking companies. While this did not immediately mark a new direction from a strictly monetary standpoint, it was significant in enabling management of the two organizations to be integrated under a single chief executive and in coordinating future financial market developments.

control the volume of funds in the system directly through open market operations. From the standpoint of monetary theory, this extended the definition of the monetary base in Hong Kong to include (1) banknotes — or the CIs corresponding to them — and (2) the Account or the Aggregate Balance.

The creation of the Account in July 1988 appeared to undermine the monetary rule — the requirement that new units of base money would be *automatically* backed by US$. The integrity of Hong Kong's currency board seemed to be compromised in the sense that the Account would not be backed by foreign currency. In fact, the EF had long ago been compromised due to the role that the EF had played since 1977 as banker to the government. The EF had been given the responsibility for investing the government's accumulated budget surpluses in overseas markets. These funds were transferred abroad from time to time by sales of HK$ in the market when the budget was in surplus, or transferred back into Hong Kong by purchases of HK$ when the budget was in deficit. The timing of such transfers was discretionary, and that meant that the authority regularly had HK$ assets on its books (in its capacity as banker to the government). The best way to view these activities from a monetary standpoint is to divide the balance sheet of the EF into a monetary segment and a fiscal segment (as shown in Ch. 5, p. 109, "Consolidated Balance Sheets for Current Hong Kong Monetary System"), confining the accumulation and investment of fiscal surpluses to the fiscal segment of the account and leaving the issue and redemption of CIs and the holding of bankers' balances in the monetary segment of the account.

Fortuitously, the Hong Kong authorities' long-standing fiscal conservatism has meant that large amounts of foreign exchange have been accumulated over the past several decades, enabling the authorities to maintain a total of foreign currency assets available to back the monetary base well in excess of the HK$ value of the base itself. Consequently, since July 1988 the foreign currency assets corresponding to the monetary base are no longer those contributed solely by the private sector when it seeks to acquire additional units of base money. In practice, the authorities designate a certain amount of their foreign currency assets from the non-monetary segment of their balance sheet and place that as backing for the part of the monetary base that has not been paid for in foreign currency by the private sector. Thus the Account and the Aggregate Balance, while not paid for in US$, could be amply covered by foreign currency, notionally transferred from the EF's fiscal accounts. (The publication of separate accounts for the monetary base has made this practice explicit since 1999.)

The issue of EFBN raises the same problem on a larger scale. EFBN are a liability of the monetary authority, denominated in HK$ and purchased by banks and other institutional investors in Hong Kong. When new issues are auctioned by the monetary authority, the HK$ reserve accounts of banks are debited. In the decade and a half from March 1990 to June 2006, the volume of EFBN outstanding had grown to exceed HK$127 billion. Should EFBN be included in the definition of the monetary base, and if so, what is monetary asset corresponding to them?

A traditional, narrow definition of the monetary base would include only banknotes (or their equivalent, CIs) plus banks' reserve accounts at the authority. EFBN would be excluded from the base and treated as part of the fiscal segment of the authorities' balance sheet. The authorities would still be able to control the total amount of base money though they would need to take into account any transfers of funds from the private sector to the authorities following the issue of EFBN, since these would inevitably drain funds from the private sector.

A wider definition of the monetary base would include banknotes (or their equivalent, CIs) plus banks' reserve accounts at the authority, plus EFBN. However, in order to maintain a 100% foreign currency backing for the monetary base, this would require substantial notional transfers of foreign currency funds from the fiscal segment of the authorities' accounts to the monetary segment of their accounts. Two problems arise with this broader definition. First, purists have argued that the issue of EFBN was equivalent to the issue of sterilization bonds by other central banks in the Asian region because, insofar as payments for EFBN were debited to reserve accounts of banks at the EF, such issues necessarily drained liquidity from the private sector in the same way as any other sterilization instrument. It is true that the bank or other institution concerned would now hold a Bill or Note issued by the EF instead of a claim on the private sector, but the liquid funds that were previously available to non-bank entities would now be absorbed by the authority. It follows that, in the absence of restrictions on the volume of issue,[4] EFBN can reasonably be viewed as a sterilization instrument.

Second, it may be claimed that the foreign exchange transferred from the fiscal segment of the authorities' accounts to the monetary segment as backing for the EFBN was not generated by the monetary rule or by payments for the EFBN (in contrast to the payment of US$ against the issue of CIs). However, insofar as all funds obtained by the government must ultimately have come from the private sector (whether through taxation, profits of government corporations, or the proceeds of government borrowing), there must always be some originating payment from the private sector to the government that would justify the notional transfer of foreign exchange from the fiscal accounts to the monetary accounts. It follows that, provided the authorities have sufficient foreign exchange to designate as backing for the monetary base, such transfers maintain the integrity of the monetary base of a currency board.

The introduction of a whole set of new instruments onto the balance sheet of the authorities in the 1990s caused the editors at AMM some concern about the risk of Hong Kong departing from the monetary rule or currency board principles. In fact the authorities never deviated from their intention to maintain a solid currency board framework, and they continued to pursue the task at hand as they saw it: managing interest rates to ensure that the exchange rate remained reasonably close to the HK$7.80 conversion rate for banknotes or CIs. Perhaps the only lapse was to allow the banks to use certain specified debt instruments other than those issued by the EF or backed by US$ as collateral for LAF loans, but the same logic about ensuring adequate foreign

---

4. A mild restriction was put in place as one of the Seven Technical Measures of September 1998 although this was modified in April 1999 to allow interest payments on EFBN to expand the monetary base. See section 3 (A) (ii).

exchange cover for EFBN applies. Although this was a departure from strict currency board discipline, it could also be said that it showed how far the authorities were prepared to go in their quest to manage interest rates in pursuit of exchange rate stability.

To summarize, the fundamental issue being addressed during these years was how to provide some degree of elasticity within the interbank settlement system — a shock absorber for sudden inflows or outflows that would prevent interbank rates becoming too volatile — while at the same time avoiding the provision of extended discount facilities that would undermine the currency board principle that base money should only be created in exchange for payments of US dollars to the monetary authority. While these developments were laudable, and would in time provide the basis for a discount window mechanism that was compatible with currency board principles, from a monetary standpoint both the authorities and AMM failed to pursue the more important option of providing convertibility for the reserves of banks held at the EF.

(iii) Prelude to Crisis

On the eve of the handover of Hong Kong to China on 1 July 1997, and immediately ahead of the onset of the Asian financial crisis, the monetary system in Hong Kong appeared stronger than it had been at any time since 1972. The note issue was now not only fully backed by US$, but incremental issues had to be paid for with US$ at the official HK$7.80 rate per US$ and could be redeemed on the same terms. Insofar as there was a lack of convergence between the wholesale foreign exchange rate and the official conversion rate for banknotes or CIs, there were now several mechanisms for the HKMA to nudge interest rates up or down to achieve closer exchange rate convergence, together with a range of new instruments (EFBN) that the banks could use to adjust their own positions, thus reducing the risk of interest rates unexpectedly spiking up or down. Moreover, the authority had ample foreign exchange reserves to ensure full cover for all its new liabilities.

In spite of this seemingly solid framework, there remained some concerns. One clue to these unspoken fears was the authorities' preference for keeping the exchange rate at a premium to the official conversion rate from 1991 onwards (see Chart 13.6). If they had been entirely confident about the robustness of the system, they could have allowed the exchange rate to trade much closer to the official conversion rate, and even fall below it, but after 1990 this never happened. Throughout the years 1990–98 the free market rate remained at a persistent premium, typically around HK$7.73–7.75 to the US unit. This was the canary in the coalmine that told the market that there was an inherent vulnerability in the system. The maintenance of the market rate at this elevated level seemed to indicate that the authorities needed a protective buffer between the market rate and the official rate — just in case something serious happened, which it inevitably did.

The handover of sovereignty from Britain to China on 1 July 1997 went remarkably smoothly. One of the less widely reported events on the first day of the new era was the unrolling of a scroll at the Hong Kong Convention Centre by Chinese Premier Zhu Rongzhi to mark the transfer back to Hong Kong of the fiscal reserves that had been built

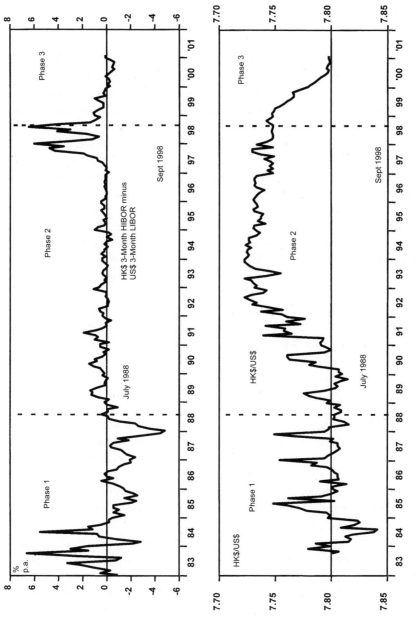

Chart 13.6 HK$/US$ Spot Exchange Rate and Interest Rate Differentials

up in the Hong Kong SAR Land Fund. These funds, representing 50% of the proceeds of land sales by the previous Hong Kong administration since 1985, had been held in trust by representatives of the PRC. The reversion of these funds to Hong Kong's control was an early sign of the PRC's commitment to the clauses in the Basic Law, passed by the National People's Congress in 1994, giving autonomy in financial matters to the Special Administrative Region (SAR) of Hong Kong.

In monetary affairs, too, there was to be a high degree of autonomy under the framework of "one country, two systems". First and foremost, the Hong Kong dollar was to continue to be the currency of Hong Kong, fully backed by a reserve fund (Article 111). The Basic Law promised that there would continue to be free movement of capital into and out of Hong Kong and that no foreign exchange controls would be imposed. Hong Kong was to enjoy fiscal independence from the PRC. These policies to maintain Hong Kong's status as an international financial centre after 1997 were clearly enshrined in the Joint Declaration, the Basic Law and the Agreed Minute on the Question of the Arrangements for the Transfer of the Exchange Fund of Hong Kong. China backed those commitments by practical cooperation with Hong Kong. For example, ahead of the handover, the PRC openly expressed support for the Linked Exchange Rate System and the issue of Exchange Fund Notes with maturities straddling 1997. The HKMA and the People's Bank of China (China's central bank) also worked closely on matters of common concern, including the establishment of a link between China's and Hong Kong's payments systems.

All these measures went into operation with seemingly little more than a change of personnel at the top of Hong Kong's administration. Instead of the British ruling Hong Kong, it was now Hong Kong people running Hong Kong, with full autonomy in all matters except defence and foreign affairs.

(iv) Onset of the Asian Financial Crisis

However, on the very next day (2 July 1997) there was a mild tremor in Asian financial markets that was to develop into a full-scale hurricane: Thailand devalued its currency from 25 baht per US$, allowing it to float downwards, reaching 56 baht per US$ in January 1998. The core of the problem was that, while Thailand maintained an essentially fixed exchange rate, the liberalization of Thai capital markets combined with an investment boom over the preceding three years had attracted substantial inflows of foreign funds into the economy.

Inevitably, monetary acceleration had pushed up asset prices and goods and service prices. At some point in 1996 or 1997, the overbuilding in Bangkok and the appearance of signs of excess capacity in the manufacturing sector across the economy as a whole triggered a reversal of capital flows. Faced with a growing capital outflow, the Thai authorities had initially supported the Thai baht in the spot market but later switched their support operations to the forward market, thus concealing the rundown of foreign exchange reserves from market participants. Ultimately, they were unable to stem the outflow and were forced to devalue. Asset prices collapsed as funds fled, and in time the economy went into a severe recession. Adding to the distress was the weakened state of the Thai banks: many went into the crisis with serious mismatches of maturities and currency positions on their balance sheets, while many experienced a rapid build-up of non-performing loans. The ultimate result was the collapse of a number of banks and non-bank institutions. In subsequent weeks and months, the Thai experience was followed by similar episodes in Korea, Indonesia, Malaysia and other economies of the region.

Hong Kong was also affected by contagion because asset prices were already at very high levels, and the territory was considered to have one of the most liquid markets in the region. Hong Kong assets were therefore viewed as a ready source of cash by investors with East Asian equity portfolios. The first wave of selling came in August, followed by a much more serious and sustained episode of selling in October–November 1997. In 1998 there were three more significant episodes of selling: in January, June, and August–September. In each case the interest rate spike and stock market downturn was triggered by investors selling substantial quantities of both Hong Kong dollar currency and equities in the spot and futures markets,[5] causing the banks in question to become overdrawn on their clearing balances. As mentioned, the rules required banks to maintain a zero or positive balance in their accounts, so a temporarily overdrawn bank would need to bid for funds in the interbank market, driving up short-term rates. When several banks did this together, rates would rise abruptly. If the rise in rates was steep enough, this would precipitate further equity declines on the expectation that the economy would be forced into an economic downturn, which would in turn damage corporate earnings. In this way, the pain of the Asian financial crisis (as it became known) was transmitted to Hong Kong.

The response of the authorities to this series of speculative attacks was conditioned by their need to maintain the credibility of the currency board system and an absolute refusal to capitulate to the speculators. To fend off these attacks and to attract financial flows back into Hong Kong it was necessary for interest rates to rise to painfully high levels. It was in this atmosphere that the HKMA restricted access to the LAF on 23 October 1997, sending a memorandum to all licensed banks warning them that repeated borrowers would be obliged to pay penalty rates. The intention was to remind banks that they could always obtain HK$ liquidity by selling US$ to the authority. Unfortunately, the memo caused panic among the banks, triggering a steep upward spiral in interbank rates. The overnight rate soared, reaching 300%. There can be little doubt that these rates, if continued for long, would have threatened the viability of the whole economy (as would be shown in 2001–02 in the case of Argentina). Yet this stance was maintained

---

5. Investors also sold Hang Seng Index futures and Hong Kong dollar forward contracts, adding to the selling pressure. The authorities were particularly concerned about these so-called "double play" transactions since they directly challenged the ability of the authorities to maintain the system. Furthermore, even if they did not succeed in causing the authorities to devalue, provided the currency sales were successful in causing interest rates to rise and the stock market to fall, the strategy would be highly profitable to the investors.

by the authorities until August 1998, when a fundamentally new approach was devised. The crisis exposed the fundamental vulnerability of the monetary edifice that had been constructed in the 1980s and 1990s in two important respects. First, it showed clearly that no matter how high rates rose, there was little if any convergence between the market exchange rate and the official parity. Second, it showed that the system was built on altogether too narrow a base: a few hundreds of millions of HK$ held by banks in the Aggregate Balance (the newly established reserve accounts of banks at the HKMA). This amount could easily prove too little in the case of sudden shifts in investor attitudes towards Hong Kong. The way these two problems were resolved forms the subject of section 3.

To treat the first it would be necessary to limit the movement of the market rate on each side of the conversion rate for banknotes; to treat the second it would be necessary to provide a degree of elasticity to the Aggregate Balance by permitting discounting against assets that were themselves backed by foreign exchange. The Seven Technical Measures of September 1998 took care of the latter, but the first was only implemented in stages between 1998 and 2005.

(B) Business Cycle Developments, 1990–98

(i) Following the US Business Cycle, 1990–97

The 92-month US expansion that had started from the trough in November 1982 peaked in July 1990, after the Fed had raised rates from 6.5% in February 1988 to 9.75% in May 1989. Following Hong Kong's mild slowdown of 1989–90 (discussed in section 1B), the US also experienced a modest 8-month US downturn between July 1990 and March 1991. Both were mainly the result of Greenspan's rate hikes of 1988–89. From a real GDP growth rate of 6.1% in 1989 Q1, Hong Kong's growth rate slowed through the rest of the year and into 1990 Q1. For the four quarters 1989 Q2–1990 Q1, Hong Kong's real GDP averaged 1.6% year-on-year (see Chart 13.2).

As in the previous expansion (1983–90), the transmission of interest rate influences from the US to Hong Kong were to set the broad shape of Hong Kong's business cycle in the 1990s, at least until 1997, when the Asian regional financial crisis intervened.

Hong Kong's recovery began a year ahead of the US recovery, averaging 4.9% in the last three quarters of 1990, and 5.7% in1991. A vigorous upturn in domestic and total exports from early 1990 helped bring about the renewed expansion phase. From this point onwards until the effects of another mid-course correction in the US began to have an impact on economic activity in 1995, the economy enjoyed a remarkably stable period of growth, averaging 5.8% p.a. in real terms (1990 Q2–1995 Q2). Compared with the sharp downturn in 1985 associated with the US mid-course correction in that cycle (discussed in section 1 (B)), the slowdown in 1995–96 was much milder. One important difference was that in 1994–95, the US dollar was substantially weaker than it had been in the early 1980s. Instead of an absolute decline in real growth, this time Hong Kong's growth rate roughly halved, from the 5.8% of the early 1990s to just 2.9% between 1995 Q3 and 1996 Q2. Thereafter the economy recovered to 5.8% for five quarters until 1997 Q3, when the impact of the Asian financial crisis started to take its toll.

(ii) Impact of the Asian Financial Crisis

The recession of 1998–99 resulting from the Asian financial crisis was by far the most severe downturn recorded in Hong Kong's post-war economic history. From a growth rate of 5.1% in real terms in 1997, the real GDP contracted in each of the four quarters of 1998 and into 1999: –3.0% in Q1, –5.7% in Q2, –7.3% in Q3, –5.7% in Q4, and –2.1% in 1999 Q1 (all figures year-on-year). In overall terms the decline in real GDP from peak to trough was 13.1%. Growth in the US was virtually unaffected by developments in Asia, the US real GDP averaging 4.4% in the three years 1997–99. Here was a clear case where, despite Hong Kong's currency board arrangements, business cycle or currency developments in the US were *not* the main driver of Hong Kong's business cycle fluctuations.

The primary mechanisms driving Hong Kong's recession in 1998–99 were twofold: (1) a large negative wealth effect coming from the sharp decline in stock market and real estate values consequent upon the capital outflows, which in turn produced a sudden decline in consumption and investment spending; and (2) an abrupt downturn in domestic and total exports, which was in part related to the sudden upward shift in the trade-weighted value of the HK$ relative to other Asian currencies. Could Hong Kong have moderated the impact of the crisis by currency management or by any other means? Currency boards can withstand external shocks of limited magnitude, but in the Asian financial crisis of 1997–98 Hong Kong was faced with 40%–50% devaluations of the currencies of several of its immediate competitor economies. It is doubtful whether any policy mix could have prepared Hong Kong for this situation, but having elected to maintain a currency board regime, it would have been disastrous if the Hong Kong authorities had capitulated by devaluing the currency. Not only would the credibility of any commitment to a future fixed rate have been jeopardized, but such weakness would have invited an endless spate of speculative flows in the event of any future adverse shocks. This does not mean that there are no exit strategies available to currency board regimes, but in the particular circumstances of the 1997–98 crisis, Hong Kong had no realistic alternative but to embark on an internal downward adjustment of prices in order to restore competitiveness.

We have covered the topic of Hong Kong's inflation during the period 1990–96 in section 2 (B). However, an additional point to note here is the gradual reduction in the CPI inflation differential between Hong Kong and the US over the years 1992–97, prior to the onset of the Asian financial crisis (see Chart 13.4). From an average differential of 6.1% between 1990 and 1995, the difference narrowed to 3.5% in 1996–97. Therefore, on the eve of the Asian crisis the Balassa-Samuelson effect which had kept Hong Kong's domestic inflation so much higher than that of the US from the late 1980s seemed already to be waning. The deflation of 1998–2004 will be discussed in section 3 (B).

3. RESTORING THE AUTO-PILOT, 1998–2005

(A) Monetary Changes

(i) Counter-attack on Speculators — Dealing with the Symptoms

The Asian financial crisis exposed some critical weaknesses of Hong Kong's currency board system despite the reforms of July 1988 and the series of innovations in the debt market and improvements in bank settlement procedures during the 1990s. The outflow of funds during the crisis (strictly, the sale of HK$, since money in this sense does not "flow out") had caused interest rates in Hong Kong to rise to painfully high levels on occasion, prompting big declines in the stock market, plunging property prices, and leading to a deep economic recession.

During the first three waves of speculative attack on the Hong Kong currency in October 1997, January 1998, and June 1998, the authorities had allowed the strain of sharply higher interest rates to feed through to the stock market and the property market. Given their predisposition towards "positive non-interventionism" the authorities were reluctant to interfere too much in the workings of the market mechanism. However, as the economy weakened further and the risk of repeated speculative attacks remained, a more confrontational attitude developed during the summer of 1998. In addition, the interest rate premium on HK$ remained high — around 125 basis points above US rates — reflecting apprehensiveness about the ability of the Hong Kong authorities to maintain the currency board when almost all other Asian currencies except the RMB and the HK$ had been devalued, further exacerbating the downturn in the Hong Kong economy. As Joseph Yam, Chief Executive of the HKMA, wrote in the summer of 1998, "There has been so much pain inflicted on the community, in terms of higher interest rates, higher unemployment, sharply lower asset and equity prices and negative economic growth" (Review of Currency Board Arrangements in Hong Kong Chapter 3, para 89). This stiffening attitude culminated in a two-stage decision in August and September 1998, first to step into the stock market and buy shares directly for the account of the EF (fiscal account), directly punishing those speculators who were short the equity market; and second to introduce more elasticity into the interbank market mechanism to enable it to deal more smoothly with sudden outflows.

Immediately following the stock market intervention, Joseph Yam wrote an article for the *Asian Wall Street Journal* to explain the reasons behind the government's market purchases, pointing out that "the actions were intended to demonstrate the Government's determination to protect the integrity of the Hong Kong dollar and the stability of Hong Kong's monetary and financial systems" (*HKMA Quarterly Bulletin*, November 1998). He emphasized the need to deter "currency manipulation by those who have built up large short positions in the Hang Seng Index futures . . .There is no doubt that there has been manipulation in our currency to engineer extreme conditions in the interbank market and high interest rates in order that profits could be made in the large short positions that have been built up in stock index futures."

In the space of ten working days, the authorities bought a total of HK$118.13

billion of equity shares and index futures, largely by drawing on the government's fiscal reserves in the fiscal segment of the HKMA's balance sheet. In defence of the move, Chief Executive Yam argued that "adherence to a monetary rule [requiring any change in the monetary base to be brought about only by a corresponding change in foreign reserves in US dollars] . . . does not preclude the government funding a budget deficit by drawing down its fiscal reserves that are held as foreign assets in the Exchange Fund. . . . Adherence to the monetary rule also does not preclude a portfolio shift outside the balance sheet of the currency board from other assets into Hong Kong stocks for whatever purpose considered to be in the best interest of Hong Kong."

The Hong Kong authorities' intervention in the stock market not only shocked and dismayed many observers on grounds of principle, but it also was a highly risky undertaking. In the event, the stock market rallied and the recovery was buttressed by three successive cuts in the Fed funds rate in September, October and November, following the downturn in US markets resulting from the Russian default and the collapse of the hedge fund Long-Term Capital Management (LTCM) in August 1998. Between November 1999 and October 2002, the government was able to sell off at a substantial profit most of the equity shares it had bought. This was done through an initial public offering and subsequent quarterly tap offerings to the public of shares in a unit trust tracker fund (TraHK).

The issue of principle is more problematic. Undoubtedly, the repeated attacks on the currency board system that featured a combination of large-scale short selling of the Hong Kong dollar and associated steep rises in interest rates did grave damage not only to asset values in the equity and property markets but also to employment and economic activity more broadly. What were the authorities to do? In the light of the recent currency devaluations in the region, investors did not have the confidence to rely on the HK$ remaining pegged and therefore made no attempt to benefit from interest arbitrage between the US$ and HK$. Also, the Hong Kong authorities did not have at their disposal a smoothly functioning discounting mechanism that would have cushioned the steep rises in interest rates. The limited tools at the authorities' disposal severely constrained their choices. In hindsight, an earlier deployment of the lower-side convertibility undertaking together with the earlier introduction of discounting arrangements for EFBN would have greatly alleviated the gravity of the situation, but these policy choices were simply not on the menu. The whole episode of stock market intervention damaged Hong Kong's reputation for its willingness to rely on market-based mechanisms, but this was one set of circumstances where leaving things to the market would have implied intolerable costs. The limits of tolerance had been breached.

(ii) Reforming the Mechanism — Dealing with the Causes, September 1998

Simultaneously with the intervention in the stock market, moves were already in preparation to solve the problems of the currency board. A Sub-Committee of the Exchange Fund Advisory Committee (EFAC) was formed (see Appendix 13.1), including a number of outsiders, the purpose being to enhance the transparency of currency board operations and to draw on the expertise of members of the banking and academic communities in Hong Kong. Then on 5 September 1998, the HKMA announced a package of measures designed to strengthen the mechanism and make it less susceptible to the disruptions of the preceding year. The Seven Technical Measures demonstrated the government's commitment to maintaining the fixed rate currency board system. In the words of the official press release, the measures comprised the following:

1. the HKMA providing a clear undertaking to all licensed banks in Hong Kong to convert Hong Kong dollars in their clearing accounts into US dollars at the fixed exchange rate of HK$7.75 to US$1. This explicit Convertibility Undertaking is a clear demonstration of the Government's commitment to the linked exchange rate system. It is the intention of the HKMA to move the rate of the Convertibility Undertaking to 7.80 when market circumstances permit;

2. removing the bid rate of the Liquidity Adjustment Facility (LAF). As the improved efficiency of the interbank payment system has facilitated liquidity management of licensed banks, the need for the LAF deposit facility to facilitate orderly interbank market activities has fallen away;

3. replacing LAF by a Discount Window with the Base Rate (formerly known as the LAF Offer Rate) to be determined from time to time by the HKMA. In determining the Base Rate, the HKMA will ensure that interest rates are adequately responsive to capital flows while allowing excessive and destabilizing interest rate volatility to be dampened;

4. removing the restriction on repeated borrowing in respect of the provision of overnight Hong Kong dollar liquidity through repo transactions using Exchange Fund Bills and Notes. Allowing for freer access to day end liquidity through the use of Exchange Fund paper which is fully backed by foreign currency reserves will make Hong Kong's monetary system less susceptible to manipulation and dampen excessive interest rate volatility without departing from the discipline of the Currency Board arrangement;

5. new Exchange Fund paper to be issued only when there is an inflow of funds. This will ensure that all new Exchange Fund paper will be fully backed by foreign currency reserves;

6. introducing a schedule of discount rates applicable for different percentage thresholds of holdings of Exchange Fund paper by the licensed banks for the purpose of accessing the Discount Window. This will ensure that the interest rate adjustment mechanism to be fully kicked in when the Hong Kong dollar is under significant pressure; and

7. retaining the restriction on repeated borrowing in respect of repo transactions involving debt securities other than Exchange Fund paper. No new issues of paper other than Exchange Fund paper will be accepted at the Discount Window. This will prevent significant liquidity to be provided to licensed banks against paper not backed by foreign currency reserves.

This package of measures did several key things. First, it created a known lower-level price at which licensed banks could convert HK$ in their clearing accounts into US$ at the HKMA. The importance of this was that banks could now count on their ability to buy US$ or sell HK$ at 7.75, using their reserve or clearing balances at the HKMA. Second, it eliminated the uncertainty over the banks' ability to discount EFBN with the authority, in the event that their clearing accounts became overdrawn. Third, in permitting EFBN to be used without restriction for discounting, it provided a hugely important shock absorber for Hong Kong's money markets against future episodes of large-scale selling of HK$ currency. Banks could now draw on as much as HK$120 billion of EFBN to act as a buffer against sudden spikes in the interbank market. Simulations conducted subsequently have suggested that if the speculative attacks of June and August 1998 had been repeated in the environment of the new discounting mechanism, overnight HIBOR rates would have reached only about 12% and 15% respectively instead of the 15% and 23.5% that they actually reached.[6] Fourth, the new framework necessarily imposed a fundamental change in the operating strategy of the HKMA. It was clearly no longer feasible to intervene at some discretionary level on the weak side, given the new fixed Convertibility Undertaking (CU) although the authorities did continue to exercise discretion on the strong side. In addition, with the abolition of the LAF bid rate and the switch to a discount mechanism that was driven by the banks and priced at the market rate plus some premium, the HKMA effectively abandoned its previous attempts to steer interest rates within a specific corridor. Finally, the effective freezing of the volume of issues of EFBN ended the possibility of using EF paper to conduct active sterilization operations or to manage the money market.

(iii) Further Refinements to the Mechanism, 1999–2005

Seven months after the successful introduction of the weak side CU, the Currency Board Sub-Committee proposed moving the rate upwards in steps of 1 pip per day (1/10,000 of a HK$) from 7.7500 to 7.8000 (or 500 pips), starting in April and ending in July the following year. This finally removed the anomaly that the CU (or previously the HKMA's intervention point) differed arbitrarily from the conversion rate for banknotes. However, the question of whether this was the optimum strategy repeatedly came up at meetings of the Currency Board Sub-Committee between October 1999 and May 2005, because the existence of a lower-side CU meant that there was still uncertainty about the upper limit for the HK$ to US$ rate and scope for discretionary intervention by the HKMA.

Discussion centred on two issues. Should there be a strong-side CU? If so, at what level should it be set? For several years, executives of the HKMA maintained the view that there should be no strong-side CU and that some "constructive ambiguity"

---

6. Guy Meredith, "Liquidity Management Under Hong Kong's Currency Board Arrangements", International Workshop on Currency Boards: Convertibility, Liquidity Management and Exit, Hong Kong Baptist University, October 1999. www.hkbu.edu.hk/~econ/99workshop/99wsMeredith.doc

was desirable because this would enable the authorities to impose costly surprises on speculators. Sometimes there was a transitional reason to maintain the status quo, as for example following the completion of the shift of the lower-side CU from 7.75 to 7.80. However, mostly the view was expressed that if a strong-side CU was set too close to the market rate, then this would undercut the operations of private foreign exchange operators, and it was an explicit requirement of the Basic Law that Hong Kong maintain an active international foreign exchange market (Article 112).

It was not until active speculation on a revaluation of the RMB in 2003–04 that the HKMA was compelled to take action, once again by market developments rather than by its own choice. Against a background of widening Chinese trade surpluses and strong capital inflows into the Mainland, many market participants, unable to purchase RMB currency directly, began to view the HK$ currency as a substitute for the Mainland's currency. Perhaps not understanding the autonomy of Hong Kong in financial matters, they expected the HK$ to appreciate in line with the RMB if that currency were to be revalued. The effect of such speculative spot and forward purchases of the HK$ was to drive down HK$ interest rates, encouraging strong upward movements in Hong Kong equities and real estate prices. Between October 2003 and 17 May 2005, the HK$ 1-year forward premium averaged 682 pips, or a premium to the spot rate of some 8.75%, while the Hang Seng Index of Hong Kong equities rose from 11,000 to 14,000, some 27%. Over the same period, the Centa-City Leading Index of transaction prices in the secondary market for selected housing estates increased 76%.

Between November 2004 and January 2005, the 3-month interbank interest rate differential with US rates had risen to over 200 basis points (see Chart 13.3), and although it narrowed in February and March, it widened again in April as speculation about a revaluation of the RMB resumed, pushing down HK$ rates again. Concerned by the risk that another extended bubble in asset prices might develop, the Currency Board Sub-Committee reviewed again the question of the indeterminate upper limit to fluctuations in the HK$/US$ spot rate. In view of the prolonged upward pressure on the RMB that seemed likely in coming years and the persistent knock-on effect that this was likely to have on the HK$ and asset prices in Hong Kong, the committee this time decided that it was preferable to end the adverse effects of strong-side speculation by introducing a strong-side CU.

Consistent with previous discussions about not restricting the activity of the local foreign exchange market, the new strong-side CU (where the HKMA would buy US dollars from licensed banks) was set at 7.75, and the weak-side CU was to be shifted from 7.80 to 7.85. The shifting of the existing weak-side CU (where the HKMA would sell US dollars to licensed banks) was to be achieved in a gradual manner over five weeks by moving the weak-side CU by 100 pips on every Monday, starting with 7.81 on 23 May 2005, until it reached 7.85 on 20 June 2005. The end result would be a symmetric band of 5 cents on each side of the 7.80 conversion rate for banknotes. However, the authorities retained the right "to conduct market operations consistent with Currency Board principles" i.e., to make discretionary interventions *within* the band between the two CU points. The announcement was made on 18 May 2005, and within days interest rates in Hong Kong returned to rough parity with US rates.

An obvious result of the modified framework for the currency board regime in Hong Kong was that it was now far more transparent and automatic and less subject to discretionary intervention. Equally important, the need for the Hong Kong authorities to use a variety of instruments to steer interest rates upward or downward in order to maintain the spot exchange rate within some undefined range disappeared altogether. There were now clear limits to the fluctuation of the spot rate on each side of the 7.80 conversion rate for banknotes. Purchases of US$ at the strong-side CU or sales of US$ at the weak-side CU would be triggered by the banks, not by the authority. Moreover, by limiting the possible range of exchange rate fluctuation, the strong-side and weak-side CU points would in turn indicate the limits of any potential loss to a bank or private investor who wished to conduct interest rate arbitrage transactions between HK$ and US$ interest rates. In combination, the implementation of these refinements in May 2005 meant that, after 22 years of experimentation, an autopilot was finally installed.

(B) Business Cycle Developments, 1998–2005

The post-Asian crisis years were a period of recession and deflation unlike anything Hong Kong had experienced in the post-war period. Not only was the sharpness and duration of the downturn unusual for Hong Kong, but the normal pattern whereby Hong Kong tended to experience an amplified version of the US business cycle trend — whether upwards or downwards — was broken for a while.

(i) Diverging from the US Business Cycle, 1998–2001

During the period from 1998 until March 2001, the US economy had continued to expand, real GDP growth averaging 4.1% p.a. in the three years 1998–2000, spurred on by strong capital investment, especially in the booming high-tech and telecom sectors (see Chart 13.2). During this period, as we have seen, Hong Kong experienced strongly negative growth rates in 1998–99 as a direct result of the Asian financial crisis, but this was followed by an astonishing growth surge in the six quarters from 1999 Q3 until 2000 Q4, during which real GDP averaged 9.3% (year-on-year). In part, the strength of the recovery reflected the depth of the preceding downturn, and no doubt it was also linked to the final stages of the tech bubble and its spillover effects on the electronics and financial sectors in Hong Kong. However, the recovery was limited to real activity; there was no recovery from deflation despite the vigour of the upturn.

Except for the SARS epidemic in mid-2003 which caused a temporary, localized downturn in the economic activity of Hong Kong and several smaller Asian economies, 2000–2001 marked the end of the US-Hong Kong divergence in growth patterns. After the Fed had raised rates from 4.75% in June 1999 to 6.5% by May 2000 (see Chart 13.3), the US economy slowed abruptly at the end of 2000 and in early 2001, entering a mild investment-led recession which lasted eight months (according to the business cycle chronology of the US NBER) from March until November 2001. In conformity with pre-Asian crisis patterns, Hong Kong's real GDP also slowed sharply, this time contemporaneously with the US. From a rate of 10% during 2000 as a whole, real GDP growth plunged to 0.6% in 2001, including three negative quarters (on a year-on-year basis) in 2001 Q3 and Q4, and 2002 Q1 (Chart 13.2).

(ii) Resynchronizing with the US Business Cycle, 2001–05

The US recovery that began after November 2001 continued until December 2007, which the NBER designated the peak of the cyclical expansion. Real GDP growth in the US picked up slowly in 2002, growing at 1.6% for the year as a whole, accelerating to 2.7% in 2003, and 4.2% in 2004. In Hong Kong's case, growth was once again stronger than in the US, real GDP recording 1.8%, 3.2% and 8.6% in 2002, 2003 and 2004 respectively. There was a sharp one-quarter downturn in 2003 Q2, when Hong Kong's real GDP declined by 0.7% (year-on-year) as a result of SARS striking numerous Asian economies, causing a reduction in business travel, tourism and hotel occupancy rates, as well as disruptions to work schedules and reduced consumer spending.

Despite the recovery of business activity in 1999–2000, there was no rapid recovery from the deflation that Hong Kong had experienced as a direct result of the Asian financial crisis. It was not until June 2004 that Hong Kong's CPI inflation rate again recorded positive rates of change on a year-on-year basis, 5 years and 8 months since Hong Kong had first started to experience deflation in October 1998 (Chart 13.4). Overall, the composite CPI had fallen by 13.5% over the whole period, in comparison with a 15.9% increase in US consumer prices over the same period, a combined difference in price movements — or a gain in relative competitiveness for Hong Kong — of almost 30%.
The deflation of the years 1998–2004 might appear to mark a significant departure from the normal relationship between prices in the anchor currency country and the currency board economy, but there is a rational and satisfactory explanation. During these years the US experienced average CPI inflation of 2.4% p.a. while Hong Kong experienced an average *decline* of –1.8% p.a. in the CPI. However, recalling the discussion above about traded goods prices remaining in line with US prices and non-traded goods prices being affected by the Balassa-Samuelson effect, it should be noted that, between 1998 and 2004, Hong Kong's productivity grew by only 1.2% p.a. (declining by –9.7% in 1998) compared with an average rise of 1.9% p.a. for the US (see Chart 13.5). In other words, given the loss of output in Hong Kong due to the economic downturn and consequently the lower growth of productivity, the Balassa-Samuelson hypothesis would suggest that Hong Kong needed to see some price declines in non-traded goods relative to the US over this period, in order to restore overall competitiveness.

4. ASSESSMENT OF HONG KONG'S POST-1983 CURRENCY BOARD

The long period of nearly 22 years between the restoration of the currency board system in October 1983 and the adoption of a two-sided, symmetric CU in May 2005, which finally enabled the system to operate with virtual automaticity, reflects the innate cautiousness of officials and bankers in Hong Kong about making radical institutional changes when the existing arrangements were — for the most part — consistent with a high degree of economic success. This dilemma — the need for systemic monetary reforms while maintaining intact Hong Kong's broader formula for past financial and economic successes — finds echoes in the sometimes ambivalent official treatment of two issues that spanned most of the 22-year period: the role of HSBC and the whole approach to interest rate management.

(i) The Role of HSBC in Hong Kong's Financial System

First, throughout the period, the size and role of the HSBC group in Hong Kong posed a long-running but often unspoken problem for the authorities. Not only was HSBC by far the largest commercial bank in the territory, but also, critically, as manager of the interbank clearing system in the years up to December 1996, it was in a quasi-public sector role that at times was potentially in conflict with its role as a profit-oriented private bank. The need to intervene in the foreign exchange market in conjunction with the EF and the willingness of HSBC to share costs in this arena has been mentioned (section 1 (A) (i)). In addition, since the provision of overdraft facilities to banks that were overdrawn on their settlement balances at the clearing house was entirely a matter for the HSBC management, the bank was clearly in a position where it could have taken advantage of its lesser rivals through denial of overdraft or discount facilities that in other jurisdictions would have been automatically provided by the central bank.

The traditional response of both the authorities and HSBC to any challenge on these grounds was the same as the oft-misquoted reply given by C. E. Wilson, then GM president, when asked in 1953 during hearings before the Senate Armed Services Committee, if as Secretary of Defense, he could make a decision adverse to the interests of General Motors.[7] As in the case of GM in the US, the stock response in Hong Kong was that what was good for HSBC was good for Hong Kong. There is some superficial merit in this response but also some obfuscation. While it might have been legitimate for a US citizen to claim that what was good for GM was good for US business in general, and therefore good for the US as a whole, unlike GM in the US, HSBC group in Hong Kong was (a) substantially larger in market share in its sector and (b) had an undeniable public sector role that created conflicts of interest such as GM never faced. Moreover, the problem is not limited to how HSBC handled the potential conflicts internally but also concerns how the dominance of HSBC influenced the setting of policy by the authorities. The concentration of the authorities on interest rate management through much of the

---

7.   Wilson had been appointed Secretary of Defense by President Eisenhower. In the hearings, he answered affirmatively but added that he could not conceive of such a situation "because for years I thought what was good for the country was good for General Motors and vice versa". Later, this statement was often misquoted, suggesting that Wilson had said simply, "What's good for General Motors is good for the country" (Source: Wikipedia).

1980s and 1990s derived in part from an underlying concern that HSBC was — at least in some degree — exercising undue dominance in the money market. This was certainly part of the motivation for the introduction of the LAF in June 1992 (since this was a scheme to enable imbalances of funds in the money market to be solved through the agency of the EF rather than through the HSBC-run clearing house). In addition, it is arguable that the sharp spikes in HK$ interest rates during the Asian financial crisis of 1997–98 might have been less dramatic had there been a more broadly competitive interbank market with more potential sources of short-term HK$ funds available to the smaller or foreign banks instead of having to rely on loans from HSBC.

However, even if the authorities had not been diverted into the creation of the ultimately unsuccessful LAF scheme, and even if there had been a more equal distribution of market shares among the main banking groups in Hong Kong, it is doubtful if the necessary core reforms would have been introduced before the onset of the Asian financial crisis in 1997. Furthermore, even after the Seven Technical Measures had been implemented in 1998, the authorities showed signs of uneasiness about the role of HSBC in the HK$ foreign exchange market, where its size continued to enable the bank to be the dominant market-maker and hence the effective price-setter.

(ii) Official Ambivalence over Interest Rate Volatility

The second issue — periodic interest rate management — was essentially a policy of last resort when other mechanisms failed. If the currency board mechanism had been more robust, in the sense that the free market exchange rate naturally and rapidly reverted to something close to the 7.80 conversion rate for CIs or banknotes whenever there was a disturbance, then there would have been little need to be so concerned about divergences of HK$ interest rates from their US$ counterparts, either in the case of short-term shocks or in the case of more extended divergences.

However, Hong Kong officials had long relied on the Interest Rate Agreement (which dated from the mid-1960s) as a method of having some influence on the setting of interest rates in the territory. The licensed banks were entitled to regulate retail deposit interest rates, subject to official approval. As a tool of policy this arrangement had numerous shortcomings (see Chapter 8, box on pp. 192–194), and indeed it had only ever really been intended as a prudential instrument to prevent excessive competition amongst the local banks.

From the start of the reconstituted currency board in October 1983 until the present day, official explanations of how the currency board worked have always emphasized the need for fully flexible interest rates. Yet, official action has seemed ambivalent, at times attempting to dampen interest rate movements (e.g. with the introduction of the EFBN discounting mechanism in 1998), and at other times encouraging wider movement of interest rates (e.g. the deregulation of deposit interest rates). Alternatively, I have described how, in 1992–98, the authorities deliberately maintained the exchange rate at a comfortable premium to the 7.80 parity, in order to provide themselves with a margin of safety in the event of a speculative attack on the currency (see p. 272).

In all probability, the authorities' fear of volatile interest rates was overdone. In many cases a sharp upward or downward movement of wholesale interbank interest rates would have served to restore stability to the exchange rate without any significant knock-on effects on retail or commercial rates affecting the real economy or inflation. Even during the Asian financial crisis, when overnight rates reached 300% p.a., it should be remembered that this represented less than 1% per day — not excessive relative to what the authorities should have been willing to allow or expect under a currency board mechanism.

But in the absence of a robust underlying mechanism tending to produce automatic or market-driven convergence of the free market exchange rate and the 7.80 parity, the official ambivalence on interest rates was understandable. Given a currency board mechanism that was predisposed to return to equilibrium at or close to the 7.80 rate, there would have been no need for back-up measures involving interest rates. However, until the convertibility undertaking for bank reserves came into operation in September 1998, there was always likely to be a nagging worry that disturbances to the exchange rate would not be truly self-correcting, and hence the authorities' need for additional lines of defence.

(iii) The May 2005 Settlement and Beyond

The combination of currency board features in force after May 2005 — foreign exchange backing for the currency in excess of 100% of the monetary base, a fixed rate for CIs, symmetrical CU bands on each side of it, and intra-day or overnight discounting of EFBNs by banks to smooth liquidity imbalances — are compatible *both* with a number of characteristic features of Hong Kong (such as the issuance of bank notes by private commercial banks, openness to large-scale free capital flows, the absence of foreign exchange controls, and the existence of a vibrant foreign exchange market) *and* with the desirable theoretical features of a modern currency board system. Having been subject to careful and incremental reforms over the two decades 1983–2005, the currency board system of Hong Kong had, by the end of June 2005, reached a state of development where the key features of its monetary aspects — as opposed to technological developments affecting (say) bank clearing or fund transfers — could be expected to pause for some years. The monetary system was now much more resilient than in 1983 and, except for two minor discretionary elements (issuance of EFBN and the possibility intra-zone intervention, i.e., between 7.75 and 7.85), was almost entirely rule-driven and automatic. The question for the next decade and a half (Chapter 14) was whether the system now had sufficient credibility and resilience to withstand two global crises (the global financial crisis, GFC, of 2008–09 and the coronavirus pandemic of 2020), and a local socio-political crisis (the street protests of 2019) that Hong Kong would encounter during the years 2005–20.

APPENDIX 13.1

EFAC Sub-committee on Currency Board Operations

As part of the announcement of the Seven Technical Measures, the HKMA included the following text:

Currency Board Operations Sub-Committee

The package of technical measures to strengthen the Currency Board arrangements of Hong Kong has earlier been examined closely by a Sub-Committee on Currency Board Operations of the EFAC established recently with the approval of the Financial Secretary. The Sub-Committee is chaired by the Chief Executive of the HKMA Mr Joseph Yam. The other members of the Sub-Committee are:

- The Hon David K.P. Li
- Mr Marvin Cheung
- Professor Y.C. Jao
- Mr Mervyn Davies as Chairman of the Hong Kong Association of Banks
- Mr David Carse, Deputy Chief Executive, HKMA
- Mr Andrew Sheng, Deputy Chief Executive, HKMA
- Mr Norman Chan, Deputy Chief Executive, HKMA

The terms of reference of the EFAC Sub-Committee on Currency Board Operations are:

(a) to ensure that the operation of the Currency Board arrangements in Hong Kong is in accordance with the policies determined by the Financial Secretary in consultation with the Exchange Fund Advisory Committee;

(b) to report to the Financial Secretary through the Exchange Fund Advisory Committee on the operation of the Currency Board arrangements in Hong Kong;

(c) to recommend, where appropriate, to the Financial Secretary through the Exchange Fund Advisory Committee, measures to enhance the robustness and effectiveness of the Currency Board arrangements in Hong Kong;

(d) to ensure a high degree of transparency in the operation of the Currency Board arrangements in Hong Kong through the publication of relevant information on the operation of such arrangements; and

(e) to promote a better understanding of the Currency Board arrangements in Hong Kong.

Since 1998, membership of the Currency Board Sub-Committee has changed from time to time, but it has always retained at least four ex-officio executives of the HKMA (including the Chief Executive of the HKMA as Chairman), the chairman of the Hong Kong Association of Banks, one or two academic economists, and one or two more external members. Initially, the committee met bi-monthly, but after 2006 it switched first to monthly "paper" meetings and quarterly "physical" meetings and later to quarterly meetings only.

CHAPTER 14

ESTABLISHING CREDIBILITY, 2005–2020

INTRODUCTION

In this new final chapter, section 1 presents a summary in balance sheet format of the monetary history of Hong Kong from the 1840s to the present. The reason for doing so is that the current structure of the balance sheets of the HKMA and the banking system have evolved to become so complicated that it is important to step back from the details to gain a clear picture of the overall framework. Underlying all the complexity is the simple and resilient currency board mechanism. However, there is also a superstructure that enables Hong Kong and its financial system to adjust more smoothly to external and internal changes. The evidence for this is that in recent years Hong Kong has successfully navigated a number of major exogenous shocks — notably the global financial crisis (GFC) of 2008–09 and the social unrest of 2019, followed by the coronavirus pandemic of 2020.

Section 2 traces the developments in the monetary system and in the economy from the monetary reforms of 2005 (laid out in Chapter 13) and how they enabled Hong Kong to weather the GFC.

Section 3 reviews the Hong Kong monetary system and economy during the post-GFC period from 2009 until the onset of the coronavirus pandemic of 2020.

Sections 2 and 3 are each divided into two segments, as in Chapter 13, covering (a) the changes that were relevant to the monetary system, and (b) an assessment of how the economy and inflation behaved under the currency board system in each phase.

Section 4 concludes with an overall assessment of the appropriate monetary system for Hong Kong in the future, extracted from Chapter 13 of the previous edition and updated for changes in the mainland Chinese economy and changes in the global financial system.

1. THE MONETARY HISTORY OF HONG KONG IN BALANCE SHEET FORMAT, 1842–2020

The monetary history of Hong Kong from 1842 begins with private commercial banks issuing banknotes under charter, but with no monetary authority. Over the nearly 180 years to 2020, there have been numerous changes in the monetary standard (i.e., in the way banknotes were issued and the backing for the notes), the role and powers of the monetary authority, the position of the banks and the monetary authority in relation to the government, as well as in the role of Hong Kong as a financial centre. To clarify the monetary, systemic and structural changes during this extended period it is useful to review the simplified, T-form balance sheets for the Hong Kong monetary and banking system chronologically.

From the 1840s to 1935 there was no central bank or monetary authority in Hong Kong. At different times, up to five commercial banks[1] were authorized under British charter to issue banknotes in Hong Kong. Under their charters, the note-issuing banks were each initially required to hold reserves in silver at a minimum level of one-third of their notes in circulation, while the total number of notes in circulation for any one bank was restricted to the paid-up capital of the issuing bank. After 1898, the government adopted a new arrangement with "authorized" issues limited to HK$30 million — of which two-thirds were required to be backed by silver, and one-third could be fiduciary (i.e., not backed by silver) issues. Any additional issues above the "authorized" amount were designated "excess" and were required to be fully backed by silver. In short, HK$10 million was the maximum fiduciary issue for any single bank.

Table 14.1.1 shows the aggregated, but simplified, T-form balance sheets for the three key sectors in Hong Kong between 1842 and 1935: the banking system, the government and the non-bank public (i.e., firms, individuals and other non-government entities such as non-profit organizations). Three features are noteworthy. First, the note-issuing function of the commercial banks is shown above the dashed line, while the normal banking functions are shown below the dashed line. Banks generally issued higher-denomination banknotes, holding a small number of issued notes in their vaults or at branches ready to exchange "on demand" against silver or against customers' deposits. Second, the government issued coins and small-denomination notes and maintained deposit accounts at one or more of the commercial banks. Third, the money supply, an asset of the non-bank public, consisted of notes and coins together with deposits at banks held by the non-bank public. Each of these items — notes, coins or deposits — was a liability of either the banks or the government.

We digress momentarily from the monetary history of Hong Kong to look at Table 14.1.2. It shows the simplified, T-form balance sheets for a standard currency board

---

1. The note-issuing banks and the dates when they started issuing HK$ banknotes are: Oriental Banking Corporation (1845); Chartered Mercantile Bank of India, London and China (1858); Chartered Bank of India, Australia and China (1862); Agra and Masterman's Bank (1865); and Hongkong and Shanghai Bank (1865).

Table 14.1.1 Free Banking in Hong Kong before the Currency Board System, 1842–1935

No Currency Board or Monetary Authority

Commercial banks issued banknotes backed by silver under British charter

Commercial Banks

Assets	Liabilities
Silver Reserves	Banknotes Issued
Banknotes (of other banks) and coin	Deposits of non-bank public
Loans	Deposits of government
Investments	Other liabilities
	Capital or net worth

Government

Assets	Liabilities
Deposits at banks	Issues of subsidiary notes and coin
Other assets	Other liabilities
	Net worth

Non-bank Public

Assets	Liabilities
Banknotes and coin	Loans from banks
Deposits at banks	Other liabilities
Investments	Net worth
Other assets	

Table 14.1.2 Simple Currency Board System – as Operated in Other British Colonies

Currency Board

Assets	Liabilities
Foreign Exchange	Banknotes and coin issued
	Net worth

Commercial Banks

Assets	Liabilities
Banknotes and coin	Deposits of non-banks
Loans	Deposits of government
Investments	Other liabilities
	Net worth

Government

Assets	Liabilities
Deposits at banks	Debt issued
Other assets	Other liabilities
	Net worth

Non-bank Public

Assets	Liabilities
Banknotes and coin	Loans from banks
Deposits at banks	Other liabilities
Investments	Net worth
Other assets	

system as operated in other British colonies in the nineteenth century and during the first half of the twentieth century. The reason for considering this system before progressing is that this was the model on which the Hong Kong variant was to be based when the silver standard was abandoned in 1935. The key feature of such a system is its extreme simplicity. The role of a currency board was simply to issue and redeem local currency on demand at a fixed price (or exchange rate) against a designated foreign currency. In the case of British colonies this was almost always the pound sterling. On the liability side of the balance sheet, the currency board only issued banknotes. It had no other meaningful liabilities; for example, it did not accept deposits from the banks or from the government.

On the asset side it held only foreign currency assets, typically government securities of the "anchor currency" country — in this case "gilts" (British government securities). A currency board generated profits (seigniorage) from the difference between the interest it earned on its reserve assets and the expense of issuing currency notes.

By design, a currency board had no discretionary monetary powers and could not engage in open market operations. It had an exchange rate policy (the fixed exchange rate) but otherwise no active monetary policy. A currency board's operations were passive and demand-driven. Since a currency board's balance sheet contained only foreign assets, and essentially no domestic assets, it could not engage in domestic open market operations either to create domestic credit or to offset inflows or outflows of foreign currency by (respectively) selling or buying domestic assets. A currency board could not act as a lender of last resort or extend credit to the banking system or to the fiscal authority. In short, a currency board maintained monetary discipline and imposed a hard budget constraint on the local government by not providing an easy borrowing option.

Currency boards have existed in more than 70 countries. The first one was installed in the British Indian Ocean colony of Mauritius in 1849. By the 1930s, currency boards were widespread among the British colonies in Africa, Asia, the Caribbean, and the Pacific islands. They have also existed in a number of independent countries, including Jordan, Estonia and Sudan. Other than in Hong Kong, they continue to exist today in several countries, most notably Bosnia and Bulgaria.

Against this background it was entirely natural and rational for Hong Kong to adopt the currency board system in 1935, when China abandoned the silver standard. It should also be noted that no orthodox currency board has ever failed.[2] Moreover, countries that

---

2. Argentina's Convertibility Scheme (1991–2001) is sometimes cited as a failed currency board, but in fact Argentina's central bank did not follow currency board rules, holding significant domestic currency assets and conducting active open market operations in domestic currency instruments. See Steve Hanke's testimony to the House of Representatives Committee on Foreign Affairs: "Venezuela's Tragic Meltdown", 28 March 2017, https://www.congress.gov/115/meeting/house/105703/witnesses/ HHRG-115-FA07-Wstate-HankeS-20170328-U2.pdf See also Schuler, Kurt, "Ignorance and Influence: U.S. Economists on Argentina's Depression of 1998–2002." Intellectual Tyranny of the Status Quo, vol. 2, no. 2, August 2005, *Econ Journal Watch*, pp. 234–278.

have employed currency boards have generally delivered lower inflation rates, smaller fiscal deficits, lower debt levels relative to GDP, fewer banking crises, and higher real growth rates than have comparable countries that have employed central banks though Singapore is a notable exception.

Since the people of Hong Kong had grown to trust the HK$ banknotes issued by banks in Hong Kong — in contrast to the banknotes issued in China — it was decided by the British authorities that the colony would continue with banknotes issued by private commercial banks instead of creating a currency board that would issue its own notes. Accordingly, when Hong Kong's Exchange Fund (EF) was created in 1935, it took on the substance of a currency board even though its form differed slightly from the orthodox model.

Table 14.1.3 covering the period 1935–72 shows how this was accomplished. The EF took over the silver reserves of the note-issuing banks, issuing HK$-denominated Certificates of Indebtedness (CIs) to the banks. Henceforth if banks wished to increase their note issues in response to customer demand, they were required to pay sterling at a fixed rate to the EF to obtain CIs (effectively authorizations to issue HK$ banknotes), and the sterling would be invested by the EF in UK government securities. The CIs authorized a specific amount of HK$ banknote issuance (see Figure 5.1, p. 110). Conversely, upon redemption, the EF would pay sterling at a fixed rate (less a small margin) to the banks in exchange for CIs, and the banks would cancel the requisite number of issued banknotes.

If the balance sheets of the EF and the commercial banks in Table 14.1.3 are consolidated, the CIs drop out, leaving the HK$ banknotes now backed by sterling securities instead of silver coin or silver bullion. Hong Kong had moved from the silver standard to the sterling standard. Except for the arrangement whereby CIs substituted for banknotes, the balance sheet of the EF was entirely orthodox.

However, over the years 1972–2020, the EF or HKMA balance sheet departed from the simple, standard currency board model in a number of ways, as shown in Tables 14.1.4, 14.1.5 and 14.1.6 and summarized in each table. It should be stressed that, after 1983, these divergences did not in any way change the underlying objective of Hong Kong's monetary policy, which remained the maintenance of a fixed exchange rate under a currency board system. Nevertheless, they do represent complicating factors which have at times caused observers to question whether the EF or HKMA was acting as a currency board or a central bank. The remaining paragraphs of this section and the discussion in sections 2 and 3 will show that the basic integrity of the currency board was maintained except for the years 1972–83.

An initial structural step along the road towards the development of the current Hong Kong currency board system was in 1977 (see p. 109) when the EF became banker or asset manager to the government. In central banking systems it is usually the case that the government maintains its deposit account(s) at the central bank, but as explained, in a standard, orthodox currency board, the government usually maintained its bank account(s) at a commercial bank.

Table 14.1.3 Hong Kong Currency Board, 1935–72

Exchange Fund created to take over silver reserves of banks and switch to sterling standard

Exchange Fund

Assets	Liabilities
Pound sterling securities	Certificates of Indebtedness (CIs)
	Net worth

Commercial Banks

Assets	Liabilities
Certificates of Indebtedness (CIs)	Banknotes issued
Banknotes and coin	Deposits of non-banks
Loans	Deposits of government
Investments	Net worth

Government

Assets	Liabilities
Deposits at banks	Debt issued
Other assets	Other liabilities
	Net worth

Non-bank Public

Assets	Liabilities
Banknotes and coin	Loans from banks
Deposits at banks	Other liabilities
Investments	Net worth
Other assets	

Table 14.1.4 Hong Kong Currency Board, 1972–88

Exchange Fund becomes banker to the government

Exchange Fund

Assets	Liabilities
Foreign Exchange	Certificates of Indebtedness
HK$ deposits at banks	Deposits of government/Debt Certificates
	Net worth

Commercial Banks

Assets	Liabilities
Certificates of Indebtedness	Banknotes issued
Banknotes and coin	Deposits of non-banks
Loans	Other liabilities
Investments	Net worth

Government

Assets	Liabilities
Deposits at banks/EF	Debt issued
Other assets	Other liabilities
	Net worth

Non-bank Public

Assets	Liabilities
Banknotes and coin	Loans from banks
Deposits at banks	Other liabilities
Investments	Net worth
Other assets	

In the case of Hong Kong, the prudence of the government under successive Financial Secretaries — notably Sir John Cowperthwaite[3] (in office 1961–71) — had led to a pattern of annual budgetary surpluses and the gradual accumulation of a substantial fiscal reserve. Table 14.1.4 shows that when the management of the fiscal reserves was transferred to the EF, Debt Certificates were issued in acknowledgement of EF debt to the Treasury of the Hong Kong government. On the asset side, the funds were normally invested abroad in foreign currency deposits and securities, while small working balances were retained in Hong Kong dollar accounts. As the overwhelming bulk of the Treasury's assets were invested abroad, it is hard to make the case that the new Hong Kong dollar accounts of the EF were intended to influence domestic credit markets.

During the years covered by Table 14.1.4 (1972–88), although there were no significant structural changes in the balance sheets comprising the monetary system, two critical decisions were made affecting the terms on which HK\$ banknotes were issued and the pricing of Hong Kong's currency in the foreign exchange markets (see also pp. 110–111). First, in 1972, after the pound sterling was floated and the Hong Kong dollar was pegged to the US dollar, the note-issuing banks were no longer required to pay foreign currency for new CIs. Second, in November 1974, the Hong Kong dollar was floated. With these two changes, the link to any anchor currency was severed.

As explained in Chapters 5 and 6, these two decisions, together with difficulties encountered in the Sino-British negotiations on the future of Hong Kong after 1997, led directly to the currency crisis of September 1983. The restoration of the currency board in October 1983 effectively reversed these two decisions by requiring the note-issuing banks to pay US\$ at the rate of US\$1.00 for HK\$7.80 (or US\$100 for every HK\$780) for new CIs. A secure external anchor was therefore reinstated — this time with the US currency instead of the pound sterling. Curiously, all this drama occurred without any changes in the legislative framework (The Exchange Fund Ordinance) underlying the currency system.

Table 14.1.5 documents the next two steps in the process. First, the authorities took the view that, through its actions as manager of the interbank Clearing House, HSBC could — and sometimes did — create credit in a manner that could be in conflict with the goal of maintaining the fixed exchange rate. Typically, this would happen if a smaller bank became a persistent debtor to the Clearing House or to other banks and was bailed out by another bank through the temporary creation of credit. Accordingly, as explained in Chapter 11 (pp. 228–241), the authorities announced in July 1988 that they would henceforth require that the balance of the banking system (i.e., the aggregate net balance at the Clearing House) be placed in a newly created account for HSBC at the EF. By varying this amount, the authorities could now manage the Hong Kong dollar money market. Second, starting from March 1990, EF Bills and

---

3.   Hong Kong's monetary system (the currency board) complemented Cowperthwaite's fiscal philosophy; the hard budget constraint put in place by the currency board helped Sir John accomplish his fiscal goals. See Monnery, Neil, *Architect of Prosperity: Sir John Cowperthwaite and the Making of Hong Kong*. London: London Publishing Partnership, 2017.

Table 14.1.5 Hong Kong Currency Board, 1988–93

Exchange Fund/HKMA takes over the Interbank Settlement System

Exchange Fund

Assets	Liabilities
Foreign Exchange	Certificates of Indebtedness
	Deposits of banks
HK$ deposits at banks	Deposits of government/Debt Certificates
	Net worth

Commercial Banks

Assets	Liabilities
Certificates of Indebtedness	Banknotes issued
Banknotes and coin	Deposits of non-banks
Deposits at Exchange Fund	Other liabilities
Loans	
Investments	Net worth

Government

Assets	Liabilities
Deposits at EF/HKMA	Debt issued
Other assets	Other liabilities
	Net worth

Non-bank Public

Assets	Liabilities
Banknotes and coin	Loans from banks
Deposits at banks	Other liabilities
Investments	
Other assets	Net worth

Table 14.1.6 Hong Kong Currency Board, 1993–2020

Exchange Fund/HKMA issues Exchange Fund Bills and Notes (EFBN); Hong Kong becomes a major international financial centre

Exchange Fund

Assets	Liabilities
Foreign Exchange	Certificates of Indebtedness
	Deposits of banks
	EFBN
HK$ deposits at banks	Deposits of government/Debt Certificates
	Net worth

Commercial Banks

Assets	Liabilities
Certificates of Indebtedness	Banknotes issued
Banknotes and coin	Deposits of non-banks
Deposits at EF	Other liabilities
EFBN	
Loans	
Investments	Net worth
Foreign Exchange Loans	Foreign Exchange Deposits
Foreign Exchange Investments	

Government

Assets	Liabilities
Deposits at EF/HKMA	Debt issued
Other assets	Other liabilities
	Net worth

Non-bank Public

Assets	Liabilities
Banknotes and coin	Loans from banks
Deposits at banks	Other liabilities
Investments	
Other assets	Net worth

Notes were gradually introduced into Hong Kong's money market (pp. 268–272) as a liability of the EF.

Table 14.1.6 illustrates the final step in the process of adding items to the EF's balance sheet while retaining the underlying integrity of the currency board mechanism. In 1996, with the advent of RTGS, it was decided to require all banks to maintain an account at the EF (by this time also known as the HKMA; see below). The HKMA was now able to conduct clearing house functions so that interbank settlements could be made across the books of the HKMA.

The only other addition in Table 14.1.6 is the foreign currency component of banks' balance sheets — shown below the second dashed line of banks' balance sheets — added at this stage although these assets and liabilities had steadily been becoming more significant ever since the 1970s. This was a direct result of Hong Kong's increasing importance as an international financial centre. In a narrow sense, the foreign currency operations of the banks did not directly affect the operations of the HKMA or the currency board. Nevertheless, it became increasingly clear that the currency board mechanism needed to be robust enough to deal with very large inflows and outflows of funds — a direct by-product of Hong Kong's role as an international financial centre — smoothly and without disrupting the domestic money markets or economy. Three sets of technical adjustments needed to meet this requirement became the subject of the subsequent 1998–2005 reforms: (1) the broadening of the monetary base, (2) the creation of a discount window relying on EFBN as collateral to act as a shock absorber for HK$ interest rates, and (3) the introduction of Convertibility Undertakings (CUs) by the HKMA to create symmetric limits on the movement of the HK$/US$ spot exchange rate.

Table 14.1.7 shows the balance sheets of the Hong Kong monetary system (the HKMA and the banks) at December 2019. After the introduction of the three refinements in May 2005, there were no significant structural changes during the subsequent decade and a half to 2020, only changes in the size of the reported items. The balance sheet of the HKMA is adapted — with some simplifications and rounding — from the Annual Report of the HKMA and could usefully be compared with the summary balance sheet of the EF for September 1983, shown in Table 5.1 (p. 109), to see how much complexity had been added.

The EF had been created in 1935 under the Currency Ordinance, later renamed the Exchange Fund Ordinance. On April 1, 1993 the Hong Kong Monetary Authority was created, signifying a historic transfer of the monetary and banking functions from the Monetary Affairs Branch of the Treasury Department of the Hong Kong government to the new entity. The name Exchange Fund, however, survives and is still used to describe various functions or activities within the HKMA, such as the business of holding and managing the territory's foreign exchange reserves, and in some contexts the name is used interchangeably with the HKMA. At the same time the HKMA also took over the role of the Commissioner of Banking with responsibility for supervising and regulating the banking system. Monetary policy, banking supervision and prudential regulation were therefore brought under one roof.

Table 14.1.7 Simplified Accounts of the HKMA, December 2019 and Simplified Accounts of the Hong Kong Banking System

Simplified Accounts of the HKMA, December 2019*
in billions of Hong Kong dollars

Assets			Liabilities		HKD
FX	Foreign Assets**	1,980	Certificates of Indebtedness	520	
			Government-issued notes and coin	10	
			Aggregate Balance of Banking System	70	
			Exchange Fund Bills and Notes (EFBN)	1,200	
			Monetary Base		*1,800*
HKD	Cash, money at call and deposits	300	Government-issued notes and coin	1,100	
			Deposits by other HKSAR government entities	320	
			Deposits by other financial institutions	50	
	Other assets (inc. invested fiscal reserves of government)	1,920	Other liabilities	190	
					1,660
			Total Liabilities	3,460	
			Net Worth	740	
Total Assets		**4,200**	**Total Liabilities and Net Worth**		**4,200**

Simplified Accounts of the Hong Kong Banking System, December 2019*

in billions of Hong Kong dollars

	Assets	Amount		Liabilities	Amount	
HKD			**HKD**			
	Certificates of Indebtedness	520		Banknotes Issued	520	
	Notes and coins	30				
	Balances at HKMA	70				
	EFBN held by banks	1,200				
	Amount due from AIs in HK	240		Amount due to AIs in HK	500	
	Amount due from banks abroad	340		Amount due to banks abroad	460	
	Loans and advances to customers	6,220		Deposits from customers	6,900	
	Negotiable CDs and debt instruments held	350		Negotiable certificates of deposit outstanding	180	
	Investments in shareholdings	160		Other debt instruments outstanding	60	
	Interests in land and buildings	220		**Capital, reserves and other liabilities**	2,120 ****	
	Other assets	620				
	Total HK$ Assets	9,970		**HK$ Liabilities and Capital**	10,740	
Fx			**Fx**			
	Notes and coins	20				
	Amount due from AIs in Hong Kong	600		Amount due to AIs in Hong Kong	600	
	Amount due from banks abroad	4,520		Amount due to banks abroad	3,900	
	Loans and advances to customers	4,160		Deposits from customers	6,900 ***	
	Negotiable certificates of deposit held	370		Negotiable certificates of deposit outstanding	620	
	Negotiable debt instruments held, other than NCDs	3,700		Other debt instruments outstanding	570	
	Investments in shareholdings	240		Capital, reserves and other liabilities	1,650	
	Interests in land, buildings and other assets	1,400				
	Total Foreign Exchange Assets	15,010		**Total Foreign Exchange Liabilities**	14,240	
	Total assets	24,980		**Total liabilities and net worth**	24,980	

* Data have been rounded.

** Adjusted to equal 110% of currency board liabilities

*** This is not an error; deposits in foreign currency were almost identical in size.

**** The consolidated banking accounts do not enable capital in HK$ and foreign currency to be distinguished. All capital is assumed to be in HK$.

Source: https://www.hkma.gov.hk/eng/data-publications-and-research/data-and-statistics/monthly-statistical-bulletin/

As explained, the major changes in the components of the HKMA's balance sheet compared with 1983 are twofold, both on the liabilities side. First, the banks now maintained reserve or settlement balances at the HKMA, often referred to as the Aggregate Balance (or AB), whereas in 1983 banks held no deposits with the EF; on the contrary, the EF was at that time a customer of the banking system maintaining accounts at the leading banks. The second important change was the addition of Exchange Fund Bills and Notes (EFBN) as a liability (pp. 268–272) on the HKMA's balance sheet from 1990.

Given that historically there was seldom any marketable government debt in Hong Kong — the government having run budget surpluses averaging 1.4% of GDP a year between 1983 and 2019 — a yield curve based on government securities was never likely to develop naturally. Accordingly, banks could not rely on the availability of liquid, short-term, essentially riskless securities of varying maturities either to manage their balance sheet positions or to use as collateral for lending or borrowing in any sale and repurchase (or repo) transaction. This was perceived as a shortcoming for a city that aspired to become an international financial centre capable of conducting all types of banking and financial business. In response, the HKMA, led by Joseph Yam, undertook the development of a market in debt instruments to be issued by the monetary authority itself.

In a formal sense, EFBN constitute direct, unsecured, unconditional and general obligations of the Hong Kong SAR government for the account of the EF and have the same status as all other unsecured debt of the government. Not only did the new instruments enable the development of a HK$-denominated benchmark yield curve for sovereign-quality (and digital or paperless) securities, but in creating an instrument that is readily convertible into deposit balances at the HKMA, EFBNs have subsequently proved critical in reducing the volatility of Hong Kong's money and foreign exchange market.

One final point to be observed from the data in Table 14.1.7 is that since Hong Kong is a major international financial centre, although the deposits in domestic and foreign currency are virtually equal in size, the foreign currency segment of banks' balance sheets, which includes a large volume of interbank balances, now exceeds the HK$ currency segment of the balance sheet by about 50%.

Chapter 13 explained (pp. 275 and 278–279) that, although there are no required reserve ratios in Hong Kong, it is a rule of the settlement system (carried over from the days of bank-operated clearing houses) that banks must maintain a positive balance at the HKMA. With real-time accounting and EFBN available as a source of cash to replenish a bank's settlement balance, banks can now adjust their clearing accounts in advance of being threatened with overdrafts, making the system much more elastic.

To summarize this section, although the balance sheet of the EF or HKMA has progressively become more complex during the decades after 1983, each step had a rationale that was based not on any intention to deviate from the currency board mechanism but on the growing needs of Hong Kong and its financial institutions. With China opening its economy to foreign investment from 1978, lower value-added manufacturing activities moved across the border, leaving Hong Kong to concentrate on higher value-added services such as design, management, finance, legal services and overseas marketing. Hong Kong therefore shifted to become the major regional financial and service hub for southern China. In turn, this implied that Hong Kong needed to facilitate a growing volume of cross-border and interbank payments, accommodate larger inflows and outflows, and build up a large and deep foreign currency market in the territory. During the 1990s the HKMA actively developed a market in sovereign-rated securities (EFBN) that served the triple purpose of providing a yield curve from which other issues and lending rates could be priced, absorbing interest rate shocks and easing the banks' ability to adjust their liquidity positions on an intra-day, overnight or term basis — all this while maintaining a fixed exchange rate at the core of the system.

2. FROM THE MONETARY REFORMS OF 2005 TO THE GLOBAL FINANCIAL CRISIS OF 2008–09

(A) The Monetary System, 2005–09

Chapter 5, "How to Rescue the Hong Kong Dollar — Three Practical Proposals," used balance sheets to explain the flaws in the Hong Kong monetary system prior to the restoration of the currency board mechanism (see Tables 5.1–5.5). Essentially, in 1983 there had been no fixed anchor in terms of quantity (no ability to control the money supply) or price (no ability to manage the exchange rate). Chapter 6 showed how those flaws were corrected by specifying the terms on which banks could obtain CIs, thus restoring a fixed exchange rate anchor for the system. Chapter 13 showed how the reforms of September 1998 (the Seven Technical Measures) and May 2005 (the Three Refinements) enhanced the elasticity of the system with respect to interest rate changes and stabilized the spot rate for the wholesale HK$ market within the CU bands (7.75–7.85). In doing so, the volatility and range of expectations about forward exchange rates was also reduced.

Banking is essentially about borrowing and lending, or the swapping of IOUs. Any currency board — including the EF or the HKMA — is fundamentally a bank whose primary business counterparties are the commercial banks.[4] In the case of a currency board, the types of transaction it can undertake are limited by design, most occurring passively. For example, the issue and redemption of CIs (the authorizations to issue banknotes) or banknotes are executed "on demand", i.e., at the initiative of the banks or their customers, not on the initiative of the monetary authority. Similarly, when the market exchange rate in Hong Kong hits or exceeds the HK$7.85 CU, it is the banks that approach the HKMA to convert Hong Kong dollars into US dollars at HK$7.85, not the other way around.[5]

---

4. Other counterparties include the government, government-owned corporations such as the Hong Kong Mortgage Corporation, and foreign official institutions such as the IMF or other central banks.

5. Banks approach the HKMA because it is more profitable for them to purchase US$ at the 7.85 CU rate than to purchase US$ in the market at (say) 7.86.

Even so, almost all the policies and transactions of the EF (or HKMA or currency board) have an impact on the balance sheets of the commercial banks, and in turn the changes in commercial banks' balance sheets have an impact on firms and households throughout the broader economy. More generally, as the American economist Hyman Minsky liked to say, the whole economy can be viewed as a network of interlocking balance sheets.

(i) The Performance of the Monetary System of Hong Kong from the 2005 Reforms to 2009

In Chapter 13 (pp. 282–285) we saw how Hong Kong's exchange rate mechanism was further refined with the creation of two CUs, ultimately set symmetrically on each side of the HK$7.80 rate for CIs or banknotes at HK$7.85 per US$ on the weak side and HK$7.75 per US$ on the strong side. As shown in Chart 14.1, the spot rate for the Hong Kong dollar remained mostly on the strong side between 2005 and 2009.[6]

Once the two CUs were in place, there was no inherent tendency to move towards the central HK$7.80 rate for banknote or CI conversion. The exchange rate tended to settle around an indeterminate equilibrium point — sometimes on the strong side, sometimes on the weak side — within the CU bands and trade there until some disturbance shocked the system, causing the exchange rate to shift to a new equilibrium.

As in earlier periods, given the fixed exchange rate and a reasonable measure of credibility in the sustainability of the fixed rate, the direction and level of Hong Kong's interest rates were largely determined by rates in the US$ market, converging to US$ rates if there was no serious event risk or other disturbance. Chart 14.2a shows Hong Kong's 3-month HIBOR (Hong Kong Interbank Offered Rate) and the US$ LIBOR (London Interbank Offered Rate), which was the benchmark rate for lending US dollars in offshore markets such as London, Hong Kong or Singapore. Chart 14.2b also shows the interest rate differential in the lower panel. Assuming credibility of the fixed HK$7.80 rate, in equilibrium — in normal economic circumstances — one would expect the two sets of HIBOR and LIBOR interest rates to be virtually identical due to arbitrage.

However, between 2005 and 2008, the HK$ HIBOR was frequently somewhat lower than its US$ LIBOR counterpart. At times there were significant deviations between HIBOR and LIBOR. Typically, the difference would be due to inflows or outflows of funds, or to expectations that the Hong Kong dollar currency might — at some stage — be revalued upwards (e.g. from HK$7.80 to HK$7.50 or HK$7.20 per US$) or more rarely downwards (towards HK$8.00 or HK$8.50 per US$). The risk of an upward move would be reflected in a lower HK$ interest rate and a forward discount for the Hong Kong currency (i.e., the 3-month forward HK$ exchange rate would strengthen

---

6.   The choice of a band between 7.75 and 7.85 rather than a single rate of 7.80 necessarily weakens the arbitrage with the anchor currency. However, the government's rationale is that this spread ensures the maintenance of an active foreign exchange market in Hong Kong. See Chapter 13 section 3 (iii).

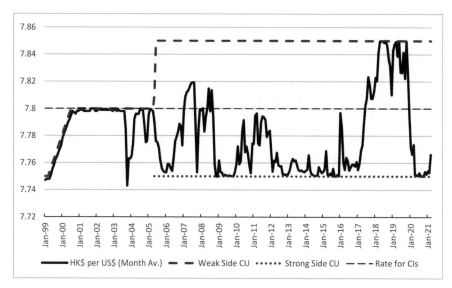

Chart 14.1 HK$/US$ Spot Rate and Convertibility Undertakings, 1999–2020

towards 7.50 or beyond) since the holder or lender would benefit from the capital gain in the currency relative to the US dollar.

Why should investors, bankers or dealers hold such a viewpoint? One such prolonged episode during the years 2005–08 was associated with (1) generalized US$ weakness when the trade-weighted DXY index for the US$ was falling continuously from 98 in September 2003 to 72 in April 2008, and (2) the revaluation and steady appreciation of the Chinese yuan from July 2005 until late 2008. Looking back on this episode, we know now that there was no revaluation of the HK$, but investors at the time were uncertain about it. The Chinese renminbi (RMB) or yuan (CNY) was revalued upwards by 2.1% in July 2005 from 8.28 to around 8.11 per US$, and it was then gradually managed upwards to 6.83 between 2005 and July 2008, passing through the arithmetic 7.80 level at which the HK$ was fixed. A frequent topic of discussion in financial markets in late 2006 was whether the HK$ would be unhitched from the US$ and fixed instead to the CNY when the 7.80 mark was reached. These rumours, although without any solid foundation, became especially prevalent as the CNY approached and appreciated beyond 7.80 yuan per US$ in January 2007, leading HK$ interest rates to remain below equivalent US$ interest rates for extended periods.

After this episode of CNY revaluation and steady appreciation, aside from a brief convergence of HIBOR and LIBOR in November 2005, HK$ interest rates generally remained below their US$ counterparts until the onset of the GFC (Chart 14.2). For the currency, too, the HK$ remained mostly on the strong side of the 7.80 rate until the GFC although it was not one-way traffic, as there were several months in 2007 and briefer periods in 2008 when the HK$ weakened below 7.80 per US$ (Chart 14.1). Overall, it

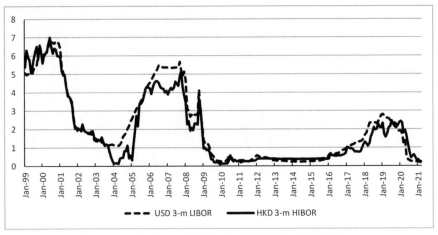

Chart 14.2a HK$ 3-Month HIBOR and US$ 3-Month LIBOR, 1999–2020

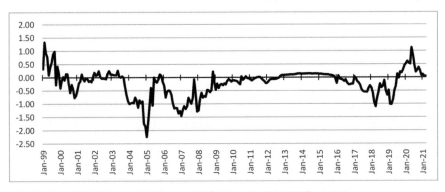

Chart 14.2b HK$ 3-Month HIBOR and US$ 3-Month LIBOR Differential

was relatively smooth sailing for the HK$, suggesting that the credibility of the Linked Exchange Rate System (LERS) due to the reforms of 1998 and 2005 had been enhanced. In short, confidence that the exchange rate would remain anchored at HK$7.80 per US$ and the greater degree of automaticity which the reforms had produced for the system were starting to pay off.

It is worthwhile closing this section with a few observations about the HKMA's transparency. There can be no doubt that financial markets benefit from transparency. Clear guidance and greater certainty about the long-term objectives of the monetary authorities reduce risk premia and lower volatility. In contrast to the attitude in earlier decades, the Hong Kong monetary authorities now embrace transparency. In addition to its very comprehensive annual report, each month the HKMA issues four press releases relating to EF data. Two relate to the balance sheet and two relate to Hong Kong's official foreign exchange reserves. The "Analytical Accounts of the Exchange Fund" is published around mid-month by the HKMA on their website, in accordance with the IMF's Special Data Dissemination Standard (SDDS) and give a snapshot of some of the key components of the balance sheet. A more detailed picture is given at month-end (for the preceding month) by a three-page document on the government's website showing the EF's Abridged Balance Sheet and Currency Board Account. This is very similar in form to the data shown in Table 14.1.7.

In addition, the HKMA practices transparency at high frequency with intra-day releases of data covering movements of the AB, cumulative past movements and forecast movements of the AB, daily data for the total monetary base and its components, as well as details of upcoming EFBN auctions and the pricing of outstanding issues. This information can all be obtained on newswire services such as Bloomberg and Thomson-Reuters/Refinitiv.

More broadly, as the HKMA's 2019 Annual Report explains, the assets of the EF are managed as four distinct portfolios. "The assets of the Backing portfolio fully match the Monetary Base, under Hong Kong's Currency Board system. The Investment portfolio is invested primarily in the bond and equity markets of the member countries of the Organization for Economic Co-operation and Development (OECD). The Long-Term Growth portfolio holds private equity and real estate investments. The Strategic portfolio holds shares in Hong Kong Exchanges and Clearing Limited acquired by the Government of the Hong Kong Special Administrative Region (HKSAR) for the account of the Fund for strategic purposes."

(ii) Adoption of Macroprudential Policies in Hong Kong and Their Effects

During the years since the currency board mechanism was reintroduced into Hong Kong in 1983, there were several major financial crises, notably the US stock and futures market crash of October 1987, the US Savings and Loan crisis followed by the US recession of 1990–91, the Asian financial crisis of 1997–98, the bursting of the technology bubble in 2000–2001, and the GFC of 2008–09. Each of these episodes created difficulties for banking sectors around the world. Either the banks were confronted with direct losses on their own portfolios, or significant numbers of their customers faced pronounced difficulty in making interest or principal repayments. The borrowers might be larger corporate customers — such as leveraged real estate developers or debt-laden shipping companies — or households that had contracted for substantial mortgage loans to buy property, or individuals who had accumulated excessive credit card debt.

The repeated experience of bankruptcy among borrowers in financial or economic downturns across the world meant that on each occasion there were widespread problems not only for the economy as a whole but also for the banks themselves, because their customers became insolvent or struggled to repay debt. Gradually, a philosophy developed among central banks and regulators around the world to deal with this recurrent problem. Hong Kong was one of the pioneers of this approach.

For our purposes we may regard the foundation of Hong Kong's macro prudential policies as dating to 1991. At that time, according to Joseph Yam, a "residential mortgage" was defined in the Third Schedule of the Banking Ordinance as a mortgage where, among other things, "the principal sum does not exceed 90% of the purchase price or the market value of the property, whichever amount is the lower".[7] This had been a matter of concern to officials, since the law prescribed a favourable capital weighting for residential mortgages even when their loan-to-value (LTV) ratios were as high as 90%. The arrangement effectively encouraged the banks to lend up to 90% of the value of a property, which appeared to regulators to be excessively risky. Instead of amending the Third Schedule to lower the 90% LTV threshold to 70% or issuing a guideline for residential mortgage lending on that basis, the authorities entered a dialogue with the banks, ultimately resulting in banks volunteering to observe a 70% LTV rule from November 1991. The 70% maximum LTV ratio was subsequently endorsed by the Hong Kong government in the Legislative Council in November 1995 as a prudential measure and has evolved into a banking industry standard intended to guard against overexposure to the property market. Later, when Basel II was implemented from 2007 onwards, capital requirements on residential mortgage lending were eased in recognition of the success of the 70% threshold for the LTV ratio.

Although the HKMA relied principally on the LTV ratio for macroprudential control, it also adopted, from January 1997, a debt servicing ratio (DSR) test. The DSR was defined as the monthly repayment obligations of the borrower as a percentage of monthly income. The ratio was required to be no higher than 50%–60% of the borrower's income though the upper end of this range was applied only to higher-income earners. Following the successful introduction of the LTV and DSR ratios as macroprudential policy instruments in the 1990s, the Hong Kong authorities began to make changes to the levels of the ratios, differentiating between types of property (residential versus commercial) and by value of the property. In addition, from time to time the government made changes in the rate of Stamp Duty as a tool to manage housing demand.

Here we summarize the experience of Hong Kong's macroprudential policy through two episodes, the Asian financial crisis that engulfed the region during 1997–98 and the GFC of 2008–09.

On the eve of the Asian financial crisis, housing prices in Hong Kong had increased dramatically — roughly doubling between 1995 and 1997 — to the point where they were widely regarded as out of line with economic fundamentals. The external shock of the Asian financial crisis and the need for realignment of Hong Kong's prices with those economies in the region which had massively devalued their currencies prompted a prolonged collapse of the property market, housing prices falling by 66% between 1997 and 2004 and consumer prices falling by 13.5% (p. 284). Despite this catastrophic decline, the mortgage delinquency ratio of the banks peaked at a strikingly low level of just 1.43% in May 2001. Thanks largely to the 70% LTV ratio there was no banking crisis and no need to bail out any of Hong Kong's banks. Macroprudential measures

7. https://www.hkma.gov.hk/eng/news-and-media/insight/2009/06/20090604/

had provided the banks with a significant cushion to absorb property price corrections while ensuring that borrowers owned a substantial equity stake and were incentivized to continue servicing their loans as long as they were able to do so.

During the years 2004–08 there were several adjustments of the LTV and DSR framework, so that although luxury housing prices roughly doubled over the period and lower-value properties increased by only slightly less, compared to previous boom-and-bust cycles there were no major signs of vulnerability in the residential property market. With the onset of the Lehman Brothers bankruptcy and other US and European financial failures during the crisis of September–December 2008, Hong Kong property prices fell in the second half of 2008 and early 2009 — housing prices by 17%, and office prices by 28% (based on the Rating & Valuation Department indices). Nevertheless, the residential mortgage delinquency ratio for banks in Hong Kong *fell* from 0.86% at the end of 2003 to less than 0.04% in the final quarter of 2009. As in the 1997–98 crisis, the cushion afforded to the banks by the 70% LTV ratio had prevented a much worse outcome.

Essentially, Hong Kong's economic fundamentals and household balance-sheet positions had strengthened over the decade from 1998, and there was no build-up of overheating pressure before the property market downturn in 2008–09. Significant imbalances in the domestic property market and banking losses were not a feature of the fall in housing prices during the GFC and largely reflected a deterioration in economic conditions.

Since the source of the problem in past crises had been excess leverage and excess credit growth, it made sense to limit leverage — of companies and individuals — through guidance or explicit regulation. If a company or individual has no borrowings — is not leveraged — at the peak of a cycle, then even if there is a major financial crisis which causes property and share prices to decline sharply, incomes and employment to fall, and total spending to decline, that company or individual may survive the crisis without facing bankruptcy. Equally important, there will be little adverse impact from such companies or individuals on the banking system.

The techniques to limit the accumulation of debt and ensure the capability to repay it have become known as macroprudential policies. As William Ryback, Deputy Chief Executive of the HKMA, explained at a conference in November 2006,

> Throughout their history central banks have aimed to ensure the overall soundness of the financial system and this followed naturally from their basic functions. Three historical developments were the key to this. In the beginning central banks were first and foremost banks — and like any bank they needed to consider the soundness and creditworthiness of their clients as well as factors in the general trading environment that might cause them losses. Second, over time, central banks developed a monopoly over ultimate liquidity, the means of final settlement, and they facilitated the settlement of interbank payments through the rediscounting of commercial bank assets and the collection of reserves in the form of bank deposits. Third, as commercial bank money progressively developed into a larger share of the money stock, the value of money became dependent on the soundness of commercial banks. In this environment the concern of the central bank for the orderly functioning and

stability of the banking system arose from the need to maintain the public goods of a stable means of payment, a unit of account and a store of value. This included last resort lending when commercial banks suffered from liquidity strains.

The success of Hong Kong's macroprudential measures during the two episodes — the Asian financial crisis and the GFC — was evident in the very low rates of loan losses by Hong Kong banks. Hong Kong's record in both stands in sharp contrast to the banking and financial crisis after the collapse of Lehman Brothers in the US and Europe, where housing prices fell by much less than they had in Hong Kong after 1997–98 but the delinquency ratios increased more sharply. In the US, for example, home prices declined by about one-third between 2006 and 2011, while the mortgage delinquency ratio increased to over 10%. Similarly, in Ireland, home prices declined by about 50% from 2008, while 90-day overdue mortgage arrears ratio rose to nearly 13%. Hong Kong's macroprudential measures had proved a good investment.

(B) Business Cycle Developments, 2005–09

(i) Deflation and Growth in the Aftermath of the Asian Financial Crisis and Ahead of the GFC

The US business cycle expansion that started in December 2001— nearly two years after the bursting of the tech bubble in March 2000 — began in anaemic fashion with low growth and a slow recovery in employment. One reason was that despite the Greenspan Fed cutting the federal funds rate to 1.0% in 2003–04 — the lowest rate since 1958 — US monetary growth was only modest (Chart 14.3).

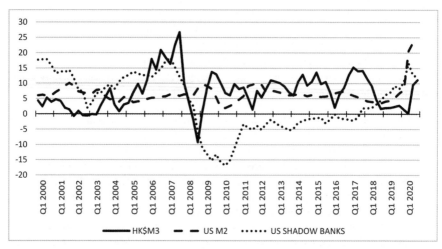

Chart 14.3 Growth of Hong Kong and US Money Supply and US Shadow Banks (Quarterly Data, % Year-on-Year)

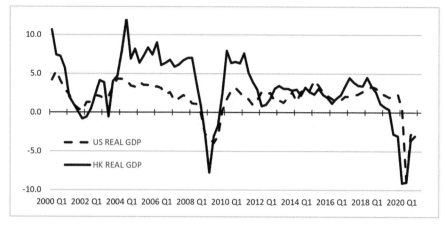

Chart 14.4 Hong Kong and US Real GDP Growth, 2000–20 (% Year-on-Year)

Indeed, the early phases of the US upswing showed only moderate real GDP growth and did not display any strong growth until mid-2003 (Chart 14.4). Observers lamented that, like the recovery of the early 1990s, this was another jobless recovery. US business activity, according to the NBER, peaked in December 2007 after an expansion of 73 months, the rate of growth of real GDP averaging 2.9% a year between the start of 2002 and the end of 2007. Against a background of M2 growth averaging 5.9% a year between 2002 and 2007, inflation also remained moderate, averaging 2.7% a year over the six-year period although it briefly increased to 4.4% year-on-year in September and October 2008 due to a jump in oil prices. The fireworks were not in the real economy but instead occurred in the financial asset markets and in housing, spurred on by leverage provided by the banks and the shadow banking system. As a result, the expansion ended with the biggest financial crisis since the Great Depression of 1931–33.

In the normal course of events, one would have expected Hong Kong's monetary growth to be strongly influenced by developments in the US, the anchor country for Hong Kong's currency. However, in the early years of the US expansion Hong Kong was still adjusting its internal price level downwards in an effort to overcome the competitive disadvantages suffered as a result of the regional currency devaluations during the Asian financial crisis. One consequence was that the Hong Kong money supply (HK$M3) grew only very slowly, recording virtually zero growth between the start of 2002 and mid-2003. It was only in 2004 that relative prices in Hong Kong had reached a level that enabled the economy to start to recover.

To understand Hong Kong's slow and difficult start to the business cycle upswing, recall that the territory, having not devalued, was left with a legacy of deflation from the Asian financial crisis of 1997–98. As explained in Chapter 13 (pp. 277 and 284), due to the depreciation of other Asian currencies such as the Thai baht, the Korean won,

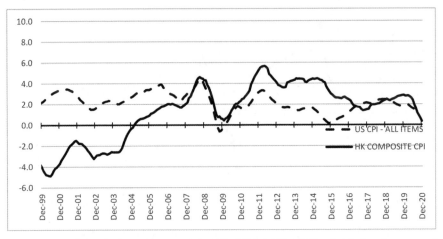

Chart 14.5 Inflation in Hong Kong and the US, 1999–2020 (12-Month Moving Averages of % Year-on-Year Change)

the Singapore dollar and the New Taiwan dollar, Hong Kong had lost competitiveness relative to other regional markets, and therefore prices and wages in Hong Kong needed to adjust downwards relative to those economies. This was also necessary for Hong Kong to regain normal growth and full employment in the domestic economy (see Chart 13.4). Given the fixed exchange rate, the process by which this adjustment of relative prices occurred was market-driven, not policy-driven.

Concretely, a business seeking to borrow from a bank would normally have presented figures showing their expanding sales and profits but, faced with the relatively stronger HK$ exchange rate, investment and new hiring became less attractive and exports less profitable. Accordingly, bankers reduced their lending, effectively restricting money growth in Hong Kong to a very low figure (see Chart 14.3). Simultaneously, so long as unemployment remained high and wage growth limited, individuals found it more difficult either to service existing loans or to take out new loans for home mortgages. The net result was sluggish bank lending growth resulting in average HK$M3 growth of just 3.7% a year between January 1998 and December 2004 – below even US M2 growth of 6.9% a year over the same period. Since the Hong Kong economy was at this time normally capable of just over 5% real growth (the average from 1991 to 1997), money growth averaging only 3.7% a year inevitably restrained nominal spending and wages, forcing prices to adjust downwards and producing deflation.

After this prolonged period of economic and price adjustment was over, Hong Kong rapidly realigned with the US economy, going into overdrive between 2004 and 2008. The resumption of strong growth was assisted by the Individual Visit Scheme implemented from 2003, which allowed Mainlanders to visit Hong Kong easily, boosting the tourist trade and retail sales, and was perhaps most broadly visible in the rapid acceleration of HK$M3 in 2005–08. The year-on-year growth rate of HK$M3 surged from 3.6% in January–March 2005 to 26.7% in the final quarter of 2007 (Chart

14.3), Hong Kong's real GDP growth averaging 6.4% a year from 2004 until the end of 2008 (Chart 14.4). With US M2 money growth continuing in the comparatively low range 4%–7% only, how was this possible?

In the author's view, the rate of US M2 growth understates the extent of monetary stimulus in these years. One of the striking features of this period was the rapid growth of securitization and shadow banking. US banks and mortgage finance companies were initiating mortgage loans — often to sub-prime borrowers — which were promptly bundled into tranches and sold as highly rated securities to off-balance sheet entities (funded in the money markets with commercial paper or other types of short-term debt issuance) such as structured investment vehicles (SIVs) or "conduits", or to other investors. Aggregated together as shadow banks,[8] the growth of this kind of intermediation greatly increased the effective rate of credit expansion and, arguably, monetary expansion (Chart 14.3). Leverage amongst households and financial institutions was also rising rapidly. Although there was no upsurge in reported US CPI inflation, asset prices such as housing, commercial property, and equities all increased strongly during these years.

In Hong Kong, which did not have a separate shadow banking sector outside the Authorized Institutions (AIs), these forces were reflected in very rapid growth of AI balance sheets and HK$M3. More fuel was added by developments in China, which also had an impact on Hong Kong's financial sector. One of these was the managed, steady appreciation of the CNY, which encouraged Chinese mainland firms to borrow US dollars or Hong Kong dollars from banks in Hong Kong, investing the proceeds in higher-yielding CNY financial assets or in onshore capital investment. As long as the CNY was widely perceived to be likely to continue to appreciate, this kind of carry trade was highly profitable for the borrower and helped to promote Hong Kong's role as a major funding centre for Mainland companies.

(ii) The Impact of the GFC on Hong Kong's Monetary System

Hong Kong entered the GFC with its economy growing very strongly. According to the NBER, the US recession started in December 2007. Nevertheless, as late as 2008 Q1, Hong Kong's real GDP was growing at 7.0% year-on-year, slowing to 4.0% in Q2 and 0.9% in Q3. With the collapse of several major US financial institutions (such as Lehman Brothers, AIG, Fannie Mae and Freddie Mac) in September and October 2008, global credit markets contracted abruptly, causing a "credit crunch" and a sharp downturn in world trade. The financial channel and the trade channel were the two main ways that the GFC shock was transmitted to Hong Kong. However, compared with the Asian financial crisis a decade earlier, the impact of the GFC on Hong Kong's financial institutions, on the currency and on interest rates and financial markets was far less damaging.

First, as discussed, Hong Kong's monetary system was now equipped with

---

8. The growth of total liabilities of shadow banks in the US is shown in Chart 14.3 as the sum of Primary Dealers, Money Market Mutual Funds, Finance Companies, Funding Corporations and Issuers of Asset-Backed Securities.

shock absorbers, preventing interest rates from rising as sharply as they had done in 1997–98. Second, Hong Kong's regulators had ensured, through sound supervision and conservative macroprudential measures, that the local banks were less leveraged than were their US or European counterparts and therefore had ample capital to withstand the adverse effects of a credit crunch, property and share price declines, and any increase in loan losses.

Between October 2007 and June 2008, the HK$ had weakened slightly from 7.75 to 7.81, but through the most intense phase of the GFC (September, October and November 2008) the currency strengthened again to 7.75 by November 2008 (Chart 14.1). Building on the reforms of 1998 and 2005, Hong Kong's more rules-based currency board was now acquiring the status of a safe-haven currency; the Hong Kong dollar was starting to be seen as a clone of the US dollar. In practice this meant that in the event of a crisis, as more risky assets in the region were sold, investors retreated to perceived strong currencies. The Hong Kong dollar, having survived the severe ordeal of 1997–98 and having not appreciated in 2005–07 when the CNY was moving upwards, was growing in credibility as a legitimate substitute for the US dollar.

During the GFC, interest rates in Hong Kong closely followed US rates (Chart 14.2). Initially, rates in both economies spiked upwards briefly in September and October 2008 before falling steeply in line with the Fed's policy of lowering the target for the federal funds rate to 0.25% in December 2008. Thereafter, as shown in Chart 14.2, except for a 3-year period between October 2012 and November 2015, the 3-month HIBOR remained below LIBOR for most of the post-GFC years. Although a popular explanation for this tendency was that there were regularly excess inflows into Hong Kong from the Mainland, such a hypothesis would be hard to prove. More objectively, the credibility of the currency board system — as reflected in forward exchange rates and longer-term yields which were also regularly below their US counterparts — was becoming more widely accepted by market participants. These premium ratings for the HK$ and HK$ interest rates continued through the start of the Fed's interest rate normalization from December 2015 onwards and remained in place until the second half of 2019.

Similarly, the growth rate of HK$M3 followed the sharp contraction in US shadow bank credit in late 2008 and early 2009, plunging from 22.0% year-on-year in November 2007 to –11.9% by November 2008 (Chart 14.3) as banks in Hong Kong called in loans and borrowers deleveraged. By contrast, the monetary growth rate for US M2 did not show this pattern. The reason was that many non-bank lenders withdrew their funds from shadow bank intermediaries, shifting them to the safety of the official banking system. In other words, there was a transfer of funds from shadow banks to member banks of the Federal Reserve System, whose deposits constituted the major part of M2. While it is true that on 25 November 2008 the Fed announced the start of a $600 billion quantitative easing (QE) plan — purchasing securities such as MBS and Agency Debt — these initial purchases were sterilized by sales of Treasury securities.[9] Moreover,

---

9. Unsterilized QE purchases by the Fed did not begin until March 2009.

US banks were already reducing their lending and suffering loan and security losses, ultimately resulting in their outstanding loans declining by US$1 trillion between 2008 and 2011. It was, therefore, the transfer of funds to the banking system, rather than any action by the Fed, that explains the upturn in reported US M2 growth between September 2008 and February 2009.

When the crisis intensified from September 2008 and the Hong Kong dollar moved to the strong-side CU at HK$7.75, banks started placing US dollars with the HKMA and receiving credits in Hong Kong dollars to their settlement accounts at the HKMA. The result was that the Aggregate Balance (AB) — the sum of all bank balances at the HKMA — started to increase very rapidly, rising from HK$5 billion in August 2008 to HK$318 billion by November 2009 (Chart 14.6). There were several consequences of these transactions. First, implicitly the increase in the AB represented a net inflow to Hong Kong of some US$40 billion (HK$313 billion at HK$7.75 per US$), increasing Hong Kong's official foreign exchange reserves by the same amount. Second, the sustained surge of funds into the AB put downward pressure on short-term interest rates in Hong Kong (Chart 14.2). Third, it should be noted that much of the increase in the AB in Hong Kong accompanied parallel increases in US banks' reserves at the Federal Reserve, as the Fed undertook successive episodes of quantitative easing (QE1, QE2, and QE3) between 2009 and 2014.

A related development was that from December 2008 onwards the issuance of EF Bills and Notes (EFBN) increased significantly. Between December 2008 and May 2010, the outstanding volume increased from HK$163 billion to over HK$650 billion, growing to just over half of total HK$ debt issuance, the majority of the new issues being acquired by banks in Hong Kong. At the same time, the HKSAR government implemented a government bond programme from 2009 onwards, promoting the

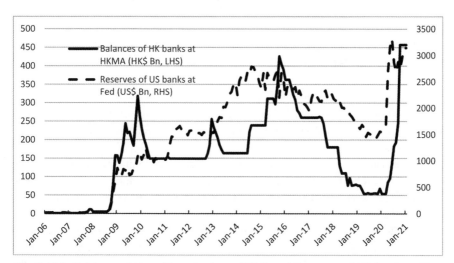

Chart 14.6 Balances of Hong Kong Banks at HKMA and Reserves of US Banks at Fed, 2006–20

development of the HK$ bond market. In an environment of very low interest rates there was a general "search for yield" among investors, which also encouraged a substantial increase in corporate bond issuance. From a monetary perspective, the increase in EFBN issuance by the HKMA, bond issuance by the government, and corporate debt by the private sector mostly added diversity to the range of instruments available for investors and institutions to hold while only the EFBN issued by the HKMA constituted part of the monetary base and could be used by banks for active management of their liquidity positions.

To conclude this section, we should ask how it was that, despite the intense financial disruptions experienced in the US and in Europe in 2008–09, Hong Kong emerged relatively unscathed from the largest financial crisis of the post-war period. First and foremost, this was due to the monetary reforms of 1998 and 2005 which had made the currency board mechanism much more robust, more rule-driven and therefore more automatic. The removal of any discretionary element in the system eliminated the need for the "constructive ambiguity" that had been deemed necessary in the 1990s and had acted as an invitation to damaging speculation. Moreover, although one or two high-profile investors did attempt to profit by short-selling the Hong Kong dollar, such attempts invariably ended in failure; the automatic, self-corrective features of the linked rate system prevented such speculators from succeeding.

Second, a strong bank supervisory regime was maintained. The HKMA's bank regulatory system ensured banking soundness while their macroprudential controls limited the amount of leverage, not only in the banking system but also in the household and corporate sectors. These measures meant that at a macro level the system could handle the trillions of dollars of inflows and outflows that passed through Hong Kong, while on a micro basis they ensured that the bulk of individuals, corporates and institutions remained financially sound and would not pose a systemic threat to the banking system.

3. POSITIONING FOR A FURTHER TEST OF THE MONETARY REFORMS, 2009–20

Over the next decade, from 2009 to 2020, there were no significant changes to the monetary framework — that is, no changes in the way the currency board system operated — and only modest or incremental changes to the regulatory framework of the banking system in Hong Kong.

As explained, the mechanism for the day-to-day functioning of the exchange rate for the HK$ had been made almost entirely automatic by the reforms of 1998 and 2005. Although there was provision for the HKMA to intervene within the convertibility bands (7.75–7.85), there was never any need to exercise that authority.

On the regulatory side, in the aftermath of the GFC, the developed world embarked on far-reaching reforms of their banking systems with the introduction, notably, of the Dodd-Frank legislation in the US and the Basel III arrangements for ensuring that the catastrophic banking losses and consequent economic collapse of 2008–09 would not be repeated. Hong Kong, however, was relatively much better placed, having insisted on banks being well capitalized and having had a strong supervisory system in place since the 1990s. The changes in the macroprudential framework and the adaptation of banks to the requirements of Basel III were therefore relatively minor in the context of Hong Kong's existing arrangements.

What could not have been envisaged was the onset in 2019 of widespread social unrest in the territory and in early 2020 of a pandemic that required the shutdown of large parts of the global economy. Both events would test the Hong Kong monetary system and its regulatory framework once again.

(A) Monetary Developments, 2009–20

(i) The Exchange Rate, Interest Rates, and the Monetary Base

Between 2009 and 2020, the HK$/US$ exchange rate operated consistently with currency board principles. It remained within the CU bands, and when market forces pushed it to those limits the HKMA either provided Hong Kong dollars at 7.75 or took in Hong Kong dollars at 7.85, consistent with its undertakings, respectively easing or tightening financial market conditions in the HK$ money markets. Chart 14.1 shows that there were significant periods when the exchange rate was at or close to the 7.75 strong-side CU between September 2008 and December 2017. The total amount of HK$ funds created and sold to the market through these episodes is documented in Table 14.2. From a level of HK$5 billion in August 2008 the amount of the AB increased to HK$426 billion in October 2015 before declining to $54 billion in April 2019 and rising again to HK$457 billion in October 2020 (Chart 14.6).

Table 14.2 Changes in the Aggregate Balance, July 2008–September 2020 (HK$ billions)

Q3 2008–Q4 2009	642.2
Q4 2012	107.2
Q3 2014	75.3
April 2015	71.5
Sept–Oct 2015	155.7
Apr–Aug 2018	−103.5
March 2019	−22.1
Apr–Sept 2020	383.5
Total	**1,435.40**

Source: HKMA, "Half-Yearly Monetary and Financial Stability Report", various issues.

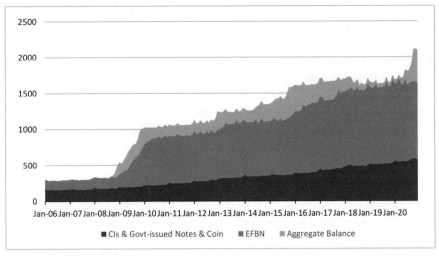

Chart 14.7 Hong Kong Monetary Base and Components, 2006–20 (HK$ BN, Monthly)

At the same time as new HK$ funds were being created by commercial bank sales to the HKMA of US$ at 7.75, the HKMA needed to make decisions about the composition of the monetary base. Recall that the monetary base (Chart 14.7) in Hong Kong consists of four items:

(A) CIs (equivalent to banknotes issued by the three note-issuing banks),

(B) government-issued notes and coin,

(C) the AB (bank deposits at the HKMA), and

(D) the amount of EFBN outstanding.

Given that the first two are demand-determined and the third (additions to or subtractions from the AB) is determined in the foreign exchange market, the only remaining element to be decided is the amount of EFBN outstanding.

Since the amount of EFBN outstanding is the only discretionary element in the composition of the monetary base, its relation to the AB deserves some elaboration. Above, we noted first the introduction of EFBN (Chapter 14, p. 297) and then after 1998 the decision to allow banks to use their holdings of EFBN to obtain funds from the HKMA, thereby introducing a shock absorber which reduced the volatility of interest rates in the HK$ interbank market. There are four main ways by which the level of the AB can be changed:

(1) additions resulting from transactions at the strong-side CU (inflows) or subtractions resulting from transactions at the weak-side CU (outflows) whenever the

CU is triggered — respectively, payments of US$ to the HKMA versus receipts of HK$ at 7.75 or receipts of US$ from the HKMA versus payments of HK$ at 7.85;[10] or

(2) since the HKMA is authorized to conduct discretionary intra-CU zone operations, there could also be similar transactions (although these are rare) at such levels; or

(3) purchases of new issues of EFBN or redemptions of EFBN by banks; or

(4) interest or coupon payments on EFBN.

As both Table 14.2 and Chart 14.6 show, inflows and outflows due to foreign exchange transactions are lumpy and erratic. Just as mechanisms have been developed to smooth out upward spikes in interest rates, the HKMA's ability to respond to banks' liquidity needs by varying the amount of EFBN outstanding is a useful smoothing tool. Nevertheless, consistent with currency board principles, the combined total of the AB and EFBN is not within the HKMA's discretion; the total is determined by net inflows or outflows of foreign exchange over time.

In general, the larger the size of the AB, the more EFBN will be required by the banks for liquidity adjustment purposes. For example, negative short-term EFBN yields tend to coincide with a large AB, indicating banks' demand for longer-term maturities. If negative yields occur, the HKMA will normally issue additional EFBN to meet banks' demand. However, in periods of relative calm in the money markets it is possible to increase the outstanding amount of EFBN while reducing the AB. Conversely, between mid-April and mid-May 2020, the HKMA gradually reduced the amount of EFBN by HK$20 billion, increasing the AB by the same amount to improve interbank liquidity. The important point, from a monetary management standpoint, is that the two items — the AB and EFBN — remain fully interchangeable. Moreover, in line with currency board principles, the combined total of items (1)–(4) above remains mainly determined in the markets by item (1), not at the discretion of the monetary authority, and fully backed by foreign exchange. The contribution of items (2), (3) and (4) to the AB is generally small.

More broadly, additions to or subtractions from the monetary base (items A–D above) mostly occur at the 7.80 rate for CIs, or at the 7.75 CU level for foreign exchange inflows, or at the 7.85 CU level for foreign exchange outflows.

(ii) Macro-Prudential Measures and Foreign Currency Markets in Hong Kong after the GFC

In an earlier section (pp. 305–308) of this chapter we outlined the important steps the Hong Kong monetary authorities had taken since the 1990s in the area of macro-

---

10. Note that the issue and redemption of banknotes via purchase and sale of CIs by the note-issuing banks at 7.80 does not affect the AB since payments and receipts are in US$, not HK$. Following discussion at the Committee on Currency Board Operations about the transferability between CIs and the AB in 2005, it was decided that such a move would not be advisable. Potentially it could re-create the problems of 1972 (see Chapter 5, p. 110).

prudential policy to improve the stability and prudential safety of the financial system. These concerns were again prominent in the post-GFC years, particularly since exceptionally low interest rates tended to promote strong asset price increases and the desire for leverage amongst investors.

In the words of Dong He, a senior economist and Executive Director at the HKMA, writing in 2014,

> After a few years of adjustment and steady recovery, housing prices in Hong Kong grew strongly [from] early 2009, with the level in Q4 2013 more than doubling that in Q2 2009. This rapid rise in residential prices reflected both low interest rates and very tight housing supply conditions. Mortgage interest rates went as low as 1 percent in the second half of 2009 and have stayed below 2.5 percent. Housing supply has fallen below the estimated demand since mid-2006, and, as a result, a large demand-supply imbalance has persisted. These developments, along with the forward guidance by the Federal Reserve that its policy interest rate will remain low for a rather long period, have led to strong expectations that property prices will keep rising. The possibility of a housing market bubble in the making has been the most important financial stability concern for the HKMA in the past several years.[11]

In response to these concerns, the Hong Kong authorities implemented seven rounds of macroprudential controls between 2009 and 2016. The purpose on each occasion was "to manage banking risks related to mortgage lending and to enhance borrowers' ability to cope with the impact of a possible property market downturn. . . . These measures helped bring down the average loan-to-value ratio for new mortgages from 64% before the introduction of the measures to around 52% more recently. The debt-servicing ratio (DSR) for new mortgages also fell by about 5 percentage points to 35%."[12] Nevertheless, property prices continued to rise until late 2018, driven by low interest rates, strong local demand and demand from mainland Chinese buyers. From an index level of 100 in March 2009, indices of residential and commercial retail properties in the territory increased to between 350 and 400 by 2018 Q3.[13]

Separately, but importantly for the financial and banking system as a whole as well as for the city's role as an international financial centre, the growth of offshore or foreign currency markets in Hong Kong continued to be very vigorous. The territory had long provided facilities for companies and individuals to deposit and borrow in leading foreign currencies such as the US dollar, the euro and the British pound. For many years the US dollar had been the pre-eminent foreign currency in Asia, and this applied in Hong Kong also. Since the Asian financial crisis in 1997–98, foreign currency deposits in Hong Kong had fluctuated in a range of 41%–53% of total deposits, the US dollar accounting for about one-third of the total deposit base.

The major innovation in the post-GFC period was the development, with the consent of the Mainland authorities, of an offshore market in RMB or Chinese yuan

---

11. https://publications.banque-france.fr/sites/default/files/medias/documents/financial-stability-review-18_2014-04.pdf

12. HKMA, "Half-Yearly Monetary and Financial Stability Report", p. 56, September 2015.

13. Based on indices compiled by the Rating and Valuation Department, author's calculations.

(CNH).[14] From 2010 onwards, RMB deposits in Hong Kong began to grow rapidly from a negligible level to peak at 12.8% of total deposits, or almost 25% of foreign currency deposits in Hong Kong by March 2014.

Two main factors explain the rapid growth of CNH deposits over these years. The first was the approval granted by the Mainland authorities for Hong Kong residents to hold RMB deposits at banks in Hong Kong (subject to some restrictions on the pace of accumulation), a decision that accompanied other moves towards the liberalization of China's financial system. The second, and seemingly more important, was the policy adopted by the Beijing authorities to terminate the fixed exchange rate that they had maintained against the USD for the duration of the GFC and to allow the steady appreciation of the CNY from 6.97 per US dollar in August 2010 to a peak of 6.10 in January 2014. The currency remained close to this level until July 2015. In a world of very low interest rates, this gave savvy depositors in Hong Kong a virtually guaranteed appreciation of up to 12% (or 33% since July 2005) relative to the HKD or USD, and it provided a motive for Chinese mainland companies to conduct "carry trades", borrowing USD or HKD and investing the proceeds in CNH or CNY.

The reason for believing that CNY appreciation was the key factor affecting the demand for CNH in Hong Kong was that after the CNY abruptly depreciated by 2%–3% to around 6.35 per US dollar in August 2015 (due to market panic triggered by a reform of the daily rate-setting mechanism by the Mainland authorities), the growth of CNH deposits in the territory rapidly went into reverse. Between August 2015 and February 2017, the share of CNH deposits at banks in Hong Kong fell from over 10% of total deposits to just 5%.

If the CNY or CNH had become a leading international currency in Asia for trade and capital transactions at this time, it is possible that the CNH would have maintained its share of the Hong Kong deposit market. However, following the mini-depreciation of the CNY in August 2015, the US dollar recovered its share from about 30% of all deposits in Hong Kong to 35% by 2016. Even at the end of 2020 the CNH share of deposits in Hong Kong remained as low as 6%–7%. Data from the IMF also showed that the US dollar accounted for 59% of global foreign exchange reserves at the end of 2020, a 25-year low but still far ahead of other currencies. The yuan's share at 2.3% confirmed that the international role of China's currency is still in its very early stages.

While the development of a CNH market in Hong Kong and other financial centres is unrelated to the functioning of Hong Kong's currency board in a narrow sense, it will be important to the long-term future of Hong Kong's currency. Until the Chinese currency becomes a truly international currency on a par with the US dollar, euro or Japanese yen, it will be hard for the authorities in Hong Kong to contemplate a switch from a US dollar-linked exchange rate system to one linked to the Chinese yuan.

---

14. Known by the currency code CNH, i.e., Chinese yuan in Hong Kong as opposed to CNY, the ISO 4217 currency code for onshore Chinese yuan.

(B) Business Cycle Developments, 2009–20

(i) Hong Kong's Recovery after the GFC

In contrast to Hong Kong's slow and painful adjustment after the Asian financial crisis, the economy's recovery after the GFC was rapid and vigorous. In the first place, Hong Kong and other Asian economies were not at the epicentre of the crisis as they had been in 1997–98; this time the crisis centred on the US, the UK, and several euro area economies such as Spain and Ireland. Second, the HKMA's macro-prudential policies had ensured that, despite a steep but brief economic downturn in 2008–09, banks survived the recession with strong capital ratios and minimal loan impairments and were therefore soon able to resupply credit to meet the needs of the economy.

Reverting to the chronology of the years 2009–20, Chart 14.2 shows that in the aftermath of the GFC interest rates remained at "the zero lower bound" between mid-2009 and December 2015, when the Federal Reserve finally started raising interest rates. Interest rate differentials between HK$ and US$ were very small through most of these years. It is worth expanding on some of the events over the period to show that, despite disturbances in the international financial system and divergent business cycles between the US and China, the reformed HK$/US$ linked rate system was able to operate smoothly and without problems.

First, on the Chinese side, the Beijing authorities, alarmed at the collapse of world trade, launched a massive CNY 4 trillion fiscal stimulus plan in November 2008, equivalent to 6% of GDP at the time. Since the central government's fiscal deficit widened only marginally — not by anything like the 6% of GDP in the headline figure — and the plan was put into operation mainly by spending at the provincial level funded by loans from the banking system, it would be more accurate to say that the plan was a fiscal stimulus in form, funded in substance by the creation of money in the banking system. Loan growth accelerated from 12.7% year-on-year in November 2008 to 35% by November 2009, and China's M2 money supply grew by an astonishing average of 23% a year over the two years 2009 and 2010. Not surprisingly, the Shanghai and Shenzhen stock markets doubled in value in 2009, the economy recovered rapidly with real GDP hitting 12.2% year-on-year in 2010 Q1, imports and commodity prices surged, and consumer price inflation increased from −1.8% in July 2009 to 6.5% by July 2011. Although arguably this gargantuan spending programme rescued significant parts of the global economy, it immediately set China and the US on differing cyclical expansion paths, testing the Hong Kong dollar's linked exchange rate system.

Second, on the US side, overleveraging of the financial and household sectors in the years to 2008 required sustained balance sheet repair. Left to themselves the banks would have reduced lending[15] so that deposits would also have contracted. In turn, this

---

15. Adjusted for changes in reporting institutions (i.e., omitting the addition of Morgan Stanley, Goldman Sachs and American Express, which all applied to become member banks of the Federal Reserve System during this period), US bank lending declined by 14% or US$1.0 trillion between 2008 and 2011.

would have given rise to a monetary contraction comparable with the Great Depression of 1931–33, when the US money supply had declined by one-third. To avoid repeating such a catastrophe the Federal Reserve, under its Chairman, Ben Bernanke, who had made his name in academia as an expert on the Great Depression, embarked on a series of quantitative easing programmes, popularly known as QE1, QE2 and QE3. By purchasing Treasury and mortgage-backed securities from non-banks, the Fed created new deposits in the banking system at a time when the banks were either reducing their loan books or reluctant to lend. The result was that the Fed's QE operations offset the tendency of US banks to shrink their balance sheets, maintaining M2 money growth at moderate single-digit rates and preventing a prolonged period of monetary contraction between 2009 and 2014. Even so, the US recovery, in contrast to China's strong upswing, was slow and widely considered sub-par, while inflation generally remained below the Fed's 2% target.

The divergence in business cycle patterns between the US and China posed the question as to which economy would dominate in Hong Kong. Although HK$ short-term interest rates converged with US rates (Chart 14.2), initially Hong Kong's economy followed China's upsurge in 2009–11, enjoying a vigorous start to the economic recovery, real GDP averaging 5.8% p.a. in 2010–11 (Chart 14.4). Subsequently, as China's growth moderated and global growth remained weak, the US resumed its domination of Hong Kong's business cycle. This was evident in the subdued demand for loans[16] — even at very low interest rates — resulting in low growth of HK$M3, averaging only 9.3% a year between 2012 and 2018 (Chart 14.3). Similarly, Hong Kong's real GDP growth slowed to an average of only 2.7% a year over the same period.

The years 2012–19 were also notable for several events and developments that could potentially have had an impact on the stability of Hong Kong's fixed exchange rate system. The first of these was the so-called "taper tantrum" — the disruption of fixed income markets and emerging market (EM) currencies following the statement by Ben Bernanke, Chairman of the Federal Reserve Board, in May 2013 that at some point the Fed would need to consider tapering its QE purchases of securities. Concerns that this might mean higher interest rates in the US triggered an abrupt and widespread sell-off of EM bonds, equities and currencies that continued through September. For Hong Kong, however, there was very little deviation of the exchange rate away from the strong-side CU (Chart 14.1). In short, the currency board mechanism and the perception of the Hong Kong dollar as a safe haven largely insulated Hong Kong from the tantrum in markets.

Another such episode was the process of interest rate normalization by the Fed. Between December 2015 and December 2018, the Fed raised the target for the federal funds rate from 0.25% to 2.5% in nine successive steps of 25 basis points on each occasion. In the US the moderate business cycle expansion continued with low inflation. In Hong Kong the exchange rate remained firmly on the strong side until early 2017, while interest rates stayed below their US equivalents, and money growth — after a brief

---

16. This refers to banks' loans for use in Hong Kong as well as for use abroad, particularly in mainland China.

slowdown in the first half of 2016 — continued at much lower rates than in the pre-GFC period. Through the entire post-GFC period HK$M3 fluctuated within moderate ranges on each side of US M2, as one would expect. Aside from a brief and mild economic slowdown in 2015 Q4 and 2016 Q1 — reflecting the knock-on effects of the taper tantrum — Hong Kong's real GDP grew at a normal pace, averaging 2.8% p.a. in 2015–18.

Inflation, too, behaved consistently with past patterns in the post-GFC period. In the early years of the recovery (2011–16), inflation in Hong Kong exceeded US inflation, partly reflecting Hong Kong's initial vigorous recovery and partly due to the Balassa-Samuelson effects referred to previously (pp. 203, 265, 278). Between 2011 and 2016, inflation in Hong Kong averaged 3.9% p.a., while US CPI inflation averaged 1.6% p.a. However, in 2017–20, the two inflation rates effectively converged, averaging 1.9% and 1.8% respectively (Chart 14.5).

(ii) Grappling with Domestic Social Disruptions and the Start of the COVID-19 Pandemic

The years between the GFC and the global pandemic in 2020–21 saw two sets of extended socio-political disturbances in Hong Kong: the largely peaceful and polite sit-in protests of the Umbrella Movement or Occupy Central Movement of September–December 2014, and the much more confrontational and violent demonstrations sometimes called the Anti-Extradition Law Movement of 2019–20. Both were triggered by legislative moves thought likely to affect democracy and civil liberties in Hong Kong. Our focus here is not on the rights and wrongs of the movements themselves but their effect on Hong Kong's exchange rate and the financial system more broadly.

The Umbrella Movement passed with almost no impact on the exchange rate. Chart 14.1 shows that the exchange rate remained close to the strong-side CU throughout the period, and Table 14.2 shows that although there had been net inflows equivalent to HK$75.3 billion in the July–September quarter of 2014 due to HKMA purchases of US dollars at HK$7.75 in response to market demand, there were none in the October–December quarter when the protests were at their peak. In addition, 3-month HK$ interbank rates remained only marginally above US$ rates before, during and after the street protests (Chart 14.2). More broadly, the willingness of the banks to lend meant that broad money growth and real GDP were not affected. The explanation is that the disruptions to day-to-day life and the scale of the protestors' demands posed no significant threat to Hong Kong's way of life or business prospects.

By contrast, the impact of the 2019–20 social unrest and the prolonged and sometimes violent demonstrations on Hong Kong's exchange rate and financial system was very different. Before the onset of any disturbances, the exchange rate against the US dollar had already moved from the strong-side CU at 7.75 in January 2017 to the weak-side CU at 7.85 by April 2018,[17] the banks placing HK$103.5 billion with the

---

17. The weakening of HKD at this time was mostly due to carry trade activity, given that HKD interest rates were at a substantial discount to their USD counterparts.

HKMA (and receiving US$ in exchange) between April and August 2018 (Table 14.2), followed by a further HK$22.1 billion in March 2019. Thereafter and during the next two years as Hong Kong's domestic troubles intensified, the HKMA was not called on to pay out any US$ against HK$; while far from weakening, the HK$/US$ rate gradually recovered towards the strong-side CU at 7.75 by April 2020 and remained close to that level for the rest of 2020 (Chart 14.1) through the period of the COVID-19 pandemic.

Nevertheless, from mid-2019, the economy weakened significantly as local consumers and tourists were deterred from visiting shopping malls and restaurants, and investment projects were put on hold — initially due to the demonstrations and after January 2020 due to the COVID-19 pandemic. With confidence in Hong Kong's future prospects temporarily undermined, banks became more risk averse; bank lending and HK$M3 growth slumped between the end of 2018 and mid-2020 (Chart 14.3). Similarly, Hong Kong's real GDP started to decline on a year-on-year basis from the third quarter of 2019, well ahead of the pandemic, and continued to do so for six successive quarters (Chart 14.4). Inflation remained in line with US inflation.

Why did the exchange rate not revert to 7.85, the weak-side CU? How can we explain the lack of any net outflows (in the sense of the HKMA sales of US dollars to the market and a decline in Hong Kong's foreign exchange reserves) during this existential crisis for Hong Kong? After all, the decline in confidence of domestic and foreign investors (reflected in the falling stock market and property prices) and the collapse of investment spending would surely suggest a simultaneous decline in capital inflows and/ or even net outflows.

One major reason was the series of large initial public offerings (IPOs) on the Hong Kong stock exchange — several heavily oversubscribed — which prompted substantial capital inflows in 2019 and 2020. A broader answer is that the slump in the domestic economy also led to a decline in the demand by Hong Kong residents for US$ or other foreign currency to pay for retained imports. Between January 2019 and August 2020, Hong Kong's imports fell by an average of 7% year-on-year, amounting to a cumulative decline of about 16%. In other words, the slump in the domestic economy led to a decline in the demand for foreign currency to pay for imports that exceeded the supply of HK$ offered by those seeking to move capital out of Hong Kong. Another factor was that foreign investors — including mainland Chinese — took advantage of the temporary decline in prices to acquire properties or equity in Hong Kong.

Irrespective of the explanation, the rock-solid performance of the HK$/US$ currency board mechanism during the 2019–20 social disturbances in Hong Kong constitutes strong evidence that the automatic adjustment properties of the system and enhanced credibility were enabling Hong Kong to ride out the political crisis without the kind of currency collapse seen in 1983 — or of the kind seen more recently in emerging market economies such as Argentina, Turkey and Venezuela. This compels us to ask, what is it about currency board systems that makes them so resilient?

At one level it is the guaranteed convertibility of currency board money — banknotes or the AB of banks at the HKMA — into the anchor currency at a fixed price. The fact that the HKMA holds foreign currency reserves equal to about twice the value of the monetary base promises a significant degree of credibility. However, the reason for the resilience of the currency board mechanism is wider and deeper than that.

In principle, faced with a future political crisis as severe as that faced by Hong Kong in 2019–20, the currency board mechanism will always induce a slowdown of real GDP growth or a decline in the stock of money and credit that will enable the economy to maintain the fixed exchange rate — by reducing the level of activity (as in 2019–20) or by lowering the price level (as in the aftermath of the Asian financial crisis in 1998–2004). The economic slowdown will either be induced by capital outflows leading to a tightening of financial conditions (by means of higher interest rates and slower money growth) or by a domestically induced slowdown (which implies consumers and businesses holding back from spending, and banks responding with lower rates of growth of lending and money growth — as in 2019–20).

To sum up, since Hong Kong restored the currency board system in 1983, the authorities have progressively enhanced both the resilience and automaticity of the fixed exchange rate mechanism. This can sometimes be difficult to see because the HKMA performs many functions that go beyond its narrow currency-board responsibilities. For example, the HKMA supervises Hong Kong's banks and provides payment clearing and settlement services. It also acts as the government's banker, as well as holding and investing its fiscal reserves. During the Asian financial crisis in 1998, the HKMA used those reserves to intervene in the stock market on a massive scale. The way to appreciate the HKMA's currency-board orthodoxy is to inspect its balance sheet and focus on its segregated currency-board account. Its currency-board operations remain largely passive and automatic.

Given that the exchange rate for the Hong Kong dollar is fixed, everything else — interest rates, money growth, domestic spending, prices and wages— will, or must, adjust to ensure that all nominal magnitudes in the economy remain consistent with the fixed exchange rate. In currency board systems these processes operate both in expansions and contractions, ensuring that equilibrium between the currency board economy and the economy of the anchor currency is maintained. Analogous to David Hume's specie-flow mechanism under the gold or silver standard, this is the magic of the automatic adjustment mechanism under a currency board system.

Hong Kong's Automatic Adjustment Mechanism
or Why Speculation against the Hong Kong Dollar Linked Exchange Rate System Always Fails

In the nearly four decades since the Hong Kong currency board mechanism or Linked Exchange Rate System (LERS) was restored in 1983, there have been numerous attempts by speculators to make money either by selling the HKD short or by buying long positions in the HKD in the hope of an upward revaluation or appreciation. While some may have profited from movements of the spot rate within the band given by the two CUs established in 2005 and set at HK$7.85 and HK$7.75, none has succeeded in pushing the spot rate outside the band. Most have ended either with their options expiring worthless, or with the investors making losses. Yet still they keep trying. Why is this type of speculation so enticing to investors and at the same time so unrewarding?

There are two reasons. Investors and commentators underestimate the power of the automatic adjustment mechanism under the currency board system. Moreover, they conflate Hong Kong's fixed exchange rate mechanism with a pegged exchange rate operated by a central bank, perceiving vulnerability where there is none.

There are two fundamental lines of defence for any currency board. First, there is the powerful, but little understood and largely unseen, automatic adjustment mechanism which operates all day and every day to keep the entire system consistent with the fixed exchange rate. Second, a currency board such as Hong Kong's maintains foreign exchange reserves in excess of 100% of the monetary base, which creates credibility for the system. Convertibility at a fixed rate is made more credible by the foreign reserve cover. Specifically, this means (1) the currency board can always meet any conceivable demand for banknotes, and (2) in the wholesale foreign exchange markets, it can exchange foreign currency for local currency bank reserves in a way that generates a self-reinforcing feedback mechanism.

Automatic adjustment mechanism

In the first case the fundamental issue is adjustment. There are two classes of things to which adjustment is required: monetary disturbances and real disturbances. How does the currency board mechanism cope with these two?

If monetary conditions[1] in the anchor currency economy (the US) become

---

1. NB: "Monetary conditions" does not refer to the commonly used Monetary Conditions Indices which are usually based on interest rates, interest rate spreads, exchange rates and stock prices but exclude quantitative measures of money and credit. Here, "monetary conditions" include sustained accelerations or decelerations of broad money and credit.

easier, HKD interest rates will, for a while, be higher than USD interest rates. Through arbitrage, inflows of capital will be attracted to Hong Kong, lowering HKD interest rates and encouraging banks in Hong Kong to lend more, thus adjusting monetary conditions in Hong Kong to monetary conditions in the US. Conversely, if monetary growth or USD interest rates tighten, HKD interest rates will, for a while, be lower than US rates. Again, through arbitrage, capital outflows from Hong Kong will be attracted into USD, raising HKD interest rates, discouraging banks from lending and slowing monetary growth to match conditions in the US. Note that the adjustment in Hong Kong extends to asset prices, economic activity, and inflation in each case, ultimately keeping Hong Kong's prices in line with US prices.

Similarly, given a positive or negative real shock which changes economic conditions or prospects in Hong Kong, the monetary system will adjust as appropriate. In the case of a positive real shock, HKD interest rates will decline, inducing a monetary expansion, and conversely for a negative real shock. An example of a positive shock is what happened when China changed the regulations easing the flow of Mainland tourists into Hong Kong from 2003, and Hong Kong's monetary growth rate expanded rapidly in 2004–07. An example of a negative real shock is what happened following the 2018 trade tensions between the US and China, triggered by President Trump's tariffs, and in 2019, as a result of prolonged demonstrations against the proposed Extradition Law and the National Security Law. These events prompted a slowdown of bank lending and money growth in 2018–20 even though HKD interest rates did not rise relative to USD rates until late 2019, and even then only in response to year-end funding and IPO demand. In an extreme case, such as a political crisis, the rise of HKD interest rates could be so steep as to attract short-term capital inflows which at least in part would counter the speculative outflows.

Most of the time, the automatic adjustment mechanism is operating in the background without the need for any response by the currency board. In Hong Kong's case, the exchange rate trades most days between the two CU limits of HK$7.85 and HK$7.75, allowing money market traders to shift positions between HKD and USD without any recourse to the HKMA.

100% foreign exchange cover for the monetary base

In the second case — relying on 100% foreign exchange cover for the monetary base — the currency board holds foreign exchange assets more than sufficient to redeem every HK$ banknote ever issued at HK$7.80 and all bank reserves. In addition, there are the two CUs whereby the HKMA will, in the event of the wholesale market exchange rate reaching either HK$7.85 or HK$7.75 respectively, purchase HK$ from or sell HK$ to the banks on demand. In the former case, purchases of HK$ by the HKMA reduce the supply of funds in the Hong Kong interbank market, driving up interest rates and squeezing monetary growth. In the latter case, HKMA sales of HK$ increase the supply of funds in the Hong Kong interbank market, lowering interest rates and inducing an expansion of lending and monetary growth. Each response reinforces the defence of the exchange rate band, easing conditions when there is an imminent breakout on the strong side at HK$7.75, or tightening conditions when there is an imminent breakout on the weak side at HK$7.85.

All the adjustments described above occur because the currency board is essentially passive and allows market forces to initiate and complete the necessary adjustments.

By contrast, in an economy with a central bank, the needed adjustments can be resisted under the guise of maintaining "stability" (of interest rates, of exports, or of some other variable). The central bank may conduct domestic open market operations or sterilize inflows, in effect concealing the growing adjustment problem. In this way disequilibria can build up — as they regularly did under the Bretton Woods system of fixed exchange rates — until the divergences are so large that a very big exchange rate change or other adjustment eventually becomes necessary.

In other words, a currency board has a fixed exchange rate policy but no monetary policy, whereas a central bank may have both an exchange rate policy and a monetary policy which can be inconsistent with each other.

In short, the currency board mechanism in Hong Kong ensures continuous, incremental adjustment, preventing the build-up of serious imbalances, in marked contrast to the behaviour of pegged exchange rates under central banks. It cannot be stressed too often that the Hong Kong LERS is, in effect, a unified monetary system with the US. The HKD currency is therefore a clone of the USD, and the Hong Kong monetary system, its economy and its price level are continuously adjusting to be consistent both with the fixed exchange rate and with monetary conditions in the US. It is therefore virtually impossible to "break" the exchange rate because market forces prevent any significant imbalance or disequilibrium from accumulating.

4.   AN OPTIMUM CURRENCY ARRANGEMENT FOR HONG KONG

The challenges facing the Hong Kong monetary authorities in future years are (a) whether the fixed rate currency board link to the US dollar alone continues to be the optimum monetary policy choice for Hong Kong, (b) whether fixing to an alternative currency such as the RMB would represent an improvement over the US$ as the anchor currency, and (c) whether a variable rate system with the currency either linked to a basket or independently managed would be superior. In the longer term it may be necessary to consider whether Hong Kong should participate in a wider Asian monetary union, but that discussion is not attempted here.

Issues (a)–(c) are very similar to those discussed by the author as far back as 1984 (see Chapter 8, "Why the HK$/US$ Linked Rate System Should Not Be Changed") although that discussion was framed in the context of the currency board system as it then operated and did not explicitly consider the RMB as a feasible alternative anchor currency. We shall therefore complete this assessment of Hong Kong's currency board by reviewing these questions in the light of the empirical experience since 1984 and in the light of some of the critiques of fixed rate systems that continue to be aired.

(a) **Fixing to the US$.** The most important consequence for Hong Kong of choosing the US dollar as the sole anchor currency for the Hong Kong dollar is that Hong Kong's business cycle — meaning asset price movements, economic activity, and inflation — will tend to be driven by the US business cycle.[18] This implies first that swings in Hong Kong's asset price movements will tend to be affected primarily by US and global factors, unless there are overwhelming regional or local events such as the Asian financial crisis of 1997–98, or the protracted political unrest that disrupted Hong Kong's growth and stock market performance in 2019–20. Second, Hong Kong's economic expansions and recessions will tend to be closely coincident with those of the US, unless there are strong regional or local forces that temporarily overpower that relationship. Third, Hong Kong's inflation rate will, subject to the Balassa-Samuelson effect discussed in sections 2 and 3 of Chapter 13, be largely determined by the underlying inflation rate in the US though this is again subject to the same qualification as in the case of asset prices or economic activity, namely regional or local force majeure.

It is sometimes argued that the US$ is an unstable anchor for Hong Kong, particularly when declines in the US$ are anticipated, but the reality is that in the past three decades the Federal Reserve has gained enormous credibility for its ability to keep inflation under control in the medium term, and therefore a substantial and prolonged

---

18. This broad view of the business cycle derives from monetary analysis. Since money growth has an impact on asset prices first, then economic activity, and finally inflation, trends in these three elements of the cycle will be transmitted from the US to Hong Kong through both financial and trade channels. Given the link to the USD, HK$M3 growth and the direction of these trends will to a degree be endogenous — sufficiently in normal times to ensure that traded goods prices align (see pp. 284–285) — but also independent enough to satisfy local idiosyncratic requirements when regional or local conditions dominate.

nominal depreciation of the US currency over an extended period seems unlikely.

As long as the US remains the pre-eminent economy in the world — in terms not only of its size but its impact on the rest of the world — and as long as Hong Kong remains a very open economy in both trade and capital flows with a high degree of dependence on external developments, it is hard to see how the impact of the US on the pattern of real growth and inflation can be avoided. If the US were to go into long-term decline and were to be replaced in global significance by, say, China, then there might be an argument for shifting from the US$ as the anchor currency to the Chinese currency as an anchor, but it is Hong Kong's openness to global influences, both positive and negative, that is the crucial issue here. As long as Hong Kong maintains a fixed rate currency board system and it remains highly externally oriented, then the optimum anchor currency will be the currency of the largest and most open economy in the world.

It is also worth repeating that while the US$ remains the pre-eminent international reserve currency and while the majority of trade and capital transactions in Asia are denominated and settled in US$, anchoring the Hong Kong dollar to the US currency will continue to bring enormous advantages to Hong Kong, helping it to maintain its role as the leading international financial centre in the East Asian time zone. For example, the pricing of IPOs on the stock market, corporate bond issues, syndicated loans and other such large-scale financial transactions can all be done in Hong Kong almost as if they were being done in US dollars in New York.

(b) **Fix to the RMB?** In view of the enormous growth of the mainland Chinese economy over the past four decades, some commentators are inclined to argue that this will mean that Hong Kong's currency anchor must inevitably be shifted to the RMB. This is to overlook both the narrow technical requirements of managing an efficient currency board and the huge benefits that a non-discretionary, depoliticized mechanism has brought to Hong Kong.

In order to ensure that the currency board mechanism is working to its best advantage, it is desirable that both domestic residents and foreigners are able freely to conduct equilibrating transactions in both the currency board economy and the anchor currency economy. This would include conducting both physical trade transactions (e.g. buying in the cheaper market and selling in the more expensive market) and financial transactions (e.g. holding deposits or bonds in the higher return market rather than in the lower return market, or borrowing in the currency where interest and hedging costs were lower). In other words, the currency board system will work best when the practice of arbitrage is feasible across the widest range of activity — goods, services or financial transactions.

It follows that the choice of an optimum anchor currency will, in practice, be restricted to freely convertible currencies. On these grounds the Chinese RMB will be at some disadvantage as a candidate currency for Hong Kong's anchor currency unless or until it becomes fully convertible. As a practical matter it may be feasible for banks in Hong Kong or the HKMA to buy or sell substantial amounts of RMB against HK$ in response to market demand (whether for issuing or redeeming CIs or for conversion at the strong- or weak-side CUs by banks), and for banks and large institutional investors to be able to do likewise. However, the lack of free capital account convertibility for the RMB, the continued existence of foreign exchange controls in China, and any restraints on interest rates in the Mainland could limit the scope of such operations.

It might also be thought that over time China's business cycle may come to dominate Hong Kong's business cycle, and if China and the US diverge, it would be better for Hong Kong to follow China rather than the US. However, as long as interest rates in Hong Kong follow US interest rates (due to the US$ being the anchor currency), and the US dominates the global business cycle, business cycles in Hong Kong will be primarily driven by the US or global business cycle. Exceptions, such as the episode discussed in section B (i) (pp. 320–321), when Hong Kong followed China in its initial recovery after the GFC rather than following the US, may occur, but these episodes will be influenced as much by the flexibility of the Hong Kong economy under the currency board mechanism as by the choice of anchor currency.

Furthermore, anchoring the Hong Kong dollar to the RMB would mean that Hong Kong's business cycle would become more subject to China's business cycle. Based on the experience of other high-growth, emerging economies, the amplitude of fluctuations of China's business cycle is likely to be at least as large as those of a developed, mature economy such as the US. Thus, while pegging to the RMB might appear to give Hong Kong the advantage of being tied to a large economy within the Asian region, in reality the benefit could be superficial compared with the possible costs.

(c) **Peg to a basket of currencies, or pursue an inflation target?** If Hong Kong were to select a basket of currencies instead of a single currency as its anchor, would the outcome be significantly different in relation to the business cycle, asset prices or the inflation effects? The answer will depend partly on the composition of the currency basket adopted and partly on the external dependence of Hong Kong's economy.

If the composition of the basket or index is still dominated by the US dollar or currencies that behave like proxies for the US dollar, then there may be no material gain from pegging to a basket. Once the RMB is liberalized and becomes fully convertible, one solution could be to set the convertibility rate for CIs at one US dollar plus an equivalent value of RMB at that time (i.e., a basket that at the start is 50% US$ and 50% RMB). Aside from losing the benefit of simplicity and straightforward arbitrage (see Chapter 8, pp. 191, 194), the problem about this and any other basket is that such baskets need to be continuously updated as trade-weights change, and they ultimately rely on a substantial measure of discretion by the monetary authority.

If there is no material reduction in Hong Kong's external dependence in the years ahead, switching to a currency basket may not bring any advantage, because Hong Kong's business cycle would still be subject to the same global influences. These forces would not be reduced by pegging to a global or a regional trade-weighted currency basket.

Finally, there is the question of setting the value of the Hong Kong currency independently. A *sine qua non* of ditching any anchor currency is that it should be immediately replaced with a credible and workable alternative monetary anchor. Hong Kong's Financial Secretary could consider two alternative anchors: a managed exchange rate, or the setting of an inflation target for the HKMA, just as the Financial Secretary currently sets the goal of the monetary authority as the maintenance of a fixed rate against the US$.

The modern, reformed Hong Kong monetary system is now robust enough for the HKMA to shift either the convertibility rate for CIs gradually over time (as it did between April 1999 and July 2000) or the strong-side and weak-side CUs. Such flexibility should theoretically permit the introduction of a managed exchange rate with systematic appreciation or depreciation, at least within limited ranges. However, the question would arise, how are such targets set in advance? It would be unwise to engineer an appreciation against the US dollar and then find the US currency itself appreciating. Similar problems would apply to setting an objective such as achieving a certain level of the nominal trade-weighted exchange rate. Consequently, few countries have ever operated such a scheme that was not at least partly discretionary.

There are other more problematic issues for an inflation target. Which price index is the relevant one? Should it be the composite CPI, the core CPI, or the GDP deflator? We have seen how the Balassa-Samuelson effect caused Hong Kong's CPI price inflation to deviate significantly from that of the US. Such deviations could easily occur again, particularly if major structural changes were to occur in China, leading to restructuring in Hong Kong. Another problem is dealing with the note-issuing banks' gains or losses from currency issues and redemptions during periods of exchange rate movement (when the rate for CIs was also moving) under a managed exchange rate system. Who should bear these gains or losses? Or, should the system of note-issuance by private, commercial banks be abandoned in favour of government note-issues despite the fact that private note-issues have been trusted and preferred to government issues by generations of Hong Kong residents? All these questions and more would need to be answered before the currency board system could be abandoned.

As the preceding discussion makes clear, none of the exit options from Hong Kong's present-day currency board are especially attractive compared with maintenance of the status quo. Although it took 22 years from the initial resumption of the currency board system in 1983 to evolve to a stage in 2005 when the system worked automatically and without regular discretionary intervention by the authorities, the system as it stands now is uniquely appropriate both to Hong Kong's status as an international financial centre that accommodates the free flow of very large volumes of capital and to Hong Kong's special position as a highly open trading economy, both as a direct trader with the rest of the world and as an intermediary serving as a major gateway to China.

INDEX